THE HOLOCAUST:
IDEOLOGY, BUREAUCRACY, AND GENOCIDE

The San José Conferences on the Holocaust, held in 1977 and 1978, were sponsored by the National Conference of Christians and Jews.

THE HOLOCAUST:
IDEOLOGY, BUREAUCRACY, AND GENOCIDE

THE SAN JOSÉ PAPERS

EDITED BY HENRY FRIEDLANDER

AND SYBIL MILTON

KRAUS INTERNATIONAL PUBLICATIONS
Millwood, New York

A U.S. Division of Kraus-Thomson Organization Limited

First Printing

Printed in the United States of America

Library of Congress Cataloging in Publication Data

Main entry under title:

The Holocaust: ideology, bureaucracy, and genocide.

   Includes index.
   1. Holocaust, Jewish (1939-1945)—Addresses,
essays, lectures. 2. Elite (Social sciences)—
Germany—Attitudes—Addresses, essays, lectures.
3. Holocaust, Jewish (1939-1945)—Public opinion—
Germany—Addresses, essays, lectures. I. Friedlander, Henry, 1930- II. Milton, Sybil.
D810.J4H644   943.086   80-16913

ISBN 0-527-63807-2

CONTENTS

VI. AFTER THE HOLOCAUST

FOREWORD

I saw my mother cry for the first time on September 1, 1939. I was twelve years old and lived safely in Washington, D.C. That was the day we learned of Hitler's invasion of Poland, the day after which we never again received wooden pecks of dried mushrooms, or ropes of dried figs from my grandmother. That was the day after which we never again saw or heard from my mother's mother, her sister, her brothers, or their children. That was the day I began to grow up, the day this particular volume began to take shape.

For thirty years I carried the Holocaust with me like an open wound, too ugly to look at, too painful to touch. I found myself unable to read what little was written of it or to discuss it with fellow Jews. It wasn't difficult to avoid, for in those thirty years few others seemed aware of its occurrence. I completed the requisite number of history courses in the University. The Holocaust didn't exist there. Years later my children too would be treated to the same indifferent view of history in public education. The Holocaust seemed to exist only in my imagination.

No intellectual examination was possible for me. On those occasions when thoughts of the Holocaust returned to haunt me, there welled from within an anger so great that it could only express itself in tears and trembling, and above all, isolation, an emotional isolation from all but those few upon whom history had placed its imprimatur of seemingly endless suffering. Those whom I could trust, Jews, were friends. All others were politely kept at arm's length and viewed through a veil of mistrust and wonder; wonder that these good people who loved their children, these

1

silent people among whom I lived, among whom my children would live, were related in fundamental fashion to those who were the murderers of Jews.

I spent those years seeking answers to the unanswerable; seeking to understand. How could beings who had been anointed by the concepts of love, mercy, compassion, tenderness, wisdom, humanity, and all those qualities that place us above all other life, have engaged in this methodically calculated orgy of slaughter? How could this barbarism, orchestrated by government, enabled by science, unhampered by law, and largely unopposed by the Christian Church, have earned the silent compliance it was so overwhelmingly granted by the rest of the world? Was Hitler right? Did no one care?

I know now that it was no accident that I was drawn to the National Conference of Christians and Jews. Unconsciously, I had searched for others who shared my anger, others who shared my tears and trembling, those significant others who were not Jews, whose hearts must also be broken because our thin veneer of civilization was so violently shattered, because my grandmother died at Auschwitz.

I have found my "thirty-six men" of Jewish lore, whose righteousness, unbeknown to themselves, sustains humanity. I found them among my NCCJ colleagues, among the ministers, priests, and rabbis who helped to restore my hope. I found righteous men who cannot influence the past, but who take responsibility for influencing the future.

I share this personal odyssey with you because it is, in a sense, the genesis of this particular examination of the Holocaust. It is from the love and the determination of righteous men that I drew the strength to face the Holocaust, and subsequently to bring together those scholars who contributed to this volume. It happened because of the years of dialogue, often painful, sometimes tearful, always loving, with the Fathers Bill Leininger, Robert Pfisterer, Arthur Hofmann; the Reverends Roy Hoch, Ralph York, Norman Thalman, Dwight Kintner, Kenneth Bell, John Arthur, and Andrew Kille; the Rabbis Joseph Gitin, David Robins, Jerry Danzig, Allen Krause, and Ben Siegel. It happened because I have been touched by the gentleness and passion of Robert McAfee Brown and Franklin Littell. It happened because of the caring, commitment, and gentle persuasion of my friend and mentor, Donald McEvoy. The love and trust that grew from my relationships in NCCJ, the concern and encouragement of President David Hyatt, the long hours of searching discussion, laughter, and comradeship with my precious friends William Pharr, Jim Lindskoog, Donald Eagle,

Frank Magrath, Robert Jones, Don Sullivan, and all the others, permitted me to look at the wound, to begin the healing.

And for one other reason I share this part of myself with you. Let there never be an examination, an account of the Holocaust that is so objective, so scholarly, so intellectual that it is without pain, for then we forget our humanity, for then we forget . . .

LILLIAN TINTER SILBERSTEIN
EXECUTIVE DIRECTOR
NATIONAL CONFERENCE OF
CHRISTIANS AND JEWS
SANTA CLARA COUNTY REGION

The National Conference of Christians and Jews gratefully acknowledges the support of all those who contributed to the success of the conference proceedings and to the editing and preparation of the papers in this volume: The National Conference of Christians and Jews, Inc., Santa Clara County Region; the University of Santa Clara; the Hoover Institution, Stanford University; and San José State University.

The NCCJ also gratefully acknowledges support from Beverly and Barnet Adelman, Dr. Robert McAfee Brown, Dr. John Bunzel, Dr. Glenn Campbell, Dr. William Donnelly, S.J., Dr. John Felstiner, Alfred Fromm, Dr. Gail Fullerton, Nathan Gierowitz, Dr. Thomas P. Hughes, Nicolai Joffe, Dr. Gavin Langmuir, Richard Levin, Dr. S. Martin Lipsett, Donald W. McEvoy, Raquel Newman, Patrick Healy Peabody, Dr. William J. Rewak, S.J., Leah and Eugene Roberts, Miriam J. Roland, Harry H. Rosenblatt, Nathan Shapell, Jack Stutman, Eli Zborowski, the Anti-Defamation League of B'nai B'rith (San José Council), the Jewish Federation of Greater San José, and the Simon Wiesenthal Center of Yeshiva University.

INTRODUCTION

HENRY FRIEDLANDER AND SYBIL MILTON

The murder of the European Jews by the Nazis during World War II has long been a subject of popular interest and scholarly concern. In February 1977, and March 1978, scholars met in San José, California, to discuss the significance of the Holocaust. This volume is a product of those two San José conferences.

Popular interest in the Nazi murder of the Jews has permeated all aspects of our culture. The Jewish catastrophe has served as a subject for novels, plays, films, and documentaries. Museums exhibit paintings, sculptures, photographs, and artifacts from the Nazi camps. Schools and universities teach about Nazi genocide. And recently the President of the United States appointed a Commission on the Holocaust. This interest in Nazi Germany and the so-called Final Solution has also manifested itself in the area where popular culture and commercial profit intersect: the Holocaust is a subject of newspaper accounts, popular lectures, television dramas, and mass market mysteries.

Scholarly concern with the origins and nature of Nazism was already evident before the end of World War II; a number of studies that appeared before 1945 are still valuable.[1] Since then, the scholarly literature on the Nazi Revolution has grown to rival that on the French or Russian revolutions. The scholarly investigation of the Holocaust—including the Nazi system of terror, the police, and the camps, as well as the so-called Final Solution—developed at a much slower rate after 1945. Still, a large number of studies, including several major works,[2] appeared during the three decades after the end of the war. But while these studies of Nazi terror illuminated the entire Nazi phenomenon, scholarship on Nazi Germany largely neglected these contributions. Only recently have scholars, writing and teaching about the Third Reich, come to appreciate the centrality of the Holocaust for an understanding of the Nazi phenomenon.

Panels on Nazi Germany have been common at scholarly conferences. At times, entire conferences have dealt with the Nazi phenomenon and with the history of the European resistance; in 1953, one of the earliest and most impressive of these conferences covered the concept and reality of totalitarianism—both Nazi and Soviet.[3] Conferences specifically treating the Holocaust have not been as common; nevertheless, a number have met since 1945. Unfortunately, most have not published their proceedings; thus we have no printed record of the 1975 conferences on the Holocaust sponsored by the Hebrew University in New York and by the International Conference of Christians and Jews in Hamburg. In part this also applies to two series of conferences: those dealing with the Church Struggle and the Holocaust, sponsored annually in New York by the National Conference of Christians and Jews, and those dealing with the teachings of the Holocaust sponsored annually in Philadelphia by the National Institute on the Holocaust, which has issued its proceedings in mimeographed form only.

However, volumes containing the papers from a number of conferences on the Holocaust have been published. The earliest of these, sponsored by the *Centre de Documentation Juifs Contemporaine,* met in Paris in 1947.[4] It served the valuable function of providing a forum where historians and archivists could exchange information about the status of the documentation of the Jewish catastrophe. Not until 1968 did another conference, meeting in Washington under the auspices of the National Archives, treat this crucial aspect again.[5]

Three scholarly conferences on the Holocaust were convened by Jewish institutions. These conferences—one sponsored by YIVO in New York, and two sponsored by Yad Vashem in Jerusalem—dealt exclusively with the Jewish dimension of Nazi genocide.[6] They were basically symposia by invitation, where scholars exchanged information and elaborated their ideas. A different, and more popular, variety of conference met in New York in 1974 at the Cathedral of Saint John the Divine.[7] Its public lectures addressed large audiences and dealt almost exclusively with the political and moral implications of the Holocaust. The conference that met at Wayne State University in 1970 combined aspects of these two types of conferences.[8] It included both academic papers and popular lectures; it provided for both public sessions and small seminars. It attempted—for the first time, but not yet with complete success—to integrate the study of the

Holocaust with the investigation of the non-Jewish dimensions of the Nazi phenomenon.

The San José conferences differed from all previous conferences on the Holocaust in several important respects. The participants, scholars actively engaged in research and writing, represented a large variety of disciplines, including history, social science, literature, theology, law, medicine, science, and technology. They exchanged ideas, but at the same time their lectures addressed a large general audience. Their papers treated the Holocaust within the larger context of the Third Reich and World War II. Scholars came from a variety of disciplines, but shared an interest in European, German, and Jewish history. For the first time, the study of the Holocaust was fully integrated with the investigation of the entire Nazi phenomenon. The first San José conference treated the significance of the Holocaust in fairly general terms. It dealt with the history of anti-Semitism as one of the roots of Nazi genocide, the psychological and theological dimensions of the Jewish catastrophe, and the methodology of teaching about the destruction of the Jews. The second San José conference used a more specific focus for its discussions. It examined the role of the educated elite and the professions in the Third Reich and Nazi-occupied Europe.

This volume contains most of the papers presented at the two San José conferences. These are not the full proceedings: a few papers as well as the unrecorded public and private discussions have been omitted. Most of the papers have been revised for publication, and their order has been rearranged to provide a logical sequence. Together, they provide a sense of the conference contents, and represent the current status of the integration of the Holocaust as a subject into the larger field of Nazi Germany and World War II.

The volume is divided into six sections, each dealing with a different aspect of the Nazi regime and the Holocaust. Section I contains six papers on the background of Nazi genocide. The first three papers trace the history of anti-Semitism. Although there was a qualitative difference between pre-modern judeophobia and Nazi anti-Semitism, there is no question but that the Nazis built upon centuries of Jew hatred. David Winston and Gavin Langmuir deal with this hatred during ancient and medieval times. Eugen Weber shows how traditional anti-Semitism was transformed into its modern variety, and how it led to a genocide impossible in pre-modern societies. The next two papers deal with the roots of Nazism in the Weimar Republic. The political, social, economic, and intellectual disintegration of German society during the years 1918–32 made it possible for the ideology and organization of the Nazi movement to grow, prosper, and finally triumph. Fritz K. Ringer traces this process through the perversion of ideas in the universities; Peter H. Merkl does so by investigating the pervasive violence of public life. In the final paper, Werner T. Angress treats the experience of the German Jews under the Nazi regime in the 1930's; he describes Jewish response to Nazi policies during the years that preceded the decision of 1941 to kill the European Jews.

Section II contains four papers on the Holocaust and its setting. The first two papers are the conference keynote speeches Raul Hilberg delivered at San José; they are included as they were presented. In the first paper, Hilberg analyzes the Nazi murder of the Jews as a process of destruction. In the second, he draws on his personal experience as a scholar and as a contemporary to attempt an assessment of the significance of the Holocaust. The last two papers in this section deal with the cultural milieu of the Holocaust. Henry Friedlander analyzes the manipulation of language by the Nazis, showing the development of two separate, though interacting, languages: one representing ideology and used by the propagandists, and one representing terror and used by the technicians. Sybil Milton analyzes the manipulation of art and artists in the Third Reich. She shows how the Nazis used art as a propaganda tool for indoctrinating the killers, and how the victims of Nazi terror used art in camps and ghettos to assert their humanity.

Section III, containing seven papers, forms the volume's largest segment. The Nazi regime needed the support of the educated classes to operate the state, to wage war, and to kill the Jews. The papers in this section analyze the outlook and behavior of this elite vis-à-vis the Nazi regime, its ideology, and its terror. Telford Taylor and Gert H. Brieger show how the legal and medical professions, usually considered bastions of independence, were in Germany predisposed to accept the authority of the state, and how this led judges, lawyers, and physicians to acquiesce step by step in Nazi political, social, and racial policies. The next two papers deal with the behavior of the scientific community: Alan Beyerchen discusses the physicists and Thomas P. Hughes the engineers. They show how these professional groups, after the purge of their Jewish and liberal members, accepted the Nazi regime as a matter of course. Although rejecting the leadership of those fellow scientists who wanted to politicize them along lines of Nazi racial ideology, they embraced an apolitical problem-solving pragmatism that made them the willing tools of Nazi policies. Christopher R. Browning treats the civil service, the most essential and willing agents of Nazi domination. He focuses his analysis on the Interior and Foreign ministries and examines, as a test case, the careers of the ambitious young bureaucrats who became the specialists in Jewish affairs, the so-called "Jewish experts" who headed the *Judenreferate*. John S. Conway applies a similar analysis to the Christian clergy, showing how their mild anti-Semitism and virulent nationalism predisposed most churchmen to accept Nazi rule; when some finally realized that Nazi doctrine was incompatible with Christian practice, they had lost their following and were forced to face Nazi radicalism alone. In the final paper, Beate Ruhm von Oppen discusses the political and cultural milieu of the educated elite in Nazi Germany; within this context she analyzes the reasons for the absence as well as the presence of rare instances of resistance.

The two papers in Section IV deal with the elites in the countries occupied by Nazi Germany. Lucjan Dobroszycki discusses the role of the Jewish elites in occupied Europe, showing how they were powerless to alter the fate of the Jews once the Nazis had decided on a policy of extermination. Nothing the Jewish Councils or the Jewish resistance could do made any difference; the fate of the Jews was determined by factors completely outside their control: the German plan, the attitude of their non-Jewish neighbors, and, above all, the status of their territory in the German scheme. Allan Mitchell examines the non-Jewish elites in occupied Europe, using three countries—Poland, Holland, and France—as his examples. He shows how Nazi ideology vis-à-vis each country regulated the treatment of the national elites, and how the relationship between the German occupation and these elites determined the fate of the local Jews. The two papers in Section V discuss the role of the United States during the Holocaust. As the democratic leader of the Western Allies, its failure to rescue any Jews remains a difficult puzzle; for those attending the conference in San José it was a question of troubling relevance. Henry L. Feingold tries to provide an answer by analyzing the politics of those who made policy; John Felstiner attempts a more personal explanation.

Section VI, containing four papers, forms the last segment of the volume. These papers deal with the postwar ramifications of the Holocaust. In the first paper, Franklin H. Littell examines today's universities in the light of the experiences of the Holocaust. The fact that men and women trained in leading universities carried out Nazi genocide forces us to challenge the credibility of higher education, unless we introduce changes to make a repetition impossible. In the next two papers, Paul van Buren and John T. Pawlikowski examine—one from the Protestant and the other from the Catholic perspective—the lessons of the Holocaust as they apply to Christian theology. In the next paper, Lawrence L. Langer discusses the impact of the Holocaust on postwar literature; he examines how the literary imagination can deal with the ultimate atrocity, the reality of the death camps.

Following Section VI, in the volume's final paper, Henry Friedlander attempts to construct a methodology for the teaching of the Holocaust; he tries to delineate the reasons why and how it ought to be taught.

The editors want to thank their fellow contributors for their patience, and Donald McEvoy and Lillian Silberstein of NCCJ for their unfailing support. Above all, they want to acknowledge the contribution of Hanna Gunther, without whose diligence and expertise this volume could not have been finished.

NOTES

1. For example, Franz Neumann, *Behemoth: The Structure and Practice of National Socialism* (London, 1942), and Konrad Heiden, *Der Führer: Hitler's Rise to Power*, trans. Ralph Manheim (Boston, 1944).
2. For example, Alexander Dallin, *German Rule in Russia, 1941–1945: A Study of Occupation Policies* (New York, 1957); Raul Hilberg, *The Destruction of the European Jews* (Chicago, 1961); H. G. Adler, *Der verwaltete Mensch: Studien zur Deportation der Juden aus Deutschland* (Tübingen, 1974).
3. Carl J. Friedrich, ed., *Totalitarianism* (Cambridge, Mass., 1954).
4. *Les Juifs en Europe (1939–1945). Rapports présentés a la première conférence euro- péenne des commissions historiques et des Centres de Documentation Juifs* (Paris, 1949).
5. Robert Wolfe, ed., *Captured German and Related Records. A National Archives Conference* (Athens, Ohio, 1974).
6. *Imposed Jewish Governing Bodies under Nazi Rule. YIVO Colloquium, December 2–5, 1967* (New York, 1972); Moshe M. Kohn, ed., *Jewish Resistance during the Holocaust. Proceedings of the Conference on Manifestations of Jewish Resistance, Jerusalem, April 7–11, 1968* (Jerusalem, 1971); Yisrael Gutman and Efraim Zuroff, eds., *Rescue Attempts during the Holocaust. Proceedings of the Second Yad Vashem International Historical Conference, Jerusalem, April 8–11, 1974* (Jerusalem, 1977).
7. Eva Fleischner, ed., *Auschwitz: Beginning of a New Era? Reflections on the Holocaust* (New York, 1977).
8. Franklin H. Littell and Hubert G. Locke, eds., *The German Church Struggle and the Holocaust* (Detroit, 1974).

THE HOLOCAUST:
IDEOLOGY, BUREAUCRACY, AND GENOCIDE

I.
BEFORE
THE HOLOCAUST

DAVID WINSTON

PAGAN AND EARLY CHRISTIAN ANTI-SEMITISM

The American playwright Maxwell Anderson once wrote: "We live in a world of shadows. We are not what we are but what is said of us." The Jews, more than any other people, have lived in such a world of shadows, shaped by mythological and theological notions of the most varied sort. We shall begin with an examination of the Greco-Roman views of the Jews.

The earliest encounter between Jews and Greeks gave rise to a series of idealized accounts, virtually Utopian in tone. Theophrastus (372–288 B.C.), Aristotle's pupil and successor, was the first Greek writer to deal expressly with the Jews. Referring in his book *On Piety* to the Jewish mode of sacrifice, he notes that "being philosophers by race, they converse with each other during the offering of sacrifices about the Deity."[1] Another pupil of Aristotle, Clearchus of Soli (ca. 300 B.C.), relates the anecdote that his master, while in Asia Minor (347–345 B.C.), had met a Jew of Coele-Syria who "not only spoke Greek, but had the soul of a Greek." This Jew, according to Clearchus, had made the acquaintance of Aristotle and his pupils because of his interest in Greek philosophy, but in the end it was they who learned from him rather than he from them. In passing, Clearchus notes that "the Jews are descended from the Indian philosophers."[2] The same estimate of the Jews as philosophers is also found in Megasthenes (ca. 300 B.C.), an ambassador of Seleucus I, who had visited India and had written an account of that country. Philosophy, he notes, is found not only among the Greeks, but also among the Brahmins in India, and the Jews in Syria. These idealizing accounts are representative of the tendency of Greek ethnographical writing to glorify Eastern wisdom.

A more realistic, though friendly, account of the Jews came from the pen of Hecataeus of Abdera (ca. 300 B.C.), a contemporary of Alexander the Great and Ptolemy I, and the author of a panegyrical exposition of Egyptian culture apparently called *Aegyptiaca*. He had obviously not read Jewish literature (the Bible had not yet been translated into Greek), but had learned something about Jewish history from a Jewish priest named Ezechias who had settled in Egypt, and whom he characterizes as Greek in spirit. He repeats Clearchus' report that the Jews are descended from the Indian philosophers. He praises the tenacity with which the Jews stick to their laws, and relates the fact that Jewish troops in Alexander's army refused to participate in the restoration of Bel's temple in Babylon. He begins his story of Jewish history with the Exodus, relating that the Jews, together with other foreigners, among them Cadmus and Danaus, were expelled from Egypt during an epidemic the Egyptians blamed on their resident aliens. Apparently this represented Egyptian reaction to claims of superiority on the part of both Greeks and Jews. Some of the aliens, led by Danaus and Cadmus (founder of Thebes) emigrated to Greece, but most went to Judaea. Moses conquered Palestine and built the Temple in the center of Jerusalem (actually in the eastern sector, but Hecataeus is here following Greek custom). Hecataeus knows nothing of the kings of Israel, and for him an unbroken dynasty of High Priests begins in Moses' time and continues until his own day. Moses divided the Israelites into twelve tribes, a perfect number, in accordance with the months of the year.[3] Hecataeus characteristically emphasizes how Moses made provision for military training, and more important, rejected the introduction of idols, in order to avoid an anthropomorphic conception of God. He implies that it was through astrophysical speculation that Moses came to the conclusion that it is the "heaven that surrounds the earth which is alone divine and rules the universe." He is apparently impressed by Moses' requirement that the Israelites rear their children, in contrast to the Greek habit of exposing infants. In contrast to the biblical narrative, Hecataeus says that the Jewish priests were not members of certain families, but were chosen on the basis of their individual talents (as are the priests in Plato's *Laws*).[4] The only critical note in Hecataeus' account is his observation that "as a result of their own expulsion from Egypt, Moses introduced an unsocial and intolerant mode of life."[5]

The first literary exponent of the anti-Jewish trend in Hellenistic Egypt was the Egyptian priest Manetho (third century B.C.), who was associated with the Ptolemaic establishment of the cult of Sarapis and was the first Egyptian writer to give an account of Egyptian history in Greek. The

Jewish version of the Exodus story called for an Egyptian reply, which Manetho supplied. According to his account, the Egyptian Pharaoh Amenhotep wished to have a vision of the gods, but was informed by an oracle that he would attain his wish only after he purified the land by ridding it of lepers. He accordingly sent eighty thousand of them into the quarries, but, under the leadership of Osarsiph, a priest of Heliopolis, they rose in rebellion and proceeded to slaughter the sacred animals of Egypt. They invited the Hyksos to be their allies, and with their aid conquered Egypt, instituting a thirteen-year reign of cruelty. They were finally expelled by Pharaoh Amenophis.[6]

The first known writer to charge the Jews with ass worship was Mnaseas of Patara (ca. 200 B.C.), who tells of an Idumaean named Zabidus who had penetrated into the interior of the Temple and made off with the golden head of the pack ass.[7] In a passage of Diodorus of Sicily, which deals with the struggle between Antiochus VII Sidetes and the Jews (134–132 B.C.), we are told that the anti-Semitic advisers of the victorious Seleucid king suggested that he should storm Jerusalem and destroy Judaism, citing as a precedent the attempt made in his time by Antiochus Epiphanes. Among other things, the advisers stated that Antiochus Epiphanes found the statue of a bearded man sitting on an ass in the Jewish Temple, and that he identified the statue with Moses.[8] Damocritus (first century A.D.) reports that the Jews caught a foreigner every seventh year and sacrificed him by carding his flesh into small pieces.[9] Apion (first half of first century A.D.) provides a more detailed version of the blood libel:

> Antiochus found in the temple a couch, on which a man was reclining, with a table before him laden with a banquet of fish of the sea, beasts of the earth, and birds of the air, at which the poor fellow was gazing in stupefaction. The king's entry was instantly hailed by him with adoration, as about to procure him profound relief; falling at the king's knees, he stretched out his right hand and implored him to set him free. The king reassured him and bade him tell him who he was, why he was living there, what was the meaning of his abundant fare. Thereupon, with sighs and tears, the man, in a pitiful tone, told the tale of his distress. He said [Apion continues] that he was a Greek and that, while traveling about the province for his livelihood, he was suddenly kidnapped by men of a foreign race and conveyed to the temple; there he was shut up and seen by nobody, but was fattened on feasts of the most lavish description. At first these unlooked for attentions deceived him and caused him pleasure; suspicion followed, then consternation. Finally, on consulting the attendants who waited upon him, he heard of the unutterable law of the Jews for the sake of which he was being fed. The practice was repeated annually at a fixed season. They would

kidnap a Greek foreigner, fatten him up for a year, and then convey him to a wood, where they slew him, sacrificed his body with their customary ritual, partook of his flesh, and, while immolating the Greek, swore an oath of hostility to the Greeks. The remains of their victim were then thrown into a pit.[10]

Lysimachus wrote that Moses had advised his people "to show good will to no man, to offer not the best but the worst advice, and to overthrow any temples and altars of the gods which they found." These decisions they put into practice:

They traversed the desert, and after great hardships reached inhabited country: there they maltreated the population, and plundered and set fire to the temples, until they came to the country now called Judaea, where they built a city . . . called Hierosyla because of their sacrilegious propensities. At a later date, when they had risen to power, they altered the name, to avoid the disgraceful imputation, and called the city Hierosolyma and themselves Hierosolymites.[11]

What were the main sources of this anti-Semitic literature? The consensus is that racial theories played little or no role in the ancient world. Tacitus did indeed speak of the Teutons' piercing blue eyes, red hair, and tall frames. The Romans were frequently overwhelmed by these huge Teutons when facing them in battle. None of these characteristics, however, are scored as peculiarities of a race which must therefore be scorned. The Romans never allowed racial considerations to govern their relationships with other peoples.[12] Some writers, however, attribute the origins of pagan anti-Semitism to a xenophobia that began mainly in Egypt, where from time immemorial there prevailed a fear of invaders from the East. The Egyptians made a distinction between "men," on the one hand, and Libyans, Asiatics, and Africans, on the other. In other words, the Egyptians were "people"; foreigners were not. At a time of national stress, we hear the complaint that "strangers from outside have come into Egypt . . . Foreigners have become people everywhere." As Wilson has pointed out, however,

the Egyptian isolationist or nationalist feeling was a matter of geography and of manners rather than of racial theory and dogmatic xenophobia. "The people" were those who lived in Egypt, without distinction of race or color. Once a foreigner came to reside in Egypt, learned to speak Egyptian, and adopted Egyptian dress, he might finally be accepted as one of "the people." Asiatics or Libyans or Negroes might be accepted as Egyptians of high position when they had become acclimatized— might, indeed, rise to the highest position of all, that of the god-king.[13]

A more important consideration is the fact of Jewish strangeness. The exotic laws and customs of the Jews and their policy of social separatism are constantly cited in Greco-Roman literature. Even the friendly Hecataeus did not refrain from noting the intolerant character of Jewish life, although he tried to provide a psychological motivation for it. In Palestinian Judaism, the separatism of the Jew is often nakedly expressed. In the Book of Jubilees, for example, the dying Abraham warns Jacob: "Separate thyself from the nations and eat not with them . . . for their works are unclean and all their ways are a pollution and an abomination."[14] The rabbis went to great lengths to create social barriers between Jews and non-Jews. "They decreed against [the Gentile's] bread and oil on account of their wine, and against their wine on account of their daughters, and against their daughters on account of 'the unmentionable' [literally, 'something else,' i.e. idolatry].[15] Even a Jewish Hellenistic writer such as the author of *Aristeas to Philocrates,* could passionately exclaim:

> When therefore our lawgiver, equipped by God for insight into all things, had surveyed each particular, he fenced us about with impregnable palisades and with walls of iron, to the end that we should mingle in no way with any of the other nations, remaining pure in body and in spirit, emancipated from vain opinions, revering the one and mighty God above the whole of creation.[16]

Among the many strange observances of Judaism, the Jewish Sabbath in particular puzzled the pagans. Josephus tells us that Ptolemy Soter entered Jerusalem on the Sabbath and thus captured the city without difficulty. In response to this, Agatharcides scornfully wrote: "That experience has taught the whole world, except that nation, the lesson not to resort to dreams and traditional fancies about the law, until its difficulties are such as to baffle human reason."[17] Juvenal and Seneca attributed the Sabbath to Jewish laziness, and complained that they lost in idleness almost a seventh of their life.[18] Tacitus even mentions the sabbatical year: "After a time they were led by the charms of indolence to give over the seventh year as well to inactivity."[19] Another custom often derided by the pagans was the rite of circumcision. Josephus notes that Apion had ridiculed this practice and then describes with glee how he had met his just deserts: an ulcer on his person rendered circumcision essential; the operation brought no relief, gangrene set in, and he died in exquisite tortures.[20] Rutilius Namatianus (fifth century) believed that circumcision was at the root of all the folly of the Jews.[21] Strabo had already looked upon circumcision as one of the fruits of the superstition into which the Jewish religion had degenerated when it

fell under the influence of superstitious men.[22] Finally, the Jewish dietary
laws also served as the butt of pagan derision. When the emperor Gaius
asked the Jewish delegation why they did not eat pork, the members of the
Alexandrian delegation burst into gales of laughter.[23]

Strangeness in itself, however, is not the whole story. The Greeks and
Romans were familiar with many foreign groups, and although they
occasionally mocked them, there was never anything like the bitter
animosity that characterized their attitude toward the Jews. The fact is, as
V. Tcherikover has correctly pointed out, that the Jews did not resemble
other aliens.[24] As long as strangers lived unobtrusively without making
demands, there was no special reason for hating them. The metics (resident
aliens) in the Greek cities, for example, enjoyed no political rights but
nevertheless undertook the various burdens of civic duty. The Jews, on the
other hand, though enjoying numerous privileges, were exempt from the
ordinary duties of most Greek citizens. They had received such privileges
directly from the kings (later from the emperors), and insisted upon the recognition of these rights by the Greek cities. Thus the Jews could not be
summoned to court on the Sabbath, were exempt from military service and
its associated taxes, as well as the liturgies or the various other city taxes.
The Jews would not contribute to the maintenance of the gymnasia, the
organization of athletic games and the building of temples, because these
were all connected with idolatry. On the other hand, they claimed the right
to collect the half-shekel and send it to Jerusalem. The Jewish refusal to
recognize the official city cult could be readily perceived as undermining
the city's autonomy. "If the Jews are really of our community," claimed the
Ionians, "let them also honor the gods whom we honor."[25] "Thus the two
peoples faced each other without being able to achieve mutual understanding."[26]

There is ample evidence of Greek hostility toward the Jews. Josephus
tells us of the Greeks of Asia Minor who wished to prevent the Jews from
observing their own customs. They forced them to desecrate the Sabbath
by summoning them to their offices on that day, confiscated the sacred
monies earmarked for Jerusalem, and imposed upon the Jews the defrayal
of urban taxes from the same monies.[27] This hostility ultimately culminated
in the Alexandrian pogrom of A.D. 37. Another period of troubles for
Alexandrian Jews came in A.D. 66, when riots again erupted, and the
prefect Tiberius Julius Alexander, a renegade Jew, let his legions loose on
the "Delta" quarter with permission to burn and loot Jewish property and
to kill the rioters. The death toll was put at fifty thousand.[28]

In the anti-Semitic mix of the Latin writers, we may identify an important additional factor that may explain the further development of anti-Jewish hatred in Rome. Moses Hadas has correctly pointed out that under the influence of Stoic theory (especially that of Posidonius) the men around Augustus formulated an official propaganda to justify the expanding power of Rome. History was seen as the working out of a divine plan, with the destiny of Rome as its central concern. Rome's mission was to pacify and civilize the world. The Romans thus constituted an elect with high privileges and equally high responsibilities.[29] The Jewish doctrine of election was thus in direct conflict with the similar conception developed by the Romans. Tacitus' biased account of the Jews may be seen as a counterblast to the Jewish presumption of divine election. When Tacitus wrote his account (ca. A.D. 100), about thirty years after the destruction of the Temple, at the beginning of Trajan's reign, Jewish proselytism was at its height. Josephus testified in A.D. 95 that "there is not one city, Greek or barbarian, nor a single nation, to which our custom of abstaining from work on the seventh day has not spread, and where the fasts and the lighting of lamps and many of our prohibitions in the matter of food are not observed. Moreover, they attempt to imitate our unanimity, our liberal charities, our devoted labor in the crafts, our endurance under persecution on behalf of our laws."[30] Alexandrian anti-Semites could complain to Trajan that the Senate was full of Jews. Angered at the failure of Rome's destruction of the Temple to stem the spread of Judaism, Tacitus sought to create a negative myth concerning the origins of the Jewish people. He finds Jerusalem's fall to be an atonement for a primordial sin going back to its founder, Moses. According to Tacitus, Moses established his influence by introducing new religious practices quite opposed to those of all other religions. "The Jews regard as profane all that we hold sacred." The chief source of Moses' religious ideas was his blind hatred of the Egyptians, which induced him to teach whatever was in opposition to Egyptian thought. Even his sublime monotheistic conception of God was not the product of a deep inner perception, but was rooted instead in his hatred of the Egyptians. The customs of the Jews are therefore base and abominable and owe their persistence to their depravity. Toward every other people the Jews feel only hate and enmity, a trait resulting from their primordial hatred of the Egyptians and their gods.[31] Since Judaism lacks all moral content and was originally established with the sole purpose of negating all other religions, the Romans were entirely justified in destroying the Temple.[32] It may be noted that the anti-Semitism of nineteenth-century Pan-Slavism was motivated in part by a similar clash between two rival claims to divine election. For the Pan-Slavs the Jew was not merely one of the many outsiders to be crushed, but, because of his counterclaim to chosenness, he was the enemy par excellence.[33]

Our analysis has shown that the roots of pagan anti-Semitism were largely social, political, and economic. The anti-Judaism displayed by early Christian writings, on the other hand, stems very largely from polemical theological considerations. The Christians sought to demonstrate that they were now the "true Israel," and that the Jews had completely misread the Hebrew Scriptures now designated as the "Old Testament." In Stephen's speech (in the opening chapters of Acts) it is asserted that the Jews had never been the true people of God. Even from the time of Moses, apostate Israel murmured against God's prophet and rejected the Law, turning to the worship of the golden calf. The theme of the "unbelieving Jew" *vs.* the "believing Gentile" is writ large in the New Testament. The Jews rejected and killed Jesus, whereas the first believer is a Roman centurion at the cross.[34] The unbelieving Jewish cities of Chorasin, Bethsaida, and Capernaum are contrasted with the believing Gentile cities of Tyre and Sidon, whose people "would have repented long ago in sackcloth and ashes," if such mighty works had been done among them.[35] The Gospels systematically play down the fact that it was quisling Jewish authorities who were involved in the death of Jesus, and that it was ultimately the Romans who executed him according to their own modes of execution. There could not be a greater discrepancy between the Pilate known from history and the feeble figure who plays such a vacillating part in the Passion drama. The Gospels are reluctant to state plainly that the death sentence was pronounced by the Roman governor. In Mark 15:15 and Matthew 27:26 we read that "Pilate delivered Jesus to be crucified"; in Luke 23:24 we find that Pilate "decided that their [the Jews'] demand should be granted"; in John 19:16 we are told that "he handed him over to them [the Jews] to be crucified." John's words are immediately contradicted, however, by the ensuing narrative, in which it is Pilate who orders the inscription on the cross (John 19:19), and where it is explicitly stated that it was Roman soldiers who carried out the crucifixion (John 19:23). By the time of Tertullian we get the bald statement: "The whole synagogue of the children of Israel killed him."[36] Tertullian could even speak of Pilate as already convinced of the Christian truth.[37]

The theme that the Jews have always killed the prophets is expressed in the parable of the vineyard, found in all three Synoptics (Mark 12; Matthew 21; Luke 20): The vineyard owner (God) leaves his vineyard (Israel) in the hands of tenants (the Jews), occasionally sending servants (the prophets) to get his share of the fruit. But these unfaithful tenants constantly beat and kill the servants. Finally the owner sends his own son, but the tenants kill him too, believing that thereby they may take perpetual squatters' rights on the vineyard. They have no real right to it. They are only tenants, not sons. What will the owner of the vineyard do? "He will come and destroy the tenants, and give the vineyard to others." (The background of the parable is Isaiah 5:1–7). The climax of this theme is found in Matthew 23:29–35:

> Woe to you, scribes and Pharisees, hypocrites! for you build the tombs of the prophets and adorn the monuments of the righteous, saying, If we had lived in the days of our fathers, we would not have taken part with them in shedding the blood of the prophets. Thus you witness against yourselves, that you are sons of those who murdered the prophets. Fill up, then, the measure of your fathers. You serpents, you brood of vipers, how are you to escape being sentenced to hell? Therefore I send you prophets and wise men and scribes, some of them you will kill and crucify . . . that upon you may come all the righteous blood shed on earth, from the blood of the innocent Abel to the blood of Zechariah whom you murdered between the sanctuary and the altar. O Jerusalem, Jerusalem, killing the prophets and stoning those who are sent to you![38]

In patristic literature there is a considerable escalation of the anti-Jewish polemic. Isidore declares that the evil nature of the Jew never changes, citing Jeremiah 13:23: "Can the Ethiopian change his color or the leopard his spots?" All the negative statements of the Hebrew Scriptures are taken out of context and read as descriptive of the Jews, thus turning Jewish self-criticism into a remorseless invective. Cain symbolizes the Jews, while Abel, killed by the elder brother and replaced by the mysterious Seth, symbolizes the murdered and resurrected Christ.

Justyn Martyr says that circumcision was given to the Jews "that you may be separated from other nations and from us, and that you alone may suffer that which you now justly suffer, and that your land may be desolate and your cities burned with fire, and that strangers may eat your fruit in your presence and not one of you may go up to Jerusalem."[39]

"The accusation that a people is deicidal," writes Rubenstein, "implies that they are utterly beyond law. This may seem a strange accusation to make against the Jews, a people who were the creators of so vast a system of religious law. This seeming paradox did not escape Justin's attention. Unwittingly this basically decent philosopher helped to create the demonological interpretation of the Jews which was to result in so much bloodshed throughout the centuries. Justin maintained that only the excessive moral weakness of the Jews made it necessary for them to be placed under the discipline of the law. This contrasted with those who experience the freedom of the Christ; they need none of the legal constraints of the Jews."[40]

The patristic polemic reaches its height in the unrestrained outburst against the Jews contained in St. Chrysostom's eight sermons (386–387), directed against the Judaizing Christians of Antioch. "The synagogue," he writes, "is not only a whorehouse and a theatre; it is also a den of thieves and a haunt of wild animals."[41] God hates the Jews, and indeed has always hated them. It is therefore the duty of Christians to hate them too.

In short, for Christianity, anti-Judaism was an intrinsic need of Christian self-affirmation. The Church taught that the religion of Israel was now superseded, the Torah abrogated, the promises fulfilled in the Christian Church.

> The Church thus provided an abiding contempt among Christians for Jews and all things Jewish. It made the Jewish people a symbol of unredeemed humanity; it painted a picture of the Jews as a blind, stubborn, carnal, and perverse people, whose history had in reality come to an end, but who were nevertheless preserved for a very special theological purpose: it was to continue to exist in a pariah status both to testify to the present election of the Church, and to witness its final triumph.[42]

The painful effect of Christian teaching concerning the Jew is poignantly felt in the case of the brave anti-Nazi Christian martyr Dietrich Bonhoeffer. As Emil Fackenheim has pointed out, his attack on the Nazi legislation against the Jews in 1933 was confined to converted Jews only. He was able to rationalize Hitler's program for faithful Jews: "The Church has never lost sight of the thought that the 'Chosen People' who nailed the redeemer of the world to the cross, must bear the curse for its action through a long history of suffering." Later, of course, Bonhoeffer's opposition to the Nazis became more complete. Still, as Yerushalmi has indicated, "if genocide were an inexorable consequence of Christian theology, it should have come in the Middle Ages. What is true, nevertheless, is that Christian anti-Semitism helped create a climate in which genocide, once conceived, could be achieved."[43]

NOTES

1. Menahem Stern, *Greek and Latin Authors on Jews and Judaism* (Jerusalem, 1976), p. 10.
2. Ibid., p. 50.
3. Cf. Plato *Laws* 771B; *Republic* 546B.
4. Ibid., *Laws* 759B.

5. Stern, pp. 20–44.
6. Ibid., pp. 62–86.
7. Ibid., pp. 97–101.
8. Ibid., p. 142.
9. Ibid., pp. 530–31.
10. Ibid., pp. 411–12.
11. Ibid., pp. 384–85.
12. Cf. Tacitus *Annales* 11.23.24.
13. John A. Wilson, "Egypt," in H. and H. A. Frankfort, John A. Wilson, Thorkild Jacobsen, eds., *Before Philosophy* (Baltimore, 1949), pp. 41–42.
14. Book of Jubilees 22:16.
15. BT Shabbath 17b.
16. *Aristeas to Philocrates,* verse 139.
17. Agatharcides, Josephus Against Apion, 209–11.
18. Juvenal, *Saturuae* 14. 105 ff.; Augustine *Civitas Dei* 6.11.
19. Tacitus *Histories* 5.4.
20. *Against Apion* 2.137–43.
21. 1.389.
22. 16.2.37.
23. Philo, *The Embassy to Gaius*, pp. 361–63.
24. V. Tcherikover, *Hellenistic Civilization and the Jews* (Philadelphia, 1959), p. 372.
25. Josephus *Antiquities of the Jews* 12.2.
26. Tcherikover, p. 376.
27. Josephus *Antiquities* 12.125 ff.; 16.27 ff.
28. Josephus *War* 2.487 ff. For the Jewish-Greek conflict in Caesarea (A.D. 61–62) see L. I. Levine, *Caesarea Under Roman Rule* (Leiden, 1975), pp. 29–30.
29. Moses Hadas, *Hellenistic Culture* (New York, 1959), p. 252. Cf. Vergil *Aeneid* 1.257–96; Livy *Histories* 1.4.1; 1.16.7; 26.41.9.
30. *Against Apion* 2.282 ff.
31. Tacitus *Histories* 5.2–5.
32. Cf. Johanan H. Levy, *Studies in Jewish Hellenism* (Jerusalem, 1960), pp. 116–96. In Hebrew.
33. Arthur Hertzberg, *The Zionist Idea* (New York, 1959), p. 34.
34. Mark 15:39.
35. Matthew 11:20–24; Luke 10:13–15.
36. *Adversus Marcionem* 3.6.2; *Adversus Judaeos* 8.18.
37. Paul Winter, *On the Trial of Jesus* (Berlin, De Gruyter), pp. 51–61.
38. Rosemary R. Ruether, *Faith and Fratricide* (New York, 1974), p. 92.
39. Justyn Martyr *Dialogue* 16.
40. Richard Rubenstein, *After Auschwitz* (Indianapolis, 1966), pp. 13–14.
41. *Or. C. Jud.* 1.3.4.
42. Gregory Baum's Introduction to Rosemary Ruether, *Faith and Fratricide*, p. 7.
43. Y. Yerushalmi, "Response to Rosemary Ruether," in Eva Fleischner, ed., *Auschwitz, Beginning of a New Era? Reflections on the Holocaust* (New York, 1974), p. 103. For Fackeuheim's remark on Bouhoeffer, see E. L. Fackenheim, *The Jewish Return into History* (New York, 1978), pp. 35–36; 74–75.

GAVIN I. LANGMUIR

MEDIEVAL ANTI-SEMITISM

The Mediterranean world of late antiquity bequeathed to the newly Germanized societies of sixth-century Europe a minority of Christians and a priesthood that sought to propagate Christianity with its corollary of anti-Judaism. Early medieval Europe also inherited dispersed Jews against whom that anti-Judaism could be directed. Both Christians and Jews were far more densely implanted in southern than in northern Europe where pagan Germans ruled themselves or dominated a population little marked by Roman culture. Half a millennium later, however, in Rashi's lifetime at the end of the eleventh century, a Christianity considerably different from that of late antiquity had become deep-rooted in both the north and south of a bellicose Europe that now thought of itself as Christendom. And the first major massacre of Jews in Europe, in the Rhineland in 1096, demonstrated that Christian anti-Judaism had, for the first time, gained merciless mass support—in northern Europe.

The Jews who died in 1096 to sanctify the Holy Name—Rabbi Judah, his young wife Rachel, their sons Aaron and Isaac, their beautiful daughters Bella and Matrona, and hundreds of others—at least had the satisfaction of dying significantly for what they were proud to be: Jews who chose martyrdom rather than apostasy, not helpless victims of a collective delusion. Yet soon, long before the coining of the term "anti-Semitism" in 1873 or the catastrophic irrationality of the Nazi camps, Jews were being killed for what they were not.

If by "anti-Semitism" we mean not only its racist manifestation, but all instances in which people, because they are labeled Jews, are feared as symbols of subhumanity and hated for threatening characteristics they do not in fact possess,[1] then anti-Semitism in all but name was widespread in

northern Europe by 1350, when many believed that Jews were beings
incapable of fully rational thought who conspired to overthrow Christendom, who committed ritual crucifixions, cannibalism, and host profanation,
and who caused the Black Death by poisoning wells—even though no one
had observed Jews committing any of these crimes. Unknown to the ancient
world, anti-Semitism emerged in the Middle Ages, along with so many
other features of later Western culture. It is one contribution to which
historians of the majority cannot point with pride, so most medievalists
have avoided discussing it.[2]

That tragedy would not have occurred, nor would an intense and
sophisticated Jewish culture have developed in Europe, had not the
presence of Jews been tolerated. And when the Babylonian Talmud was
being formed in the East, and the Roman Empire was drawing to an end in
the West, that possibility was uncertain. After Christianity had been
recognized as a licit religion in the Roman Empire, gained political
influence, become the official religion in 391, and secured the official
suppression of paganism, the future of Judaism hung in the balance. Partly
because most Christian laymen got on only too well with Jews, many
bishops and monks wanted to extirpate that contaminating influence and
destroyed synagogues in various places across the Empire. Saint Ambrose,
bishop of Milan, threatened the Emperor Theodosius II with excommunica-
tion if he punished the perpetrators of one of these incidents. Ambrose
declared that it was right to destroy synagogues and that Christians had a
duty to disobey any law that forbade their destruction.[3] But imperial
reluctance to change Roman law, supported by Pauline theology about the
providential role of the Jews, preserved the synagogues, albeit with a
lowered status.

That restricted toleration was finally made the official policy of the
Western Church about 600 by the man who has been described both as the
last of the church fathers and the first of the medieval popes. Gregory I held
that non-believers should be led to the faith by clear reasoning pleasantly
presented, not by persecution, and that those who acted otherwise were
pursuing their own ends, not those of God. It was Gregory the Great who
formulated the statement that was to appear in the preamble of all the papal
bulls of general protection for Jews from 1120 to the end of the Middle
Ages: "Just as license ought not to be allowed for Jews to do anything in
their synagogues beyond what is permitted by law, so also they ought to
suffer no injury in those things that have been granted to them." For better
or worse, Gregory declared the right of Jews to live as Jews in western
Christian societies.[4]

Solomon Grayzel has commented that "it is not difficult to imagine what the fate of Jews would have been had not the popes made it a part of church policy to guarantee the Jews life and rights of religious observance."[5] But, fatally, that policy was never vigorously enough pursued by popes or strongly enough enforced by local prelates to be decisive in time of need. Once Europe had fully accepted medieval Christianity, the expulsion of Jews began in earnest: from England and southern Italy in 1290, from France first in 1306 and finally in 1394, from many parts of Germany by 1350, and from Spain in 1492 and Portugal in 1497. While these expulsions were the work of secular authorities impelled primarily by secular motives, no pope spoke out against them, and by 1492 much of Europe was *judenrein*. Although Jews were never expelled from Rome itself, the principle that Jews and Judaism existed legitimately in Europe was never fully accepted in Christendom at large. The toleration extended by churchmen to those whom they considered both their forefathers in righteousness and Christ-killers was too ambivalent and half-hearted to provide reliable protection. The possibility of extirpation was always open.

I have thus far presented what may be considered the traditional picture of the Christian Middle Ages, in which the teaching of contempt of Jews by churchmen was carried to extremes of expulsion and massacre by religious fanatics and laymen incapable of understanding the religious subtleties. But let us not be so naive as to reduce history to the conflict of religions or to think that every action of people labeled Christians or Jews was dictated by their religions. Granted that the church designated Jews within Christian society as an inferior religious out-group, why did many inhabitants of European Christendom treat Jews in ways that were either not prescribed by Christian doctrine or explicitly prohibited by it? Why did people in northern Europe go far beyond the official anti-Judaism and create anti-Semitism?

Until about the year 1000, hostility against Jews was purely anti-Judaic and generally insignificant. Some Mediterranean clerics did try to instill anti-Judaic attitudes in the minds of laymen, particularly rulers, but they were rarely successful in a barbarized Europe where Christianity was only a thin veneer.[6] Anti-Judaic laws were intermittently promulgated, and in some localities Jews were sometimes given the choice of baptism or exile. An excellent example of this kind of cleric is the Spaniard, Archbishop Agobard of Lyons, one of the most rational and conscientious Christians of the first half of the ninth century. He was shocked that in the avowedly Christian society of the Carolingian Empire the common people and nobles seemed to favor Jews as much as Christians, and he tried to persuade

Charlemagne's successor to enforce the anti-Judaic laws of the church—without success.[7] For there was no significant animus against the descendants of the prophets and the warriors of the Old Testament in that heavily Germanized and warlike society." Within the next two centuries, however, the situation had changed radically.

By 1000, the second wave of great invasions—by Saracens, Vikings, and Magyars—had been repulsed; the parish network had been completed; Benedictine monasteries were richly endowed across Europe; and Europeans had become self-consciously Christian in their own way. During the eleventh century, political stability and economic development had progressed sufficiently for Europeans to go on the attack against their non-Christian neighbors in Spain, eastern Germany, and the Holy Land—and to do so under the sign of the cross. Christian symbols had become accepted as the banner of European culture and of the European expansion that began with the first crusade in 1096 and continued for centuries.

The first great massacre of Jews in Europe in 1096 marked the beginning of a new and tragic phase in Jewish history and demonstrated a radical change in the pattern of European hostility toward Jews. Those massacres were not committed by official crusading armies but by bands consisting primarily of peasants, which set out from northern Europe before the official forces. The worst hostility was no longer Mediterranean, ecclesiastical, and official; it was northern, popular, and defied both ecclesiastical and secular prohibitions. The unofficial crusaders came from that area where Mediterranean influences were most directly confronted by Germanic culture: northeastern France and the Rhineland. Here illiterate people, whose Germanic conception of religion emphasized warfare and drew little distinction between sacred and profane activities, had finally learned to define their cosmos in terms of salient Christian symbols and rituals. To them it seemed ridiculous to go and kill distant Moslems before dealing first with God's worst enemies close at hand, the Jews who had killed their Christ. Yet although the Christianity of this ignorant and brutal rabble differed notably from that of Ambrose of Milan, the massacres were nonetheless still primarily anti-Judaic in motivation, an overflow of animus in an atmosphere of religious war.

The nature of the hostility was old; its new pervasiveness and intensity, however, forced the Jews to adopt new forms of conduct which, in turn, aroused new kinds of hostility. A self-fulfilling prophecy had been set in motion: the intense pressure of the majority increasingly circumscribed voluntary Jewish conduct and forced Jews to adapt to their more perilous situation. Before 1100, Jews had been considered fundamentally inferior because they could not recognize Christ's truth and had killed him, but most of the restrictions imposed by ecclesiastical law to separate Jews from Christians had been unenforceable. But after 1100, in an ever more self-consciously Christian society, those old restrictions were more strictly enforced and new ones were imposed because now laymen as well as clerics had discovered that they could exploit the Jews.

In 1100, Jews were not concentrated in moneylending and were not stereotyped as usurers.[8] But in the twelfth century, the commercial revolution brought to northern Europe the development of towns, monopolistic merchant and craft guilds, more financial transactions, and a demand for credit. Wealthier Jews, excluded from their former participation in long-distance trade and from local production, began to concentrate disproportionately in moneylending. In the second half of the twelfth century the church became seriously concerned with the new importance of credit. Its prohibitions fairly effectively stopped the monasteries, the first great suppliers of credit, but only forced Christian merchants to camouflage their lending operations. Yet if Jews were never the first, the only, or—except briefly in parts of northern Europe—the principal lenders, nonetheless they came to concentrate openly and very disproportionately in northern Europe in the unpopular but needed activity of pawnbroking and contract loans. The needs and pressures of the majority had forced Jews to engage in new conduct.

Their increasing unpopularity as unbelieving Christ-killers and usurers in turn made Jews more dependent on the protection of secular authorities. In return for a large share of the profits, kings and princes were willing to protect Jews and their moneylending, despite ecclesiastical admonitions; as a result, Jewish lenders in northern Europe reached their greatest prosperity around 1200.[9] Later on, as Italian lenders came to provide an alternative source of credit, rulers discovered that protecting unpopular Jews was a political liability of decreasing economic value. The period of expulsions was approaching.

As pressure mounted in the thirteenth century, Jews in northern Europe were increasingly identified as town-dwellers constricted to certain quarters, marked by distinctive clothing, denied the right to bear arms, forbidden to leave their lords' jurisdiction, concentrated in moneylending, and forced to rely on money and bribery for self-protection. Now they were not only seen as Christ-killers but were also stereotyped as usurers, bribers, and secret killers. And since thirteenth-century people did not realize that the new stereotypes were a result of majority pressure, Jews now seemed even more inferior than they had in the fourth or eleventh century. Jews were not inferior because they had killed Christ; rather, their killing of Christ was only one, if the most important, manifestation of an underlying essential inferiority that was also evident in such apparently unconnected conduct as usury, bribery, and military incapacity. It was now much easier to think of Jews as less than fully human and to treat them accordingly.

The anti-Jewish stereotypes mentioned thus far, which I shall call xenophobic stereotypes, all had a kernel of truth. (It should be remembered that, so long as it was safe, Jews always acknowledged that they had legitimately killed the heretic, Jesus.) But now a new kind of stereotype appeared, which I shall call chimeric. These chimeric stereotypes had no kernel of truth; they depicted imaginary monsters, for they ascribed to Jews horrendous deeds imagined by Christians, which no Jew had ever been observed to commit. "The Jews" were used as a symbol to express repressed fantasies about crucifixion and cannibalism, repressed doubts about the real presence of Christ in the Eucharist, and unbearable fears of the bubonic bacillus that imperceptibly invaded people's bodies. Individuals poorly integrated in their societies and within themselves could express their internal tensions as a conflict between good and bad people, between Christians and Jews. These psychologically troubled people discovered that they could even gain social approval for their struggle to support generally accepted values against hidden menaces by accusing and attacking Jews.

The first European fantasy of Jewish ritual murder was created at Norwich about 1150 by the cumulative irrationality of a superstitious, insignificant priest and his wife, a mendacious Jewish apostate, and an unimportant monk who sought to overcome his sense of inferiority. They transmuted the fact of a cruel murder of a boy by an unknown killer into a fantasy that Jews throughout Europe conspired to crucify a Christian child once a year as a sacrifice and to show contempt for Christianity. Despite much initial skepticism at Norwich, the fantasy gradually gained acceptance because people wanted a new, local saint to work miraculous cures, and because local churchmen welcomed profitable new relics. As the rumor spread, other churchmen in England and northern France claimed that bodies discovered in their localities were also martyrs and erected shrines for them. Still other clerics chronicled these purported crucifixions as facts. One century later, in 1235, Germany contributed its own variation: the fantasy that Jews killed Christians for ritual cannibalism. Such rumors, followed by massacres, became so frequent, particularly in Germany, that they provoked official investigations by the German emperor and then by the pope. But although both denied that ritual cannibalism was part of

Judaism, no pope ever condemned the crucifixion fantasy, for it too conveniently supported Christian doctrine about the Jews. Consequently, when Henry III, the weakly pious king of England, investigated the alleged crucifixion of young Hugh of Lincoln in 1255, nothing inhibited his superstitious credulity, and he became the first major authority to execute Jews for ritual murder.[10] Although many members of the tiny educated class remained skeptical, it was becoming hard for peasants not to believe accusations supported by such authoritative confirmation.

By the end of the thirteenth century, when the fantasy of ritual murder had become firmly rooted in northern Europe, a new fantasy suddenly appeared. Christians had long debated whether and how Christ's body and blood were present in the consecrated bread and wine of the Eucharist. In 1215, the Fourth Lateran Council tried to settle the issue by promulgating the dogma of transubstantiation. Though doubts continued, the cult of the body of Christ, of the consecrated host, was massively developed. In 1264, the new feast of Corpus Christi was made official for the whole church; and during the troubled fourteenth century, the need for the reassurance of Christ's concrete presence drove people to witness the Mass, some even rushing from church to church just to see the priest elevate the consecrated wafer. But was Christ really present? The best indication that hidden doubts continued was the way Jews, who assuredly did not believe this dogma, were exploited to prove its truth. By a strange coincidence, only at the end of the thirteenth century, when so much had been staked on the reality of Christ's physical presence in the Mass, were Jews suddenly accused of torturing Christ by profaning the consecrated host. By that time, the Jews had been expelled from England and France, but the new fantasy spread like wildfire through Germany and Austria. Hundreds and hundreds of Jews were slaughtered and new shrines were erected for the allegedly profaned hosts. Proof was supposedly provided by blood or cries emanating from the miraculous, tortured host or, more naturally, by the discovery of a mutilated wafer in a Jew's house—evidence that in at least one case is known to have been planted by a priest. In fact, as one skeptical intellectual of the fifteenth century, Nicholas of Cusa, pointed out, the fantasy contradicted the dogma of transubstantiation, which declared that the visible characteristics of the bread and wine did not change, only their underlying substance. However, this did not prevent waves of persecution which only stopped with the emergence of Protestantism.[11]

Thus, by the early fourteenth century, Jews were no longer slaughtered as a side-effect of the crusades, out of anti-Judaic animus; instead they were killed by lower-class mobs, organized to avenge ritual murders and profaned hosts. Many now saw the Jews as inhuman beings who secretly conspired to commit the worst atrocities on defenseless hosts and children and to undermine Christendom. Anti-Semitism was firmly implanted. When the Black Death broke out in Europe between 1347 and 1350, it was all but inevitable that Jews would be accused of poisoning the wells in order to overthrow Christendom and be slaughtered in thousands despite papal prohibition.

It is significant that although xenophobic stereotypes were current throughout Europe, chimeric fantasies were largely restricted to northern Europe, especially to the least Romanized regions. Although militant friars and other clerics tried to implant these fantasies in Mediterranean Europe, they had little success—as the Nazis similarly failed to convert the Fascists to the Aryan myth.[12] In the Middle Ages, as in modern times, the heartland of anti-Semitism was northern Europe.

The chimeric fantasies had been developed in England, northern France, and Germany by a minority of anxious Christians who used the label "Jew," and the persons so identified, as a menacing symbol of their own weaknesses, their own guilt, doubt, and fear. Social confirmation through shrines and executions then convinced many more rational people (who already believed the xenophobic stereotypes) that the chimeric accusations were true. But by the end of the Middle Ages, Englishmen and Frenchmen were denied this irrational way of dealing with weaknesses in their societies and in themselves because the Jews had been expelled from those kingdoms. Even though the label "the Jews" retained its chimeric symbolism in French and English culture,[13] other explanations for personal and social failure had to be found.

From Germany, however, Jews had never been completely expelled, and in this region people seem to have retained a need for an undifferentiated religion—or ideology—that would encompass and explain all experience. Here, perhaps because of that need, Jews had first been massacred in large numbers in 1096. Here, partly because of the guilt and fear aroused by those initial massacres of the defenseless, occurred most of the killing incited by chimeric fantasies during the Middle Ages. Here, from the later Middle Ages to Hitler, there was not only "The Jew" embedded in religion, literature, and art[14] as a symbol of depravity and subhumanity; there were also real Jews whose isolation in the ghettos made it all the easier for people outside to perceive them, not as individual humans, but as walking symbols of those social and personal weaknesses which people could not confront in themselves but could attack directly when projected on Jews. And here it was that Protestantism had the least effect on attitudes toward Jews.

Although Martin Luther broke the unity of medieval Christendom, and was briefly optimistic that his understanding of Christianity would convert the Jews, he soon returned to a virulent repetition of the medieval chimeric fantasies about them.

Later, when *Der Stürmer* cautioned parents to keep their children away from Jews at Passover and reprinted medieval woodcuts of ritual murders, a popular edition of Luther's pamphlet *The Jews and Their Lies* was issued simultaneously (1935). One violent passage among many stands out in that pamphlet:

> We do not curse them but wish them well, physically and spiritually. We lodge them, we let them eat and drink with us. We do not kidnap their children and pierce them through; we do not poison their wells; we do not thirst for their blood. How, then, do we incur such terrible anger on the part of such great and holy children of God? There is no other explanation for this than . . . that God has struck them with "madness and blindness and confusion of mind." So we are even at fault in not avenging all this innocent blood of our Lord and of the Christians which they shed for three hundred years after the destruction of Jerusalem, and the blood of the children they have shed since then (which still shines forth from their eyes and their skin). We are at fault in not slaying them.[15]

In contrast to Calvinist tolerance in Holland and England, German Lutheranism only reinforced the medieval anti-Semitism that, together with its future victims, the Ashkenazim, was already so deeply rooted in German culture.

NOTES

1. Gavin I. Langmuir, "Prolegomena to any Present Analysis of Hostility Against Jews," *Social Science Information*, vol. 15 (1976), 689–727.
2. Gavin I. Langmuir, "Majority History and Post-Biblical Jews," *Journal of the History of Ideas*, vol. 27 (1966), 343–64.
3. Marcel Simon, *Verus Israel*, 2nd ed. (Paris, 1964), pp. 239–74.
4. Bernhard Blumenkranz, *Juifs et chrétiens dans le monde occidental, 430–1095* (Paris, 1960), pp. 98–99, 105, 311–12.
5. *The Church and the Jews in the XIIIth Century*, rev. ed. (New York, 1966), p. 81.
6. See Heinrich Fichtenau, *The Carolingian Empire*. Peter Munz, trans. (Oxford, 1957), pp. 47–65.
7. Bernhard Blumenkranz, *Les auteurs chrétiens latins du moyen age sur les juifs et le judaísme* (Paris, 1963), pp. 152–68.
8. Despite retrospective stereotyping in some modern histories, e.g., Marshall W. Baldwin, ed., *A History of the Crusades*, vol. I: *The First Hundred Years*, (Madison, 1969), p. 263.
9. See H. G. Richardson, *The English Jewry under Angevin Kings* (London, 1960); Robert Chazan, *Medieval Jewry in Northern France* (Baltimore, 1973). In Germany, however,

Jewish moneylending prospered up to the early fourteenth century: Salo W. Baron, *A Social and Religious History of the Jews*, 2nd ed. (New York, 1952–73), vol. 12, p. 150.

10. "The Knight's Tale of Young Hugh of Lincoln," *Speculum*, vol. 47 (1972), 459–82.

11. For an excellent brief survey, see Sister Marie Despina, "Les accusations de profanation d'hosties portées contre les juifs," *Rencontre*, 22 and 23 (1971), 150–73, 180–96.

12. See my "L'absence d'accusation de meurtre rituel à l'ouest du Rhône," *Cahiers de Fanjeaux*, vol. 12 (1977).

13. See Léon Poliakov, *The History of Antisemitism* (New York, 1965–75), vol. 1, 172–245; Bernard Glassman, *Anti-Semitic Stereotypes without Jews* (Detroit, 1975).

14. E.g., Isaiah Schachar, *The Judensau: A Medieval Anti-Jewish Motif and its History* (London, 1974).

15. Martin Luther, *Works*, Jaroslav Pelikan and Helmut T. Lehman, eds. (St. Louis, Mo., 1955–75), XLVII, 267.

EUGEN WEBER

MODERN ANTI-SEMITISM

The Holocaust is not about anti-Semitism, but it is (and it is about) the fallout of anti-Semitism.[1] When one asks about the origins of the Holocaust, one really asks how an infection latent in Western Christian society for centuries could become a murderous plague just when that society had become least Christian and most orderly. And the answer to this sort of question must refer to cultural tradition.

Societies produce stereotypes (which are the height of artifice), and then consume them as commonplaces (which are the height of naturalness). That is how bad faith can pass for good conscience. That is how religious distinctions and cultural stereotypes can lead to murder—which is not an unusual case in history but unusually gruesome and shocking when practiced on the scale that marks the Holocaust.

Hence the desperate attempts to understand, or, more correctly, to comprehend, in the sense of taking in and rendering intelligible a phenomenon so inapprehensible by its nature. Let me say at once that understanding something (or understanding just a bit better) is simply the satisfaction of a curiosity. I do not believe that, in the popular phrase, to understand all is to forgive all. Indeed, it is one of the weaknesses of contemporary thinking to act as if one could understand all, and as if one could or should forgive all. Nor can we really understand. Social scientists are silly if they think that to explain all is to understand all. We cannot explain everything, and we understand even less.

Others have tried before us, of course. So much has been written on

Reprinted with permission, from *Historical Reflections/Réflexions Historiques,* Vol. 5, No. 1 (Summer, 1978).

the subject that it is hard to say anything new—anything that is not already a platitude. A dip into even one or two representative books—for instance, Rudolph Loewenstein's *Christians and Jews*, or Hannah Arendt's *Origins of Totalitarianism*—will provide all the basic interpretative themes: Jewish peculiarity and particularism; the association of Jews with the death of Christ, with usury, and with dark, mysterious, implicitly threatening forces; the ubiquity of the Jew as *other* in so many places and at so many social-economic-cultural levels; and finally the resentment against Jewish pretensions and upstartness. These are also the basic explanations that I should advance for anti-Jewish sentiment. And I shall treat them in due course.

More interesting, though, and more debatable, is another point I want to raise, one that stems from the fact that anti-Semitism does not necessarily imply genocide, or even mass murder. But a desire for riddance from what is regarded as alien and potentially menacing can lead to such conclusions, as may be seen in a well-known document, whose accuracy is debatable but whose contents are revealing. In Book I of Exodus (1:7–10), Joseph, under whose aegis the Jews had prospered in Egypt, dies:

> And the children of Israel were fruitful, and increased abundantly, and multiplied, and waxed exceedingly mighty; and the land was filled with them.
>
> Now there arose up a new king over Egypt, which knew not Joseph.
>
> And he said unto his people, Behold, the people of the children of Israel are more and mightier than we:
>
> Come on, let us deal wisely with them; lest they multiply, and it comes to pass that, when there falleth out any war, they join also unto our enemies, and fight against us, and so get them up out of the land.

Pharaoh, as we know, tried persecutions of all sorts and, when these did not work, he began to have all male children killed at birth—which is the beginning of the story of Moses.

A few hundred years later the story repeats itself, and the text is even more suggestive. In the Book of Esther (3:8–9), we find the Jews in Babylonian exile, that is, essentially in Persia:

> And Haman said unto King Ahasuerus, There is a certain people scattered abroad, and dispersed among the people in all the provinces of thy kingdom; and their laws are diverse from all people, neither keep they the king's laws: therefore, it is not for the king's profit to suffer them.
>
> If it please the king, let it be written that they may be destroyed.

A rather similar dec·sion, though more piecemeal, is reported by Tacitus for the reign of Tiberius: send the men of military age to Sardinia to fight the bandits. "If they perished as a result of the unhealthy climate, it would be no great loss. The remainder would have to leave Italy if they had not abjured their profane rites before a set date."[2]

And why all this? Why such extreme measures? The sources suggest the extent to which apparently modern arguments and criticisms were articulated hundreds of years before Christ. For one thing, the Egyptians and their friends had to find an explanation for the embarrassing events of the twelfth century (whether they had occurred or not). And so in the third century B.C. we find the Egyptian Manethos, and also the Greek Hecateus of Abdera, accusing the Jews of contagious maladies, subversion, rebellious-ness, and lack of piety[3]—and these are all dangerous to the realm; but they also accuse them of misanthropy and misoxeny.[4] And here we come to the crux of the matter, especially when we read that the Jews, chased from Egypt for their lack of piety, perpetuated in Jerusalem their hatred of men, of mankind, of strangers: "This is why they instituted special laws, like never to sit at table with a foreigner and to show them no kindness."[5]

Here is one leitmotif, one major theme among many, that one runs into all the time: in the first century B.C. Posidonius of Apamea thinks that "the Jewish race alone of all nations refused to have any social relations with the other people and considered them all as enemies."[6] More explicit is Philostratos of Lemnos, another Alexandrian Greek, writing around A.D. 200:

> For this people had long raised itself not only against Romans but against humanity in general. Men who have imagined an unsociable life, who share with their fellows neither table nor libations, neither prayer nor sacrifices, are further from us than Susa or Bactria, or even the farthest Indies.[7]

Finally, Juvenal repeats some of these charges but makes explicit two of their implications: suspicion growing out of a sense of mysterious doings among the suspect; and resentment of a people that insists on having its own way and does not participate or share in some of the essential aspects of its neighbors' lives. Juvenal accuses the Jews of spurning Roman law and revering only their own which, he says, Moses passed on "in a mysterious volume: not to show the way to the traveler who doesn't practice the same ceremonies; to point out a fountain only to the circumcised." And to spend the seventh day doing nothing "without sharing in the duties of life."[8]

One last quotation, to show how many familiar themes had been developed two thousand years ago: in 59 B.C., Valerius Flaccus, a corrupt Roman official who had served in Palestine, was accused of having appropriated the gold that Jews all over the Empire sent for the upkeep of their temple. Flaccus hired Cicero, who was the best lawyer in town; and Cicero argued that, in confiscating the Jewish gold, Flaccus had merely opposed a barbarian superstition and an uneconomic drain on Roman resources. And here again a familiar note creeps in: Flaccus, says Cicero, in effect, *a bien mérité de la patrie*, because it takes a brave man to take on the Jews: "You know how numerous their gang, how they support each other, how powerful they are in the assemblies . . . to despise in the interest of the Republic this multitude of Jews . . . is proof of a singular strength of mind."[9]

So here we have a people (or sect) whose insistent particularism arouses strong resentments—which will be further reinforced by Christian experience and Christian tradition. And this brings me to my first component of modern anti-Jewishness: religious indoctrination.

I shall not insist on it, because it is obvious; yet it is basic.[10] By the nineteenth century, traditional religion was no longer a dominant component of high culture—sometimes not even of official culture. But religious tradition was; and religious tradition in its most basic form shaped the mentality and conditioned the reflexes of most people—especially simple people.

One thing everybody knew was that the Jews had killed Jesus. The crime and its implications were reiterated in liturgy and catechism, generation after generation and year after year, at the very least in Easter Week services which often included the wreaking of symbolic retribution on the Jews, either during the Tenebrae service on Maundy Thursday, or on Good Friday. Symbolically, beating "the Jews" with hammers or cudgels or fists, extinguishing them with candles, burning them in bonfires—these were practices that survived in France until around 1900, and elsewhere, I suspect, longer than that.[11]

The memory of alleged Jewish "crimes" was also preserved in the legends of a number of saints whom the Jews were supposed to have martyred, like St. Hugh of Lincoln, or St. Verney in Auvergne—who had been crucified head down by local Jews—whose official or officious worship lent authority to the legends of ritual murder that kept reviving into the twentieth century.[12]

In 1892–93, a French friend of the Jews, Anatole Leroy-Beaulieu, wrote a book about and against anti-Semitism, in which he remarks that "races conserve for a long time at the instinctual level repugnances whose cause they do not really know very well."[13] I am convinced that the firm base of visceral anti-Semitism in the West was laid down by this long-persistent conditioning that made suspicion and condemnation of Jews integral parts of prejudices and aversions that could be evoked almost at will. Two references to Hannah Arendt's work will illustrate this.

At one point, talking about the time of the Dreyfus Affair, she says: "There can be no doubt that in the eyes of the mob the Jews came to serve as an object lesson for all the things they detested."[14] The point is well made, but it begs the question: could that have happened without preparation? If Dreyfus had been an Armenian, or even a Turk, could the press campaign against him have achieved so much so quickly? The ground had to be prepared, and Arendt herself tells us about the preparation, though that is not her purpose in this passage: "For thirty years," she writes, "the old legends of world conspiracy had been no more than the conventional stand-by of the tabloid press and the dime novel, and the world did not easily remember that not long ago . . ."[15] One may notice here a rather haughty disparagement of the most widely diffused creators and expressors of popular lore, because they are cheap and vulgar; and the mistaken assumption that "the world" did not easily remember, when in effect it had never forgotten.

This is the sort of protective self-delusion that can also be found in Rudolph Loewenstein's preface to his book in which this very able analyst refers to his surprise in 1940 (having completely identified himself with France for many years) "suddenly to find himself morally rejected by his adopted country because he was a Jew."[16] It is difficult to understand how an intelligent man living in the France of the 1930's could find his rejection by his adopted country *sudden*.[17] But, whatever the psychological interpretations, it is hard to miss the readiness with which potential rejection becomes actual. Which makes anti-Semitism an excellent recruiting agent.

Hannah Arendt perceives a "grand strategy of using anti-Semitism as an instrument of Catholicism."[18] This is very debatable—and the more so because the idea was first mooted by the anti-Clericals, notably in a famous open letter of Emile Zola (January, 1898), in which he argues that anti-Semitism was the Church's handle for rechristianizing the masses. The Catholics, says Zola, were trying to regain popular support by founding workers' clubs and organizing pilgrimages, but belief would not return. It was only when they started to appeal to anti-Semitism that they began to win back the masses. The people, says Zola, still do not believe, "but is it not the beginning of belief to make them want to burn the Jews?"[19]

This brings me very conveniently to my second argument, because the idea that, while anti-Semitism may be beside the point, it can be put to use—an idea Zola attributed to the Catholics—was also explicitly shared by the Socialists. It was a Socialist who condemned anti-Semitism as the

Socialism of fools. But plenty of Socialists also believed that it could be useful in winning them a hearing, in introducing the politically illiterate to integral Socialism. One of the great figures of the French Left (Augustin Hamon) said this quite explicitly in an interview of 1898: "With the petty bourgeois especially, anti-Judaism is the road to Socialism . . . the stage through which the petty bourgeois passes before becoming a Socialist."[20] But for the Left as for the Catholics, anti-Jewishness was far more than just a recruiting device: the utilitarian argument itself probably the rationalization of more profound sentiments.

Until a few years ago, to talk about an anti-Semitism of the Left seemed like a contradiction in terms. By now we know much about the equation of money power, banking, capitalism, and usury, with Jews; and how this notion was symbolically incarnated in the Rothschilds. The fact is that, in France at least, most of the great anti-Jewish works (great in size and impact, of course, not in their contents, which are largely a farrago of nonsense) came from the Left: Fourier, Proudhon; and, in a major key, Toussenel, Chirac; even, in some ways, Drumont. Which is understandable if we remember that, through most of the nineteenth century, the historic Left was *against* what we used to call progress, i.e., the development of capital and industry.

The Left probably remained the most audible source of attacks on Jews until the 1890's, with frequent anti-Semitic articles in officious publications like the *Revue socialiste,* in which the use of terms like "parasites" and "microbes" was nothing exceptional.[21] In 1894, *Le Chambard socialiste* (March 24) still called the Jews *youpins.* The popular rebellion against the hardships of the modern world found in the Jew a convenient symbol. But I would argue that the economic component of anti-Semitism is not crucial in itself: only as alimented by, and alimenting, basic cultural tensions and (again) cultural stereotypes.

For example, one cannot help being struck by the epidemic nature of prejudices that came out even in the opponents of anti-Semitism, like Anatole France, or Marx's son-in-law Paul Lafargue who, when he attacked Drumont, could not find anything better to call him than a "dirty Jew!"[22] Even Jean Jaurés allowed himself derogatory remarks about *la juiverie,* notably about the Jewish race, "subtle, concentrated, always devoured by the fever of gain. . . ."[23] And if one reads Marx's notorious essays on the Jewish question (of which the second is the only really hostile one) one will find that their interest does not lie in their anti-Jewish statements, but in the fact that Marx, like his contemporaries, identified the Jew with "gross and unrelieved commercialism"—with huckstering and money-grubbing.[24]

If Marx is considered a hostile witness, let us take a more acceptable figure: Bernard Lazare, himself a sephardic Jew from Nîmes, and one of the heroes of the Dreyfus Affair, contrasts *israélites de France* and *juifs* (of whatever race) and describes the latter as "dominated by the single preoccupation of rapidly making a fortune . . . by fraud, lying, and trickery." If only anti-Semites would become specifically *anti-Juifs*, he says, a lot of Israelites could join them. As for the French Israelites, they should leave the Alliance Israélite Universelle and work to stop the "continual immigration of these predatory, rude, and dirty Tartars [East European Jews] who come to feed upon a land that is not theirs."[25] Lazare changed his mind about these things, but his first position is revealing. Nor was Lazare's view an isolated one, because as late as the winter of 1898–99, when the leading anti-Semitic paper in France, *La Libre Parole*, launched its notorious subscription to build a monument to Colonel Henry (the man who had forged the papers incriminating Dreyfus), quite a few Jews sent contributions including one who described himself as *"un israélite dégoûté des juifs."*[26]

Whatever one may think about Lazare's description of these "rude and dirty" aliens, it is a fairly mild reflection of a widespread reaction to people who looked, spoke, acted very differently—in consequence easy to perceive as ugly, grubby, unmannered—essentially uncivilized because essentially different. Even a friend like Leroy-Beaulieu had to admit that "It is true that the race is neither strong nor handsome." And he repeats: "The race is not handsome," before he goes on to quote a young Russian woman: "They are so ugly that they deserve all their troubles."[27] Leroy-Beaulieu attributes Jewish unpopularity with "so many women" to their ugliness. But the remark, insofar as it is significant or revealing, does not necessarily apply to women alone. Karl Marx once described a boring woman he met during a visit to Germany as "the ugliest creature I ever saw in my life, a nastily Jewish physiognomy."[28]

In this context it is useful to remember that Jewish emancipation itself carried very equivocal implications; that its advocates had seen emancipation in terms of assimilation—a contractual demand for fusion in exchange for freedom. This vision had been inspired, it is true, by belief in the rights of man; but the rights of man not so much to *be* what he will, but to *become:* secularized, homogenized, "civilized," like his fellow citizens.

To the extent that Jews refused the implications of this tacit understanding; to the extent that they hesitated or tarried; to the extent that unassimilated Jews tarred the assimilated with the brush of their difference (their "ugliness"), the promises of emancipation itself turned into a new source of resentment and criticism—and even into the source of a certain liberal anti-Semitism.

We are talking of an age and of societies that are culturally imperialistic, for which cultural integration and homogenization are basic principle and active practice. And here are the Jews—who, on one hand, take some time to assimilate and, on the other, are continually irrigated by fresh streams of immigrants whose presence and whose strangeness help to stress their difference-by-association.

And so another factor of irritation is the insistent persistence of cultural difference, of Jewish particularism, or apparent particularism willy-nilly, whose results, again, are well-reflected when Leroy-Beaulieu has to admit and to justify the incomplete integration and assimilation of the Jews. The change from Jew to Frenchman or Englishman, he says, "has been too sudden to be complete." They have sometimes for us "something that jars, something discordant"—"a look, a word, a gesture, suddenly bares the old Jewish base. . . . Scratch an Israelite, one of my friends said to me, and you will find the ghetto Jew. That is not always true. What we take for the Jew is often only the stranger. . . . What one does feel coming through in the civilized Israelite, is not so much the Jew as the parvenu. . . . Parvenus! Most of the Jews we know are certainly that." And he lists their characteristics: pretentious, conceited, vain, lacking distinction or elegance or tact, revealing bad taste, bad manners, bad breeding, their excessive ways, their tendency to be either over-familiar or over-diffident, the trouble they have in showing the measure of men of the world. [29]

The justice of such charges is quite irrelevant; the fact that they reflect the perceptions of a friend and defender is not. But this aspect of the Jew— which Leroy-Beaulieu cites as a venial drawback, only to explain it as a passing phase—brings tremendous grist to the mill of anti-Semites. Hence my third point, best introduced with another quotation from Hannah Arendt: "The anti-Semite tends to see in the Jewish parvenu an upstart pariah." [30] The upstart pariah is at the center of many a hostile paroxysm and, given the guilt-by-association syndrome, all Jews who act as if they thought themselves the equals of their fellows may be so considered.

Here is another opportunity to articulate griefs founded in feelings that remain inarticulate. Jewish emancipation creates passional problems not very different from those aroused by the legal emancipation of the Blacks, which was roughly contemporary. Here are people who (until Louis XVI abolished the practice), paid the same tolls on entering towns as those charged on cattle. [31] This group, so traditionally and so obviously inferior, is declared equal to all. What is worse, its members declare themselves to be equal and act as if they believed it. Indignation at such pretensions made North Africa (where Jews had been a particularly despised and disadvantaged community) a hothouse of anti-Semitism, both French and Muslim. It also contributed to European anti-Semitism—whether at the benign level one can find in Leroy-Beaulieu, or at the bumbling redneck level, or at increasingly explicit levels—a fund of more or less articulate indignation, also very available, also very easy to exploit.[32]

Were one trying to be exhaustive, one would have to include every personal maladjustment that could find expression in some anti-Jewish rationalization. That is not my purpose. But I would add that anti-Semitism proved useful not just for diverting social tensions, but for arguing the case of national unity against the divisions and dissensions that could be declared artifcial and attributed only to Jews or to their influence. To those who wanted to avoid or play down class issues and antagonisms, anti-Semitism could be useful, because it translated economic resentments and revendications from a class to a national or racial context. Other national groups beside the Jews could provide scapegoats for economic distress and social crisis, but Jews were the most widely available and traditionally designated villains of the piece.

In this context, anti-Jewishness was not merely the identification of a scapegoat, but a rallying cry in the precise sense of the term: the assertion of unity and community, in terms of an appeal to common stereotypes and, hence, at least by implication, to common interests more powerful than any divisive factor.

Here we have an out-group whose inferiority and noxiousness have become a cultural commonplace; whose cultural difference, constantly reaffirmed by themselves and by their critics, is a constant irritant, a constant reconfirmation and reinforcement of prejudice, and an invitation to further rejections. Any deliberate campaign—whether motivated by concrete resentments or private paranoia—could build on prejudice, could make the latent manifest or, at least, could expect to be greeted with understanding. There was nothing extraordinary in the fact that Jews should provide an object of prejudice and persecution, whether continuous or sporadic, according to circumstances and to the interests a given situation suggests. What is extraordinary is that they managed to survive so long.

There is not even anything illogical about taking such attitudes to one possible conclusion, which is the elimination or extermination of the rejected out-group. Especially when the Christian Church, which needed their presence, was losing its grip![33] The Old Testament provides precedents, and so does history.[34] The only thing about such precedents is that the means of execution available in pre-modern times (whether to Pharaoh, or to Louis XIV, or to the Young Turks) were imperfect. And the execution of almost any scheme tended to be piecemeal and incomplete at best.

On the other hand, pre-modern societies, living on the margin of subsistence, offered great incidental opportunities for the destruction of rejected individuals or groups; because any such who were placed "without the law" tended to be removed from access to food, to shelter, to the means of keeping alive. Mortality rates were already very high. They were vastly higher for the outlaws. Which meant that the mere decision to destroy, however inefficiently executed, tended to have self-fulfilling effects.

Modern society, by contrast, could be far more exhaustive and efficient. Its dominant values operated against the destruction of human groups, at least in times of peace. But when such moral prohibitions were suspended, destruction could be surpassingly thorough. It also had to be more thorough, because the modern policed state (i.e., a well-regulated state) had mitigated the operation of natural processes of selection and destruction. No modern society could accept the kind of disorder that its predecessors took for granted, and that permitted these "natural laws" to operate. Nor would modern sensibilities accept it. Even if it had been possible, the social hygiene of the modern policed state could not tolerate great numbers of people starving in public places, dying in ditches, bleeding on somebody's threshold, corpses cluttering up the sidewalks or the highways, the impediments to shopping and traffic, the possibilities of infection and disorder, or even, simply of violence as private enterprise.

If an out-group had to be eliminated, the ad hoc possibilities of earlier times, occasions built into the pre-modern economy but also into the nature of pre-modern society and state, were excluded. Social hygiene prescribed something more orderly, and something that could proceed without contaminating the regularities of policed society. Natural forces could no longer be trusted to operate "naturally": first, because they no longer did; but also because if they did they would be far more destructive of the social fabric than in the earlier, looser context of the pre-modern state.

So there is a logic to concentration camps and extermination camps. If extermination is going to take place, it has to take place in isolated centers. This was not a consideration in more bucolic days.

One can see this clearly if one compares other great massacres of the twentieth century with that of the European Jew. All but this last have taken place in backward, undeveloped societies. In India, in Bangladesh, in various parts of Africa, hundreds of thousands of people at a time have been massacred by traditional means; or simply driven out by the millions.

Patchy but impressive examples of what artisanal methods can achieve when the preservation of social order is not a high priority. The best illustration of this is to be found in what happened to the Turkish Armenians in 1915.

It is a good illustration because Christians living in Turkey were also a subject, inferior race, and traditionally designated as dogs.[35] The reformed state of the Young Turks had declared Christians and Jews to be equal citizens with Muslims. But the nationalist passion for Turkification also demanded the extinction of separate communities, including the Arabs, but especially when, as in the case of certain Christian communities, these existed as distinct colonies and cultures.

The war of 1914–18 provided opportunities for extreme action that would have been difficult in times of peace; and the geographical situation of the Armenians on the Russian border designated them for this sort of action. Precisely what the Turkish Government, the Turkish authorities, wanted to do to the Armenians remains the subject of debate. What they did is less debatable. The men were disarmed, and then butchered. U.S. Ambassador Henry Morgenthau tells how at Ankara all Armenian men between fifteen and seventy were sent off on the Cesarea Road, bound in groups of four and massacred by a mob of Turkish peasants "in a secluded valley" where "their bodies, horribly mutilated were left" to be "devoured by wild beasts."[36] The young and the old and the women were deported, mostly on foot and mostly to various desert places. Morgenthau reports that out of one such convoy of about eighteen thousand souls only about one hundred fifty women and children reached Aleppo. Fridtjof Nansen makes this three hundred fifty, but he tells us about another convoy from Erzerum that had eleven survivors out of nineteen thousand.[37]

The description of what happened to the convoys is very repetitive; a few extracts taken from German and American witnesses, mostly missionaries, will convey the gist. Here is one American in 1916: the deportees were driven to die by the roadside, left to bleed to death, or to commit suicide, many women and children were raped, many others were sold cheap or given away to peasants. Arnold Toynbee and others mention that hundreds of thousands died of hunger, thirst, exposure; or if turning from the road, were shot or speared, hunted down by Kurds and Turkish peasants.[38] After the American, here is a German eyewitness writing about the deportees driven into the great limestone deserts of Asia Minor, into the wilderness and semi-tropical marshes of Mesopotamia, barefoot, part-naked, starved: newborns buried in dungheaps, severed heads rolling about the roads (and there are photographs that can compare with concentration camp ones!), "fields strewed with swollen blackened corpses, infecting the air with their odors, lying about desecrated, naked . . ," and about those who were driven into the Euphrates bound back to back.[39]

As in the India of my day (1946–47), river crossings were favorite places for massacres. One report says: "In a loop of the river, near Erzinghan . . . the thousands of dead bodies created such a barrage that the Euphrates changed its course for about 100 yards."[40] And everybody notes the intolerable mess along the routes: dead, dying, sick people spreading epidemics, bodies unburied or only halfburied, with vultures and dogs tearing at them, occasional corpses thrown in wells, and so on. I am not trying to insist on the horrors, but on what would seem to us the disturbance involved, and to show how much can be done just by encouraging private enterprise when the circumstances are right. But one has to note, too, that these haphazard methods missed a lot of people. Thus, Toynbee estimates that there were about 1.8 million Armenians in Turkey when the war broke out and that about equal numbers "seem to have escaped, to have perished, and to have survived deportation in 1915."[41] That is scarcely thorough. And even this limited success depends on high tolerance for disorder, and the availability of large waste spaces.

It is hard to tell how much of this was deliberate and how much just to be expected in the semi-primitive Turkish context aggravated by the wartime breakdown of almost everything. But one can see that it could be quite destructive in its way.[42] One can also see that it could never have been tolerated in a Western country—especially in that model of the policed state that was Germany!

I conclude that if you determine to eliminate an out-group today, the logic of that determination suggests that this be done in isolation; and the technological and administrative means at your disposal are bound to make the process itself very efficient. Platitudes perhaps, but platitudes to which a lot of Armenians probably owe their lives.

One last consideration arises: before the Jews could be isolated and exterminated, they had to be divested of the human qualities with which emancipation and liberalism had endowed them like other members of modern societies. There were certain things one could do to people in the old world, and that people did to each other all the time before didactic civilization put its mark on us, that one could no longer do after the nineteenth century had humanized and refined our sensibilities. There were certain things Turks could do to Armenians that Europeans could not normally regard as anything but crimes. So there were things one could not do to Jews, and murder was certainly one of them. The rights of man, however diffuse the concept, were also the rights of Jews, as long as Jews were recognized as men and women. This is where the logic of the situation demanded that the Jew be dehumanized. And the didactic and exemplary process of isolation and dehumanization was able to draw on the whole treasury of prejudice and resentment that has been chronicled.

But then, if the Jew was less than human—and harmfully so, of course: a microbe or a parasite—it was not enough to expel him from society, from this country or that. One had to rid the world of him. The logical conclusion of his dehumanization was his extermination. The rest is history. And, to the extent that it has become a part of history, it suggests that the humanization and sensibilization of man may have been a transitory phase: the generalization of particular and limited experiences treated as irreversible by people who took the exception for the norm.

The question remains, and it continues to obsess or fascinate our time: how could an apparently civilized society, an ordered modern society, produce and condone the mass murders that we describe as genocide? I believe that this is a false question. If an earthquake leveled a city and killed most of its inhabitants, we would say: "How could this happen?" Scientists could answer our question in terms of general laws and particular conditions, but that would not satisfy us; because our words are really an expression of shock and horror at the very notion of such destruction—and of destruction on such a scale!

The fact is that the question of Jewish genocide can also be answered in matter-of-fact terms, too banal to satisfy. Tragedies on this scale seem to defy the trivialization that explanations inflict upon them; and almost reject the attempt to explain as a sort of insult. That may be right, because explanation is sometimes advanced as an exorcism (and that is an evasion), or as an excuse (and that is inexcusable). But explanation is also advanced at times as if it could help to prevent similar tragedies in the future. And it may be a last question one might wish to consider: whether that is not a form of naïveté.

NOTES

1. The term seems to have been coined by the German journalist Wilhelm Marr, in the popular pamphlet, *The Victory of Judaism over Teutonism,* published in the wake of the German stock exchange crash of 1873. It really means anti-Judaism, of course; but I shall use it in its accepted sense.
2. Theodore Reinach, *Textes d'auteurs grecs et romains relatifs au judaisme* (Hildesheim, 1963), p. 295.
3. Ibid., pp. 14–15, 27.

4. Ibid., pp. 17, 30. This would be repeated by many Greek authorities on the Jews and, after them, by Romans as late as Rutilius Namatianus in the fifth century.

5. Posidonius of Apamea, quoted in Reinach, *Textes*, p. 57.

6. Ibid., p. 56.

7. Ibid., p. 176. See also Angelo Segré, "Anti-Semitism in Hellenistic Alexandria," *Jewish Social Studies*, VIII, 2 (1946), 127–36.

8. Satire XIV; Reinach, *Textes*, p. 293.

9. Cicero, *Pro Flacco* 67, cited in Reinach, *Textes*, p. 238.

10. It has been thoroughly treated in Jules Isaac, *Jésus et Israel* (Paris, 1948); Léon Poliakov, *Du Christ aux juifs de cour* (Paris, 1955) and a host of other works. For a brief treatment, see George La Piana, "The Church and the Jews," *Historia Judaica*, XI, 2 (October, 1949), 117–44.

11. For example, see *inter alia* Robert Jalley, *Le folklore du Languedoc* (Paris, 1971), p. 151; Dieudonné Dergny, *Images, coutumes et croyances ou livre des choses curieuses* (Brionne, 1885), *1, 330–42*; Charles Beauquier, *Traditions populaires: Les mois en Franche-Comté* (Paris, 1900), p. 44. In Corsica, in 1914, "Le jeudi saint, à la lecture de l'évangile de la Passion, on voit des hommes entrer en fureur quand Ponce-Pilate livre Jésus aux Juifs. Ils injurient le pusillanime procurateur de Judée; ils tapent sur les bancs à casser leurs bâtons." Albert Quantin, *La Corse* (Paris, 1914), p. 257. In the opening scene of his novel *The Last of the Just,* André Schwartz-Bart has described the effect of Good Friday services on the Jews of rural Poland.

12. The Feast of St. Verney, patron of the winegrowers of Beaumont (Puy-de-Dôme), was a great event. See Francis Gostling, *Auvergne and its People* (New York, 1911), pp. 25–26.

13. Anatole Leroy-Beaulieu, *Israel chez les nations* (Paris, 1893), p. 16.

14. *The Origins of Totalitarianism* (New York, 1958), p. 108.

15. Ibid., p. 94.

16. *Christians and Jews* (New York, 1951), p. 11.

17. This may have been due to "the philosemitism of the liberals" of the circle in which he moved. (Arendt, *Origins*, p. 335). Lucient Rebatet exaggerates when he claims that in the four or five years before the war "Paris était antisémite à 80% de sa population capable d'une idée," but he cannot have exaggerated much, and Arendt seems to confirm it. As Rebatet says, simplistic anti-Semitism was much more widespread "dans la petite bourgeoisie, dans les couches populaires que chez les intellectuels." *Cahiers de l'Herne,* Special number on Céline (Paris, 1963), p. 44.

18. Arendt, *Origins*, pp. 116–17.

19. Emile Zola, "Lettre à la France," January 6, 1898, in René Rémond, *L'histoire de l'anticléricalisme* (Paris, 1976), p. 206.

20. François Bournand, *Les juifs et nos contemporains* (Paris, 1898), p. 215.

21. For more detailed treatment see Edmund Silberner's numerous writings, notably, "French Socialism and the Jewish Question, 1865–1914," *Historia Judaica* XVI, 1 (1954), 3–38; and, more recently, Zeev Sternhell, *La droite révolutionnaire, 1885–1914* (Paris, 1978).

22. Silberner, ibid., pp. 21–24. Some socialists, like Réne Viviani who once remarked that "anti-Semitism is the best form of social struggle," had picked up their anti-Semitism in Algeria, which was a hothouse of anti-Jewish feeling. See *Journal Officiel, Chambre des députés, Débats* (February 21, 1895), 592–93. For the influence of Algerian anti-Semitism on metropolitan socialists see Charles Robert Ageron, *Les Algériens musulmans et la France* (Paris, 1968), 1, p. 583.

23. For Jaurés, see ibid.; Stephen Wilson, *Wiener Library Bulletin*, 1972, No. 3/4, 34; also *Dépêche de Toulouse*, May 1, May 8, 1895.

24. See Robert Tucker, ed., *The Marx-Engels Reader* (New York, 1972), pp. 46–51.

25. Bernard Lazare, *Entretiens politiques et littéraires* (Paris, 1890) I, pp. 177, 179, 232, and *passim*.

26. P. Quillard, *Le monument Henry* (Paris, 1899), p. 476. For Charles Péguy, writing in 1900, three quarters of the Jewish upper bourgeoisie, half of the Jewish middle class, a third of petty bourgeois Jews are anti-Semitic. *Oeuvres en prose, 1898–1908*, p. 290. This appears confirmed when Arthur Meyer, *Ce que mes yeaux ont vu* (Paris, 1910), pp. 124, 134, expresses his admiration for Drumont and insists that nowadays "one can, one must be anti-Semitic." For this and more see Stephen Wilson, "Anti-Semitism and the Jewish Response in France during the Dreyfus Affair," *European Studies Review*, VI (1976), 237.

27. *Israel chez les nations*, pp. 175–76.

28. Quoted by Hugh Lloyd-Jones, "The Books that Marx Read," *Times Literary Supplement*, February 4, 1977, 119.

29. *Israel chez les nations*, pp. 253–54.

30. Arendt, *Origins*, p. 118. Compare with the remarks of E. F. Gautier, *Un siècle de colonisation* (Paris, 1930) on the "exemple quotidien et contagieux du mépris musulman pour le juif!" On top of which Algerian Jews are "natives". Ageron, *Les Algériens musulmans*, p. 589, also speaks of their "nativeness" *(indigénat)*, which prevented the *colons* from accepting them as equals, and refers to "the atavistic contempt of the Muslims . . . which surrounded them with a sort of blemish, constantly renewed."

31. Leroy-Beaulieu, *Israel chez les nations*, p. 31, makes much of this. See Joseph Lemann, *L'Entrée des israélites dans la société française* (Paris, 1886), Ch. 1.

32. Thus Alsatians (and Lorrainers), who despised Jews as much as Algerians did, settled heavily behind the Gare de l'Est, around La Villette where in the 1880's and thereafter Parisian anti-Semites recruited their toughest supporters. Emile Durkheim, born at Epinal in 1858, could testify that in 1870 it was the Jews who were blamed for the defeat, just as in Alsace they suffered from the 1848 Revolution. See his contribution to Henri Dagan, *Enquête sur l'antisémitisme* (Paris, 1899), p. 60.

33. While trying to hold on, meanwhile, the Catholic Church sponsored a lively revival of anti-Jewish fantasies brought up to date. See Pierre Sorlin, *La croix et les juifs* (Paris, 1967), and Pierre Pierrad, *Juifs et catholiques français* (Paris, 1970). Catholic publications supported Drumont and spread wild anti-Semitic accusations. Anti-Semitic literature was widely used in Catholic schools.

34. In 1898, Jules Guérin's Ligue Antisémitique advocated a "Saint-Barthélémy des juifs" and invited the French to imitate those Galicians who had burnt a Jewish family alive. Wilson *Wiener Library Bulletin* 1972, No. 3/4, 34.

35. Compare this with certain explanations of Algerian anti-Semitism. Ageron, *Les Algériens musulmans*, p. 589, explains that Algerian Jews, long isolated in their *mellahs*, lived in narrowly endogamic communities and were recognized as a Jewish "nation," governed by its own law.

36. *An Anthology of Historical Writings on the Armenian Massacres of 1915* (Beirut, 1971), p. 118.

37. Ibid., pp. 126, 194.

38. Herbert Adams Gibbons, *The Blackest Page in Modern History* (New York, 1916), pp. 15–17: Arnold Toynbee *Armenian Atrocities* (New York, 1917), p. 22.

39. Armin T. Wegener, *The Turkish Armenocide: An Open Letter to President Wilson*, (reprinted AHRA, 1965), p. 76.

40. *Anthology*, p. 123.

41. Ibid., p. 70. For many details, see the British White Book, *The Treatment of Armenians in the Ottoman Empire, 1915–16*, edited by Viscount Bryce (London, 1916); and, further, Henry Morgenthau, *Secrets of the Bosphorus* (London, 1918), Chs. 23–27.

42. Note that the Turkish persecution of Armenians sacrificed even military interests and the

efficient pursuit of war to the superior aim of their destruction: blocked roads, spreading typhus, loss of rare skilled personnel—doctors, government and railroad officials, bank clerks, drivers, artisans, even army effectives, were sacrificed to a higher passion. The German Ambassador commented: "It looks as if the Turkish government wants to lose the war!" Johannes Lepsius, "The Armenian Question," *Muslim World* (London), X (1920), p. 350. Morgenthau, *Secrets of the Bosphorus*, p. 223, quotes Talaat Pasha: "We care nothing about the commercial loss."

FRITZ K. RINGER

THE PERVERSION OF IDEAS
IN WEIMAR UNIVERSITIES

During the decades before World War I, German Jews sent a significantly larger proportion of their children to secondary schools and universities than did German Protestants and Catholics.[1] This circumstance may have been due to the relatively high concentration of the German Jewish population in the cities and in commercial and industrial occupations, or it may have been due to the cultural traditions of German Jews.[2] In any case, when Jewish students reached the universities, the existing prejudices effectively barred them from the official careers that attracted many of their non-Jewish colleagues. As a result, much Jewish talent flowed into the more genuinely "liberal" professions, especially into medicine, journalism, and the literary and artistic occupations. Within the academic world itself, the position of instructor *(Privatdozent)* offered a perfect opportunity for the young Jewish intellectual, because unlike higher academic ranks, it was not a civil service position. Thus in 1909–10, when Jews made up about 1 percent of the German population, almost 12 percent of the instructors at German universities were of the Jewish religion, and another 7 percent were Jewish converts to Christianity *(Getaufte)*.[3] Jewish instructors must have been unusually able men, since they had to earn the *venia legendi*, the right to teach at a German university, from prejudiced examiners. Even after passing that hurdle, however, they found it difficult to advance into the official and salaried academic ranks of associate and full professor *(Extraordinarius* and *Ordinarius)*. In 1909–10, less than 3 percent of full professors at German universities were of the Jewish religion, and another 4 percent were converts. Protestants and Catholics held over 93 percent of the full professorships, although they supplied less than 81 percent of the instructors. In Berlin, the biggest and most prestigious German university, there was not a single Jewish full professor in 1909–10. These figures, together with a number of individual instances of delayed promotion for Jewish university teachers,[4] demonstrate beyond any doubt that some form of anti-Semitism was a palpable reality within the German academic world well before the beginning of the Weimar period.

The objective situation of German Jews at German universities probably did not change much between 1910 and 1930.[5] However, the climate of opinion they faced grew much worse after World War I. Although a few German academics publicly stated their anti-Semitic views well before 1914, the central strands in the anti-Semitic doctrines of the prewar era were developed mainly outside the universities.[6] This was true of the political anti-Semitism of the late 1870's and 1880's, which was subsequently integrated into the platforms of the conservative parties. It was also true of the *völkisch* theories articulated by such non-academic literati as Paul de Lagarde and Julius Langbehn and echoed, at an even less coherent level, by certain sectors of the German Youth Movement around the turn of the century. And it was certainly true of those forms of racism supposedly grounded in biological theory that emerged toward the end of the nineteenth century. This biological anti-Semitism was the work of a few marginal intellectuals, and received little explicit support within the German universities until the advent of National Socialism. Fully explicit anti-Semitic theories within the German academic community became much more common after 1918; they were associated less with biological racism than with a larger cluster of social and cultural anxieties that must be analyzed in all its complexity.

One of the main ingredients in this cluster of anxieties was a deep-seated fear of modern class society and of modern democratic politics. The majority of German academics, as well as most highly educated Germans, were deeply disturbed by the social changes that accompanied the extraordinarily rapid and disruptive industrialization of Germany during the later part of the nineteenth century. They had been accustomed to the high social status of learned notables in an early industrial society, and had enjoyed considerable influence under the political system of the bureaucratic monarchy. Suddenly, after about 1890, they found themselves socially and politically overpowered by new wealth on the one hand, and by the emergence of democratic mass politics on the other. This made them particularly sensitive to some of the more problematic aspects of modern social and political life. They loathed the politics of undisguised interest bargaining and class conflict, the replacement of conviction and principle by what struck them as rampant materialism. They lamented the loss of "community," of social harmony based on shared ideals, and the dissociative and alienating aspects of modern existence.[7] At the same time, they felt that the advent of the machine age and mass society would be a threat to the inherited high culture for which they stood, and even to individual creativity itself. They suspected that the emerging mass culture would be shallow and trivial. Creative individuals and creative elites would find themselves at once ignored by the mass and numbed by the all-pervasive rationalization of modern technology and modern social organization. Learning itself would lose its ancient significance as a search for pure truth, for meaning, wisdom, and personal fulfillment. Its place would be taken by a purely utilitarian and instrumental rationality, by a predominant concern with means instead of ends, and by the ultimate identification of progress with comfort.

Obviously, these concerns were neither groundless nor unique to the German academic community, but they were felt much more intensely in Germany than elsewhere. Indeed, these problems gave rise to works of lasting interest by such distinguished German thinkers as Thomas Mann, Georg Simmel, and Max Weber. Even during the Weimar period, a creative minority among German university scholars tried to deal with these issues in a spirit of intellectual discipline and restraint. The members of this creative minority realized that neither modern technology nor modern democracy could or should be wished out of existence, so that a way had to be found to adapt the most enduring values of the German cultural tradition to a changing environment.[8]

While a minority thus sought realistic solutions to the so-called cultural crisis, the majority of German academics, those I have elsewhere called "orthodox mandarins,"[9] allowed themselves to be driven ever further into the realm of illusion and unreason, hysteria and hate. Before and during World War I, this orthodox majority of German university professors sponsored a particularly rabid form of authoritarian nationalism, preaching the unquestioning submission of the individual to the national "community" as the only alternative to modern egotism and materialism. It did not trouble these self-appointed prophets of nationalist "idealism" that their rhetoric was also a defense of a repressive social and political system against all efforts to reform it. They saw themselves as unpolitical men, morally above the petty squabbles of the political parties and the emerging class conflict between workers and capitalists. Yet their patriotic moralizing was itself a contribution to the class war; it was directed almost exclusively against Social Democrats and determined liberals, and it discarded all restraints on an aggressive foreign policy.

The defeat of 1918, the revolution that followed, and the establishment of the Weimar Republic thoroughly disoriented the orthodox mandarins. Most of them now became violent enemies of the Republic, of democracy, of Enlightenment rationalism, and of everything that seemed vaguely Western, liberal, modern, or otherwise associated with technological "civilization." In countless "patriotic" speeches and polemical essays against the new regime and social order, they paraded their despair at Germany's fall from greatness, at the moral and intellectual corruption of the age, the death of idealism, the triumph of materialism and of envy. The only alternative they ever offered their audience was a total revolt against modernity: a spiritual revival, a rebirth of idealism, or a national revolution that would simultaneously erase the Treaty of Versailles and create a new Germanic community beyond the horizons of either capitalism or social-ism.[10]

It is in this context of willful despair and revivalist illusion that the comparatively mute anti-Semitism of prewar days rose to the surface and became explicit within the German academic community of the Weimar period. While biological racism as such was rarely expressed, the Jews were made symbols of modern evils in two important ways. First, as in *völkisch* ideology, the Jew generally symbolized economic calculation and utilitarian rationality; he represented the "bad," "unproductive," and uprooting aspects of the commercial and industrial revolution. Particularly for those who dreamt of a non-socialist alternative to capitalism, a corporate community, or an even more vaguely "idealistic" escape from modern materialism, the symbol of the Jew was used to cover up the lack of any more realistic assessment of modern choices. Second, the Jew represented the critical aspects of modern thought, the acids of analysis and skepticism that helped to dissolve the moral certainties, patriotic commitment, and social cohesion of former times.

This identification of the Jew with critical thought became explicit in the polemical writings of some orthodox mandarins. They used the word *Zersetzung* (dissolution) to suggest the destructive and dissociating impact of rational analysis on traditional convictions and social bonds. For example, here are some passages by the historian Karl Alexander von Müller:

> We are surrounded on all sides by the destructive and the low-
> mindedly iconoclastic [*das Zerschwätzende*], the arbitrary and formless,
> the leveling and mechanizing of this machine age, the methodical
> dissolution [*Zersetzung*] of everything that is healthy and noble, the

ridiculing of everything strong and serious, the deriding of everything godly, which lifts men up in that they serve it.

In a series of essays on nineteenth-century German history, Müller wrote about the growth of factories and big cities, the decline of rural Germany, the race for profits, the growth of an uprooted proletariat, and the modern tendency to rationalize human relations in purely economic or utilitarian terms. He linked these developments with the emergence of opportunistic mass parties and newspapers, and with the appearance of a socially and politically radical literature. He described what he considered the increasing predominance of criticism over constructive thought, the decline of poetry and the birth of popular journalism; and he explicitly associated "the first noisy outbursts of a new radical literature" during the early nineteenth century with "the first appearance of liberated Jews in literature": "the faiths intermingle; the Israelites are emancipated. Then iron and coal begin their victory procession." [11] "As the classic party of national decomposition," the historian Georg von Below added, "the Jews gained influence over the proletariat": "From Moses Hess to Landauer, Toller, and Eisner, it has been the Jewish fashion to acquire influence by indulging and arousing the instincts of the proletariat and to use this influence for unpatriotic politics." [12] Another reactionary professor, Michael Doeberl, also thought it significant that Marx was Jewish, suggesting that this accounted for his "ruthless logic and acid [*zersetzend*] criticism." [13]

Of course, anti-Semitic sentiments had appeared not only in Weimar Germany, but also in other times and places. We already noted the relatively mute anti-Jewish prejudice that confronted Jewish instructors at German universities around 1910. (I wonder what comparable statistics would show for American colleges and universities at that time.) What was peculiar to Weimar Germany was not the existence of anti-Semitism as such, or even the symbolic identification of the Jews with modernity, but the passionate intensity of the emotional revulsion against the machine age and mass society, and the profound need to escape from a realistic analysis of social alternatives into the dream of a national and spiritual revival. The grounds for these neurotic dispositions are not easy to identify. One can cite the rapidity of German industrialization, the lack of a strong tradition of participatory politics, and an almost habitual blindness to the social realities in the German philosophical and scholarly heritage. One can also cite the Treaty of Versailles, the devastating impact of runaway inflation in 1923 on certain sectors of the German middle class, and the singularly overt character of class and party conflicts that buffeted the Weimar Republic throughout its short existence.

Without pursuing these larger causal questions, however, I would like to touch briefly on a somewhat narrower issue that lies closer to hand, since it deals with the configuration of the German intellectual community between about 1890 and 1933. I refer to the grain of truth in the orthodox mandarins' caricature of the Jewish intellectual as a strictly critical thinker. Sigmund Freud once observed that the prejudice and hostility encountered by a young Jewish intellectual might well cause him to develop "a certain independence of judgment."[14] If one joins this highly plausible observation to what I said earlier about the obstacles put in the path of highly educated German Jews before World War I, one begins to see a possible connection.

The political scientist Roberto Michels, a student of Max Weber, once remarked on the relatively large number of Jews among the intellectual supporters of the socialist movement.[15] In his excellent book on *Die Weltbühne* and its circle, Istvan Déak reports that this leading non-academic journal of left liberal and social democratic opinion was largely the work of a brilliant group of young Jewish intellectuals, whereas *Die Tat*, the *Weltbühne*'s counterpart on the young neo-conservative right, drew its collaborators largely from among the offspring of non-Jewish members of the German educated elite.[16] Similarly, in his essay on *Weimar Culture*, Peter Gay makes a distinction between those who were "outsiders" and those who were "insiders" within the social and cultural establishment of Wilhelmian Germany. Gay suggests that after 1918 the former "outsiders" became "insiders," at least for a brief period, during which they produced the brilliant modernist experiments we now regard as the most vital aspects of "Weimar culture."[17] Though Gay does not actually say so, this cultural efflorescence took place almost exclusively *outside* the German academic community; it was much more cosmopolitan in character than the official culture of the universities, and German Jewish artists and intellectuals played a very important role in it. In my own study of German academic opinion, I was struck by the courageous maverick stance of those I called "radical modernists."[18] These were the most determined critics of mandarin orthodoxy; they were prominent among the innovators in various disciplines; they often had contacts in the world of the non-academic intelligentsia, and many of them were Jews.

To reiterate: explicit anti-Semitism at the German universities of the Weimar period was part of a larger complex of attitudes, which amounted to a cultural war against every aspect of modernity. Of course, this is a generalization. There certainly were many cultural and social conservatives, fervent patriots, and even hyper-nationalists among German Jews, just as there were many non-Jews among the radical critics of mandarin orthodoxy.

Still, the republican government and the parties of the liberal and socialist Left were relatively more popular among Jewish than among non-Jewish Germans.[19] In any case, the explicit anti-Semites among German university professors conceived their attack on the Jews as an integral part of their opposition to the Republic and to the vulgar materialism of the day. It was Friedrich Nietzsche who first described the German anti-Semites (disapprovingly) as "these newest speculators in idealism."[20] This phrase was as true and important in the 1920's as in Nietzsche's time, though it may strike us as absurd and repellent. In some vague way, German anti-Semites were widely considered "idealists." After all, they were working for a national and spiritual revolution against an age of egotism, dissociation, and cultural decadence.

One consequence of this widespread attitude was the benevolent tolerance with which the majority of German professors regarded the brutal tactics of hyper-nationalist and anti-Semitic students during the 1920's. Whenever a lecturer expressed anything resembling pacifist or socialist views, there was a student riot against him, particularly if he was Jewish. Though a courageous minority tried to stem the tide, most German academics did little to protect their unorthodox colleagues. On at least one important occasion the semi-official Corporation of German Universities publicly supported the anti-Semitic German Students' League in its conflict with the republican authorities in Prussia.[21] Naturally, in this climate of opinion all standards of academic freedom and civility simply melted away.

In the meantime, the so-called "crisis of learning" (Krise der Wissenschaft) raised havoc with the standards of scholarly clarity and precision. Although perfectly respectable in its intellectual antecedents, this crisis developed from a series of philosophical and methodological innovations at the end of the nineteenth century. One example was the new emphasis on hermeneutic interpretation in the humanistic disciplines that grew out of Wilhelm Dilthey's work. Another example was the phenomenological method of Edmund Husserl, which lent itself to dangerously loose adaptations by second-rate imitators. In the historical disciplines, the so-called "problem of historicism" raised the specter of an inescapable moral relativism. Most important of all was the neo-Kantian revolt against nineteenth-century scientism and "positivism" that soon inspired new forms of post-Kantian Idealism.[22]

While certainly not objectionable in themselves, these currents of thought became dangerous when they converged in a general revolt against what was vaguely called "positivism." That pejorative label, in turn, became ultimately so inclusive that it covered almost the entire realm of specialized empirical research. There was a growing consensus that excessive specialization was primarily to blame for the failure of modern scholarship—and of the academic elite—to exert the inspiring influence it had once exerted, especially during the days of the great German idealists and neo-humanists. The result of this conviction was a call for "synthesis" and for a "revolution in learning" that reached its climax in the revivalist atmosphere of the 1920's. In almost every discipline, an outdated, overly specialized, and vaguely "positivistic" direction was declared responsible for a profound "crisis" that was then promptly "overcome" through new forms of "synthesis." There was much talk of "intuitive understanding," of a "viewing of essences," of holistic and organic approaches that were to replace outdated mechanistic models. Above all, a renewal of idealism was represented as the potential source of a more meaningful, value-saturated, and therefore spiritually compelling direction in learning. And so the quest for more engaged and influential forms of scholarship ultimately joined and reinforced the demand for a new social and political idealism and for a spiritual revolution against cultural decadence.[23]

Of course the whole process was much more complicated than this brief summary can explain. I am especially sorry that space does not permit me to discuss men like Max Weber, who warned early and urgently against the replacement of scholarship with prophecy and the consequent loss of intellectual discipline.[24] It is my impression that the crisis of learning was like a semantic disease. Words became mere emotional stimuli that trailed ever larger clouds of implicit meanings. Thus audiences were trained to respond to an expanding circle of vaguely anti-modernist and anti-positivist allusions. The resulting intellectual chaos robbed even good minds of their critical resistance. It is not surprising that the vulgar polemicist Ernst Krieck escaped the problem of relativism by identifying everything as good and true that supported Germany's national uprising against its internal and external enemies; but it is shocking to find that Martin Heidegger said much the same in a slightly more philosophical way.[25]

When I seriously consider what the German universities contributed to the rise of National Socialism and the horrors that followed, I generally think first of all of the orthodox mandarins' escapist revolt against modernity, and their support for the pseudo-idealism of the so-called "national revolution." I also think of their anti-Semitism, which was an integral part of that irrational revolt. But above all I blame them less for what they consciously instigated than for what they failed to prevent. I do not believe that more than a handful among them really wanted the National Socialist regime with all it implied. But many of them certainly disarmed themselves in advance against whatever form the "national revival" would take. Indeed, their own emotional and intellectual excesses destroyed everything that might have protected their civilization against the dark forces that finally overwhelmed it: I mean reason, civility, common sense, and common humanity. Their total failure as teachers is demonstrated by the behavior of their students during the last years of the Weimar Republic, and by their own response to that behavior.

In 1929, the National Socialists began a concerted drive for control of the German student organizations. They sought to wrest power from right-wing nationalist and *völkisch* elements, and they achieved these ends by 1931.[26] Thus the Third Reich triumphed among the students two years before it captured the rest of the nation. Brown shirts and swastikas appeared more and more frequently in German academic buildings. Exploiting an already well-established tradition of "patriotic" protest, National Socialist students openly used the brutal tactics of the storm troopers against Jewish, internationalist, or liberal professors. Many academics, including some of the orthodox enemies of the Republic, now began to suspect that this was not the sort of revival they had sought. But even if they counseled restraint at this late date, much of their earlier rhetoric enfeebled their voices; they had left themselves little to fall back on. For some of them, the old illusions simply persisted. As late as 1955, the well-known professor of philosophy and pedagogy Eduard Spranger published an extraordinary explanation for his reluctance to censure National Socialist students in 1932. Though "undisciplined in its form," he wrote, "the national movement among the students" was "still genuine at the core."[27] I do not quote this staggering sentence because Spranger stood out among German university professors as a particularly violent nationalist, an outspoken anti-Semite, or one of the early supporters of the *völkisch* movement or of National Socialism. He was in fact a rather average, orthodox member of the German academic community, and not without influence. His remark about "the genuine core" can therefore be taken to epitomize everything that was wrong with the German universities—and with much of the German intellectual elite—during the years before 1933.

NOTES

1. Wilhelm Ruppel, *Über die Berufswahl der Abiturienten Preussens in den Jahren 1875–1899: Eine statistische Studie* (Fulda, 1904), pp. 14–15; for the Weimar universities, see Hubert Graven, "Gliederung der Studentenschaft nach statistischen Ergebnissen," in Michael Doeberl, Otto Scheel, et al., *Das akademische Deutschland*, vol. III (Berlin, 1930), pp. 326–29.

2. Peter G. J. Pulzer, *The Rise of Political Anti-Semitism in Germany and Austria* (New York, 1964), pp. 3–15; Esra Bennathan, "Die demographiche und wirtschaftliche Struktur der Juden," in Werner E. Mosse, ed., *Entscheidungsjahr 1932: Zur Judenfrage in der Endphase der Weimarer Republik* (Tübingen, 1965), pp. 87–131.

3. Alexander Busch, *Die Geschichte des Privatdozenten: Eine soziologische Studie* (Stuttgart, 1959), p. 160; Bernhard Breslauer, ed., *Die Zurücksetzung der Juden an den Universitäten Deutschlands* (Berlin, 1911).

4. Examples in Fritz K. Ringer, *The Decline of the German Mandarins: The German Academic Community, 1890–1933* (Cambridge, Mass., 1969), pp. 136–37.

5. The subject deserves further study. Important and pertinent primary material on the characteristics and careers of German academics is available through Professor Dietrich Goldschmidt, Max-Planck-Institut für Bildungsforschung, Lentzeallee 94, 1 Berlin 33.

6. Basic in this entire field, in addition to Pulzer, *Rise of Political Anti-Semitism,* are George L. Mosse, *The Crisis of German Ideology: Intellectual Origins of the Third Reich* (New York, 1964); George L. Mosse, *Germans and Jews: The Right, the Left and the Search for a "Third Force" in Pre-Nazi Germany* (New York, 1970); Fritz Stern, *The Politics of Cultural Despair: A Study in the Rise of the Germanic Ideology* (Berkeley, 1961).

7. Ringer, *Decline of the German Mandarins,* pp. 113–43.

8. Ibid., pp. 162–80, 202–13, 253–82.

9. In *The Decline of the German Mandarins* the term mandarins is used simply to describe people whose status of upper-middle-class notables was based on educational qualifications rather than on wealth, and who developed a characteristic ideology of "cultivation." Among German university professors (mandarin intellectuals), the "orthodox" were those who developed the reactionary and escapist potential of the ideology of cultivation.

10. Ringer, *Decline of the Mandarins,* pp. 213–27.

11. Karl Alexander von Müller, *Deutsche Geschichte und deutscher Charakter* (Stuttgart, 1926), pp. 26, 60–61, 158.

12. Georg von Below, *Die Hemmnisse der politischen Befähigung der Deutschen* (Laugensalza, 1924), pp. 18–19.

13. Michael Doeberl, *Sozialismus, soziale Revolution, sozialer Volksstaat* (Munich, 1920), p. 12.

14. Sigmund Freud, *Selbstdarstellung,* 2nd ed. (Vienna, 1936), p. 8.

15. Roberto Michels, "Intellectual Socialists," in George B. de Huszar, ed., *The Intellectuals: A Controversial Portrait* (Glencoe, Ill., 1960), pp. 316–21.

16. Istvan Déak, *Weimar Germany's Left-Wing Intellectuals: A Political History of the Weltbühne and Its Circle* (Berkeley, 1968), esp. pp. 23–24.

17. Peter Gay, *Weimar Culture: The Outsider as Insider* (New York, 1968).

18. Ringer, *Decline of the German Mandarins,* esp. pp. 239–40.

19. Friedrich Meinecke reported a general impression that republican students were often Jewish. See the passage cited in *Decline of the Mandarins,* p. 240.

20. In the "Genealogy of Morals." Friedrich Nietzsche, *Werke in drei Bänden,* ed. Karl Schlechta (Munich, 1966), vol. II, p. 896.

21. Ringer, *Decline of the German Mandarins,* pp. 250, 215–218, and literature cited there.

22. Ibid., pp. 295–351.

23. Ibid., pp. 367–418.

24. Ibid., pp. 352–55.

25. For Krieck, see Ringer, pp. 357–58.

26. Karl Dietrich Bracher, *Die Auflösung der Weimarer Republik: Eine Studie zum Problem des Machtzerfalls in der Demokratie,* 4th ed. (Villingen, 1964), pp. 146–49.

27. Ringer, *Decline of the Mandarins,* p. 439.

PETER H. MERKL

THE CORRUPTION OF PUBLIC LIFE IN WEIMAR GERMANY

How was it possible that in a civilized society like Weimar Germany, public life could become so ugly and vindictive? How could the educated elite of Germany become so callous toward the most elementary principles of fairness and human decency that they would tolerate—and often even support—political violence and prejudice? Only when these questions are answered, will it be possible to pinpoint the factors that corrupted the ethos of Weimar public life.

The public climate of the Weimar Republic was not that of a normal, peaceful society. It was turbulent, crisis-ridden, and ever-changing. There was a sense of fundamental cultural change, especially among the young World War I generation. The old class structure and the old institutions were in a state of disintegration; the values and restraints observed by their elders no longer seemed to apply. A great number of new causes and movements were springing up: Utopian Communism, revolutionary Social-ism, the Youth Movement,[1] the *völkisch*[2] movement. Masses of people were being mobilized, and new prophets appeared every day. After the grand spectacle of the Russian Revolution and Mussolini's March on Rome, every little upstart wanted to become another Lenin, or another fascist leader. There was a pervasive climate of nationalism, to the point of quasi-racial notions of nationality. There was a great passion for national expansion *(Lebensraum)*, a wave of national indignation and enthusiastic superpatriotism. All Weimar parties—from right to left—favored a revision of the Treaty of Versailles and the secret rearmament of Germany. Finally, there was a corrosive climate of hatred, violence, and prejudice in the

Weimar Republic long before the Nazis played a significant role—and certainly long before the Third Reich was established. It was a climate of latent civil war.

In the German cultural tradition, a great myth has always existed about the word *Not*.[3] There are many popular sayings in connection with it, such as *"Not kennt kein Gebot,"* i.e., "emergency knows no rules." When Germans believe that their fatherland is in great danger, they rally and, in their panic, tend to accept whatever measures a willful minority or a demagogue may propose. In such an emergency, constitutional restraints, human rights, even human decency, are suspended.

What was the great emergency that existed in the minds of many Germans at that time? There was, first of all, World War I, which most Germans naïvely saw as a great patriotic war of defense against Allied encirclement, a proud rallying around the flag of the fatherland in its hour of need. In their indiscriminate reaction to this great emergency, many Germans were willing to cloak all sorts of excesses with the mantle of well-meaning patriotism. Even in 1917 and 1918, when hunger and exhaustion had dampened the passions of war, the rantings of Pan-Germans and ultra-conservatives of the Fatherland Party against the peacemakers were viewed as patriotism. Later, their facile lies about the army having been "stabbed in the back" by the "November criminals" were widely believed. These same Pan-Germans and ultra-conservatives were the founders and financial backers of numerous postwar militant right-wing organizations—especially *völkisch* groups—that preceded and later merged with the Nazi Party.[4] The peacemakers—Socialists, Democrats, and Catholic Centrists—were their first victims in the early years of the Republic, when men like Matthias Erzberger and Walther Rathenau were murdered.

The war had shattered the moral values of a whole generation of educated Germans. Youngsters torn from their *Gymnasium* or university became hardened killers, or were spiritually broken by the ruthless slaughter of trench warfare. The moral certainties of a decent, civilized bourgeoisie turned into the nihilism of killing and survival. Hundreds of thousands made a virtue of necessity and became professional officers or officer candidates. When they came back from the war—assuming they did come back—they seemed fit only for a military career. But since the Treaty of Versailles permitted Germany an army of only one hundred thousand men and four thousand officers, they did not have much of a future—unless they could overthrow the Republic and rescind the Treaty. Consequently, by 1920–21, they joined the paramilitary Free Corps and the Citizens' Defense League.[5] When these organizations were dissolved, they became members of the paramilitary armies of the Right, such as the *Stahlhelm* (Steel Helmet) veterans and the SA (Nazi Stormtroopers), in order to fight the paramilitary armies of the Left, such as the Communists. They gave Weimar politics an air of latent civil war, in which normal rules of democratic life had no chance to prosper.

To many Germans, the sense of need, of national emergency, came with the sudden collapse and defeat of 1918. The fall of the monarchy and of Imperial institutions hit especially the older military men and civil servants, whose lives had been bound up with their pride in the Empire. Now the Kaiser had fled, the army was demobilized, people were tearing off the insignia of returning officers, and the media were besmirching the honor of German soldiers. The Navy was seized or being scuttled, German colonies were taken over by the victors, and substantial territories ceded to neighboring states—some of them populated by formerly subject minorities. To the military and the civil servants of the old regime, this was a shattering experience,[6] which a belief in the legend of the "stab in the back" made easier to bear. This experience drove them into the arms of the right-wing parties, which were looking for scapegoats. The first and most obvious scapegoat was the Jew. Yet the German wartime army included thousands of German Jews; many lost their lives for the very cause of those who now maligned them. In advertisements, grieving Jewish mothers implored other German mothers to stop this slander, but to no avail.[7]

The defeat and collapse of the Empire was not the only event that upset conservative Germans; other occasions provoked their false sense of patriotism. The Treaty of Versailles was so broad in its impact that even a long-time pacifist and Socialist like Philipp Scheidemann spoke in indignation of shouldering a rifle and going back to fight for the fatherland in its hour of need. All political parties denounced the Treaty. The government-in-office that finally signed it was henceforth blamed for this alleged "act of treason," just as every subsequent Weimar government was blamed for every act of cooperation with the Treaty and the victorious Allies. When French and Belgian forces invaded the Rhineland in 1923, in order to exact the reparations due them in kind, this was again seen as an "hour of need" of the fatherland, and whole armies of indignant patriots were mobilized—proving how many potential recruits there were for the Nazi Party. The same was true in 1929, when the right wing mounted a campaign against the Young Plan of Reparations that had been signed by the government. All these events gave unprecedented respectability to the Nazi Party, which had taken part in them, together with the conservative German nationalists and the *Stahlhelm* veterans. The warlike spirit of 1914–18 seems never to have died. As the German historian Ludwig Dehio pointed out a quarter of a century ago, World War I did not end in 1918; it continued to smolder under the ashes of German national indignation until its final resolution in 1945—a modern thirty-years-war, and every bit as devastating.[8]

Perhaps none of the "national emergencies" were as easily abused as the threat of Bolshevism during the first years of the Republic. It was easy to expand an anti-Communist crusade into a vendetta against everyone who disagreed with one's point of view, Communist or not. In 1918–19, the provisional government called upon the Free Corps and other military units—including terrorist groups such as *Organisation Consul*—to put down the revolutionary insurgents who had taken over Munich and Berlin. They were eager to oblige, and did so in the most brutal manner. The wave of white terror that followed went beyond the original purpose of restoring constitutional order: there were mass arrests, lawless killings, and executions; innocent citizens were harassed and terrorized—some of them were Jews, because anti-Semitism was rife in the Free Corps. Among the Free Corps members of those days were many who later became notorious Nazi killers: Auschwitz Commander Rudolf Höss, Heinrich Himmler's right-hand man Reinhard Heydrich, and Martin Bormann. Emil Gumbel, a mathematician and courageous civil rights advocate, wrote a statistical study computing the political murders during the early years of the Republic. He documented four hundred such murders during the first four years, 95 percent of them committed by the right wing. Four out of five murderers went scot-free, including several self-confessed killers. Others received nominal punishment, averaging four months in jail per murder.[9] The conservative judges and prosecutors of the Weimar Republic were ready to excuse even murder as a mere excess of patriotism—even when the victims were public officials and honorable members of republican parties.

This climate of hatred and murder was constantly fueled by slanderous attacks in the right-wing press, which instigated the assassination of government leaders, launched smear campaigns of vilification and hatred against local republican mayors, city councillors, and regional officials, attacking them with scurrilous law suits, slander, and lies; every means fair or foul was used to discredit them and remove them from office. Anyone who was shocked, ten years later, by Nazi propaganda calling for the persecution of Jews, need only look at the right-wing campaign calling for the assassination of Erzberger and Rathenau. Even at that time, hatred and prejudice had won the day.

The Republic barely survived the first tumultuous years of murder and putsches. Yet anyone who thought that the climate of hatred might have abated during the quieter years of 1924–29, was sorely mistaken. Many World War I and Free Corps veterans withdrew from active political involvement, but their hatred and prejudice became encapsulated in the anti-republican parties and paramilitary organizations of the Right: German Nationalists, Nazis, *Stahlhelm* veterans; and of the Left: the Communist Red Front. Many joined the large number of youth organizations, veterans groups, and partisan youth groups, and indoctrinated others with their militant romanticism, their prejudices and venom. In this connection, it is important to realize the problem youth posed for the Weimar Republic. Due to the high prewar birth rate, great numbers of young people reached political and economic maturity during the height of the Depression, when jobs were extremely rare and youthful paramilitary armies waged battles in the streets and meeting halls. Many of them joined youth groups of every conceivable kind: political, religious, sports, trade union, etc. In 1927, official estimates put the number of organized youth at nearly five million. Most of them were alienated from adult society and from the democratic politics of Weimar.[10] As they grew up, these alienated youths became politicized in a millenarian direction, joining either the Nazi stormtroopers or the militant Communists—the two major antagonists of the street fights of the early 1930's. Political violence dominated electoral campaigns at a time when the Reichstag and several state legislatures had already been turned into circuses by the combined majority of Nazi and Communist deputies. Every year, the police had to intervene in thousands of rallies and demonstrations that were attacked or broken up by stormtroopers or Communists. Every year, many on both sides were killed or seriously wounded. During the seven-week campaign preceding the Reichstag elections of July 1932, there were 461 political riots in Prussia alone. Eighty-five people were killed and 400 seriously injured.[11]

What happened to all these violent passions and violent men after Hitler came to power in 1933? Is it surprising that many found employment by the new regime? Is it surprising that the educated public, having experienced illegal violence for years, having lived through many national emergencies, was ready to welcome an end to chaos at almost any price?

In conclusion, it could be said that it was the never-ending sense of national emergency which eased the way for the Third Reich, having robbed the Republic of the normal defenses any civilized society should have been able to marshal against the savage onslaught of the Nazi state.

NOTES

1. On the German Youth Movement, see esp. Walter Z. Laqueur, *Young Germany* (New York, 1962).
2. The term *völkisch* denoted a literary and political movement, which combined national and agrarian romanticism with populism and racial prejudice. See, for example, Martin Broszat, *German National Socialism, 1919–1945* (Santa Barbara, Cal., 1966), pp. 11–67.
3. The English word "need" is only a pale copy of the deep emotions and survival instincts aroused by the German word *Not* which is more accurately translated as "emergency," "crisis," or "clear and present danger".
4. See Broszat, pp. 34–35.
5. The Free Corps were volunteer army units formed by the government immediately following the war to combat left-wing revolutionaries and threats to the German Eastern borders. The Citizens Defense Leagues *(Einwohnerwehr)* were local vigilante organizations formed spontaneously for the same purpose. Both were disbanded a few years later.
6. See Peter H. Merkl, *Political Violence Under the Swastika: 581 Early Nazis* (Princeton, N.J., 1975), pp. 159–88. This book is a study of autobiographical essays collected in 1934 by Professor Theodore Abel.
7. Many of the early Nazis of the Abel Collection report a mental breakdown: like the outbreak of rabid anti-Semitism, a *Judenkoller,* in 1918–19, presumably resulting from their reactions to the German defeat and the fall of the old regime. Merkl, Ibid., pp. 499–517.
8. In *Deutschland und die Weltpolitik im 20. Jahrhundert* (Munich, 1955). See also Karl Dietrich Bracher, *The German Dictatorship* (New York, 1970), pp. 28–34.
9. See Emil Gumbel, *Verräter verfallen der Feme. Opfer, Mörder, Richter 1919–1929* (Berlin, 1929).
10. For details see Peter D. Stachura, *Nazi Youth in the Weimar Republic* (Santa Barbara, Cal., 1975), pp. 89–108 and 112–16.
11. See Chapter 2 of this writer's *The Making of a Stormtrooper* (Princeton, N.J., 1980).

WERNER T. ANGRESS

THE GERMAN JEWS, 1933–1939

A week after Hitler's appointment as chancellor, a future professor of history, Ernst Simon, wrote from Palestine to his friend and teacher Martin Buber about an article on Zionism he was writing. At the end of the letter was a brief question: "Does the Hitler thing [*Hitlerei*] affect you *directly?* And what's your prognosis?"[1] Buber replied on February 14 from Heppenheim—after a very thorough analysis of Simon's essay—that the "Hitler thing" had so far done nothing to him, although he was prepared for anything. As for a prognosis, he felt that this would depend on the outcome of the anticipated conflicts between the Nationalists and the Nazis within Hitler's coalition government. A shift of the present power constellation in favor of the Nazis, even if they should succeed in further strengthening their parliamentary basis, was unlikely to be granted by the Nationalists, who held an overwhelming majority in the Cabinet. In that case, according to Buber,

> the Hitler people will either remain in the government, regardless; then they'll be sent into battle against the proletariat which will split their party and will render them harmless. Or they'll quit [the government]; then there will be presumably a state of siege in which . . . the technical superiority of the army vis-à-vis the . . . [Nazis] will undoubtedly win the upper hand. As long as the present coalition prevails, any real persecution of Jews [*Judenhetze*] or anti-Jewish legislation is unthinkable. . . .

Buber added that administrative nastiness could be expected, but legislation against Jews would only become possible if the present power constellation in the government should shift in favor of the Nazis, which seemed unlikely. Open persecution of the Jews would merely occur between the time the Nazis quit the government, and the proclamation of a stage of siege.[2]

Buber's prognosis proved to be wrong, of course, but he was by no means alone in misjudging the situation. Like the majority of the nation, most German Jews—there were five hundred and thirty thousand of them in January 1933[3]—underestimated Hitler's skill in political maneuvering, and few believed that his regime would last long or that, if it did, any far-reaching anti-Jewish measures would materialize. Such optimism rapidly evaporated within a few weeks after the so-called seizure of power, although the real extent of the dangers faced by the Jews remained obscured by what one historian recently termed "creeping persecution."[4] As the party had failed beforehand to devise any definite policy on how to solve the "Jewish Question" once in power, its efforts to eliminate the Jews from all spheres of national life gradually proceeded from 1933 to the end of 1938 without a recognizable pattern of coordination.[5] Thus during the first five years of the Third Reich, both the Party and the rapidly Nazified bureaucracy operated on the hazy assumption that some solution would have to be found to rid Germany of her Jews as quickly as possible. But how this was to be accomplished remained for years subject to improvisation. Nevertheless, during the first six months of 1933, when Hitler consolidated his power and elbowed his Nationalist coalition partners into political limbo, the first drastic anti-Jewish measures were taken. Following Boycott Day on April 1, which was staged as a protest against what the Nazis termed "atrocity propaganda" fostered abroad by "international Jewry," decrees were passed which led to the dismissal of Jews from the civil service, and shortly thereafter from the courts and the public health service.[6] These measures were accompanied throughout the Reich by what Party officials fondly called "spontaneous outbursts of the outraged public against Jewish impudence and arrogance," a euphemism for "hooliganism," usually organized by stormtroopers against individual Jews, their houses of worship, their cemeteries, and their places of business. Over the next few years, Jews were driven from the schools and universities—both teachers and students—and ultimately from Germany's economy.[7]

Given these developments, it soon became obvious that some sort of leadership would have to be provided within German Jewry in order to present its collective concerns to the regime, render counsel and assistance to those who were losing their livelihood, and, as far as this was possible under the circumstances, chart a course for the immediate future in an attempt to respond to the deteriorating situation of the Jews. Not surprisingly, this task fell to men and women of the educated Jewish elite.

Who belonged to this elite? Though any answer is bound to be somewhat arbitrary, we may include first of all members of the professions, all of which required a firm educational basis, usually with university training. This category included the medical and legal professions, educators on all levels, scientists, engineers, rabbis, etc. To these must be added persons from cultural and artistic life, i.e., writers, publishers, journalists, theater directors, actors, painters, and musicians. Finally, a good number of Jewish businessmen, notably bankers, industrialists, and prominent merchants, tended to be well educated, had attended either six or nine years of secondary schools, and not infrequently held a university degree, usually a doctor of law or philosophy. A rough estimate of their number in 1933 would be thirty thousand.[8]

It was precisely this category of Jews—for convenience's sake I shall call them intellectuals—that suffered the first massive dismissals as a result of anti-Jewish legislation passed in April 1933. Deprived of their livelihood as civil servants, state attorneys, judges, teachers, and professors, a relatively large number of them—the exact number is difficult to determine—emigrated during the first year of Hitler's chancellorship. They were joined by Jews not in government employment, whose livelihood and safety were also threatened: writers, journalists, entertainers, and left-wing politicians. A few wealthy business people who viewed the future with misgivings also decided to leave the country while "the going was good."[9] Although more Jews, including many educated people, emigrated in 1933 than in any other year prior to 1938–39, many educated Jews remained.[10] They assumed positions of leadership on the national and local levels and attempted to help German Jewry adjust to the drastic changes that had occurred since Hitler had become Chancellor. Few of them realized at the time that more than readjustment was involved, and that they would, in fact, be called upon to preside over the breakup of the Jewish community in Germany.

Their task was formidable from the outset. Attempts had to be made to establish contact with the new regime in order to ascertain what National Socialism held in store for the Jews, and what role, if any, the Jewish leadership would be allowed to play in what they initially assumed would be a process of readjustment. As already mentioned, nothing was known in 1933 about any definite policy the regime may have had in connection with the so-called solution of the Jewish Question. This was not surprising because, as we now know, no such policy existed at the time.

Aside from establishing some working agreement with the regime, several major areas affecting the Jews demanded the attention of their leadership. All those dismissed from the civil service, the legal profession, and all subsequent victims of *Gleichschaltung* (aryanization or nazification), which since April 1933 had affected Jews in most areas of public life, had to be retrained either to enable them to find a new livelihood in Germany, or to prepare them for emigration. Both retraining and emigration, initially thought to be essential primarily for the young generation, had to be organized. People unable to find jobs because of the process of *Gleichschaltung*, and those either too old or too sick to be retrained, had to be supported by the Jewish community which had to raise the necessary funds from among its own members since Jews were no longer eligible for state aid. Finally, the educational, cultural, and spiritual needs of the Jews had to be met in the face of their rapid and relentless isolation within society.[11]

All these tasks required unity and cooperation which, in the approximately one hundred years since emancipation, had always been a weak point with Germany's Jews. Divided among different religious traditions—Orthodox, Conservative (in Germany, Liberal), and Reform—and since the turn of the century also into assimilationists and Zionists (to name but the most obvious divisions), they had never succeeded in creating an all-encompassing organization that could represent and speak for the Jewish community as a whole.[12] When Hitler took office, the bulk of German Jewry was organized—often with overlapping membership—in the *Centralverein deutscher Staatsbürger jüdischen Glaubens* (Central Association of German Citizens of the Jewish Faith), or CV, and the *Reichsbund jüdischer Frontsoldaten* (National League of Jewish Frontline Veterans), or RjF. Both were decidedly non-Zionist. The Zionists, who were until 1933 a very small minority, had their *Zionistische Vereinigung für Deutschland* (German Zionist Federation). The various Jewish congregations were loosely organized in the German-Israelite Congregational League. In addition, there existed two small but vociferous organizations of superpatriots, the *Verband nationaldeutscher Juden* (League of National-German Jews) and *Deutscher Vortrupp* (German Vanguard). I shall say more about these later on.[13]

It was not until September 1933 that an umbrella organization, the *Reichsvertretung der deutschen Juden* (Reich Representation of German Jews), was established. Representing all Jewish religious and secular factions, this organization grew out of a less comprehensive *Reichsvertretung der jüdischen Landesverbände* (Reich Representation of

Jewish Regional Associations) founded in 1932.[14] *Reichsvertretung* and CV were run by men and women of the educated elite, both at the main offices in Berlin and in the regional branches. The *Reichsvertretung* was jointly directed by Dr. Otto Hirsch,[15] formerly an official in Württemberg's Ministry of the Interior, and by Rabbi Dr. Leo Baeck.[16] Most of the other members of the board also had the title of doctor, a trademark of German Jewry's upper crust. It was similar in the CV, whose board consisted almost entirely of lawyers, and whose newspaper, the *CV-Zeitung*, was edited by Dr. Alfred Hirschberg and Drs. Hans and Eva Reichmann. Many of those who assumed the burden of leadership responded to the formidable challenge they faced partly from a feeling of *noblesse oblige*, and partly because they had been ousted from their jobs in the civil service, the press, the law courts, or non-Jewish private enterprise. Left with few choices, they had flocked into the exclusively—and constantly shrinking—Jewish sector where they joined forces with rabbis and a score of prominent business people who had traditionally volunteered their services to the boards of congregations or regional CV and Zionist chapters.[17]

During the first two and a half years of the Third Reich, until the passage of the Nuremberg racial laws in September 1935, spokesmen for the principal Jewish organizations as well as the Jewish press took a somewhat precarious dual approach in dealing with the Nazis. While registering their protests against anti-Semitic insults by Party newspapers and speakers, they simultaneously assured the regime of German Jewry's unquestioned loyalty to the fatherland.[18] The objective was to reach some sort of acceptable accommodation with the new rulers. Thus shortly after the April 1 Boycott Day, and after the subsequent passage of legislation ousting Jews from the civil service, the *CV-Zeitung*, the most widely circulated assimilationist newspaper, responded to the recent events by stating that Jews no longer enjoyed equal rights with the rest of the nation. The ideology of Aryan racial superiority and the imputed unsuitability of Jews for state service was now law, and although the Jews disagreed, they would have to bow to the facts. Yet despite these developments, the paper stated, Germany remained their homeland, and "it is our objective to maintain the German-Jewish community in Germany materially, phys- ically, and spiritually unbroken in its strength."[19] Shortly before Boycott Day, assimilationist and Zionist spokesmen had voiced their dismay at the upcoming boycott to the government. The Nazis justified the boycott as a defense against the lively press campaign abroad which charged Hitler's regime with unrestrained violations of Jewish rights. This "atrocity propa- ganda," as they chose to call it, the Nazis attributed to the "machinations of international Jewry." In view of this situation, the Jewish spokesmen accompanied their protests with emphatic assurances that Germany's Jews strongly disapproved of, and disassociated themselves from, the anti-German agitation abroad.[20] It was a bizarre situation. Inside Germany, leading representatives of the Jewish community, which had been exposed to countless indignities and sporadic physical outrages ever since January 30, now found themselves compelled, for reasons of political prudence, to disavow the accuracy of the charges raised abroad, although they knew only too well how true many of them were. Worse yet, the charges did not only appear in the major newspapers of neighboring countries but also in detailed and well informed accounts published in German-language emigré journals then springing up in Paris, Prague, Amsterdam, and elsewhere. Their contributors and editors were mostly Jewish intellectuals who had left Germany with the first wave of refugees in the spring and summer of 1933. They may have meant well, these knights of the pen, but their good intentions were viewed with mixed feelings by the embattled Jews still residing along the banks of the rivers Rhine, Spree, Elbe, and Main rather than along those of the Moldau, Amstel, Thames, or Seine.

Since 1933, responsible representatives of the Jews, notably the *Reichsvertretung,* tried with considerable tact and restraint (and, one might add, with diminishing success) to protect the Jewish community at least from unauthorized violations of their rights while attempting simultaneously to discover, equally unsuccessfully, what place, if any, within German society the regime would allot the Jews. A less balanced approach toward seeking an accommodation with the Third Reich was taken by a few men who headed organizations with a pronounced German-patriotic stance. There was, first of all, Dr. Leo Löwenstein, a scientist by profession, a captain in the Bavarian Army Reserve, retired, and chairman of the Jewish War Veterans (RjF).[21] For over two years he tried to persuade Hitler by mail to allow patriotic Jews, and the young generation in particular, to be absorbed into the German *Volksgemeinschaft;* settle as farmers on German soil; participate in athletic contests with non-Jewish youth; and, after the announcement of German remilitarization in March 1935, to serve in the German armed forces. Hitler never replied, and none of these requests was ever granted.[22] However, Löwenstein did succeed in April 1933, through an appeal to the aged President von Hindenburg, in having Jewish civil servants with frontline service during wartime exempted from losing their jobs. It proved a dubious achievement because it created two classes of Jews, privileged and non-privileged. Moreover, the exemptions were honored only until Hindenburg's death in August 1934.[23]

While Löwenstein ruffled a lot of Jewish feathers, Dr. Max Naumann, a lawyer and chairman of the League of National-German Jews, succeeded in offending most of his co-religionists by his even crasser attempts to curry favor with the regime. He and his supporters, for the most part respectable members of the professions, publicly de-emphasized their Jewishness while stressing their German heritage. They also drew a clear line between themselves and those of their fellow Jews whom they disdainfully labeled Cosmopolitans, Leftists, Zionists, and Eastern Jews. All those falling within these categories were not worthy of being called Germans, according to Naumann, whereas his group was, and therefore should not be subjected to discriminatory racial laws.[24] Less offensive but equally nationalistic was the attitude of the *Deutscher Vortrupp* (German Vanguard) led by Dr. Hans-Joachim Schoeps, a brilliant albeit eccentric young theologian.[25] Unlike Naumann's group, Schoeps and his disciples were avowed Jews but also fiercely nationalistic, and they tried hard to sell this ideological blend to an utterly unreceptive regime. Both organizations were ordered dissolved by the end of 1935, while the Jewish War Veterans League survived until the end of 1938.

I chose these selected examples to show how far some Jewish leaders were prepared to go to achieve possible accommodation with the regime. Needless to say, they all failed; but so did the more judicious efforts of the *Reichsvertretung* and the CV in trying to obtain assurances from the government that at least those Jews unwilling or unable to leave would be allowed to stay in Germany.

Whatever hopes the Jewish leadership still had for an acceptable accommodation with Hitler's regime were shattered in September 1935 with the passage of the Nuremberg racial laws. Yet even earlier, in the spring of that year, after Hitler had announced Germany's remilitarization, the provisions of the new defense act of May 1935 excluded Jews from active service. This made it clear to all perceptive observers that Jews were now officially regarded as barely tolerated second-class citizens. The Nuremberg Laws merely substantiated this new status through specific and humiliating definitions. The Nuremberg Laws signaled in legal terms what had been evident *de facto* since 1933: the end of Jewish emancipation in Germany.

This fact was not lost on the Jewish leaders, and they acted accordingly. Two days after the announcement of the racial laws the chief organ of the Zionists, the *Jüdische Rundschau*, demanded that immediate measures be taken to step up emigration, especially for the young generation. A week later the *CV-Zeitung* also suggested the establishment of systematic and coordinated plans for the emigration of Jewish youth. Thus, assimilationists and Zionists, whose traditional feuds had gradually abated after 1933, still implied in their respective statements that while the young no longer had a future in Germany, the older generation of Jews might be permitted to stay—though under highly restrictive and humiliating conditions—until natural attrition would solve the "Jewish Question" in Germany once and for all.[26]

Yet before long that hope, too, began to dissipate. Besides embarking on an intensified program of financial assistance for the growing number of impoverished Jews, of counseling, and of occupational training projects, the *Reichsvertretung*, with the assistance of the CV and the Zionist Federation, also accelerated the search for every available avenue of emigration. It had become apparent soon after passage of the Nuremberg Laws that the initial expectation of restricting emigration efforts mainly to the young generation was unrealistic. Toward the end of 1935, the *Reichsvertretung* prepared a program for mass emigration which, given the worldwide economic Depression and the widespread aversion of most countries to admit large numbers of Jewish refugees, proved to be extremely difficult.[27] We cannot dwell on the details of these efforts, important though they were. What concerns us here is that Jewish emigration was planned, coordinated with the Nazi authorities, and the necessary funding was secured by that educated segment of German Jews that in 1933 assumed the thorny task of organizing what proved to be the liquidation of a Jewish presence in Germany, which had existed there for two thousand years. Their efforts enabled more than half of Germany's Jews—roughly two hundred and seventy thousand—to emigrate. Unfortunately, many of them merely went to neighboring countries rather than overseas and were ultimately caught in the dragnet of Hitler's European-wide Final Solution.

We have so far been concerned with the response of the Jewish leaders to the most pressing practical needs their community faced after 1933. But besides dealing with such vital matters as emigration, occupational retraining, and welfare, they also recognized the importance of educational and cultural needs, two additional spheres within German society from which Jews were gradually but relentlessly excluded. But it was not merely necessity that gave rise to educational and cultural programs. A number of intellectuals, inspired largely by Martin Buber, saw the crisis the triumph of National Socialism had created for their community as a challenge. It provided an opportunity for the rediscovery of Jewish values and traditions and, with it, the age-old commitment to learning. With these considerations in mind, an intensive adult education program was launched in 1933,

first in Buber's *Lehrhaus* in Frankfurt am Main, and subsequently—
sponsored by the *Reichsvertretung*—in all cities with a sizable Jewish
population.[28] The curriculum varied widely and was by no means restricted
to religious studies. Philosophy, history, economics, music, and literature
were taught by such prominent scholars as Franz Oppenheimer, Ernst
Kantorowicz, Arnold Berney, and Hans Liebeschütz. Thus various courses
which Jews could no longer take at German universities were taught by
Jewish academicians no longer allowed to teach at German universities. In
addition to as well as within the context of traditional disciplines the courses
did emphasize Jewish themes in an attempt to rekindle pride and self-
respect among men and women who, because of their religion and alleged
racial inferiority, were daily exposed to humiliations and slurs on the part of
their neighbors and the media. The signal for this short-lived Jewish
renaissance—it lasted until the end of 1938—at a time when the ties with
the beloved German homeland were irrevocably dissolving had been given
on April 4, 1933, in response to the boycott, by Dr. Robert Weltsch, editor-
in-chief of *Jüdische Rundschau*. "Wear it with pride, the yellow spot!" read
the headline of his editorial which urged the Jews to affirm their
Jewishness.[29]

In addition to the adult education program and, after the fall of 1935,
the rapid expansion of Jewish elementary and secondary schools to
accommodate the mounting number of youngsters barred from attending
regular state schools a separate cultural program was instituted in 1933.[30] As
Jews were ousted from the stage, the film industry, the art academies, and
the conservatories, and as Jewish audiences found it increasingly unpleasant, and eventually impossible, to attend theaters, concert halls, or opera
houses frequented by the general public, the Jewish *Kulturbund* (literally,
"cultural alliance") was founded.[31] At branches in all the larger cities Jewish
actors, singers, and musicians performed for exclusively Jewish audiences
until even this segregated cultural phase was terminated following
Kristallnacht, the "Night of Broken Glass," in November 1938.[32] Performances had to be confined to works of foreign or non-Aryan playwrights and
composers, although non-popular works by German Aryans and those with
specific Jewish themes, like Lessing's *Nathan the Wise*, were also permitted. The same held true for musical performances. Beethoven and Wagner
were forbidden, Mahler and Mendelssohn were not. At a time of constant
fear, uncertainty, and stress for most Jews, evenings at the *Kulturbund* with
performances of high quality provided much more than entertainment.
They also gave comfort, brief respite from the pressures outside, and pride
in the achievement of Jewish artists.

Until June 1939, after most of the remaining Jewish organizations had
been banned and after the *Reichsvertretung* had been deprived of whatever
independence it had still possessed by being renamed *Reichsvereinigung
der Juden in Deutschland* (Reich Association of Jews in Germany) and
turned into a Gestapo-controlled organization,[33] the men and women who
then composed the Jewish leadership enjoyed a considerable degree of
leeway in taking initiatives and making decisions. Faced by what they
gradually realized was the last stage of German Jewry's existence as an
identifiable entity, they worked unsparingly to turn this human catastrophe
into a dignified and orderly process of dissolution. Their responsibilities
were varied and heavy: they represented Jewish concerns to the German
authorities; they planned and organized emigration; they assumed the
burden of caring for the rapidly rising number of people reduced to
poverty; they arranged for occupational retraining and both general and
Jewish education for adults and children; and they created an ambitious
and, until its termination, highly successful series of rich cultural programs.

Throughout the period, from 1933 until the summer of 1939, when the
last remaining possibilities for independent action had been taken away
during the months following *Kristallnacht,* the Jewish leadership was
guided by two basic rules. The first pertained to the prevention of discord
among the traditionally divisive Jewish factions so as to present a common
front when dealing with government or Party officials. The second required
the adoption of an unemotional, businesslike manner in all communications
with either the Nazi authorities or the Jewish community, and in all
contacts with the former a display of dignity and self-restraint. These rules
were never spelled out in so many words, but they were quietly adhered
to.[34] To be sure, the Jewish leadership had to make certain rather painful
concessions when communicating with the ministries and Party offices of
the Third Reich, because letters and memoranda had to be phrased in such
a way as to make allowances for the peculiar Nazi mentality.[35] In a few
instances, moreover, some leaders of Jewish organizations violated these
rules, as has been shown earlier. One might add to these infractions the less
than edifying hanky-panky that went on between some Zionist leaders and
the Gestapo, involving attempts by the former to attain preferential
treatment for those Jews who wanted to emigrate to Palestine.[36] Nor would
it be amiss to mention the, still undetermined, number of rabbis who
shortly after Hitler's "seizure of power" left their congregations and
removed themselves, thanks to the benevolent assistance from rabbis
abroad, with what is known in diplomatic parlance as "indecent haste" to
new pulpits in Adelaide, Cincinnati, Johannesburg, Los Angeles, New

York, and other places. Yet aside from these few examples, the men and
women entrusted with the organization of this difficult dissolution process
handled their responsibilities with what in retrospect appears as a remarkable display of courage and discipline—attributes that the Nazis always liked
to arrogate exclusively to themselves. And while many Jewish intellectuals
who had served their dying community faithfully since 1933 joined the last
and largest emigration wave between November 1938 and September 1939,
a small but dedicated number of them who also might have saved
themselves stayed on, literally to the bitter end, because they considered it
their moral obligation to do so.[37] Was it Immanuel Kant's categorical
imperative that inspired them to do so—and steeped as they were in
German culture they knew their philosophers—or did they recall the words
of the prophet Habakkuk:

> I will stand at my post,
> I will take up my position on the watch-tower,
> I will watch to learn what he will say through me,
> and what I shall reply when I am challenged. . . ?

We shall never know.

NOTES

1. Martin Buber, *Briefwechsel aus sieben Jahrzehnten*, vol. 2 (Heidelberg, 1973), p. 463.
2. Ibid., pp. 465–67.
3. These figures are rough approximations and pertain only to Jews who listed themselves as
   Glaubensjuden, i.e., Jews who professed their faith. The 1925 census recorded 564,379
   Glaubensjuden in Germany; by June 1933, six months after Hitler's appointment as
   Chancellor, the census established a figure of 499,682 *Glaubensjuden*. See Esra
   Bennathan, "Die demographische und wirtschaftliche Struktur der Juden," in Werner E.
   Mosse and Arnold Paucker, eds., *Entscheidungsjahr 1932. Zur Judenfrage in der
   Endphase der Weimarer Republik*. Schriftenreihe wissenschaftlicher Abhandlungen des
   Leo Baeck Instituts, 13 (Tübingen, 1965), pp. 87–88. The figure 530,000 in January
   1933—again a rough estimate—is based on compilations from the following studies:
   Werner Rosenstock, "Exodus 1933–1939. A Survey of Jewish Emigration from Ger-
   many," in *Year Book of the Leo Baeck Institute*, vol. I (1956), pp. 373–90 (hereafter cited
   as *LBI Year Book*); Wilhelm Treue, "Die Juden in der Wirtschaftsgeschichte des
   Rheinischen Raumes 1648–1945," in *Monumenta Judaica* (Cologne, 1964), pp. 458–59;
   Helmut Genschel, *Die Verdrängung der Juden aus der Wirtschaft im Dritten Reich*
   (Göttingen–Berlin–Frankfurt–Zürich, 1966), pp. 274, 291; and Bennathan, *passim*.
4. Genschel, *Die Verdrängung der Juden*, p. 4.
5. This is evident from the findings of Karl A. Schleunes, *The Twisted Road to Auschwitz.
   Nazi Policy Toward German Jews 1933–1939* (Urbana–Chicago–London, 1970) and Uwe
   Dietrich Adam, *Judenpolitik im Dritten Reich* (Düsseldorf, 1972). See also Hans
   Mommsen, "Der nationalsozialistische Polizeistaat und die Judenverfolgung vor 1938:
   Dokumentation," *Vierteljahrshefte für Zeitgeschichte*, X (1962), 76. But cf. the older

account in Karl Dietrich Bracher, Wolfgang Sauer, Gerhard Schulz, *Die na-tionalsozialistische Machtergreifung. Studien zur Errichtung des totalitären Herrschafts-systems in Deutschland 1933–34* (Cologne and Opladen, 1960), p. 277. On the genesis of anti-Jewish legislation predating the "seizure of power" see ibid., pp. 411–13, and Saul Esh, "Designs for Anti-Jewish Policy in Germany up to the Nazi Rule," *Yad Vashem Studies on the European Jewish Catastrophe and Resistance*, VI (1967), 83–120, esp. 115–20 (hereafter cited as *YVS*).

6. Bracher, Sauer, Schulz, *Die nationalsozialistische Machtergreifung*, pp. 278–79; Schleunes, *The Twisted Road to Auschwitz*, pp. 62–91; Genschel, *Die Verdrängung der Juden*, pp. 43–59.

7. Adam, *Judenpolitik*, pp. 51–71, and *passim;* Schleunes, *The Twisted Road to Auschwitz*, pp. 95–114, and passim; Bracher, Sauer, Schultz, *Die nationalsozialistische Machtergrei-fung, pp.* 277–86, 496–503; Hans Mommsen, *Beamtentum im Dritten Reich. Mit ausgewählten Quellen zur nationalsozialistischen Beamtenpolitik.* Schriftenreihe der *Vierteljahrshefte für Zeitgeschichte*, XIII (Stuttgart, 1966), 48–60.

8. This estimate is based on Bennathan, in *Entscheidungsjahr 1932*, pp. 111–12, and Genschel, *Die Verdrängung der Juden*, p. 287.

9. Rosenstock, in *LBI Year Book* I (1956), pp. 377–80, esp. p. 378; Schleunes, *The Twisted Road*, p. 199; Genschel, *Die Verdrängung der Juden*, p. 291.

10. Rosenstock, in *LBI Year Book* I (1956), pp. 373–74, 377; Genschel, *Verdrängung*, p. 291.

11. Friedrich S. Brodnitz, "Die Reichsvertretung der deutschen Juden," in Hans Tramer, ed., *In zwei Welten. Siegfried Moses zum 75. Geburtstag* (Tel Aviv, 1962), pp. 106–13.

12. Marjorie Lamberti, "The Attempt to Form a Jewish Block: Jewish Notables and Politics in Wilhelmian Germany," *Central European History*, III (1970), 73.

13. Bracher, Sauer, Schulz, *Die nationalsozialistische Machtergreifung*, p. 262. On the origins of the CV see Ismar Schorsch, *Jewish Reactions to German Anti-Semitism 1870–1914* (New York-London, 1972), pp. 117–48, and Arnold Paucker, "Zur Problematik einer jüdischen Abwehrstrategie in der deutschen Gesellschaft," in Werner E. Mosse and Arnold Paucker, eds., *Juden im Wilhelminischen Deutschland 1890–1914*. Schriftenreihe wissenschaftlicher Abhandlungen des Leo Baeck Instituts, 33 (Tübingen, 1976), pp. 480–548. On the RjF see Ulrich Dunker, *Der Reichsbund jüdischer Frontsoldaten 1919–1938. Geschichte eines jüdischen Abwehrvereins* (Düsseldorf, 1977); Ruth Pierson, "Embattled Veterans: The Reichsbund jüdischer Frontsoldaten," *LBI Year Book* XIX (1974), pp. 139–54. On the RjF, and also on the *Verband nationaldeutscher Juden* and the *Deutscher Vortrupp*, see Carl J. Rheins, "German-Jewish Patriotism 1918–1935: A Study of the Attitudes and Actions of the *Reichsbund jüdischer Front-soldaten,* the *Verband nationaldeutscher Juden,* the *Schwarzes Fähnlein, Jungenschaft,* and the *Deutscher Vortrupp, Gefolgschaft deutscher Juden,*" unpubl. Ph.D. Diss., State University of New York at Stony Brook, 1978, *passim*. On the origins of the *Zionistische Vereinigung* see Jehuda Reinharz, *Fatherland or Promised Land. The Dilemma of the German Jew, 1893–1914* (Ann Arbor, 1975), pp. 90–143, and *passim*.

14. Brodnitz, in *In zwei Welten*, pp. 106–13; Hugo Hahn, "Die Gründung der Reichsvertre-tung," ibid., pp. 97–105; Franz Meyer, "Bemerkungen zu den 'zwei Denkschriften,'" ibid., pp. 114–18, and "Zwei Denkschriften," ibid., pp. 120–27; Max Gruenewald, "Der Anfang der Reichsvertretung," in Robert Weltsch, ed., *Deutsches Judentum, Aufstieg und Krise. Gestalten, Ideen, Werke* (Stuttgart, 1963), pp. 315–25; Hans-Erich Fabian, "Zur Entstehung der 'Reichsvereinigung der Juden in Deutschland,'" in Herbert A. Strauss and Kurt Grossmann, eds., *Gegenwart im Rückblick. Festgabe für die jüdische Gemeinde zu Berlin 25 Jahre nach dem Neubeginn* (Heidelberg, 1970), pp. 165–68. For two rather critical Zionist views of the *Reichsvertretung*, see Kurt Jakob Ball-Kaduri, "The National Representation of Jews in Germany—Obstacles and Accomplishments at

its Establishment," *YVS*, II (1975 [1958]), 159–78, and Abraham Margaliot, "The Dispute Over the Leadership of German Jewry (1933–1938)," ibid., X (1974), 129–48.

15. For a brief sketch of Hirsch's life, see Leo Baeck, "Gedenken an zwei Tote," in *Deutsches Judentum*, pp. 312–13, and Ernst G. Lowenthal, ed., *Bewährung im Untergang. Ein Gedenkbuch* (Stuttgart, 1965), pp. 71–74. See also Annedore Leber, *Das Gewissen entscheidet: Bereiche des deutschen Widerstandes von 1933–1945, in Lebensbildern* (Berlin-Frankfurt/Main, 1957), pp. 12–17.

16. The literature on Baeck is growing steadily. Here it will suffice to list some of the earliest and some of the latest publications. The former consist of several short sketches by Siegfried Moses, Hans Liebeschütz, Eva Reichmann, and Wolfgang Hamburger, under the heading: "In Memorium Leo Baeck," *LBI Year Book* II (1957), pp. 3–34; among the latter is Leonard Baker, *Days of Sorrow and Faith. Leo Baeck and the Berlin Jews* (New York, 1978). For a rather polemical exchange on Baeck's image, see Ball-Kaduri, "Leo Baeck and Contemporary History. A Riddle in Leo Baeck's Life," *YVS*, VI (1967), 121–29; and Ernst Simon, "Comments on the Article on the late Rabbi Baeck," ibid., pp. 131–34.

17. Brodnitz, in *In zwei Welten*, p. 111. In *Bewährung im Untergang*. Lowenthal, in his series of brief biographies, presents 178 men and women who served the Jewish community in Germany either in Berlin or on the congregational level in the provinces, and who perished in the Final Solution. Of these, 50 were rabbis, 46 jurists, 24 educators on all levels, 15 businessmen, 8 physicians, and the remainder former public officials, journalists, architects, or full-time employees of Jewish congregations. Lowenthal makes it clear in the introduction that this is by no means a complete list but merely a "representative" one as he was unable to secure the names and data of everybody who served in a similar capacity, and perished.

18. Bracher, Sauer, Schulz, *Machtergreifung*, pp. 282–83; Brodnitz, in *In zwei Welten*, p. 108; see also the two "Denkschriften," ibid., pp. 120–27, and Gruenewald, in *Deutsches Judentum*, p. 320. For a succinct survey of this reaction as it affected the various Jewish organizations, regardless of religious or ideological orientation, see Dunker, *Reichsbund jüdischer Frontsoldaten*, pp. 115–24.

19. *C.V.-Zeitung*, XII, 15 (April 13, 1933).

20. See, for example, the appeal by the (old) *Reichsvertretung* in conjunction with the Executive of the Berlin Jewish Congregation to Hitler, dated March 29, 1933, in Klaus J. Herrmann, *Das Dritte Reich und die deutsch-jüdischen Organisationen 1933–1934*. Schriftenreihe der Hochschule für Politische Wissenschaften München, Neue Folge, 4 (Cologne-Berlin-Bonn-Munich, 1969), p. 61. See also Dunker, *Reichsbund*, pp. 121–22 (for the CV); Jakow Trachtenberg, *Die Greuelpropaganda ist eine Lügenpropaganda, sagen die deutschen Juden selbst* (Berlin, 1933).

21. On Löwenstein, see Rheins, unpubl. Diss., pp. 21, 207, and *passim*; Herrmann, *Das Dritte Reich*, p. 18.

22. Dunker, *Reichsbund*, pp. 132–44, 173–75; Herrmann, *Das Dritte Reich*, pp. 18–21, 49–52, 66–67, 69, 92–105, 119–23, 126–27, 132–42; Rheins, pp. 177–79.

23. Dunker, *Reichsbund*, pp. 133–34; Schleunes, *The Twisted Road*, pp. 95–96, 104–5; Mommsen, *Beamtentum*, pp. 48, 54, 59; Adam, *Judenpolitik*, p. 64; Gruenewald, in *Deutsches Judentum*, p. 320.

24. On Naumann and the VndJ see Rheins, pp. 58–101; Hermann, pp. 12–13, 21–31, and *passim*.

25. Rheins, pp. 147–90, and the following autobiographical books by Hans-Joachim Schoeps: *Die letzten dreissig Jahre: Rückblicke* (Stuttgart, 1956); *Ja—Nein—und Trotzdem. Erinnerungen—Begegnungen—Erfahrungen* (Mainz, 1974); and the documentation, *"Bereit für Deutschland." Der Patriotismus deutscher Juden und der Nationalsozialismus. Frühe Schriften 1930–1939*. (Berlin, 1970).

26. *Jüdische Rundschau*, XXXVIII, 75 (September 17, 1935); *C.V.-Zeitung*, XIV, 39 (September 26, 1935).

27. Hahn, in *In zwei Welten*, pp. 108–9; Dunker, *Reichsbund*, pp. 159–60; Margaret T. Edelheim-Muehsam, "Die Haltung der jüdischen Presse gegenüber der nationalsozialistischen Bedrohung," in *Deutsches Judentum*, pp. 376–77. For a tentative assessment of Jewish emigration patterns, including the role played by the Hitler regime, see Schleunes, *The Twisted Road*, pp. 169–213. This topic is still in need of further investigation.

28. For this and the following see Ernst Simon, *Aufbau im Untergang. Jüdische Erwachsenenbildung im nationalsozialistischen Deutschland als geistiger Widerstand*. Schriftenreihe wissenschaftlicher Abhandlungen des Leo Baeck Instituts, 2 (Tübingen, 1959), esp. pp. 1–75; Richard Fuchs, "The 'Hochschule für die Wissenschaft des Judentums' in the Period of Nazi Rule. Personal Recollections," *LBI Year Book* XII (1967), pp. 3–31.

29. *Jüdische Rundschau*, XXXVIII, 27 (April 4, 1933).

30. Solomon Colodner, "Jewish Education under National Socialism," *YVS*, III (1975 [1959]), 161–85; Hans Gaertner, "Probleme der jüdischen Schule während der Hitlerjahre, unter besonderer Berücksichtigung der Theodor-Herzl-Schule in Berlin," in *Deutsches Judentum*, pp. 326–52.

31. A thorough study of the *Kulturbund deutscher Juden*, later *jüdischer Kulturbund*, remains to be written. A good, succinct appraisal is Herbert Freeden, "A Jewish Theatre under the Swastika," *LBI Year Book* I (1956), pp. 142–62. See also Elisabeth Flessen, "Nathan der Weise im Staate der Nazis," *Die Zeit*, October 14, 1977, and "Flamme des Geistes in der Zeit der Not," ibid., October 21, 1977; and Erwin Lichtenstein, "Der Kulturbund der Juden in Danzig 1933–1938," *Zeitschrift für die Geschichte der Juden*, X (1973), 181–90.

32. On *Kristallnacht*, see Lionel Kochan, *Pogrom. November 10, 1938* (London, 1957); Erich Lüth, "Die Reichskristallnacht," in Friedrich-Ebert-Stiftung, ed., *Die Reichskristallnacht. Der Antisemitismus in der deutschen Geschichte* (Bonn, 1959), pp. 9–18; Ball-Kaduri, "The Central Jewish Organizations in Berlin During the Pogrom of November 1938 ('Kristallnacht')," *YVS*, III (1975 [1959]), 261–81; Genschel, *Die Verdrängung*, pp. 177–86; Hermann Graml, *Der 9. November 1938, "Reichskristallnacht"* (Bonn, 1953); Wolfgang Scheffler, *Judenverfolgung im Dritten Reich*. Zur Politik und Zeitgeschichte, 4 (Berlin, 1964), pp. 29–32.

33. Adam, *Judenpolitik*, pp. 230–31; Fabian, in *Gegenwart im Rückblick*, pp. 165–79; Ball-Kaduri, "Von der 'Reichsvertretung' zur 'Reichsvereinigung,'" *Zeitschrift für die Geschichte der Juden*, I (1964), 191–99; Shaul Esh, "The Establishment of the 'Reichsvereinigung der Juden in Deutschland' and its Main Activities," *YVS*, VII (1968), 19–38.

34. Gruenewald, in *Deutsches Judentum*, pp. 320–21, 324–25.

35. Gruenewald, ibid., p. 320; Brodnitz, in *In zwei Welten*, p. 108.

36. The crassest case is that of Georg Kareski. See Herbert S. Levine, "A Jewish Collaborator in Nazi Germany: The Strange Career of Georg Kareski, 1933–1937," *Central European History*, VIII (1975), 251–81. For evidence of preferential treatment of Zionists by the Nazi authorities, see Mommsen, "Polizeistaat," *Vierteljahrshefte*, esp. Documents No. 2, 5, 8, and 9.

37. See Lowenthal, *Bewährung im Untergang*.

II.
THE SETTING OF THE
HOLOCAUST

RAUL HILBERG

THE ANATOMY OF
THE HOLOCAUST

In the middle of the war a remarkable man by the name of Franz Neumann, who worked in the Office of Strategic Services and the Department of State, wrote a book about Nazi Germany called *Behemoth*. The first edition came out in 1942, the second in 1944. Each edition was written without the benefit of any original documents, any of the captured materials which became available after the collapse of Germany and which constitute the major source of our knowledge about the destruction process. Franz Neumann worked from newspapers, from published decrees, from journal articles that were somehow transmitted across the ocean, through Switzerland to the United States. He worked intuitively, and he analyzed the structure of the Nazi regime with singular insight. He called Germany a "non-state," a "behemoth" but not a state. He identified four hierarchical groupings as operating virtually independently of one another, and occasionally coming together to make what he sarcastically called "social contracts." Those four hierarchies were the veritable pillars of modern Germany, as they have occasionally been described by German constitutional lawyers and historians: the German civil service, the German army, the later emergent industrial conglomeration of various giant enterprises, and finally, the Nazi Party and its machinery.

Several years later, when the war crimes trials were begun in Nuremberg, most particularly after the very first one, more and more documents were turned up here and there, a paper residue of a vast bureaucracy. The primary problem was to make a few piles of them so that one could at least break down this mass of tens of thousands and even hundreds of thousands of materials into manageable quantities. The records were labeled roughly by subject matter: "NG," "NI," "NO," and "NOKW." "NG" stands for Nazi government, in the main correspondence produced by the civil service; "NI" is Nazi industry; "NO," Nazi organizations, that is to say, Party documents; and "NOKW" stands for Nazi *Oberkommando der Wehrmacht*, the high command of the armed forces. Independently of Franz Neumann, the archivists and researchers preparing the Nuremberg trials had developed the identical scheme of things as they looked at these documents. They, too, concluded that there were four major hierarchies.

Fortunately, I came under Neumann's influence very early, while I was a beginning graduate student at Columbia University. Neumann was not a very approachable man, and I did not want to tell him that I was about to embark on the study of the destruction of the Jews. Therefore I said that I wanted to investigate the role of the German civil service in that destruction. He nodded his head, and that was as much conversation as he made because he was hard of hearing. Actually, I was preparing to do more—I was going to write about all the other hierarchies as well, because somehow I felt that each was involved in the destruction process in some way. And then I realized that I would have to write four stories, paralleling one another. That wouldn't do. Consequently I had to come upon another scheme, another anatomy, to describe that development. At that very moment I came across an analysis by an extraordinarily shrewd observer who was in Hungary during the war. Rudolf Kastner, a Jew who made audacious attempts to negotiate with the Germans in 1944 for ransoming the Jews of Hungary (efforts that by and large failed), wrote an affidavit on his experiences and perspectives at Nuremberg right after his liberation. In that 18-page summation he said words to the effect: For years, we sat there in Hungary surrounded by other Axis countries. We watched the Jews disappear in Germany. We watched them disappear in Poland. We watched them disappear in Yugoslavia and many other places. And then we noticed—meaning in essence *he* noticed—that everywhere the same events seemed to be happening, that certain steps followed in sequence. In a crude way he outlined these steps. And it suddenly occurred to me that the destruction of the Jews was a process.

In the administrative process, the path of a bureaucracy is determined, not by blueprints or strategies, but by the very nature of the undertaking. Thus, a group of people, dispersed in a larger population over an entire continent, will not be concentrated or seized until after they have been identified and defined. One step at a time, and each step dependent on the preceding step. The destruction of the Jews transpired in this manner; it had an inherent logic, irrespective of how far ahead the perpetrators could see and irrespective of what their plans were. They could have stopped at any one moment and at any one place, but they could not have omitted steps in the progression or "escalation" of the process. They had to traverse all of these routines. They had to sever, one by one, the relations and ties of the Jewish community with the surrounding population in every region of German-dominated Europe. Step one, in the analytical scheme of things, was thus the undertaking of defining Jews as such. It would appear to have been a simple matter, but it was not. There is a Jewish definition of the term "Jew," but that would not serve the Germans. To them, an adherence to the Jewish religion, or descent from a Jewish mother, was not decisive because there might have been recent converts to Christianity, or half-Jews with a Jewish father who were not Jewish in Jewish eyes but who could not be German in the Third Reich. Above all, if Jewry were defined in accordance with religious criteria alone, Jews might convert overnight and, by doing so, immunize themselves from the effects of the destruction process, a medieval approach adequate enough in an earlier age, but one that was not proper in a racial environment. Yet everyone knew that Jews could not be identified in every case by physiognomy. Definition could not rest on measurements of faces. The whole notion of race had an ideological tinge, but very little administrative utility.

It was an official in the Interior Ministry (originally in the customs administration) who wrote the final version of the definition decree that we associate with the Nuremberg Laws. The original Law, the very first in which measures were taken against Jews, the Law for the Restoration of the German Civil Service, had specified "non-Aryan." The phrase had come down from the nineteenth century. It resulted in a protest by the Japanese government, which felt insulted. The Germans replied, "Wait. We do not mean that different races are necessarily different in quality. They are just different in kind." But even with this explanation, that concept was in trouble.

Non-Aryan, at any rate, was any person with a single Jewish grandparent. That grandparent only had to belong to the Jewish religion. A person with a Jewish grandparent could be dismissed from a post in the civil service or from the teaching profession. Yet in the escalating destruction process, such a definition, embracing individuals who were three-quarters German, was too harsh. It was up to Bernhard Lösener, the customs official transferred to the Interior Ministry, to define the term Jew. He had to do so urgently because at Nuremberg a law had been issued, a criminal law, in which "Jews" were forbidden to marry Germans, and "Jews" were forbidden to have extramarital intercourse with Germans, and "Jews" were forbidden to employ in their household German women under the age of 45. And Jews were not defined in that criminal law.

Thus, an implementation decree had to be issued that would contain that missing definition. It was to provide that a person was to be considered Jewish if he had three or four Jewish grandparents. That person was Jewish regardless of his own religious adherence. He could have been brought up as a Christian, his parents might have been Christians, but if most of his grandparents were Jewish by religion, then he was Jewish in accordance with this new definition. If an individual had two Jewish grandparents, he would be classified as Jewish only if he himself belonged to the Jewish religion at the time of the issuance of the decree, or if—at that moment—he was married to a Jewish person. The critical factor in every case was in the first instance the religion of the grandparents. That is the reason for a new profession that came into being all over Germany, the *Sippenforscher,* specialists in genealogy who were providing evidence of the religion of grandparents by means of records found in state offices or baptismal certificates furnished by churches.

The definition decree had the effect of targeting the Jews automatically in that it precluded them from doing anything at all to change their status and thereby to escape from the impact of all the destructive measures that were to come. The very next step in the unfolding destruction process was economic, primarily the expropriation of Jewish business firms, a process known as "Aryanizations."

At the beginning, the "Aryanizations" were "voluntary." German companies, aided by regulations of the Economy Ministry, would bid for Jewish enterprises, always at levels below market value. Still, we can clearly see a struggle being waged by Jewish owners attempting to obtain a meaningful price, and by German interests competing for Jewish property against each other, attempting to enlarge their over-all strength or influence in a sector of the economy. However, this phase of acquisition came to an end, by and large, at the end of 1938 with the firing of the synagogues. At that point the Aryanizations were no longer voluntary, but compulsory. Jewish firms could be sold or liquidated by German "trustees" and Jewish employees in these concerns lost their jobs.

The very next step was concentration, the physical separation and the social isolation of the Jewish community from the German. Actually the very first Nuremberg decree prohibiting new marriages between Jews and Germans was an initial step in that direction. There followed others, including measures that placed the machinery of the Jewish community under German command. Henceforth, in the Reich as well as in newly conquered territory, the Germans would employ Jewish leaders and Jewish community personnel for housing segregation, personal property confiscation, forced labor, and even deportations. In the wake of the violence and the arrest waves of November 1938, Hermann Göring and several other Nazi personalities discussed the question of whether one ought to form ghettos inside Germany. The idea was rejected, most particularly by that expert policeman Reinhard Heydrich, who was to head the German Security Police and Security Service, on the ground that so long as the Jews were not inside a wall, out of sight of the German population, every German could act as an auxiliary policeman, every German could watch the Jews, every German could keep track of them.

Less than one year after that conference, war broke out. Poland was invaded, and several million additional Jews came under German jurisdiction. A concentration process in Poland began almost immediately; the medieval ghetto came into existence once more. The largest was the Warsaw ghetto, the second largest was the ghetto of Lodz, and there were hundreds of others. All were captive city-states, with a variety of functions including mundane as well as extraordinary tasks. That is a history so varied, so diversified, so complex as to demand attention in and of itself. In the great work of Isaiah Trunk, *Judenrat*, you may discover the history not only of the Jewish Councils, but of the entire structure of the ghettos, their social, economic, and political problems under the Nazis.

There was an ambiguity in the very formation of the ghettos. What was going to happen to the Jews inside the walls? The death rates slowly began to climb. We have detailed statistics from Lodz and from Warsaw, though not from most of the other ghettos. Because those two ghettos were very different, the Lodz ghetto having been stratified and centralized under a kind of Jewish dictatorship, even as the Warsaw ghetto remained laissez-faire with private enterprise, it is instructive to note that in both starvation and illness they were roughly comparable, and that the death rates rose at an almost uniform rate to 1 percent of the population per month.

By 1940 the Germans attacked the western countries: France, Belgium, Holland. They won a quick, decisive victory on the ground and contemplated a peace treaty with England. Were that treaty to have come into being, it would automatically have been made also with France, and France was to have ceded the African island of Madagascar to the Germans. That island was to have been governed by the police, and all the Jews of Europe would have been shipped there. Such, at least, was the fantasizing in certain sections of the German Foreign Office. But the British did not make peace. When that fact began to sink in, toward the end of 1940, there was a transition period of greatest importance in German thinking. Up to that moment there really had been only two policies in all history against the Jews, the first being the conversion of the Jews to Christianity, the second being the expulsion of the Jews from a country in which they lived. Expulsion was now becoming impossible. In the middle of a war, millions of people cannot be expelled. Forced emigration was no longer feasible. Hence the idea of "a territorial solution" emerged. How? What form was it to take? That was not spelled out in 1940 or even in early 1941. Everyone was waiting with some anticipation for a decision.

Then came the planning of "Barbarossa" (the attack on the Soviet Union). The onslaught was being contemplated in a military conference held as early as July 22, 1940, and plans were taking shape in directive after directive, order of battle after order of battle, and in negotiations with Axis partners. In the course of these preparations a document was being drafted in the High Command of the Armed Forces. The order contained a cryptic sentence to the effect that the armed forces would be accompanied by special units of the SS and Police, which were to carry out certain state-political tasks in occupied territory. That was the beginning of the first massive killing operation. It has its origin in a social contract, as Neumann would have called it, between the German army and the SS and Police. The arrangement was hammered out in a series of agreements between the Quartermaster General of the German Army, Edward Wagner, and representatives of the Security Police, particularly Heydrich and Schellenberg. On June 22, 1941, when the German armies spilled into Russia, the Security Police units—called *Einsatzgruppen*—also moved in and started killing Jews on the spot.

The *Einsatzgruppen* sent daily reports to Berlin. In consolidated form, this revealing material was routed to many recipients, but only one set of copies was discovered after the war. As for the original reports from the field, very few are still around. From the Soviet Union came one report of a single commando that operated in Lithuania. A commando was a company-sized unit augmented by native helpers. The commando of which I speak killed 135,000 Jews in its area between June 1941 and January 1942.

The occupied territories of the U.S.S.R. were the scenes of massacre after massacre. Sometimes the *Einsatzgruppen* commanders would return to the same place again and again, shooting Jews en masse. In White Russia, a substantial number of victims fled to the woods; few were the survivors of roundups and shootings in the Ukraine.

But shooting operations had their problems. The Germans employed the phrase *Seelenbelastung* ("burdening of the soul") with reference to machine-gun fire or rifle fire directed at men, women, and children in prepared ditches. After all, the men that were firing these weapons were themselves fathers. How could they do this day after day? It was then that the technicians developed a gas van designed to lessen the suffering of the perpetrator. It was simply a vehicle, or a van, strictly speaking, with an exhaust pipe turned inward so the carbon monoxide would kill the seventy people inside even while they were being driven to their graves. The gas vans began operating in the east for women and children, but the unloading was very dirty work.

In 1941, some six weeks after the attack on the Soviet Union, a letter was written by Hermann Göring to Reinhard Heydrich, charging Heydrich with the Final Solution of the Jewish problem in Europe. I have always regarded that letter as the signal for the total destruction of European Jewry, the decisive step across the threshold. Although Göring was not specific about the time or manner in which his directive was to be implemented, his words implied finality and irreversibility.

How was the killing set into motion? As of November 1941, there was some thinking about deporting Jews to the *Einsatzgruppen* so they could be killed by these experienced shooters. That is why German Jews were transported to Minsk, Riga, and Kovno. In the long run, however, the shooting of millions would be an insurmountable problem; there would be too many witnesses, too many bodies, too many soul-burdened members of the SS and Police. Some of the deportees were consequently sent to the crowded ghettos of Poland. The ghettos themselves were to be dissolved soon. In various parts of the occupied Polish territory, the Germans were erecting facilities for the silent killing of Jews—the gas chambers. There were pure killing centers, including Kulmhof, Treblinka, Sobibor, and Belzec, the object of which was nothing except the gassing of people on arrival. A more complex camp was Auschwitz because it had industry as well as killing facilities. At Auschwitz, death was administered by hydrogen cyanide. The crystals were poured from a canister by an SS man wearing a gas mask with a special filter. In the crowded chamber the solid material became a gas.

The Jews had to be transported from all over Europe, always to the "East." We now know of the very expensive preparations that were required for these deportations. The Foreign Office negotiated and actually made treaties with satellite countries promising, as it were, that the Jews would be leaving for good, but that their property would be left behind. Some of the countries allied with Germany would not agree. The

Romanians, although at first very enthusiastic killers in Russia, balked, and by the fall of 1942 rescinded an agreement to hand over their Jews, while Bulgaria procrastinated, allowing the deportation of Jews from Bulgarian occupied territories in Yugoslavia and Greece, but not permitting the deportation of Jews from Bulgaria itself.

The French Vichy regime adopted a compromise: negotiations were conducted with a view to protecting Jews of French nationality, while foreign Jews were surrendered to the Germans. "How can an occupied country," said French Premier Pierre Laval, "be a country of asylum?" The Italians not only did not deport their Jews, they refused to allow the deportation of Jews under Italian jurisdiction in other Mediterranean regions, including France, Greece, and Yugoslavia. The Germans never let up. You may find correspondence about twelve Jews in Liechtenstein. "What are they doing there?" Or Monaco. Several hundred Norwegian Jews were being deported from Oslo and Trondheim; they were gassed in Auschwitz.

It was wartime, and transport itself was a problem. Movement to killing centers took place by railroad for the most part, occasionally over long distances, as in the case of deportations from southern France or southern Greece. For the Transport Ministry, the movement of the Jews was a financial as well as an operational matter. In principle, each passenger transport had to be paid for. Jews were "travelers" and the Gestapo paid the railroads one-way fare (third class) for each deportee, half price for each transport of more than four hundred. The railroads were accommodating that way. The Gestapo on its part attempted to collect the necessary funds from the Jewish communities themselves. Although such "self-financing" took place in contravention of normal budgetary procedure, the Finance Ministry acquiesced in the practice.

The operational problem was even more complex. For each death transport, central and regional railway offices had to assign scarce rolling stock and time on tracks. Yet these transports seldom had a priority rating. A classification would have identified them for what they were. Instead they were being dispatched whenever possible. The timetables, written for each of them, placed them behind and ahead of regularly scheduled trains. Thus it was that with the intensification of the war, and even after the climax of Stalingrad, the Germans were pursuing ever more relentlessly and ever more drastically the one operation they were bound and determined to finish. They were going to solve the Jewish problem in Europe once and for all.

By the end of 1942, the death camp of Belzec had fulfilled its mission and was dismantled. Six hundred thousand Jews had died in Belzec; there was but one known survivor. At Sobibor and Treblinka there were uprisings. The survivors numbered in the dozens, but the dead of these two camps were about one quarter of a million and three quarters of a million, respectively.

The one camp that remained in operation throughout was Auschwitz. It was the farthest west, not in the path of the advancing Red Army. It was maintained, and even built up, in 1944. The year 1944 is of interest to us because no one could pretend not to know what was going on at that moment. The Jews knew. The Germans knew. The British knew, the Americans knew, everyone knew. There had already been escapes from the Auschwitz camp, and information was gathered also by the War Refugee Board in the United States. Despite that dissemination, no serious ransom negotiations were attempted by the Allies, no strategy of psychological warfare was developed, and no bombs were dropped on the gas chambers.

The Germans continued to destroy the European Jews, even under bombing, even while the Soviet forces were breaking into Romania and eastern Poland, and even as Allied landings were begun in France. To the end, we see the alignment of the German army, the German SS, the German Transport Ministry, the German Foreign Office, as well as financial agencies, all completing the work of solving the "Jewish problem" in Europe. Now we see the results. Here they are, in plain statistics.

I believe the Jewish death toll to be slightly above five million. I arrive at this figure not by subtracting the postwar population from the prewar figures, but by adding numbers that I find in German documents, and extrapolating from them the unreported data. The deaths in camps were roughly three million. Auschwitz had over a million dead; Treblinka on the order of seven hundred to eight hundred thousand; Belzec about six hundred thousand; Sobibor, two hundred to two hundred fifty thousand; Kulmhof, one hundred fifty thousand; Lublin (also known as Maidanek) some tens of thousands. In addition, tens of thousands of Jews were shot by the Romanians in camps between the Bug and Dniester rivers, thousands of Jews were killed at Semlin and other places in Yugoslavia. There were a number of additional camps where Jews suffered heavy losses, but in Holocaust statistics, thousands and even tens of thousands may be lost in footnotes.

About one million four hundred thousand Jewish victims were shot or died in mobile operations of one sort or another. Six hundred thousand died in ghettos.

The heavy concentration of dead is in Eastern Europe. Polish Jewry has virtually disappeared; dead are three million. Soviet Jewry, which was subject to shooting, lost seven hundred thousand within pre-1939 boundaries of the Soviet Union and another two hundred thousand in the Baltic area. In Western Europe the number of dead was proportionally smaller—in France, Belgium, and Italy, the survival rate was relatively high.

Today, the distribution of Jews is radically changed. The United States now has the largest Jewish population in the world, followed by almost equally sized Jewish communities in Israel and Russia. In these three countries live three-quarters of all the Jews remaining in the world. Europe is, for Jewry, a graveyard, and this, after a presence, on that continent, going back to the Roman Empire, of some two thousand years. That is the anatomy. And that is the statistic.*

*This paper is an edited transcription by Raul Hilberg of his speech at San José.

RAUL HILBERG

THE SIGNIFICANCE OF
THE HOLOCAUST

My topic is the significance of the Holocaust for Western civilization. This is quite an assignment. I know that many Holocaust researchers, compartmentalized in their own academic disciplines, have not been in touch with one another. Only in recent years have theorists turned to history and have asked themselves in more detail, "What happened?" By the same token empiricists like me, who have always been concerned with concrete questions, are now becoming more contemplative as we address the larger issue of meaning. Still, it would be difficult, if not impossible, to spell out the import of the Holocaust in an evening. Perhaps it could be defined and even refined in that time but the task would not be finished in a lifetime. Understanding of these matters comes slowly and sometimes not at all. Thus, I will try only to present an outline, one which, incidentally, I have never before attempted. Let us characterize this event in three ways. My approach may sound a little professorial, but it helps to reduce the awesomeness of the topic so that one may, in a certain sense, confront it.

The first consideration, and the foremost one, is the obvious—or perhaps not so obvious—fact that the Holocaust was irreducibly distinct from any other historical event or phenomenon. One cannot explain it in terms of anything else. One cannot submerge it in the campaigns of World War II, or in the aims of the Germans in that war. One cannot drown it in scapegoat theories of government. The Holocaust was *sui generis*. That is the reason it cannot be simply a part of a study of persecutions or of dictatorships. It demands its own literature and its own sources. We must always remember that the Holocaust was pursued relentlessly by its perpetrators from 1933 to 1945; that it had its own momentum, and that it was pressed to its logical conclusion even after it had become evident during the battle of Stalingrad in January 1943 that the war would be lost. The destruction process was implemented regardless of its costs, not for any material gain and not for any military purpose. Even those Jews that may have been needed by the German war industry in a variety of sectors were killed. It becomes increasingly apparent, from the sheer examination of the evidence itself, that the destruction of the Jews of Europe was willed for itself and was accomplished for its own sake. That is the quality of the Holocaust which presents us with some of its most profound implications.

A second feature of the process is the circumstance that the Germans, embarking on ever more drastic measures against the Jews, were coming into conflict with fundamental prohibitions in law, mores, and morality. The confrontation with these rules was personal and immediate. Within the bureaucracy, the Holocaust became an increasingly sensitive topic. Rationalizations broke down. Notwithstanding the continuous bombardment of words which accompanied the destruction of the Jews, the endless propaganda that was intensified even as more and more of the victims were dead, those of the perpetrators who were closest to the scene of action could no longer justify their actions—they had to repress them. They knew that they had now taken an unprecedented step that no other bureaucracy, and no other nation, had dared. They had moved beyond the limits; they had crossed the threshold; they were in forbidden territory. Never would they be able to justify what they had done.

We see the long-term consequences of this venture in the nature of relations visible to this very day which Western countries, not only the Jews, have with Germany. Once, before the end of World War II, there were men in the United States and Great Britain for whom the reports of what was transpiring in Axis Europe meant very little, for whom persecution of any kind meant very little, until they underwent the shock of seeing something with their own eyes in 1945. They saw the camps. The questions that were raised then have been perpetuated through the years within the United States and throughout the Western world.

Most intensive, however, are the effects of this massive transgression in Germany itself. I was there in 1976, and I found to my utter astonishment that men in the judiciary, in railroad offices, even in the customs administration, introduced themselves to me somewhat as follows: "My name is Schultze. I am 38 years old." "My name is Krause. I was born in 1939." What a strange introduction. Such is the division in Germany between the generations. In some respects, it is deeper than the political division between East and West. It cuts across both of these entities. Yet, on occasion, a younger hand reaches toward the older perpetrator, a taboo is suddenly broken, and a weird concordance is established with the past.

Take a single example that I witnessed in 1976. I was the guest of the Central Administration of the German Provinces in Ludwigsburg, which investigates remaining war crimes. I was cordially received. I was shown documents that I wanted to see and I was given a very special treat. A forbidden film was being shown, a propaganda film going way back to the Hitlerite period, dealing with the theme of *Jud Süss*, a Jew who takes over Stuttgart in another age, exploits the German people, and is finally put to death. I watched this film, of which only two or three prints were alleged to remain. Very well. The office closed, as usual, at 4 or 4:30 P.M. I had nothing to do. I browsed in a bookstore, and I found a book, a paperback published by Suhrkamp, one of the major publishing houses. And here was a new play written by someone born after the war, about a Jew who in the middle of the 1970's takes over the city of Frankfurt and exploits it, while the Germans watch helplessly. In the text there is a monologue that sounds like so very many that had been written in the past but with one line added: "They forgot to gas him." Thus the play by the German playwright Rainer Werner Fassbinder, since withdrawn from circulation, I understand, because of mounting criticism by the press.

We know, of course, that just as there has been a subtle forbearance by Western countries, and not only by Jews, in their dealings with Germany, there is also a very special relationship of all Western nations, and not only Germany, with the Jews. It manifests itself in a variety of ways, including the difficult, and continuing existence of Israel, which is a post-Holocaust phenomenon par excellence.

The Holocaust is an irreducible phenomenon. It was a deed that sent shock waves, with long-term consequences, through our society. It was also, at the time of its occurrence, an unexpected event.

The first to be affected by that unexpectedness were the victims themselves. At the moment of extreme danger, they could not perceive impending disaster. They could not envision a Western civilization that would ever be capable of launching a "Final Solution." That is one of the reasons why, in the Jewish Councils all over Europe, nothing was done. Even as rumors of ominous developments began to multiply on the desks of the chairmen of Jewish Councils, they could not believe the country of Beethoven, the home of Goethe, to be capable of deliberate mass destruction. Thus in the summer of 1942, it was the turn of the Jews of Warsaw to be deported. The chairman of the Council of the Warsaw ghetto,

Adam Czerniakow, left a diary, a daily series of entries of incomplete sentences from September 1939 to the moment that the deportation began. He recorded all the news, all the reports that reached him, actually from Germans he was in contact with, that is, his own persecutors. The rumors multiplied during January, March, and April 1942. Finally, everyone within the ghetto was aware that something was going on, and at this point he went to the Gestapo and asked the crucial question: "Is it true?" "No." "Is there any basis for the rumors?" "No." He was not satisfied. He went to another official. "Is it true?" "I haven't heard anything." "Is it true?" he asked for a third time. "No." "Can I deny the rumors?" "Yes." He went about his business for another day or two. Then he swallowed the poison he had had in his drawer from the beginning. Some months later, the chairman of the Jewish community in Vienna, Dr. Josef Löwenherz, who presided over the deportation of some tens of thousands of people, also had to ask himself the inevitable question. He went to the office of the Gestapo in Vienna, where he spoke to the Gestapo man Dr. Karl Ebner. Löwenherz wanted to see the Chief of the Vienna Gestapo himself to verify the reports of the Jews being put to death. Ebner thought Löwenherz would have a "bad time" with the Chief if he asked about such matters. The Jewish chairman was, however, admitted to the chief's office; then he was asked to wait outside while a phone call was to be made to the Chief of the Gestapo in Berlin. Then the Vienna Gestapo Chief denied the reports.

Two incidents; there were more. The leadership of the Jewish people in 1942 and 1943 would not believe the worst. Neither, by the way, did the Allied Powers, despite the indications that were coming in, in some profusion, from occupied Europe. They kept checking, and in the final analysis not much was said and less was done during the most lethal hours of European Jewry. Remember, again, that the basic question was whether a western nation, a civilized nation, could be capable of such a thing. And then, soon after 1945, we see the query turned around totally as one begins to ask: "Is there any western nation that is *incapable* of it?"

The problem was verbalized by an attorney, Edwin Sears, in an article that appeared in two issues of the *Jewish Forum* during 1951. More than a decade later, the British writer Frederic Raphael inserted in his novel *Lindmann* a three-page fantasy of Jews being deported by a British bureaucracy from British cities. His depiction of that hypothetical event is particularly startling because the characters are British, their thoughts are British, and the mode in which they speak is—far from any German model—typically and completely British. Finally, I should mention the famous experiment at Yale University by Stanley Milgram who showed that people will, under the influence of authority, push buttons. Once I went to New Haven and, remembering that Milgram had drawn his experimental subjects from that city, asked several of my hosts: "Tell me, are you capable of it? Do you believe it could happen in New Haven?" One woman, who had just moved there from another state, said: "Not in our country, not anywhere in the United States, but perhaps it could happen in New Haven." Another, a Jewish dentist, told me: "Now here is something I want you to know. There was a participant in the experiment who refused to cooperate in it, and that man was a dentist."

In 1941 the Holocaust was not expected and that is the very reason for our subsequent anxieties. We no longer dare to exclude the unimaginable from our thoughts. Yet, our analytical powers to measure the destructive propensities in all of mankind are too meager for adequate prediction. Hence, our current assessments of possible danger are much less the product of systematic probing than a matter of personal disposition and feeling. To put it simply, if you believe that only Germans are capable of such mass destruction as we have seen between 1933 and 1945, you are an optimist. If you think that many nations have that potential, you are pessimistic indeed.

There is one conclusion we may draw from the past. A destruction process is not the work of a few mad minds. It cannot be accomplished by any handful of men. It is far too complex in its organizational build-up and far too pervasive in its administrative implementation to dispense with specialized bureaucrats in every segment of society. The perpetrators who were responsible for "The Final Solution of the Jewish Question in Europe" came from all parts of Germany and all walks of life. One should not assume that a man who may have been an essential individual in these destructive operations is instantaneously recognizable. Let me tell you a small story as a means of giving you a small illustration.

In my quest for railroad documents I went to the headquarters of the German railways in Frankfurt on Main. After the usual bureaucratic encounters with various offices, I was directed to an annex building in the heart of the section of the city where pornographic materials are sold. That is where the documents center was. A center, incidentally, without documents. By the time I got there it was half-past-eleven in the morning. I stood in the hallway and two gentlemen came by. "What would you be interested in?" they asked. I said, "What I'm interested in is a bit of World War II history." "Ah," they said, "Military trains?" "No, civilian passenger traffic on special schedules." "Ah," said one of them, "Auschwitz! Treblinka!" Somewhat astonished by the quick recognition of what I was asking for from my sheer expression of interest in special trains, I asked him how he could know? And he said, "Oh, railroad people get around." He had seen ghettos. He had been to Katyn. He was the first one there when the grave, with all those Polish officers shot by the Soviets, was opened. I listened for ten minutes. Then the other one, who had been quiet, said, "Look. We're having an early lunch. Why don't you come with us to the commissary? If you eat by yourself it will cost you twelve mark, and with us it will cost you three." "That's very kind."

We came back to the office. He xeroxed cards of books he thought would interest me. He patiently explained to me why German railroad cars had four wheels rather than eight. It has to do with superior German metallurgy. He explained to me technical matters pertaining to how trains were routed through timetable zones. And then I chanced to ask him about a person named Geitmann, whom you would not have heard of even though he was, in the 1960's, a member of the four-man directorate running the *Bundesbahn,* the German railroads. This man Geitmann was, during the war, a railroad director of Oppeln, which included the death camp of Auschwitz. Like so many of these railroad people, even like the German railroads themselves that never stopped running, he had made a magnificent career after the war. I said, "Well, what can you tell me about Geitmann, perchance?" My host, a rugged, tall man, around the age of sixty, said, "I know Geitmann." Interesting. "How? Where? When?" He said, "I was in the railroad directorate of Oppeln." We went on talking, this way and that. The hour was getting late, but he did not go home. He stayed with me. And then he said, "I have seen Auschwitz." I said to myself: Perhaps this is a German who made a pilgrimage after the war. Aloud I said, "Did you make a pilgrimage?" "Oh, no. I was there, then." "What did you do there?" "I put up the signal equipment." "Are you an engineer?" He said, "Yes." He wanted me to know. He had no need to tell me. I had walked in off the street. He knew who I was and what I was doing, though the word "Jews" was never mentioned. He told me, and I saw the perpetrator. Was he so very different from all the accountants, all the engineers, all the professionals who by reason of something that touched their jurisdiction were drawn into the destructive work? I am speaking not of volunteers but of men who at some point had to deal with the Jews because the matter was at the stage that required their attention, expertise, and efficiency. Amazing to me, after involving myself for thirty years in this research, is still the question: Why were they not inefficient?

When Milgram performed his experiment at Yale, his model comprised an authority figure and men who did as they were told. How accustomed we are to thinking in these terms about the administrative process in totalitarian systems. The reality, however, was much more complex. The bureaucracy that destroyed the European Jews was remarkably decentralized, and its most far-reaching actions were not always initiated at the top. Officials serving in middle or even lower positions of responsibility were producers of major ideas. Every once in a while, a particular set of recommendations would be approved by a superior and become a policy, authorization, or directive. Such, often enough, was the genesis of an "order."

Consider a crass but not isolated illustration from the middle of 1941, at a time when the "Final Solution" was in the offing. A letter was dispatched by an SS-major in Lodz to his comrade Eichmann about several hundred thousand Jews in the Lodz area. The major thought that during the following winter many Jews would be starving to death in their ghettos. He therefore suggested a quick working device to relieve the unproductive older men as well as women and children of their misery. We cannot determine the exact effect of that communication, but we know that within months "devices" in the form of gas vans were in operation near Lodz and elsewhere. By then, memoranda were hardly even necessary; there was no further need for words. Everyone, in every segment of the bureaucracy, knew what had to be done. Few were the dissenters, fewer the deserters.

You have all heard the saying that a bureaucrat is merely a cog in the wheel—it turns whenever the wheel is turning. As a political scientist, I have a different view: The bureaucrat *drives* the wheel—without him, it would not turn. And who were these drivers? They were, by and large, like the men in the railroads, trained representatives of a society, rather than its aberrants, deviants, or outcasts. Even Heinrich Himmler, Chief of the German SS and Police, may be said to have been typical of a particular class, place, and time. In a biography written by Bradley Smith, we learn of his upbringing in a reasonably well-to-do family, his formative years with a governess, his childhood illnesses, and his education. Smith possessed a diary kept by the young Himmler from the time he was about twelve to the age of twenty-six. Himmler had had his problems and frustrations, but he had not lost his senses or his ability to make calculated judgments. He was not demented. Now, wouldn't you be happier if I had been able to show you that all of these perpetrators were crazy?

They were educated men of their time. That is the crux of the question whenever we ponder the meaning of Western civilization after Auschwitz.

Our evolution has outpaced our understanding; we can no longer assume that we have a full grasp of the workings of our social institutions, bureaucratic structures, or technology.

Should we wait for comprehension? Should we suspend our analysis until we have more documents, from more countries, of that period? Should we defer to another generation that may bring to the task its own new perspective? I do not think so. Those of us who have lived during the destruction of the Jews or who have first-hand knowledge of something that transpired at that time will read records with a contemporaneous interpretation of their contents. We may identify nuances, allusions, references that may be puzzling to those who come after us. We can therefore make our special contribution to an understanding of this event because we were part of it.*

---

*This paper is an edited transcription by Raul Hilberg of his speech in San José.

HENRY FRIEDLANDER

THE MANIPULATION
OF LANGUAGE

Hitler's Third Reich was a totalitarian state where propaganda and terror
imposed the ideology of National Socialism. But the ideology could not
operate in a vacuum: it had to use language as a vehicle for its slogans and
commands. This article is an attempt to explore the use of language to
manipulate the mass audience in Nazi Germany.[1]

The Nazis used two languages. One was the public language, the
language of the propagandists. The other was the bureaucratic, hidden
language, the language of the technicians. While the language of the
technicians remained hidden from public view until the postwar years, the
language of the propagandists stood for all Nazi language during the twelve
years of the Third Reich. Hitler pronounced it, Goebbels refined it, and
every Nazi functionary copied it. This public language—used to guide the
followers, convince the subjects, and intimidate the opponents—eventually
penetrated all aspects of public and private life.[2]

Nazi language exhibited great poverty. While normal languages
appealed to both reason and emotion, it appealed exclusively to emotion.
Devoid of reason, it became a kind of exorcism. Transforming clichés into
reality by repetition, it used the tone of the barracks square (or the
concentration camp parade ground) to shout slogans and drown out the
opposition.[3]

Nazi language was a language of motion and action. We can see this
best when we look at the insignia of the SS. Today we write this with a
double Latin S, but the Nazis wrote it with a symbol copied from Teutonic
runes ⚡⚡ and they had special letters for it on official typewriters. These

two stylized S's were *zackig*, a military term from World War I that can best be translated as both "jagged" and "snappy." It reminds us of the Prussians' goose step and their rigid form of salute. But at the same time it represented lightning: this symbol (S)—usually in red—has traditionally been a warning for high-tension wires. The SS used two of them; silver symbols on a black field. Here the language merged into picture writing to provide dynamic impact.[4]

Motion and action were further bolstered by the constant use of exaggerations, by the absolute refusal to accept any limitations. This exaggeration is demonstrated by the use of enormously large numbers—numbers of records set, demonstrators assembled, weapons produced, enemies killed. But this game of fanciful statistics was also an attempt to defraud and stupefy. Thus during the war in Russia the military constantly announced the capture of hundreds of thousands of prisoners of war; there were instances when they reported that two hundred thousand Russian soldiers had been surrounded, and shortly thereafter released the news that the same pocket had yielded six hundred thousand prisoners. Eventually, large numbers were not enough and were replaced, even in sober army communiqués, with terms like "innumerable" and "unimaginable."

On the other end of the scale were small numbers, also a kind of impressive exaggeration. At times, very small numbers can have a greater impact than very large ones. Thus in 1941 Ribbentrop announced that Germany could wage war for yet another thirty years. In 1942 Hitler boasted that his armies had fought in Russia at minus 45 degrees centigrade, while Napoleon's had only done so at minus 25 degrees.[5]

Tied to these kinds of exaggerations was the word "total." The phrase "total war" was used often, but the Nazis also used the word in many other ways. Thus "total war" led to "total peace," and "total politics" to "total revolution." Goebbels spoke of the "total educational situation," the Party demanded "total commitment," and a toy manufacturer marketed a "total game." In the same way the Nazis used and devalued the words "historic" and "unique." Every meeting they sponsored became a "historic event," and if Hitler appeared, it was transformed into one of "world historic" proportions. The same applied to the word "unique"; every speech, every conference, every decision had to be "unique." Thus after the victory over Poland Hitler elevated twelve generals to the rank of field marshal: each for a "unique" act of military genius. Along with "unique," the Nazis abused the word "genuine." Everything proclaimed "unique" was also declared "genuine." The Führer affirmed his "genuine concern," the Party its "genuine solidarity," and the police its "genuine alarm." Only "genuine uniqueness" (*echte Einmaligkeit*) was missing.[6]

While the Nazis used exaggeration to advertise their own accomplishments, they employed defamation to denigrate those of their opponents. They defamed the November Revolution of 1918 that created the Weimar Republic as a "revolt of deserters" (*Deserteurrevolte*); they denounced the revolutionaries as "agents of the stab-in-the-back" (*Dolchstossleute*) and the republican leaders as "November criminals" (*Novemberverbrecher*). Whenever the Nazis mentioned democratic parliamentary deputies, they referred to them as the "so-called representatives of the people." In written form, the "so-called" was represented by quotation marks. Thus they wrote about Soviet "strategy," American "statesmen," and Jewish "scholars." The Nazis also assembled new words by attaching a pejorative adjective to the noun representing a hated institution or concept. Thus they created new defamatory words like "money-bags republic" (*Geldsackrepublik*), "fraudulent democracy" (*Schwindeldemokratie*), and "profiteering philosophy" (*Schieberphilosophie*). Finally, they combined their three leading enemies—Jewry, capitalism, Communism—into a composite code word: *jüdischer Finanzbolschewismus*.[7]

Nazi ideology demanded motion and exaggeration; it also called for commitment. The word most often used to describe this commitment was "fanatic" (*fanatisch*). Webster defines fanaticism as "excessive enthusiasm or unreasoning zeal," especially as applied to religion. The term has usually had a pejorative meaning. Although the Romantics celebrated "passion," the word fanaticism retained its pejorative meaning until 1933. The Nazis changed this. They gave the word a positive meaning and used it constantly. It started with Hitler's *Mein Kampf*: "The state will be protected by the living wall of men and women who are filled with the greatest love of fatherland and *fanatic* national enthusiasm." Soon every Nazi used it. Thus Goebbels: "Behind every army stands the home front, which defends its national life with *fanatic* heroism." The word often appeared in combinations: "fanatic pledge" (*fanatisches Gelöbnis*), "fanatic confession" (*fanatisches Bekenntnis*), "fanatic belief" (*fanatischer Glauben*). And sometimes it appeared in everyday and non-heroic usage: "fanatic animal lover" (*fanatischer Tierfreund*). Eventually it appeared in army communiqués, formerly too sober to include this kind of language: "fanatically fighting troops" (*fanatisch kämpfende Truppen*). As is usual with words that are overexposed, they tend to lose their effectiveness. Thus adjectives were added to fanaticism, creating curiosities like "wild fanaticism" (*wilder Fanatismus*).

At first the Nazis also used "fanatic" in a pejorative sense when applied to their enemies. Thus *Mein Kampf* contained the following: "The most terrible example of this kind is found in Russia; there the Jews murdered

and starved thirty million human beings with truly *fanatic* ferocity." But
the term "fanatic" had become so positive in Nazi usage, that it could no
longer be applied to Jewish ferocity. Therefore, in the 1943 edition the
term "satanic" was substituted for "fanatic," to read: "with truly *satanic*
ferocity."[8]

The word "idealistic" (*idealistisch*) was closely related to "fanatic" in
Nazi language. In Webster an idealist is a visionary and dreamer, and in
German dictionaries he is also defined as someone motivated by ethical
aims. But even in the Weimar Republic judges had freed right-wing
assassins because they considered them "idealists" who sacrificed themselves for the national cause. After 1933 the term "idealistic" was applied to
SS-men because their duty demanded that they kill women and children.[9]

Two words—"system" (*System*) and "organization" (*Organisation*)—
symbolized the difference between the ideology of the Nazis and that of
their predecessors. The former word they detested; the latter one they
cherished.

For the Nazis, "system" applied to the democratic, constitutional, and
parliamentary republic. For them the Weimar Republic was "the System,"
and the period 1918–33 was the "system years" (*Systemzeit*). The term was
used to defame the German democratic experiment. But in addition the
Nazis rejected everything the term "system" implied. A system is a logical
and rational construct. In the United States we have a constitutional system
of government. There is the Kantian system in philosophy and the
Copernican system in astronomy. A system demands thought, and we often
say that we think in a systematic fashion. For the Nazis a system was an
artificial, intellectual, theoretical, and thus alien (*volksfremd*) creation. The
Nazi philosopher Alfred Rosenberg spoke for them all when he referred to
"the intellectual garbage dump of purely schematic systems."[10]

But even the Nazis needed something to describe their own system.
For this they used "organization." Rejecting "system," the Nazis appropriated the word "organization," and proceeded to "organize" absolutely
everything. There were organizations for every purpose, from the most
important to the most mundane; there were Party and SS organizations,
and there were organizations for bicycle riders and devotees of flowers.

While a "system" represented intellect and abstract thought, the
"organic" was based on intuition and faith. A "system" was an artificial
construct, but an "organization" was a biological organism that grows,
swells, sprouts, and germinates from the inner essence of the racial soul.
Thus the Nazis did not systematize with their intellect; they seized secret
knowledge from the organic. After 1933 the Nazis "organized" everything,

and the verb "to organize" rapidly became popular. Generals "organized" victory, editors "organized" the news, teachers "organized" examinations, and auto mechanics "organized" tune ups. Soon usage devalued the word. The *vox populi* eventually used the verb to describe any activity that required individual skill or stealth; finally, "to organize" implied to finagle, to contrive, to cheat. During the war people "organized" a safe job, extra rations, or a second cup of coffee.[11]

As we have seen, Nazism rejected reason and took its models from the organic; and this should not surprise us, because biological racism was central to its outlook. For the Nazis, virulent anti-Semitism served to express their racial ideology. In their biological interpretation of history the idealized Nordic racial type, the so-called Aryan, symbolized "good," while the stereotype of the Jew represented "evil." Julius Streicher, the editor of the *Stürmer,* was Nazi Germany's leading anti-Semitic propagandist. In his articles and speeches he combined racial fantasies and pornographic anti-Semitism to produce vicious diatribes. One example will suffice:

> "Alien albumen" is the sperm of a man of another race. During copulation the male sperm is completely or partially absorbed by the fertile female and thus enters her blood. One single episode of intercourse between a Jew and an Aryan woman is sufficient to poison her blood forever. Together with the "alien albumen" she has absorbed the alien soul. Never again will she be able to bear pure Aryan children, even when married to an Aryan; but only bastards with two souls in one body and the physical appearance of a mongrel race. Also their children will again be mongrels, that means ugly people with unsteady character and a tendency for physical disease. This process is called "impregnation."[12]

Hitler described the Jews as "the enzyme of decomposition" (*Ferment der Dekomposition*), and Nazi usage compared the Jews to parasites, applying to them terms like "international maggots and bedbugs" (*Völkermaden und Völkerwanzen*). Obviously, the Nazis needed one word to symbolize the supposedly omnipresent power of "international Jewry" (*Weltjudentum*). They invented the word *Alljuda:* a combination of the German word *All*, meaning universe or cosmos, and the archaic word *Juda*, designed to remind the audience of Judas Iscariot. Long before World War II, Nazi propaganda spoke of the war against *Alljuda*, and after 1939 it always argued that Germany was fighting a defensive war against *Alljuda*, who was using Americans and Russians to fight for world Jewry. This was Nazi Germany's so-called "Jewish War"; it served as Hitler's ideological justification for genocide.[13]

As part of their racial ideology, the Nazis resurrected archaic words of Germanic origin, and substituted them for accepted words of later vintage of foreign extraction. Thus they used *Amtswalter* instead of *Beamter* for civil servant; *Gau* instead of *Bezirk* for district; *Gefolgschaft* instead of *Belegschaft* for staff; *Schriftleiter* instead of *Redakteur* for editor; *Sippe* instead of *Familie* for family.[14] But at the same time Hitler and his followers often used words of foreign extraction for emphasis even when acceptable German equivalents existed. Thus the Nazis used *Aktion* instead of *Unternehmung* or *Kampfhandlung* for operation; *Dynamik* instead of *Schwung* for dynamic; *Fanal* instead of *Flammenzeichen* for signal; *Garant* instead of *Bürgschaft* for guaranty; *gigantisch* instead of *riesenhaft* for gigantic; *heroisch* instead of *heldenhaft* for heroic; *Instinkt* instead of *Gefühl* for instinct; *säkulär* instead of *weltlich* for secular; *total* instead of *gänzlich* or *vollständig* for total.[15]

The same ambivalence that distinguished the Nazi use of words of foreign extraction also characterized their attitude toward other aspects of modernity, especially toward industry and the city. Publicly, they denigrated all urban existence, using the code word "asphalt" to describe it. They attached it as a pejorative prefix to defame aspects of cosmopolitan city life. Thus Jewish newspapers were *Asphaltblätter;* Weimar pluralism was *Asphaltdemokratie;* Weimar culture was *Asphaltkultur;* anti-Nazi authors were *Asphaltliteraten;* and the Berlin masses who voted for the parties of the Left were simply *Asphaltmenschen*.[16]

At the same time, however, Nazism also embraced the most mechanical aspects of technology. Its aim, revealed in its language and realized in its concentration camps, was to reduce mankind to the level of robots. Thus it took technological terms and applied them to human beings.

The term *Gleichschaltung* symbolized this application of technology and dominated the early years of the Third Reich. In most studies it has been translated as "coordination," an unassuming word that is not too objectionable. It is also an inaccurate translation. *Gleichschaltung* is a combination of two words: *gleich* meaning "same" or "equal," and *schalten* meaning "to switch" or "to shift." Used in technology, it is best translated as "synchronization." Now we can appreciate the word's true meaning as applied in Nazi Germany. It appeared first "to synchronize" institutions: the national, state, and local governments, in the spring of 1933. Soon the Nazis "synchronized" everything they had just "organized." Eventually it was applied to people, as the Nazis "synchronized" everyone—from army generals to postal clerks.[17]

Those who used this mechanical language no longer dealt with human beings, but only treated them as inanimate objects; the German term for this process was *Menschenbehandlung*.[18] It formed the link between the public and the hidden bureaucratic language of the Third Reich. So far we have discussed the language of the propagandists, men like Goebbels and Streicher. They created the atmosphere and provided the ideology that justified genocide. But they did not plan and implement the physical destruction of the Jews, the ill, the gypsies, or the Russian prisoners of war. This was the task of the technicians; men of the SS and the police, supported by experts from the civil service, the armed forces, and industry. While the technicians often used the public propaganda language, especially when justifying or rationalizing their behavior, they also used a special bureaucratic language designed to disguise their criminality. The language of the technicians related to the language of the propagandists in the same way as the regime's terror related to its propaganda: they complemented each other.

The propagandists did not hesitate to use clear and inflammatory language when speaking about the enemies of Nazi Germany. They called for the "extermination" (*Ausrottung*) of the Jews and for the "eradication" (*Ausradierung*) of Rotterdam and Coventry.[19] The Nazi technicians never used such explicit terms; instead, they used code words to hide their true intentions. These code words, alone or in combination, made up the deadly vocabulary of the Holocaust.[20]

The code word most widely known and used was *Aktion* (operation). First introduced during the 1930's as *Polizeiaktion* (police operation), it was used to describe mass arrests. During World War II the modifying "police" was dropped, and *Aktion* alone stood for a variety of operations: roundups, deportations, thefts, and killings. Most often it meant the murder and despoilation of the Jews; such operations were called *Aktionen* and sometimes *Judenaktionen*. One example will suffice:

> On 13 April 1943 the former German dentist Ernst Israel Tichauer and his wife, Elisa Sara Tichauer, née Rosenthal, were delivered into the prison by the Security Service (SS Sergeant Ruebe). Since that time all German and Russian Jews who were committed to the prison had their gold bridgework, crowns, and fillings pulled or broken out. This happens always one to two hours before the respective operations (*Aktionen*).
> Since 13 April 1943, 516 German and Russian Jews have been eliminated (*erledigt*). On the basis of a definite investigation, gold was taken only during two operations (*Aktionen*); on 14 April 1943 from 172,

and on 27 April 1943 from 164 Jews. Approximately 50 percent of the Jews had gold teeth, bridgework, or fillings. SS Sergeant Ruebe of the Security Service was always personally present and he also took the gold with him.[21]

Aktion appeared in a large variety of combinations; *Säuberungsaktion* (cleansing operation) and *Befriedungsaktion* (pacification operation) were only two of many such examples. *Aktion Reinhard* was the cover designation for the murder of Polish Jews; *Aktion Kugel* was the code for the killing of escaped prisoners of war.[22] The deportation of Dutch students was called *Studentenaktion;* the incarceration of Polish intellectuals was known as *AB-Aktion;* and *M-Aktion* stood for the systematic theft of art treasures in occupied Europe.[23] A large-scale operation, like the destruction of the Warsaw ghetto, was a *Grossaktion;* a small operation, involving the murder of "only" a few, was a *Kleinaktion;* and a murder committed by a single individual on his own initiative, was an *Einzelaktion.*[24]

Sonder (special or extraordinary) was another important code word in the language of the technicians; appearing in combination with other words, it almost always served as a euphemism for murder. Its most common form was *Sonderbehandlung* (special treatment). One example will suffice:

> One transport of Jews, which has to be subjected to special treatment (*Sonderbehandlung*), arrives weekly at the office of the Commander of the Security Police and the Security Service of White Ruthenia. The three S-vans (*S-Wagen*) located there do not suffice for this purpose. I request assignment of another S-van (5 tons). At the same time I request the shipment of 20 exhaust hoses (*Abgasschläuche*) for the three S-vans on hand (2 Daimond, 1 Saurer), since the ones on hand are leaky already.[25]

The term *Sonderbehandlung* was so widely used, that in Auschwitz-Birkenau the initials "SB" indicated that the person after whose name they appeared had been sent to the gas chamber. In addition, units that did the killing were *Sonderkommandos* (special commandos) and had received their orders in the form of a *Sonderaufgabe* (special assignment).

Sonderbehandlung was not the only euphemism the technicians used for murder. A variety of other code words served the same function as *Sonderbehandlung: deportieren* (deport), *aussiedeln* (evacuate), *umsiedeln* (resettle), *aussondern* (select), *transportieren* (transport).[26] Sometimes the Nazis also used the more explicit *liquidieren* (liquidate), writing an "L" after the name of the Jews they had murdered. This word came from the language of the market place, and the SS liquidated human beings the way others liquidate a business.[27]

Nazi language was a prison language. Both jailers and convicts spoke it. Not only the perpetrators, but also the victims spoke the language of Nazi totalitarianism.[28] In the camps the inmates spoke a language not too different from that spoken by the guards. Thus the term "to organize," so popular in the Third Reich, penetrated every ghetto and every camp. There too everyone "organized" another piece of bread or another bowl of soup.

Of course, the camps also developed their own language; new code words emerged to describe the extraordinary conditions of the camps. Thus a prisoner who had stopped fighting for survival, one of the emaciated walking dead, was called a "Musulman." This term was derived from "Moslem," because these inmates seemed to resemble stereotyped pictures of Arabs: brown skin, huge eyes, always wrapped in blankets. Another term used in the camps was *Kapo*. Its origin is not fully known, and its official use might have derived from the German word *Kameradenpolizei* (comrade police); but it probably came from the Latin *capo*, meaning "head," long used as a title by Mafia chieftains and supposedly introduced into Dachau by Italian migrant workers employed in Bavaria. Another code word, common in Auschwitz, was *Kanada*. It was a designation for the place in Birkenau where the belongings of the newly arrived were sorted and stored for the SS. It also symbolized, like the country Canada, a place of great riches—as such it is still used in modern Poland.

The language of the technicians penetrated into every ghetto and every camp. Every victim understood the Nazi code words that served as the euphemisms for the killings. They used the German code words, only changing them to fit their own language. Thus the Jews in Eastern Europe used the word *akzya* to describe the brutal roundups. The shipment of victims to the death camps was known as *transport* (in French as *transport noir*). *Selekzya* described the process of choosing the victims for the gas chambers, and *sortyrer* the SS officer who did the choosing. Thus dehumanized code words—*Aktion*, transport, selection, and sorting—described the killings in Yiddish as well as in German.

A fascinating variation is the word for *Aktion* used by the Lithuanian Jews. Lithuania had been occupied by the Germans in 1941 after more than one year of Soviet occupation. Lithuanian Jews used the Russian word *shystka*, meaning "clean up." This code word was used in Stalin's Russia as a euphemism for the "purges," and is still used in this way throughout Communist Eastern Europe. Here we see how the Jews borrowed a code word from the language of one totalitarian system and applied it to the murders committed by the other.

NOTES

1. Portions of this paper appeared in *Shoah* I, 2 (Fall 1978), 16–19.
2. Victor Klemperer, *LTI. Die unbewältigte Sprache. Aus dem Notizbuch eines Philologen* (Munich, 1969), p. 9 ff. and p. 17 ff. (Originally published in East Berlin in 1946.) Klemperer's abbreviation LTI stands for *Lingua Tertii Imperii*.
3. Klemperer, pp. 26–30; Eugen Seidel and Ingeborg Seidel-Slotty, *Sprachwandel im Dritten Reich. Eine kritische Untersuchung faschistischer Einflüsse* (Halle, 1961), pp. 1–8.
4. Klemperer, pp. 71–76.
5. Ibid., 218–27.
6. Ibid. Also Dolf Sternberger, Gerhard Storz, and W. E. Süskind, *Aus dem Wörterbuch des Unmenschen* (Hamburg and Düsseldorf, 1968), pp. 51–56.
7. Klemperer, pp. 77–78; Manfred Pechau, *Nationalsozialismus und deutsche Sprache* (Greifswald, 1935), pp. 24–29, 50, 85–87. Pechau's 1934 dissertation was the first attempt by a Nazi to describe the language of the regime.
8. Klemperer, pp. 62–66; Cornelia Berning, *Vom "Abstammungsnachweis" zum "Zuchtwart." Vokabular des Nationalsozialismus* (Berlin, 1964), pp. 74–78.
9. See for example Himmler's Posen speech, October 4, 1943: Nuremberg Document PS 1919.
10. Klemperer, pp. 102–4; Berning, pp. 179–81. See also Pechau, p. 30.
11. Klemperer, pp. 104–7; Sternberger, Storz, and Süskind, pp. 137–42.
12. Streicher's article, January 1, 1935: [my Trans.]. Nuremberg Document M 020. The German text reads as follows:

    "Artfremdes Eiweiss" ist der Same eines Mannes von anderer Rasse. Der männliche same wird bei der Begattung ganz oder teilweise von dem weiblichen Mutterboden aufgesaugt und geht so in das Blut über. Ein einziger Beischlaf eines Juden bei einer arischen Frau genügt, um deren Blut für immer zu vergiften. Sie hat mit dem "artfremden Eiweiss" auch die fremde Seele in sich aufgenommen. Sie kann nie mehr, auch wenn sie einen arischen Mann heiratet, rein arische Kinder bekommen, sondern nur Bastarde, in deren Brust zwei Seelen wohnen und denen man körperlich die Mischrasse ansieht. Auch deren Kinder werden wieder Mischlinge sein, das heisst hässliche Menschen von unstetem Charakter und mit Neigung zu körperlichen Leiden. Man nennt diesen Vorgang: "Imprägnation".
13. Pechau, pp. 66–67; Klemperer, pp. 175–84. Although *Alljuda* was already used in earlier anti-Semitic polemics, the term entered common usage only during the Nazi period. Berning, pp. 9–10.
14. Berning, pp. 11, 86–88, 168–69, 171–74, 207; Klemperer, p. 239 ff.
15. Berning, pp. 59, 74, 85–86, 91–92, 106, 167; Seidel and Seidel-Slotty, p. 65, 109, 123–28; Klemperer, p. 253 ff.
16. Berning, pp. 26–28; Pechau, pp. 64–65.
17. See Klemperer, p. 52 ff.; Berning, p. 95; Seidel and Seidel-Slotty, pp. 60–77; Sternberger, Storz, and Süskind, p. 94 ff. The most common Nazi term borrowed from technology was *Kontakt*. This is also the word most often used in this manner in English. Thus we once "met people," but now "contact people."
18. Sternberger, Storz, and Süskind, p. 126 ff.
19. The word *ausradieren* actually meant "to erase." After the destruction of Coventry, the Nazis also used the term *coventrieren*. See Seidel and Seidel-Slotty, p. 44.
20. See Joseph Wulf, *Aus dem Lexikon der Mörder. "Sonderbehandlung" und verwandte Worte in nationalsozialistischen Dokumenten* (Gütersloh, 1963).
21. Report of prison administrator *(Strafanstaltsverwalter)* Günther concerning *Judenaktionen*, Minsk, May 31, 1943: Nuremberg Document R 135.
22. For *Aktion Reinhard*, see Nuremberg Document PS 4024; for *Aktion Kugel*, see Nuremberg Documents PS 1650 and L 158.

23. For the *Studentenaktion,* see Nuremberg Document F 665(i); for the *AB-Aktion* (*Allgemeine Befriedungsaktion,* or general pacification operation), see Werner Präg and Wolfgang Jacobmeyer, eds., *Das Diensttagebuch des deutschen Generalgouverneurs in Polen 1939–1945* (Stuttgart, 1975), p. 26; for the *M-Aktion,* see Nuremberg Document L 188.

24. For *Grossaktion,* see *The Stroop Report: "The Jewish Quarter of Warsaw Is No more!";* facsimile edition with translation by Sybil Milton (New York, 1979); for *Kleinaktion,* see Nuremberg Document L 180; for *Einzelaktion,* see Nuremberg Document M 034.

25. Cable, June 15, 1942, from BdS Ostland to RSHA II D 3 A: Nuremberg Document PS 501.

26. For some of these terms, see Nuremberg Document L 018.

27. *Justiz und NS-Verbrechen,* 19 vols. (Amsterdam, 1968 ff.), IX, No. 298b, p. 10.

28. For the camp and ghetto language of the victims, see Nachman Blumental, "Di yidishe shprakh un der kamf kegn natsi rezhim," *Bleter fun geshikhte,* I, 3–4 (August–December 1948), 106–24; David Diamont, "Folklor in di lagern," *Pariser shriftn,* 2–3 (March 1946), 70–74; M. I. Feigenbaum, "Geto-vertlekh un anekdotn," *Fan letztn khurbn,* VI (August 1947), 72–76; Shmuel Glube, "Geto un katset vertlekh," *Fun letztn khurbn,* X (December 1948), 131–36; I. Kaplan, *Dos folks-moyl in natsi-klem* (Munich, 1949).

SYBIL MILTON

ARTISTS IN THE THIRD REICH[1]

During the twelve years of the Third Reich, Nazi artists produced nothing of longevity or of creative importance. They placed all art in the service of barbarism, creating a cultural vacuum in which opportunism and mediocrity were rewarded with political security and economic privileges. The regime they served conceived of art and visual symbols as an effective means of social mobilization, a way of changing people's behavior by giving them standards to imitate. The standards of the Third Reich included the glorification of militarism and racial anti-Semitism. By intensifying the political message of art, the Nazis removed the distinctions between art and propaganda. New technologies led to the mass distribution and reproduction of art as posters and postcards; increasing government patronage of artists and museums led to greater control of all visual arts. These developments provided the Nazi regime with the means to manipulate mass culture.[2]

Total control of the production and distribution of all forms of popular culture guaranteed stylistic homogeneity. This control was institutionalized in the bureaucracy of the *Reichskulturkammer* (Reich Chamber of Culture). This organization was created on September 22, 1933, as a branch of the Ministry of Propaganda and Popular Enlightenment under Dr. Joseph Goebbels. The subordinate Reich Chamber for Fine Arts (Department IX of the Propaganda Ministry) was national in scope and controlled all aspects of artistic life. Its jurisdiction included every aspect of the production, exhibition, and commercial distribution of painting, sculpture, architecture, interior decoration, landscape gardening, and crafts. It also controlled art and antique dealers, auction houses, art publishing, arts and crafts education, and gallery and museum exhibitions; even the retail vendors of canvases, oil paints, paintbrushes, and other art supplies were forced to join the Reich Chamber of Fine Arts. Membership in the Chamber was compulsory and included approximately one hundred thousand "art workers" by 1936.[3]

The Nazi state's patronage of the fine arts involved a combination of economic rewards, legal restrictions, and physical intimidation. Racial and political enemies were blacklisted, expelled from teaching positions in the universities and memberships in the academies of fine arts, banned from selling or exhibiting their works, and often even prohibited to paint in the privacy of their own studios. This latter prohibition, the so-called *Berufsausübungsverbot,* was frequently enforced by the Gestapo. Emil Nolde, Otto Dix, and Käthe Kollwitz reported that Gestapo officers visited their studios, felt the canvases and paintbrushes for signs of dampness, and attempted to harass and intimidate them into silence, isolation, and inactivity.[4]

Although neither style nor subject matter were dictated by the Party or the Reich Chamber for Fine Arts, certain stock themes recur in the official art of "national socialist realism." These included: romantic landscape paintings; peasants with large families; suckling infants in their mothers' arms; formal portraits of leading Nazi personalities, especially Hitler; stylized Nordic racial prototypes in heroic military or athletic poses; pseudo-erotic classical allegories of nude female "muses"; still lifes; genre paintings; and blatant plagiarisms from the works of the Old Masters.[5] Although National Socialist artists travestied the very traditions they claimed to live by, often reducing them to an unintended parody, their work appealed to vast numbers of people who had no specialized interest in, or knowledge of, art. Their works glorified the virtues of the Nazi state and invoked the imagery for Hitler's words: "Art is a lofty mission that requires the artist to be fanatical; German artists must now answer the call to help undertake the proudest defenses of the German *Volk* by means of German art."[6]

The conventions and clichés of Nazi art are exemplified in the works of Richard Klein. Klein was an important Party functionary, Director of the Munich Academy of Applied Art, and one of the publishers of the glossy official NSDAP art journal, *Die Kunst im Dritten Reich*. Klein's idealized pen-and-pencil study from 1937 reveals many of the stock themes of National Socialist art: Aryan racial prototypes, farmland, fertility, production, and progress. In the foreground is a stylized naked Aryan male, whose right arm is bent to his chest as though pledging loyalty; his left hand holds a sword pointing downward; and his eyes stare off into the distance. Despite clear anatomical detail, the obviously virile male is almost sexless in his rigid pose. An oversized imperial eagle clutching a swastika in its talons is perched on his left shoulder. The background contains several miniscule scenes: a farmer pushing a plow, a factory complex with smoking chimneys, and laborers constructing a house. These same motifs recur in many of the heroic friezes and free-standing sculptures common to Nazi design and public architecture. The motifs of the eagle, the swastika, the SS insignia, and the nude male Aryan were vivid, dynamic, and often repeated elements of non-verbal design in Nazi Germany. Many of these non-verbal symbols were astonishingly dull when applied to fine art; however, they were arousing and effective when subordinated to the mass pageantry of the Nuremberg Party rallies.

The elaborate and aggressive ideological edifice of Nazi propaganda was reinforced by the militant use of museums and exhibitions as vehicles for mass indoctrination and popular entertainment. The museum was turned into a surrogate university for mass education in racial politics. The Nazis took the educational responsibility of the museum very seriously; they rejected the traditional elitist view of museums as passive repositories of unique aesthetic objects collected independently from the community. Using the financial power of the state, the Nazis turned the traditional, somewhat austere, art museum into a circus of traveling media events that sacrificed the needs of art to ideology. This new and modern use of the museum was evident in three exhibits that opened in 1937, "German Art," "Degenerate Art," and "The Wandering Jew."[7]

The inaugural gala exhibit of German Art opened on July 18, 1937, at the recently completed Haus der Deutschen Kunst in Munich. The display included almost nine hundred paintings and sculptures by dogmatic Nazi sloganeers, old-fashioned academic painters, and traditional landscape and portrait artists. Retrospective content analysis has divided the exhibit into the following main categories: landscapes, 40 percent; idealized Aryan types, 20 percent; portraits of leading Nazi personalities (often against the background of Nazi architecture), 15 percent; animals, 10 percent; still lifes, 7 percent; peasants (including rural mothers and infants), 7 percent; urban industrial workers, .5 percent; and pseudo-classical erotic works, .5 percent.[8] The fanfare of advance publicity for this exhibit featured a work entitled "The Muster on February 23, 1933" by Elk Eber.[9] Eber's painting shows two uniformed stormtroopers, one closing his collar, the other fully dressed. In the right-hand corner of the picture is a swastika flag. Both brown shirts are drably realistic and in the militant pose common to SA and SS recruiting posters. The colors are drab browns, except for the bold geometric design of the swastika flag: a pitch-black swastika in a white circle, surrounded by a field of blood red. The picture appealed to an audience of the convinced; it was supposed to be a representative example of German art.

Elk Eber was typical of the Nazi artists featured in this exhibit of German art. Born in 1892, he was an early member of the Party and carried membership card number 1307. He participated in Hitler's abortive Munich putsch in 1923, and was rewarded with a professorship after 1933. During the 1920's, Eber worked as a staff illustrator for the Nazi Party's newspaper *Völkischer Beobachter*, and also as house artist for its publishing house, Franz Eher Verlag. After 1939, he served as a combat artist on the eastern front; in 1941, a posthumous retrospective exhibit of his Polish campaign sketches was held in Berlin.[10]

Despite elaborate publicity, this first major show of German Art was an anticlimactic failure. It was overshadowed by the concurrent rival show of Degenerate Art *(Entartete Kunst)*, located in a gallery directly across the street from the House of German Art in Munich.[11] Over two million visitors viewed this Munich exhibit between July 19 and November 30, 1937; forty-two thousand viewers were counted on one peak day that fall. The *New York Times* reported on August 6, 1937, that the crowds at the Degenerate Art exhibit were three times as large as at the rival show of German-Aryan Art. The crowds included many German art students, who used the exhibition as a last chance to study otherwise proscribed and confiscated works of modern art and avant-garde sculpture. Guards were instructed to keep people moving rapidly through the exhibit halls, a restriction inhibiting genuine study of the works and reinforcing the propagandistic intentions of the Party. Crude, written slogans on the walls explained Nazi objections to the work of "physical and mental defectives," the artistic products of "Jewish and Bolshevik disintegration and sedition."[12] The cover of the exhibit catalog showed an abstract stone sculpture by the Jewish artist Otto Freundlich, then a refugee in Paris. Freundlich was later deported to Lublin-Maidanek, where he perished in 1943.[13] The catalog also denounced the works of other twentieth-century avant-garde artists, such as George Grosz, Otto Dix, Max Beckmann, Paul Klee, Lyonel Feininger, Oskar Kokoschka, and others.

Decadent art was defined as: 1) works produced by Jewish artists; 2) works with Jewish themes, even if by Aryan artists (e.g., Rembrandt); 3) works with pacifist subjects or art that didn't glorify war (e.g., Otto Dix and George Grosz); 4) works with Socialist or Marxist themes, and works by other political enemies; 5) works and objects with ugly faces and distorted figures, which depicted supposedly inferior Negroid or Jewish types; 6) all expressionist works; 7) all abstract art, especially anything from the Bauhaus; and 8) works that any Nazi bureaucrat found objectionable. Most works that fell into these categories were destroyed; some were looted or purchased at artificially low prices for Göring's private art collection. By 1937, sixteen thousand "degenerate" paintings had been confiscated from German museums, galleries, and private collections. Almost five thousand additional works were burned in a public bonfire at the Berlin Fire Department on March 20, 1939. The experts trained to purge German art extended their looting operations across all of occupied Europe after 1941. Art was subordinated to the toxic worship of the "*Stahlhelm* (steel helmet) as the most perfect form and beautiful shape created in modern times."[14]

The third exhibit, The Wandering Jew (*Der ewige Jude*), was a pseudo-historical exhibit that opened in the Library Building of the German Museum in Munich on November 8, 1937.[15] It was touted as a "political and educational spectacle" showing two thousand years of Jewish history in the virulent tabloid style of the *Stürmer*. According to a report published in the *Völkischer Beobachter* on November 11, 1937, one hundred and fifty thousand people viewed this exhibit during the first three days. The exhibit contents are revealed in the anonymously designed exhibit poster.[16] A fat stereotyped Jew dominates the poster; he is placed somewhat off-center against a yellow-gold background. He is dressed in a dark brown caftan, his face dominated by a hooked nose and thick protruding lips. His chin is covered by an unkempt beard. The Jew does not face the spectator; his eyes are half shut and his forehead wrinkled with concentration as he glances at gold coins in his right hand. Under his left arm is a light brown map of the Soviet Union imprinted with a red hammer and sickle; a whip is held firmly in his left hand. The red letters at the bottom of the poster, *Der ewige Jude* (The Wandering Jew), are printed in mock-Hebrew style calligraphy. Words are almost redundant on this poster, which also served as the cover for the exhibit catalog. The stylized anti-Semitic cartoon figure recalls two major themes of Nazi propaganda: the Jew as capitalist profiteer, and the Jew as Communist. The Jew is portrayed in a sinister and loathsome manner, isolating and alienating him from the spectator. The pseudo-educational guise of the exhibit was intended to reinforce vilification of the repugnance for Jews in Nazi Germany. Similar exhibits were exported throughout Nazi-occupied Europe after 1939, and a "documentary" film of the same name was released in 1940.[17]

The film was made on location in the Lodz ghetto and premiered in Berlin on November 28, 1940. It was produced by Fritz Hippler, a civil servant who headed the Film Department of the Propaganda Ministry.[18] Although the film showed conditions created by the Nazi occupation of Poland, the Nazi narrator presented the documentary as an accurate portrayal of prewar Jewish "criminal life and filthy pestilence." The film was shown in occupied France, Holland, and Poland, and used for the calculated indoctrination of native populations, soldiers, police, and SS-units, who were to implement the policies of internment, deportation, and annihilation of European Jewry. The propaganda art of *Der ewige Jude* coordinated museum exhibits with the implementation of the Final Solution. The banal vulgarity of Nazi art merged into propaganda for genocide.

The art of the victims was produced in exile, in hiding, and in the ghettos and concentration camps of Nazi-dominated Europe. The victim-creators of the years 1939–45 differed from the socially conscious protest artists of other periods. Historically, artists from Goya to Picasso possessed some distance from the political and social victims of oppression depicted in their works.[19] This distinction between artist and victim was obliterated for the professional artists incarcerated in the ghettos and camps of Europe. The artist and victim were one and the same person.

Traditional artistic concerns were scarcely possible in the world of consciously imposed dehumanization and agony. The usual concerns of artists—prospective clients, commissions for works, the cost of supplies, ateliers, and a prosaic sense of pride in a finished work—obviously disappeared in the camps. Creative freedom to determine style, technique, and sometimes even subject matter, were also obvious casualties of the camp conditions. Faced by torture, starvation, and death, the artist-victim worked furtively and clandestinely. It is remarkable that over eight thousand works which rendered the world of atrocity survive.[20]

The works were done in any media available: pencil, charcoal, ink, homemade paints, coffee grounds, tree twigs and barks, etc. The artists occasionally used canvases, but more often the only material available was wrapping paper, cloth, the blank backs of official camp flyers, toilet paper, and even the empty margins of postage stamps. Most works were small in size, so that they could be concealed during searches by the Nazi guards. Some of the art produced was traded for food and clothing. Other works were smuggled out to relatives or friends living in hiding or in the relative safety of mixed marriages. Most works were hidden underground, vulnerable to deterioration and damage from insects and moisture. Most artists tried to save their work for posterity, so the dead would "live at least on paper."[21] Esther Lurie buried pottery jugs containing two hundred drawings of life in the Kovno ghetto; only eleven survived. Zoran Music hid hundreds of drawings in a Dachau factory complex, where he worked as a slave laborer. The factory was later bombed and only thirty-five drawings survived. Leo Haas "pried out part of the wall in his room to wall in the drawings about life in Terezin." Almost all of these works survived the war. Alfred Kantor smuggled out several drawings from Schwarzheide with the help of a friend. He destroyed most of the sketches because of "menacing surveillance."[22]

Although it is impossible to estimate the total number of these clandestine eyewitness drawings, a very large number survived from West European transit camps and from East European ghettos. Fewer works come from the death camps. The surviving scraps of paper do not permit the reconstruction of even one artist's full œuvre during these years. There are no biographical dictionaries or sources which establish the names of the deported and murdered artists. Despite the massive monograph and memoir literature about concentration camps, information about the artists is fragmentary and incomplete.

A substantial body of art survives from the internment camps of unoccupied Vichy France. Like the Germans, the French used euphemisms to disguise their actions. Therefore, official documents referred to internment camps as "reception centers" (centres d'accueil) and "supervised lodging centers" (centres d'hébergement). Conditions in these camps became known through novels and memoirs, such as Arthur Koestler's Scum of the Earth, which described forced labor at Le Vernet:

> In Liberal-Centigrade, Vernet was the zero-point of infamy; measured in Dachau-Farenheit it was still 32 degrees above zero. In Vernet beating-up was a daily occurrence; in Dachau it was prolonged until death ensued. In Vernet people were killed for lack of medical attention; in Dachau they were killed on purpose. In Vernet half of the prisoners had to sleep without blankets in 20 degrees of frost; in Dachau they were put in irons and exposed to the frost.[23]

Conditions in Vernet were similar to those in Gurs.

Gurs was one of the largest Vichy internment camps, and housed over fifteen thousand internees by late 1940. It was located on swampy land in the foothills of the Pyrenees, close to the Spanish border near Pau. Gurs was first used as a "reception center" for Spanish Republican refugees and members of the International Brigade. After June 1940, it was used as a transit camp for Jewish refugees displaced by the German occupation of

France and Belgium. In October 1940, over seven thousand Jews from Baden and the Palatinate were deported to Gurs. Deportations from Gurs to Auschwitz and other Eastern death camps lasted from July 1942 to the summer of 1943. Accounts by survivors and official reports by relief agencies describe conditions in Gurs as worse than in the camps located in Nazi-occupied Northern France.[24] Overcrowded damp barracks, mud, lice, inadequate food, insufficient clothing, and the fascist *garde mobile* provided the atmosphere and subject matter for the interned artists.

Art supplies and musical instruments were donated to the inmates of Gurs by the YMCA and other international relief agencies. Thus, during 1940 and 1941, the artists of Gurs had adequate supplies of canvas, paper, sketch pads, pencils, paints, and paintbrushes. Two large art exhibits were held in the barracks of the men's compound during the spring and summer of 1941. The art works on display even attracted buyers from the surrounding region. Among the works on display were sketches by Felix Nussbaum and Karl Schwesig.

One of the most powerful drawings of concentration camp life is Felix Nussbaum's pencil and watercolor study "Camp Gurs" from 1940. He inscribes it in the lower left-hand corner, "a study for a painting." This work is done in pastel shades of blue, dark yellow, and gray. A group of men and one woman in tattered clothing are seated on packing crates huddled round a blank globe. The plight of the displaced refugee, isolated without hope and deprived of their possessions, is symbolized by the desolate background of barren land and barbed wire. One figure in the background to the far left is hunched over facing the barbed wire, an unattended viola leaning against the crate. In the foreground is a bleached bone and a tattered pair of shoes lying on the sandy ground. A world of gaunt, emaciated, and hopeless people is clearly portrayed. Nussbaum captures the alienation and desperation of the refugees as they endure the collective tragedy of deportation and death.[25]

Felix Nussbaum was born in a comfortable middle-class Jewish family in Onasbrück in 1904. He studied painting and art history at the academies in Hamburg and Berlin and won the prize of the Prussian Academy of Art in 1931. This prestigious prize for his work "Der tolle Platz" enabled him to study in Rome for two years. In 1933, he was forced to emigrate to Belgium, where he married a student friend from Berlin, Felka Platek. In 1940, Nussbaum was arrested in Belgium and deported to Gurs. After two months in Gurs, he escaped and returned to Belgium, where he lived in hiding. He continued to paint and his works in hiding repeat the motifs of the distraught figure on a crate, ragged refugees, and blank globes. He was supported by friends, but was able to earn a small irregular pittance by illustrating textbooks. He and his wife were recaptured by the Germans in 1943; they were both deported to Auschwitz. Both are believed to have perished in Auschwitz in 1944. Many of Nussbaum's paintings from 1940 to 1943 have survived; they were shown in major retrospective exhibits held in Onasbrück.[26]

Another artist interned in Gurs was Karl Schwesig. Schwesig was a hunchback, a dwarf, a Communist, and partly Jewish. He was born in 1898 in Gelsenkirchen and studied at the Academy of Fine Arts in Düsseldorf. During the 1920's, he was a member of "The Novembrists" and the *Rheinische Sezession*. He joined the Communist Party in the late 1920's and was imprisoned for sixteen months when the Nazis came to power in 1933. Upon his release, he was granted political asylum in Belgium. During 1935 and 1936, he lived in Antwerp, Brussels, and Amsterdam. Schwesig went to Moscow in 1937. During the same year, the Nazis placed his name on the *Ausbürgerungsliste*, revoking his citizenship and confiscating his property. In 1938, Schwesig moved to the Pyrenees and designed posters for the Spanish Republicans and children's aid in Spain. After the German invasion of France in 1940, Schwesig was interned in St. Cyprien, Gurs, and Noé. He escaped repeatedly from these Vichy camps during 1943. He was arrested by the SS and brought to Paris. In 1944, he was once again freed by his friends in the resistance and fled to northern Germany. He was again captured by the SS in 1944 and placed in Ulmer Höh Prison in Düsseldorf, where he was finally liberated by American troops in 1945. He resided in Düsseldorf until his death in 1955.[27]

During his internment at Gurs, Schwesig drafted twenty-seven mock postage stamps, drawn in colored ink on the blank perforated margins of real stamps. The dimensions of the stamps were 1½ inches by 1 inch, and were dated March 1941. They were small enough to escape detection during body searches by camp guards. The stamps are a powerful indictment of conditions in Gurs: rats, lice, mud, epidemics, black market, etc. The three stamps subtitled "Liberty-Equality-Fraternity" parody the motto of France behind the barbed wire at Gurs. All the stamps carry spurious postal denominations.[28] Schwesig's larger sketches from Gurs and Noé reveal the same precise draftsmanship as the Gurs postage stamps. Despite its obvious effectiveness, Schwesig's work is more simplistic in concept and handling than Nussbaum's works from this same period. Although Schwesig does not reveal a doctrinaire Communist vision, his

camp works are closer to the style of John Heartfield's photomontage anti-
Nazi newspaper exposés.[29]

The unofficial and illegal art of Terezin is best known because of
numerous publications available in English. It is also one of the locales for
the television docu-drama *Holocaust*. The art of Terezin included the works
of Alfred Kantor and Leo Haas. Haas's work shows the nightmarish world of
gaunt faces, semi-clothed emaciated bodies, and disfigured humans rather
than the "model ghetto" of Nazi propaganda.[30] A second type of art was also
produced in Terezin; it was an art that evaded atrocity rather than
rendering it. Such were the nostalgic and tranquil watercolors of Fritz
Fabian, a Berlin architect deported to Theresienstadt on November 5,
1942.[31] His works from 1943 and 1944 were painted in warm yellow and
green hues, sunny pastels, and bright colors. Some of the sketches are
purely architectural, showing the façade of the old Bohemian garrison
village and the untouched Bohemian countryside outside its gates. Fabian's
works are not examples of collaboration; rather they reveal the professional
artist evading and escaping reality by showing the nostalgic exterior of
Maria Theresa's garrison town Theresienstadt.[32]

Art supplies were relatively accessible in Theresienstadt. Artists who
painted official portraits, family trees, and did camp posters for their SS
tormentors had access to paper, pencils, ink, and other drawing materials.
They obviously could and did siphon off extra supplies for their "unofficial"
work. Ghetto artists also made signs, ghetto currency, decorations for
visiting Red Cross delegations, and stage sets for Nazi propaganda films.[33]
The intensive cultural life in Theresienstadt provided a certain amount of
protective cover for securing illegal paper and art supplies. It became
increasingly difficult to obtain paper by 1944 and 1945, and some works
were done on wrapping paper from packages and parcels occasionally
delivered to the inmates. Conditions in Theresienstadt differed from other
camps in one crucial respect. Artists were able to communicate with each
other as a loose community; they were not as isolated as in the other camps
and ghettos.

The last artist to be considered in this paper is the Hungarian-Jewish
lithographer and book illustrator Bertalan Göndör.[34] Most of Göndör's
prewar works were macabre black and white expressionist graphics and
linocuts. His drawings from 1944, when he was conscripted into Hungarian
forced labor service, were humorous, cartoon-like, and wryly bittersweet.
They resemble the illustrations to *Good Soldier Schweik* drawn by Czech
cartoonist Joseph Lada. Eight illustrated postcards survive from March 11,
1944 to May 28, 1944.[35] The postcards are all postmarked and censored.
Göndör addressed them to his wife in Budapest from his forced domicile,

Battalion 109/37 of the Front-Line Labor Service Company at Volocz in Bereg Province in Carpathian Ruthenia. The sketches drawn on the backs of each postcard reveal Göndör's conscious concern with the plight of the artist. The postcard dated May 19, 1944, shows the *Atelier Göndör,* a ramshackle and makeshift studio. Göndör's easel is a rickety table, propped up by carefully balanced stacks of wood and bricks. The style on these postcards was deliberately light to escape censorship, and only hints at the realities of the Hungarian camps in 1944. In March 1944, Germany invaded Hungary and the Nazis took control of the Hungarian ghettos and camps. Deportations to Auschwitz were begun on May 15, 1944. Göndör was deported to Poland and Harka in late 1944. He perished in March 1945 in Mauthausen.

The nature of creativity under duress and deprivation has not been explored in either the psychological or artistic literature. It is unclear whether artists consciously opted to chronicle the grotesque world of every concentration camp in *Festung Europa,* or whether they continued to paint because they were professionals, and art and survival were psychologically synonymous. Artist-survivors of the Holocaust continue to paint their nightmare memories in the postwar world. The works of Zoran Music still deal with his experiences in Dachau; the illustrations of Corrado Cagli replay memories of Buchenwald; and Adolf Frankl paints vividly colored scenes from Sereth, Birkenau, and Auschwitz.[36] Other artistic witnesses of the Holocaust have drawn on subjects and themes from the concentration camps. Modern artists who have dwelt on the unhealed wounds of Nazi Europe include Ben Shahn, Rico Lebrun, Mauricio Lesansky, and Audrey Flack.[37] The art created by victims during World War II is beginning to find a place in postwar art.

The art of the Nazis has mostly disappeared. There is no major political or creative group that imitates it, and the Homeland—East and West Germany and Austria—has rejected it.[38] The impact of their opponents has been far greater. Refugee artists have helped spread modern avant-garde art to the United States. While the refugee- and victim-artists have not changed the world or halted atrocities, their works have been of lasting historic and creative importance. Their work is slowly being incorporated into a viable postwar post-Holocaust artistic tradition.

NOTES

1. Portions of this paper appeared in *Shoah,* I, 2 (Fall 1978), 10–15; and Josephine Z. Knopp, ed., *International Conference on the Lessons of the Holocaust* (Philadelphia, 1979), pp. 87–136,

2. See George L. Mosse, *The Nationalization of the Masses. Political Symbolism and Mass Movements in Germany from the Napoleonic Wars through the Third Reich* (New York, 1977); Anthony Rhodes, *Propaganda. The Art of Persuasion: World War II* (New York-London, 1976); and Ward Rutherford, *Hitler's Propaganda Machine* (Hong Kong-London-New York, 1978).

3. For background information on the politics and development of Nazi art, see: Hildegard Brenner, *Die Kunstpolitik des Nationalsozialismus* (Reinbek bei Hamburg, 1963); Berthold Hinz, *Die Malerei im deutschen Faschismus. Kunst und Konterrevolution* (Munich, 1974); Hellmut Lehmann-Haupt, *Art under a Dictatorship* (New York, 1954); Robert R. Taylor, *The Word in Stone. The Role of Architecture in the National Socialist Ideology* (Berkeley and Los Angeles, 1974); Joseph Wulf, ed., *Die Bildenden Künste im Dritten Reich. Eine Dokumentation* (Gütersloh, 1963); and Frankfurter Kunstverein, *Kunst im 3. Reich. Dokumente zur Unterwerfung* (Frankfurt/Main, 1974).

4. Diether Schmidt, ed., *In letzter Stunde, 1933–1945; Schriften deutscher Künstler des zwanzigsten Jahrhunderts,* Band II (Dresden, 1964); and Akademie der Künste, *Zwischen Widerstand und Anpassung; Kunst in Deutschland 1933–1945* (Berlin, 1978).

5. Paul Vogt, *Geschichte der deutschen Malerei im 20. Jahrhundert* (Cologne, 1976), pp. 269–340; and Hinz, *Die Malerei im deutschen Faschismus,* pp. 193–288. For example, Werner Peiner's "German Soil" is reminiscent of Breughel's "Hunters in the Snow" and "Return of the Herd." Other Nazi artists used blatant plagiarisms from the works of Albercht Dürer, Caspar David Friedrich, Gustave Courbet, Ferdinand Hodler, Wilhelm Leibl, and Anselm Feuerbach.

6. This quote is from a cultural address by Hitler to the NSDAP on September 1, 1933. The text of this speech is found in: Wulf, *Die Bildenden Künste,* pp. 64–67. An excellent analysis of Nazi usage, including the word "fanatic," is: Henry Friedlander, "The Language of Nazi Totalitarianism," *Shoah,* I, 2 (Fall 1978), 16–19. A revised edition of this article entitled "The Manipulation of Language" appears in this volume; p. 103.

7. For an analysis of the public role of the art museum, see: Barbara Y. Newsom and Adele Z. Silver, eds., *The Art Museum as Educator. A Collection of Studies as Guides to Practice and Policy* (Berkeley-Los Angeles-London, 1978). For Nazi museums, see: Wulf, *Die Bildenden Künste,* pp. 55–63, 337–86; and Hinz, *Die Malerei im deutschen Faschismus,* pp. 18–47.

8. Brenner, *Kunstpolitik,* pp. 112–13; and Hinz, *Die Malerei im deutschen Faschismus,* pp. 43–47.

9. There seems to be no special significance to Eber's date. The painting is featured on the front page of *Völkischer Beobachter* on July 17, 1937; it is also discussed in Adolf Dresler's pamphlet *Deutsche Kunst und entartete "Kunst"; Kunstwerk und Zerrbild als Spiegel der Weltanschauung* (Munich, 1938), pp. 38–39.

10. Werner Rittich, "Zum Tode von Prof. Elk Eber," in: *Völkischer Beobachter,* August 15, 1941.

11. See Franz Roh, *"Entartete" Kunst. Kunstbarbarei im Dritten Reich* (Hannover, 1962). This volume contains a facsimile of the exhibit catalog *Führer durch die Ausstellung Entartete Kunst.* Another relevant volume is Haus der Kunst, München, *Entartete Kunst. Bildersturm vor 25 Jahren* (Munich, 1962).

12. These phrases were used in Hitler's and Adolf Ziegler's inaugural speeches at the exhibit opening on July 19, 1937. Both speeches are found in Wulf, *Die Bildenden Künste,* pp. 319–24.

13. See: Guenter Aust, *Otto Freundlich, 1878–1943* (Cologne, 1960); Wallraf-Richartz-Museum, Cologne, *Otto Freundlich, Gemälde-Graphik-Skulpturen, 1878–1943* (Cologne, 1960); and Edouard Roditi, "The Fate of Otto Freundlich," *Commentary,* XX, 3 (1955), 248 ff.

14. This remark is from a speech by SS Major Cout Klaus Baudissin. Baudissin was born in 1891, received his Ph.D. in Art History from Heidelberg University, and became director of the Folkwang Museum in Essen in 1934. He headed the committee that listed "Degenerate Art" to be confiscated by Nazi officials. This speech is undated, and is quoted in: Frederic V. Grunfeld, *The Hitler File; A Social History of Germany and the Nazis, 1918–1945* (New York, 1974), pp. 247–48.

15. Wulf, *Die Bildenden Künste*, pp. 317–20.

16. Anthony Rhodes, *Propaganda*, p. 49.

17. Information about the film *Der ewige Jude* is found in: Leif Furhammar and Folke Isaksson, *Politics and Film*, trans. Kersti French (New York-Washington, 1971), pp. 116–20. See also, Erwin Leiser, *Nazi Cinema*, trans. Gertrud Mander and David Wilson (New York, 1975), pp. 84–88; and Roger Manvell and Heinrich Fraenkel, *The German Cinema* (New York, 1971), pp. 88–90.

18. Hippler's biography is found in: Furhammar and Isaksson, *Politics and Film*, pp. 119–20.

19. Paul von Blum, *The Art of Social Conscience* (New York, 1976); Theda Shapiro, *Painters and Politics. The European Avant-Garde and Society, 1900–1925* (New York and Amsterdam, 1976); and Ralph E. Shikes, *The Indignant Eye. The Artist as Social Critic in Prints and Drawings from the Fifteenth Century to Picasso* (Boston, 1969).

20. Six exhibit catalogs of surviving concentration camp and resistance art contain extensive but unsystematic selections of names and drawings. These are: Musée d'Art Juif, *Oeuvres d'artistes morts en deportation*. February 28-March 12, 1955. (Paris: Galerie Zak, 1955), 11 pages; Yad Vashem Exhibitions, *January-March 1960: Works of Jewish Artists in Concentration Camps and Ghettos* (Jerusalem, 1960); Union of American Hebrew Congregations, *Spiritual Resistance, Art from Concentration Camps*, from the collection of the Kibbutz Lochamei HaGhettaot, Israel (New York, 1978); Centro di Documentazione Ebraica Contemporanea, *Aspetti di una resistenza ebraica al Nazismo; comunicazioni visive dai campi di concentramento* (Milan, 1979); *Arts in Terezin, 1941–1945* (Memorial Terezin, The Small Fort, 1973); and Mary Costanza and Nora Levin, eds., *The Living Witness: Art in the Concentration Camps*, special exhibit at the Museum of American Jewish History, October 18-December 30, 1978 (Philadelphia, 1978). See also: Erhard Frommhold, ed., *Kunst im Widerstand. Malerei, Graphik, Plastik, 1922 bis 1945* (Dresden, 1968), and Nelly Toll, *Without Surrender. Art of the Holocaust* (Philadelphia, 1978).

21. This quote comes from a letter from Halina Olomucki, a survivor of the Warsaw ghetto and Auschwitz-Birkenau, written to Miriam Novitch, Director of the Museum at the Kibbutz Lochamei HaGhettaot. This letter is quoted in: Costanza and Levin, *The Living Witness*, p. 39.

22. Costanza and Levin, *The Living Witness*, pp. 11–13; Alfred Kantor, *The Book of Alfred Kantor* (New York, 1971); Leo Haas, "The Affair of the Painters of Terezin," in: Council of Jewish Communities in the Czech Lands, *Terezin* (Prague, 1965), pp. 156–61; and Leo Haas, *Ghetto Terezin, Catalog* (Pamatnik Terezin, 1969).

23. Arthur Koestler, *Scum of the Earth* (New York, 1941), p. 94.

24. Hanna Schramm, *Menschen in Gurs, Erinnerungen an ein französisches Internierungslager (1940–1941)*, mit einem dokumentarischen Beitrag zur französischen Emigrantenpolitik (1933–1944) von Barbara Vormeier (Worms, 1977); and Gilbert Badia, et al., *Les barbelés de l'exil. Etudes sur l'emigration allemande et autrichienne (1938–1940)* (Grenoble, 1979). See also the Archives of the Leo Baeck Institute, New York, which hold several collections about Gurs: Concentration Camps France Collection, 1939–1944; the Darmstädter Collection; the Eugen Neter Collection; as well as materials about the deportation of Jews from Gailingen, Baden-Baden, and Mannheim to Gurs.

25. This picture is 11¾ inches × 18¼ inches unframed and is located in the Art Collection of the Leo Baeck Institute, New York. A completed oil painting on the same subject is located at the Kulturgeschichtliches Museum in Osnabrück (letter Dr. Meinz, Director of the Osnabrück Museum to me on August 28, 1978.)

26. Biographical information on Nussbaum is found in: Kulturgeschichtliches Museum, Osnabrück, *Felix Nussbaum, 1904–1943*. *Gemälde aus dem Nachlass* (Osnabrück, 1971); and a series of articles offprinted from a local Osnabrück newspaper by Wendelin Zimmer, *Versuch über Felix Nussbaum*. The articles carry the following subtitles and dates: I. *Eine widersprüchliche Revolte*, March 20, 1971; II. *Auf der Suche nach dem eigenen Stil*, March 21, 1971; and III. *Symbole gegen den Verfall*, April 3, 1971. Other biographical information on Nussbaum is found in the Nussbaum Collection in the Archives of the Leo Baeck Institute, New York.

27. Biographical information on Schwesig is found in: Frommhold, *Kunst im Widerstand*, p. 570. Supplementary information was provided by Brigitte Bruns of the International Biographical Dictionary Project at the Institut für Zeitgeschichte, Munich; Louise Forsyth of the International Biographical Archives and Dictionary of Central European Emigrés, 1933–45, located at the Research Foundation for Jewish Immigration, New York; and Miriam Novitch of the Kibbutz Lochamei HaGhettaot, Israel. There is an extensive biographical file on Schwesig in the Archives of the Leo Baeck Institute, New York. His works are located at the Leo Baeck Institute, New York; the Museum of the Kibbutz Lochamei HaGhettaot, Israel; and the Städtische Kunsthalle, Düsseldorf.

28. These stamps are found in the Schwesig Collection at the Leo Baeck Institute, New York.

29. See: John Heartfield, *Photomontages of the Nazi Period* (New York, 1977); and Wieland Herzfelde, *John Heartfield: Leben und Werk* (Dresden, 1971).

30. See footnote 21, and also: H. G. Adler, *Die verheimlichte Wahrheit, Theresienstädter Dokumente* (Tübingen, 1958), copiously illustrated with the works of Theresienstadt artists; and Gerald Green, *The Artists of Terezin* (New York, 1978).

31. Fritz Fabian was born in Berlin in 1877 and died in Switzerland, December 1967. Further biographical information and art works are located at the Leo Baeck Institute, New York. Printed data about Fabian is found in: Costanza and Levin, *The Living Witness*, pp. 18–19; and Sybil Milton, in *International Conference*, pp. 99–100.

32. Slide show at the Museum of American Jewish History, Philadelphia, during the exhibit *The Living Witness;* and the Art Collection of the Leo Baeck Institute, New York, which contains numerous works of Fabian from these years.

33. Council of Jewish Communities in the Czech Lands, *Terezin;* and H. G. Adler, *Die verheimlichte Wahrheit*. See also H. G. Adler, *Theresienstadt, 1941–1945* (Tübingen, 1960); and Zdenek Lederer, *Ghetto Theresienstadt* (London, 1953).

34. See Bertalan Göndör Collection at the Leo Baeck Institute, New York. Further biographical data about Göndör is found in: Bertalan Göndör, *Emlekkigllitasa* (Budapest, 1962), *Bertalan Göndör, 1908–1945* (Budapest, 1947); Sybil Milton, "Concentration Camp Art and Artists," *Shoah*, I, 2, p. 13; and conversations with his widow, Mrs. Lily Gondor, New York.

35. All eight postcards are reproduced in Nelly Toll, *Without Surrender*, pp. 60–62. The original cards are located in the Göndör Collection at the Leo Baeck Institute, New York.

36. Music's works are found in Costanza and Levin, *The Living Witness*, pp. 34–35; Frommhold, *Kunst im Widerstand*, p. 561 and illustrations 473–74. See also: Marcus Smith, *Dachau: The Harrowing of Hell* (Albuquerque, 1972). Information about Corrado Cagli is found in: Frommhold, *Kunst im Widerstand*, p. 533, and the catalog *Arte e resistenza in Europa* (Bologna and Turin, 1965). An exhibit catalog of Adolf Frankl's works is: Walter Huder, ed., *Visionen aus dem Inferno* (Vienna, 1974).

37. Rico Lebrun, Mauricio Lesansky and Ben Shahn's works are discussed in Shikes, *The*

Indignant Eye, pp. 348–62. See also Mauricio Lesansky, *The Nazi Drawings* (Philadelphia, 1960); and the review of Audrey Flack's exhibit at the Meisel Gallery in New York, "A painting that is difficult to forget," in: *Art News*, 77, 4 (April 1978), 150–51.

38. *Art News*, 77, 10 (October 1978); special issue on West Germany.

III.
THE PROFESSIONS IN NAZI GERMANY AND THE HOLOCAUST

TELFORD TAYLOR

THE LEGAL PROFESSION

One of the trials at Nuremberg, for which I was partly responsible, was a
trial in which the main defendants were lawyers and judges. Thanks to the
rather odd combination of the Columbia Broadcasting System and producer
Stanley Kramer, that particular trial has attained notoriety with the general
public.

I do not pretend that I will be able to give any definite answers to the
question what role the bench and the bar played in the rise of Nazism, and
in its programs, including the Final Solution. Obviously, there was no
major sector of the German social or political organization that was not
significantly involved. There is no point in searching for first causes, either
philosophically or practically. Whatever factors or circumstances we pick
out to explain the involvement of the bar—or of any other sector—in the
atrocious events of that time, we would only find that they, in turn, had
been caused by other events that preceded them, and this tree of causation
would branch out and expand about as rapidly as a genealogical tree does.

To avoid this, I would like to break into the chronological sequence and
rather discuss the two reasons why there was not more opposition to Hitler
and to Nazism. The first reason was essentially that Hitler gave the
Germans what they wanted. I think this is undeniable. The fact that he
stressed, for instance, Versailles and rearmament, enabled him to persuade
the two major sectors of real power in Germany at the time, that is to say,
heavy industry and the army, to support him. These values were widely
cherished by Germans in general. The second reason was, simply, fear; fear
that if you protested, the consequences would be severe. That certainly was
also true. Even before 1933, there were considerable hazards attached to

133

criticizing the Nazis. After 1933, it became even more hazardous. Yet, on June 17, 1934, Franz von Papen, whom we do not ordinarily consider a model of civic courage, did indeed deliver a speech in Marburg, in which he criticized much of what had been going on.

In the first place, it is important to differentiate between the willingness of the people to support Hitler because he was advancing goals they wanted to achieve, and in which there was nothing inherently criminal, and their willingness to follow him when he embarked on policies and actions that were obviously and flagrantly unlawful.

How well equipped was the German legal system to cope with the onslaught of Nazi lawlessness? A short and simple answer is: It was not very well equipped. I'm sure some of you are old enough to remember one of George Bernard Shaw's less successful dramas, *Too True to be Good*, which has a prologue spoken by a symbolic character called The Microbe. The Microbe, who is a spokesman for Shaw, ends the prologue with these words: "Ladies and Gentlemen, the play is now virtually over, but the actors will discuss it at length for three more acts." I feel a bit like that myself, because having said: not very well equipped, I've really shot my bolt. What I can add are mainly details, examining why I think that it was poorly equipped. In order to do this, it will be necessary to examine the German legal profession as it existed before Hitler, and to compare it with other legal systems, notably the Anglo-American system, but also with other Continental legal systems. I think we will see that the defects, the flaws, the weaknesses in the German legal system were in part the result of its intrinsic structure—which was essentially no different from other Continental systems—but in part also due to the special circumstances in Germany at the time.

I think it is significant that the German legal system was much younger than that of any other major European country, or the United States, or, indeed, most of South America. There really was no German legal profession, no German legal system before the 1870's. Prior to that, as we know, Germany was a collection of princedoms and kingdoms, some of them small, many of them very backward, and the dispensation of justice— similar to the way it was in feudal England—was a prerogative of the local barons or, sometimes, of the king. The court was not an institution separate from other manifestations of sovereign rule. There was, properly speaking, no legal profession. There were counselors, there were people who assisted the authorities in ironing out disputes, but to call it a profession would be going much too far. There were no bar associations, no bar examinations, nor anything like that.

Now compare this with traditional American law. If you walk around the Harvard Law School, you are surrounded by portraits of famous justices, going back to the sixteenth and seventeenth centuries. No such tradition of a high-level profession existed in Germany.

There was a partial emancipation of the bar in the 1870's. The system had begun to get creaky. In 1848 efforts had been made to establish bar associations and to professionalize the administration of the law. These efforts were not really successful until the founding of the German Empire. But several of the results are very significant for us. The bar was emancipated in the sense that it no longer was an activity into which you had to earn your way by royal appointment, by state appointment. Admission to the bar was opened up, a national law was created; a Supreme Court of the Reich and a bar association called the *Anwaltsverein* were created. As a result, there was an enormous increase in the number of lawyers in Germany, beginning in the 1870's, and among those who entered the profession were a great many Jews. Indeed, they came in in such quantities that just after the turn of the century, around 1905, the Jews made up about 14 percent of the legal profession, as compared to less than 1 percent of the population; in Berlin they were even in the majority.

What kind of an ambiance, what kind of social and political level had the bar achieved in these roughly thirty years since its foundation in the 1870's? I think it can best be described as a sort of petty elite. Yes, lawyers were better than tradesmen, they were better than small merchants, they were better than lots of people. But they were not as good as bankers, they were not as good as high-level civil servants, they were certainly not as good as army officers. And so the bar found itself professionalized, but really up in the air, trying to keep up with the Joneses, trying to emulate the occupations and callings that were far more honorific. Some lawyers were lucky enough to get honorary titles, such as *Geheimrat*—rather meaningless titles, but they gave them much pleasure. However, the bar was, in fact, a bunch of social climbers. That briefly describes the German bar as it entered the twentieth century.

After World War I, there were a great many German reserve officers, civilians who held reserve commissions. Most of them valued their reserve commissions much more than anything else they had. Many reserve officers were lawyers, and they loved to be called *Hauptmann der Reserve*. There were hardly any Jews among the reserve officers. The legal profession became overcrowded, more and more Jews were pressing into it, the older members of the bar who antedated these developments became increasingly hostile. The bar, being basically conservative, emulating the military professions and other conservative callings, became sharply divided.

Let us now turn to the structure and other appurtenances of the legal profession. In the first place, legal education in Germany, as in most Continental countries, meant taking law courses as part of a general university education; any subsequent training depended very much on where you wanted to go. There were four fairly well-defined groups in the legal profession.

First, there were lawyers in private practice, as we know them in the United States; they made their living by taking clients and, hopefully, doing something for them.

Second, there was the judiciary and the office of public prosecution. This was a very important segment of the profession and was basically part of the civil service. In the United States, there are various ways to become a judge. In some instances, I regret to say, you may get a judgeship by purchase; you may get it by election, you may get it by eminence, you may get it by having friends in high places. But the theory is that you become a judge if you are an eminent lawyer. That is not the case in Germany or, generally speaking, on the Continent, where the judicial profession is part of the civil service. This means that you can train to be a judge and spend your life as a judge, getting promotions, transfers, etc., as in other branches of the civil service.

The composition of the bar in Germany is totally different from ours. In the United States, about three quarters of the members of the bar are practicing lawyers who live independently by taking clients. In Germany, the proportion of practicing lawyers is about one quarter. In the United States, the judges compose perhaps 3 percent of the legal profession; in Germany, closer to 20 percent. Germans are very litigious. They appeal repeatedly, and therefore there are very many Appellate Courts. Although there was a great deal of legal business, it was not enough for an overcrowded bar.

The third group—about 20 percent of the German bar—worked for the government in one capacity or another: as public prosecutors, or as lawyers in one of the many government departments.

Finally, about another 20 percent worked for private corporations. Whereas in the United States these so-called house counsels, government attorneys, and judges make up less than 25 percent of the profession, in Germany they account for 75 percent; and practicing lawyers number only about 25 percent of the profession. That means, of course, that a very much larger proportion of the bar is government dominated, dependent on the government for its livelihood.

There were other factors that affected the ability of the German bench to resist the onslaught of Nazi lawlessness. Despite professional pride, the German judge does not have the opportunities to achieve the kind of distinction characteristic of either England or the United States. In the United States, names like Holmes, Brandeis, Frankfurter, Black, Harlan, and Douglas are household words. There is no equal possibility for individual pre-eminence in most Continental countries. They act in a collegial capacity. There are few dissenting opinions; and decisions are not written with either the informality or logical sequence of American opinions. Furthermore, the judges, being civil servants rather than people who have achieved some degree of eminence in their profession, do not see themselves as public figures.

For all these reasons, it is quite clear that the German bench is not the kind of institution we think of when we think of the U.S. judiciary. On our own bench, there may be many judges we do not consider the most courageous in the world; others, however, act very independently. The same holds true for the bar. In Germany, the bar was overcrowded, divided, frequently anti-Semitic, conservative, wishing they were in uniform.

The role of the German lawyer in court is also very different. It is less important than in the United States because of differences in the rules of evidence. This is especially true of criminal law, where the process consists mainly of a preliminary government inquiry before an investigating magistrate (*Untersuchungsrichter*), and the purpose of the trial is largely to clear up points of doubt. In a criminal trial, the prosecuting attorney sits on the same level as the judge, while the defense attorney sits way down in the well, with the defendant, who is usually presumed guilty, anyhow. All this makes a great deal of difference, of course, in the prestige and the feeling of responsibility.

Unlike Germany, there are several stereotypes of legal heroes in the United States. One of them is, of course, the crusading district attorney, who throws the rascals out, finds corruption, causes people to resign, and then is elected Governor. The prototype in this century: Thomas E. Dewey. Another folk hero of the law is the courageous attorney who takes on unpopular causes and proves, like Abraham Lincoln, that the moon wasn't shining that night. The prototype in this century: Clarence Darrow. The third type is the very able lawyer, in a corporate sense, who, to be sure, makes a lot of money but also participates in large business ventures and perhaps even becomes a corporate director or president. An example is Albert Gary, who became president of U.S. Steel.

I have tried to sketch the different kinds of status the bar and the bench had in Germany as Nazism came to power. I will now spend a much shorter time on one secondary feature: How did it all come about? What was the response of the bench and the bar in the 1920's and 1930's, before Hitler achieved power? We might start with the trial of Hitler himself, after the abortive putsch in Munich in 1923, before a Peoples' Court in Munich. Let's look at the opinion rendered by Judge Georg Neithardt at the end of the trial: He made it perfectly plain that under no circumstances was he going to convict General Ludendorff—he was a general. As far as the others were concerned, although he did sentence some of them to as much as five years, he described them as noble, patriotic, selfless men. There was a statute that explicitly required that any alien convicted of treason was to be banished, or deported. Hitler was an Austrian. But—and this is most unusual in Continental law, where the judges are very much wedded to the letter of the law, the letter of the code—Judge Neithardt said: Well, he served in the German army, he thinks of himself as a German, and therefore we will not impose this penalty of banishment. It's nice to speculate what difference to history it might have made, had Judge Neithardt banished Hitler to Austria. Probably he would have found his way back, but much might have been changed. In almost every case in which the defendant was nationalist or right-wing, the judges tended to deal with him leniently. The case of Carl von Ossietzky was quite another matter. He received a long prison term. Throughout that period the bench and the bar had exhibited an affinity for the kind of nationalist sentiment that was the initial source of Hitler's success.

The means by which, after 1933, all this was translated into the total demolition of the legal system in Germany really merits only a few words. The bar association crumbled rapidly. In 1928, the National Socialist Bar Association had approximately two hundred and fifty members; in 1930, it had about one thousand three hundred members; in 1933, after less than a year of Hitler's power, there were over eighty thousand members. The Lawyers' Association, the pre-existing bar association, in March, a few weeks after Hitler came to power, passed a resolution disavowing discrimination "against our Jewish colleagues." But the resolution published in the papers did not say anything about that. And a few weeks later, a law (Law for the Restoration of the Civil Service) was passed, requiring that no Jew could be an attorney unless he had served in World War I, or had been a lawyer since before 1914, or had lost a relative in World War I. All others were legally disqualified, and after that the German Bar Association crumbled completely. The German lawyers were all dismissed, and in 1936 the prohibition on Jewish lawyers was made complete. Within the space of a few months—and this was much the same as in the medical profession— the expulsion of the Jews took place with hardly a whimper.

There is only one other point that is perhaps worth commenting on: There was one remaining problem; there was going to continue to be a lot of legal business between Aryans, and it was necessary to have some reasonably orderly means of settling such disputes. Therefore there had to be some courts that functioned in a reasonably predictable way. It would be a little bit odd to have courts that were functioning like courts in some matters, and then, all of a sudden, simply became tools of the government in other matters. Therefore, most of the political cases were handled before special courts, set up for political cases.

I do not want to give the impression that everybody crumbled immediately. There was, after all, the Reichstag Fire Trial in 1934, in which all the defendants except van der Lübbe were acquitted, despite the fact that Göring himself had been a witness for the prosecution and it was perfectly plain that the government wished to convict all of them. But, although that was to some extent a symbol of continuing independence, the result was the creation of the Peoples' Court, before which treason trials were to be held from then on. After 1934 and the Röhm purge, everything came out into the open, Hitler declared himself supreme judge, he put his blessing, and the Reichstag then put its blessing, on the killings that were taking place during the purge. By 1935 we find sentences like this from the periodical *Deutsche Justiz,* the official organ for magistrates: "The judge is his own legislator, he is no longer subject to the law, the judge is only subject to the orders given him by the Führer." The independence of the courts seemed definitely to belong to the past. One might as well use that for an epitaph, but worse was to come. As soon as war came, special legislation was passed depriving first Poles and Jews of ordinary legal protection, forbidding either Poles or Jews to challenge judges on the ground of partiality, and putting them under other great disadvantages in conducting litigation of any kind. Then, a few years later, the Poles and the Jews were separated and the Jews were removed even from the protection of that statute, and it was declared that Jews were to be punished by the police. End of law. Total end of law.

What remains to be said? I do not want to give the impression that in my opinion the U.S. legal system is foolproof. I have tried to point out some

significant differences—some of them structural, some of them historical—
that account for the basic flaws and weaknesses of the German legal system.
I think it would be fair to say that if in 1933 we had been looking for a
source of probable opposition to Hitler, the last place we would have looked
to would have been the bench and the bar.*

*This paper is an edited transcription by the editors of Telford Taylor's speech at San José.

GERT H. BRIEGER

THE MEDICAL PROFESSION

As a professional outsider, I feel privileged to have my paper included in this volume. The late American historian Allan Nevins once began a lecture at the Library of Congress by noting that when the British Empire went to war in 1914, the Cabinet, sitting anxiously in Downing Street, was astonished by a crisp message from one of its outlying dependencies. It read: "Barbados is behind you!" My role is humbler than that of Barbados in 1914. I am a historian of American medicine and do not have a broad knowledge of the literature of recent German history. Yet from the reading I have lately been able to do, some questions have emerged that seem to me pertinent to the subject of this book.

There is one topic so pertinent that it has to be mentioned at the outset: The story of the so-called doctors of infamy. This ghastly aberration in the history of an otherwise humane profession is so well known that I do not intend to dwell on it. Besides, of the approximately ninety thousand German physicians probably less than 350 were involved in these medical crimes. It is the rest, the 89,650, that we must try to understand.

There are four points that bear emphasis. The first is one that was eloquently made by a German physician, Dr. Alexander Mitscherlich, in his book *The Death Doctors* (which surely deserves a prize for the poorest translation of a German book title; its original title was *Medizin ohne Menschlichkeit* [Medicine Without Humanity]). What horrified Dr. Mitscherlich, as it did the rest of us, was that the crimes of cruelty, malice, and blood-lust, as he called them, "were at the same time organized with such professional bureaucratic efficiency, that the reader can only feel the deepest shame as he realizes that human beings could be capable of such acts."[1]

The second point has to do with what Dr. Leo Alexander called the beginning of corrosion occurring in microscopic proportions.[2] Thus the beginnings of much that happened in the early 1940's may be seen in the sterilization and euthanasia programs, first for the chronically ill, then for the so-called socially unproductive, and later as eugenic measures.

The third point concerns a statement by the late Dr. Andrew Ivy, and others, to the effect that the perpetrators of these gruesome and amoral concentration camp experiments could not even claim that the results obtained were in any way scientifically useful.[3] This entirely misses the point. Even if highly useful results had been obtained; the means to their end deserve nothing but utter condemnation in the strongest possible terms.

Finally, there is today a growing movement known as bioethics. Beyond a simple awareness of human rights, the influence of the civil rights movement, consumer activism, and the growing interest in ecology and conservation, it was the Nuremberg trials, followed by the Declaration of Geneva, that helped to spark—or, more properly, to rekindle—an interest in the age-old problem posed by the ethics of medicine.

If you ask medical historians what were the world's leading centers in the last decades of the nineteenth and the first decades of the twentieth century; whence came many of the important diagnostic and therapeutic advances; where were the so-called basic sciences of medicine, anatomy, physiology, biochemistry, and pharmacology most successfully pursued; and where did most of the avid young American physicians who wished to round out their medical education or engage in actual research seek additional training, the answer will surely be Germany—or the German-speaking part of Europe. Thousands of Americans headed for Berlin, Leipzig, Heidelberg, Würzburg, and Vienna to observe the great surgeons, walk the wards with the great internists, or to learn at the laboratory benches of the physiologists and pathologists. There is little doubt that from about 1860 until 1914 German medicine was pre-eminent in the world. German scientific as well as social advances in medicine were studied and copied all over the world.

Although by the 1930's the United States had begun to assert world leadership in medicine, the German medical profession and medical-care system was still probably second to none. How did a profession with such a glorious historical tradition, such a heritage of excellence and strength, permit such great atrocities in the name of medical science? This is at the heart of what Ralf Dahrendorf calls the German question.[4] Unfortunately, my colleagues in medicine were not very different from their non-medical brethren. This should not really surprise us. Nevertheless, the question remains: Why did the German medical profession seem to ignore the danger signals?

In the 1930's, German medicine still lived off the fruits of its earlier pre-eminence. Americans were still arriving in German centers for postgraduate training—some, ironically, because of a *numerus clausus* in some of our own medical schools.

Ideally, medicine ought to be value free and beyond political reach. Yet it is perfectly clear, both from the history of medicine and from a quick glance around us, that medicine is culturally and socially influenced, if not determined, and medical care is an eminently political issue. This was certainly true around the middle of the nineteenth century, when physicians were quite well represented on the Berlin barricades during the 1848 Revolution. The young Rudolf Virchow was destined to be Germany's leading medical figure in the second half of the century. He was a spokesman for his profession as well as an eloquent spokesman for liberal causes, social justice, and an outspoken foe of anti-Semitism. Together with several colleagues he published a radical journal. In its short life from mid-1848 to mid-1849, *Die medizinische Reform* was really a weekly set of editorial statements. The misery of poverty, the lack of proper sanitary provisions, poor housing, and the lack of government interest in the people's health and welfare in general, were constantly decried by Virchow.

With the failure of the Revolution the outspoken journal ceased publication, and its principle founder was virtually banished from his hospital position in Berlin to the much less prestigious medical school in Würzburg. There Virchow continued to write scientific articles and books, and by 1859 he returned triumphant to his own institute of pathology in Berlin. He subsequently became an elected member of the Berlin city council and of the German parliament, and he was an implacable foe of Bismarck. Yet despite Virchow's fine example, the German medical profession followed him only in its scientific bent, leaving to others the attempt to solve social problems. In the later decades of the nineteenth century, German medicine became seemingly much less political, even apolitical.

In 1847, the year before Virchow founded *Die medizinische Reform*, he and another co-worker began a journal that still exists as *Virchows Archiv*. Here he published his 1848 article about an outbreak of typhus in Silesia which the government had sent him to investigate. The young graduate of the prestigious military medical school in Berlin hardly behaved like a dutiful government functionary. For ten years the *Archiv* continued to carry editorials about various social issues. In 1858 the editorials ceased, and the *Archiv* became a purely scientific journal, perhaps the prime example in its field. The historian's quest for political expression from the leaders of German medicine becomes increasingly frustrated.

When I try to understand the American medical profession's response to any question, be it a scientific development, a new form of therapy, a different way of paying for medical care, or a reform attempt in medical education, my primary sources of information often are the proceedings of medical societies and editorial comments in medical journals. Much to my surprise, I found the leading German medical journals of the 1930's devoid of editorials. Medical news of advances in therapy or diagnosis are certainly plentiful. Comments on political questions are simply not there, or at least my initial search has not found any. British and American journals would yield quite a different picture.

This absence of editorial comment might explain an earlier episode of German medicine not entirely unrelated to the events of the 1930's. Germany had long been hailed as the pioneer in social legislation, especially as it pertained to medical care, and it had been the model that many countries followed. In 1883, after two years of intense debate and much political wrangling, Bismarck was finally able to push his bill for health insurance through the legislature; it was soon followed by industrial accident insurance. Knowing of the debate carried on by the British Medical Association over Lloyd George's proposed insurance bill of 1911, and the great campaign waged by the American Medical Association against Medicare in the early 1960's, it is of interest to ask what was the attitude of the German medical profession toward health insurance in 1883. Henry Sigerist, who studied this episode in some detail, pointed out many years ago that he was somewhat surprised to find no comments on the intense debate going on in the Reichstag, either in medical journals or in biographies. I am no longer surprised at all that the medical journals were silent.[5]

German medical societies of the 1920's and early 1930's were not political in any sense. There were local scientific medical societies as well as specialty societies, but their meetings appear to have been devoted solely to technical or medical discussions. In the United States—until recently, at any rate—the AMA was known as the voice of American medicine. I have been unable to find any association in Germany that might be called the voice of German medicine. This does not mean that German doctors had no opinions, it means only that they seem to have kept them safely to themselves.

The history of the rise of National Socialism, the resistance to it, the story of Germany during World War II, and much else has been amply treated by historians. But where are similar discussions about the medical profession? They are seemingly not at hand. Nor have German historians paid much attention to the profession. With the notable exception of Professor Fritz Ringer's work on education, and Professor Michael Kater of York University,[6] I find that much new ground must be ploughed. The role of the German medical profession in German life during the period of 1930–45 certainly is worthy of a book, and I hope someone will write it.

In the meantime, what can we say? It is well known, for instance, that on March 31, 1933, Jewish physicians holding university hospital or faculty positions were told they need not appear for work the following day. According to Gerhard Jaeckel's history of the Charité in Berlin, the hospital lost that day forty-seven out of one hundred doctors of internal medicine, fourteen out of fifty-seven in surgery, eight out of forty in obstetrics and gynecology, seven out of seventeen in psychiatry and neurology, five out of seventeen in dermatology, eight out of twenty-six in pediatrics, and seven out of twenty in pathology.[7] Altogether ninety-six Jews were dismissed, leaving one hundred and eighty-one Gentiles behind. None of these, Jaeckel claims, raised his voice in protest, though many wrote helpful letters of recommendation to colleagues abroad.

Dr. Gustav von Bergmann, one of Germany's leading professors of internal medicine and director of the University Clinic in Berlin, was apparently dismayed at having to carry out these orders. According to Dr. Frank Gassman of San Francisco, Bergmann begged him not to ask any questions, but just to go.[8] Most of the non-Jewish physicians were very kind, but could do, or at least did, very little to help. The atmosphere was one of uncertainty and great fear. Dr. Gassman well remembers that the man who succeeded to his position at the Charité, a man with whom he had had a friendly relationship for several years, would not even shake the departing doctor's hand, lest he be seen sympathizing with a Jew in the hallways of the Charité.

Bergmann is the author of a widely acclaimed textbook of medicine published in 1932. On the title page, in print only a little smaller than that of the author's own name, was that of his acknowledged *Mitarbeiter* Dr. Martin Goldner. The second edition, issued in 1936, no longer carried Dr. Goldner's name, although I am told that he continued to receive some royalties. In a vein rather typical of German physicians, Bergmann introduced the second edition by noting that Germany stood at the brink of a revolutionary epoch—but one in which there would be clinical reformation, not one on which political comments needed to be made.

Bergmann's equally famous Berlin colleague, the surgeon Ferdinand Sauerbruch, joined the resistance to Hitler—albeit somewhat late. One of his principle assistants, Rudolf Nissen, was a Jew whom he treated very well. Despite all Sauerbruch's attempts to retain him on his staff, he was unable to do so. Yet perhaps the most revealing line in Sauerbruch's autobiography is the one beginning the description of an incident in which he refused to fly the new flag from the rooftop of his clinic. He wrote: "In time, the Third Reich penetrated even the quiet sanctuary of our surgical clinic."[9] One is left wondering what would have happened if this gifted man, who perfected the pioneering method of open chest surgery, could have stepped out of his quiet sanctuary; if he and many others had come out of their sanctuaries, would they have influenced events? This question is especially appropriate when applied to Sauerbruch, because he was an immensely powerful figure who ran his service in the old tradition of an absolute ruler, and who was considered a tyrant by many who came in contact with him. Sauerbruch was an authoritarian—but he was not the best judge of people; perhaps he was not such a good judge of political events either. According to Werner Forssmann, Sauerbruch referred to one of his assistants as "that idiot Domagk."[10] Gerhard Domagk later won a Nobel Prize for the introduction of sulfa drugs. Forssman was not well received either by his teacher. In 1932 Sauerbruch let him go because he had too little scientific initiative. Three years earlier Forssmann had passed a catheter into his own heart and taken an X-ray picture of himself to record it for posterity, a feat that would earn him a Nobel Prize in 1956.

Forssmann, incidentally, joined the Nazi Party very early, claiming he was swayed by a colleague. In a sense, he abrogated responsibility by saying that his generation was young and accustomed to obeying authority. He denied that he and his colleagues were capable of passing political judgments. Thus he typified the apolitical physician.

Can one say, though, that those German physicians who joined the Party were indeed apolitical? In a paper on the sociological aspects of the Nazi Party, Michael Kater has shown that between 1933 and 1945, 31 percent of German physicians took out membership in the Reich's Physicians' League, an adjunct Nazi Party organization. He found that certain academics, especially physicians and jurists, were over-represented in the SS as well—at any rate, up to seven times greater than their national quota. An important distinction still needs to be made: Was the joining of one or another group a politically motivated act, or was it only a politically expedient, hence a naïve act? However, an over-representation in the SS cannot simply be dismissed.

We also do not know enough about the socio-economic situation of the average German physician around 1930. As Michael Kater has pointed out, it is not surprising that pauperized German physicians and lawyers, along with many of their economically suffering compatriots, eagerly joined the Nazi Party in 1932. But what was the average medical income? While physicians suffered along with everyone else during the Depression, they were by and large better off than many others. William Allen, in his book *The Nazi Seizure of Power*, a detailed analysis of one town, found that in 1930 a senior laborer earned 1500 marks per year, while a physician's income was 9600 marks.[11] The average German physician of 1930 was indeed economically far better off than the average working man. Thorough studies of the recruitment patterns of physicians and their financial status will have to be made and compared with other professions and their responses to political pressures, before the medical profession as a whole can be properly assessed.

Autobiographies of physicians do exist, but they were not written by average physicians—or, at least, few if any of them were published. Those whose stories did find their way into print either give fairly vague reasons for joining the Party or circumvent the whole issue. I venture to say that only through large-scale, computer-assisted studies will we be able to arrive at more than the usual, purely impressionistic conclusions.

Just as the human experimentation so callously carried out by some concentration camp physicians may be an aberrant condition when one considers the whole German medical profession of the time, the numerous ideological medical writings are probably not indicative of mainstream thinking either. How many German physicians could follow Hanns Löhr's 1935 book about the place of medicine in the National Socialist state? Löhr proclaimed that, "The social upheaval of the present time will help us to turn from an undue concentration on individual symptoms and organs to the consideration of the 'whole' human being, and thus will lead to truly medical-biological thinking."[12] This sounds very much like today's fascination with holistic medicine. Yet if one continues with Löhr's argument, one comes to realize what he really meant: The National Socialist physician had an obligation to the state, not merely to the individual patient. The physician had to be an alert biological soldier: "We university teachers," Löhr concluded, "are obliged to teach the student that the health of the *Volk* stands above the health of the individual as the ultimate aim of the art of medicine, hence to be a doctor to the people is more important than science itself."[13] "Adolf Hitler and his associates have shown the way to the German medical profession."[14]

If George Mosse is correct when he says that the boundaries between public and private activities were abolished, then I suppose it is true that the boundary between professionalism of the physician and life in Nazi-ruled Germany could also be blurred.[15] Scientists may be quoted in a similar vein as I have quoted Löhr, but all this does not yet convince me that the average physician–patient encounter was profoundly changed. This is another question that cries out for more work.

Considering how much work remains to be done, only a very superficial summary can be made at this point.

Since the medical profession was traditionally open to Jews, it is not surprising that they were heavily represented. It is difficult to assess the reaction of the Gentiles in the profession to the mass dismissal of Jews from hospital posts in 1933, the prohibition of Jews treating insurance fund cases after 1934, and their subsequent loss of licenses. Virtually no comments exist in the few places I have been able to check. There may be several possible interpretations. The most charitable one would be that the bulk of German physicians, many of them with the mentality of small functionaries, were simply running scared and convinced there was nothing they could do. There is doubtless some truth in this, and one must remember that aside from the groups of physicians on the various faculties who had potential strength, the profession as a whole was not organized as it is in the United States. It was certainly not organized for political purposes.

Physicians, by their nature and training, are a conservative lot. This is as it should be, because when we seek aid as patients, we do not want our own doctor to be anything but conservative when it comes to his prescription for our treatment. Therefore, one cannot expect physicians as a group to be in the vanguard of reform or resistance. Furthermore, to resist meant to be deviant, and that is difficult in the best of circumstances.

A less charitable interpretation—but one that doubtless has some validity—is that economically non-Jewish physicians could only benefit when their Jewish colleagues could no longer compete with them for positions and patients.

There are, however, further possible interpretations, some of which may well be appropriately invoked to explain the apparent lack of reaction from the German medical profession. Ralf Dahrendorf has pointed out that Germans lack an awareness of social inequality. "The question of how the other half lives," he claims, "is rarely raised in Germany. Existing conditions are accepted without protest: they are as they are and nobody can do much about them."[16] But another of Dahrendorf's ideas appeals to me more as a possible explanation for the medical profession's seemingly quiet acquiescence in what was happening in their surrounding world. Perhaps as was true in the political realm, no really self-confident leadership ever followed the medical elite of the older generation. As Dahrendorf puts it, "the cartel of the anxious" always presents an invitation to the less anxious to put an end to indecision by arbitrary definiteness.[17] Thus the men who were the potential leaders of the profession did act by not acting; nor did they stand firm for their Jewish colleagues, until it was too late for all. If it was later true that most doctors did not know what was going on in the concentration camps, it is also true that they did not ask.

But our task is to explain, not to assign blame. I do not have any evidence that the German medical profession on the whole behaved differently from other so-called educated elites. Probably many a German physician could well have echoed the words of Albert Speer, who said, "Whether I knew or did not know, or how much or how little I knew, is today unimportant when I consider what horrors I ought to have known about and what conclusions would have been the natual ones to draw from the little I did know. . . . No apologies are possible."[18]

NOTES

1. Alexander Mitscherlich and Fred Mielke, *The Death Doctors*, trans. James Cleugh (London, 1962), p. 9. The German original was published in 1949 and an American version appeared as *Doctors of Infamy: The Story of the Nazi Medical Crimes* (New York, 1949).

2. Leo Alexander, "Medical Science Under Dictatorships," *New England Journal of Medicine*, 241 (July 14, 1949), 39–47. See also Lucy S. Dawidowicz, *The War Against the Jews 1933–1945* (New York, 1975; paperback reprint, 1976), pp. 175–80; and Richard L. Rubenstein, "The Health Professions and Corporate Enterprise at Auschwitz," Chapter 4 in his *The Cunning of History, The Holocaust and the American Future* (New York, 1975; paperback reprint, 1978).

3. Andrew C. Ivy was a distinguished professor of physiology at the University of Illinois School of Medicine who was involved in the postwar investigation of Nazi war crimes. His own career ended tragically when he became a strong proponent of Krebiozen as a cure for cancer. His comment about the lack of utility of the medical experiments is surprising in view of his strong statements about and deep understanding of the medical crimes. See Mitscherlich, *Doctors of Infamy*, p. xi.

4. Ralf Dahrendorf, *Society and Democracy in Germany* (Garden City, N.Y., 1976).

5. Henry E. Sigerist, "From Bismarck to Beveridge; Developments and Trends in Social Security Legislation," *Bulletin of the History of Medicine*, XIII (April, 1943), 365–88.

6. Fritz K. Ringer, *The Decline of the German Mandarins: The German Academic Community, 1890–1933* (Cambridge, Mass., 1969); Michael H. Kater, *Das "Ahnenerbe"*

150 GERT H. BRIEGER

der SS 1935–1945 (Stuttgart, 1974); Michael H. Kater, "Sociological Aspects of the Nazi Party, The Stormtroopers and the SS: Towards a Social History of the National Socialist Movement until World War II"; typescript kindly provided by Professor Kater; see also Stephan Leibfried and Florian Tennstedt, "Die Auswirkungen der nationalsozialistischen Machtergreifung auf die Krankenkassenverwaltung und die Kassenärzte," working paper, Universität Bremen, 1979, and other works by professors Leibfried and Tennstedt which are in progress. Theirs will be the most complete study of the German medical profession of the 1930's. Unfortunately, little of it was available at the time of the Conference in San Jose.

7. Gerhard Jaeckel, *Die Charité: 250 Jahre Medizin und Sittengeschichte um das berühmte Krankenhaus* (Munich, 1965).
8. Personal conversation with Dr. Frank Gassman of San Francisco, March 8, 1978.
9. Ferdinand Sauerbruch, *Master Surgeon*, trans. F. G. Renier and A. Cliff (New York, 1958), p. 200.
10. Werner Forssmann, *Experiments on Myself: Memoirs of a Surgeon in Germany*, trans. Hilary Davies (New York, 1974), p. 127.
11. William S. Allen, *The Nazi Seizure of Power: The Experience of a Single German Town 1930–1935* (Chicago, 1965; paperback reprint, 1973), p. 15.
12. Hanns Löhr, *Über die Stellung und Bedeutung der Heilkunde im nationalsozialistischen Staate* (Berlin, 1933); excerpted and translated in George L. Mosse, *Nazi Culture* (New York, 1966), p. 232.
13. Mosse, ibid, p. 334.
14. Ibid.
15. Ibid., p. xx.
16. Dahrendorf, *Society and Democracy*, p. 104.
17. Ibid., p. 368.
18. Albert Speer, *Inside the Third Reich*, trans. Richard and Clara Winston (New York, 1970; paperback reprint, 1971), p. 163.

ALAN BEYERCHEN

THE PHYSICAL SCIENCES

When teaching courses in twentieth-century history, I am disturbed by the popular belief I repeatedly encounter that the Third Reich sponsored a great deal of successful scientific research and was thus to a large extent "pro-science." The examples of such successes are usually technological feats like the V-1 and V-2 rocket projects or the ME-262 jet fighter. My students usually have to be taught that science and technology are different pursuits before it can be explained that despite the admiration of Hitler and his followers for technology and applied science, the objective, disinterested quest for knowledge we call "pure" science was held in low esteem in the Third Reich.

Nothing brought this fact to light more dramatically than the dismissal of large numbers of highly competent academic scientists as part of the purge of the civil service beginning in April 1933. Through 1935, at least 18 percent of the natural science faculty members had been forced from their positions. The best available figures indicate that 13 percent of academic personnel in chemistry, 20 percent in mathematics, and over 25 percent in physics were driven from their posts.[1] The qualitative toll of the "intellectual decapitation"[2] of German science was even more startling. No fewer than twenty contemporary or future Nobel laureates were dismissed or resigned their positions during the Third Reich, including Hans Bethe, Felix Bloch, Max Born, Albert Einstein, James Franck, Dennis Gabor, Gustav Hertz, Victor Hess, Erwin Schrödinger, Otto Stern, and Eugene Wigner in physics as well as Peter Debye, Fritz Haber, Gerhard Herzberg, and George de Hevesy in chemistry.[3]

Although the dismissal process affected the scientific community only as a side effect of the Nazi aim of ridding the civil service of potentially uncooperative elements, the leaders of the National Socialist government were not unaware of the damage they were causing. Max Planck, physics Nobel laureate and elderly president of the Kaiser Wilhelm Society, visited Hitler in late May or early June 1933 and tried to make the Führer understand the magnitude of the loss being incurred by German science. Hitler was completely unapproachable on the topic, however, and the story circulated afterward that Planck had been told bluntly:

> Our national policies will not be revoked or modified, even for scientists. If the dismissal of Jewish scientists means the annihilation of contemporary German science, then we shall do without science for a few years.[4]

The Nazis, not content to eliminate Jews and other "politically unreliable" persons from positions of public trust, also sought to align all aspects of German organized life with the National Socialist movement. The university administrations were quickly Nazified, of course, but so were many professional scientific societies, such as the prestigious German Chemical Society. The tone of the process was clear in the address of the president of the National Mathematical Federation at that organization's annual meeting in September 1933.

> We thus wish to conform to the spirit of the total state, and to cooperate loyally and honestly. Unconditionally and joyfully, we place ourselves— as is a matter of course for every German—at the service of the National Socialist movement and behind its leader, our Chancellor Adolf Hitler. And we hope that we have something to offer.[5]

Very few professional societies were able to resist the pressure to conform to the pattern dictated by the new government.

But even this did not satisfy the radicals within the Party, whose goal it was to inject racist ideology into the content and conduct of each scientific discipline. Thus an empirical "Germanic" astronomy was discovered among the ancient Teutons, and the general theory of relativity was decried in articles such as "Albert Einstein's Attempt to Overthrow Physics and Its Inner Possibilities and Causes."[6] Hence the effort by Erich Jaensch to generate a psychological theory of perception differentiating a deductive, formalistic-thinking (and ostensibly) Jewish type of personality structure from an inductive, data-oriented (and just as ostensibly) Aryan type.[7] And thus also the noted Berlin mathematician Ludwig Bieberbach announced different forms of mathematical creation, contrasting the formalism of Jewish types with the intuition of Aryan types.[8]

Perhaps the most notorious effort to inject racism into the nature and practice of one of the physical sciences was the "Aryan physics" propounded by the Nobel prizewinners Philipp Lenard and Johannes Stark, and supported by a small band of radicals and ideologues composed mostly of their pupils and political allies. Lenard (born in 1862) had by 1905 been awarded the Nobel Prize for his experimental research into cathode rays. Stark was considerably younger (born in 1874) and won the 1919 award for his discovery of the doppler effect in canal rays and the splitting of spectral lines in a magnetic field. Both men were thus well established scientists of international reputation by the beginning of the Weimar period, when they both became alienated from their professional community. Lenard resorted to racist ideology as a consequence of his unsuccessful efforts to rouse his fellow physicists in defense of nineteenth-century aether theory against the acceptance of Einstein's relativity. Stark turned to *völkisch* politics as a result of an abortive bid to wrest control of the professional organizations and journals from the leaders of the physics community in Berlin. The personal animosities he generated in this fight made him such an academic pariah that from 1922, when he resigned his post in Würzburg, to the Nazi seizure of power in 1933, he was unable to secure another university position. Already by 1924 Lenard and Stark were so thoroughly alienated from their peers that they published a joint declaration of support for Hitler in a small, Pan-German newpaper.[9]

Lenard's primary concern was to create a properly Germanic under-standing of physical science, especially a true *deutsche Physik*. In orthodox mandarin fashion—to categorize his outlook in Fritz Ringer's terms—he completely rejected nineteenth-century mechanistic materialism. It is noteworthy that a scientist, particularly a physicist, would do so, because the popular belief was that the epistemological foundations of the physical sciences (such as causality) provided the deterministic basis for material-ism—which, in turn, provided the basis for atheistic Marxist socialism. In the popular mind all this went back to the seventeenth-century scientific revolution, and especially to the work of Isaac Newton. Although Lenard repudiated the results to which Newton's mechanistic world view had led, he did not find fault with Newton himself. For Lenard, Newton's universe was still animated by mystery and spirit *(Geist)*. The popularizers of the succeeding generations, however—particularly the Enlightenment *philosophes*, had corrupted Newton's work by divorcing spirit from mechanics and attributing rationalistic omniscience to science. Lenard deplored the outcome and maintained:

> The eradication [of spirit from nature] has still not been overcome to this day. It has produced an arrogant material craze (materialism) which sees above all technology and the mastery of nature as the successes of natural research. [10]

That the German *Volk*, with its intuitive understanding of nature, had succumbed to such delusions was easily explained: An "alien spirit" had infected the physical sciences in recent times. The "powerful penetration" of the Jews into positions of academic authority had caused the masses instinctively to lose faith in science so that only respect for technology remained. In May 1933, at the height of the dismissals, Lenard applauded Stark's appointment as president of the Physikalisch-Technische Reichsanstalt (PTR), the largest state-supported laboratory in Germany. He was pleased to report:

> The specter has fallen into ruin; the alien spirit is already voluntarily leaving the universities, and indeed the country—that alien spirit which was able to manage [only] so uncomfortably on the firm foundation of the natural sciences, [namely] that created by the pure Aryan spirit in work lasting down through the centuries. It means nothing that those who have left also possess Nobel Prizes; these prizes of late have unfortunately become of increasingly contestable spiritual value. [11]

The alternative to mechanistic materialism advocated by Lenard, Stark, and their disaffected followers was an essentially organic universe that could only be properly perceived by Germanic intuition and observation. To attempt to rationalize this universe and claim true human understanding of it was unnatural and arrogant. Physical reality could be understood to a limited extent by mechanics, but the laws governing material events were not the result of matter in motion; they were the result of spirit in action and therefore reflected the infinite interconnectedness and mysteriousness of nature rather than the power of the human intellect. According to Lenard, this was especially clear in regard to the aether. Mechanisms in the aether eluded man because it was the realm linking matter and energy, governed by spirit. Since no human being could comprehend even its own spirit, the fundamental causal agent in nature was qualitatively beyond our ken. [12]

The muddled tenets of *deutsche Physik*, or "Aryan physics" as it was called, followed from these beliefs. Relativity theory and quantum mechanics were decried as propagandistic, arrogant, abstract formalisms abhorrent to nature. Quiet, humble, patient experimentation was hailed as the key to scientific investigation, with sound theory only following afterward on the basis of established, empirical data. Stark, in particular, contrasted a deductive, Jewish, dogmatic approach to physics with an inductive, Aryan, pragmatic way of doing things.[13] (These racial stereotypes reflected, of course, the personality structures asserted by Jaensch and Bieberbach, and made it possible to brand political or professional enemies proponents of "Jewish thought" even if their lineage was impeccably Aryan.) Science thus perceived was thoroughly subjective: In properly "Aryan physics," objectivity was regarded as a fiction which weighed all possibilities equally, without a firm commitment to the truth; and science was recognized only on the basis of national characteristics of racially kindred researchers. The entire notion of the internationality of science was held to be nothing more than a Jewish-Liberal-Marxist fraud.[14]

After his appointment as president of the PTR, Stark had tried to gain control of the entire physics community under the Nazi leadership principle. But he found his path blocked by his old professional antagonists. In particular, Max von Laue, professor of theoretical physics in Berlin, Nobel laureate, and close friend and supporter of Einstein, emerged as Stark's most determined opponent among scientists. He managed to turn back Stark's drive to be named president of the German Physical Society and to be given editorial review power over the professional journals.[15] Although he was not able to prevent Stark's appointment in 1934 as head of the *Notgemeinschaft der deutschen Wissenschaft* (Emergency Association of German Science, an important research funding agency founded during the inflation of the early Weimar period), von Laue realized this might not be a total loss. As he noted to a colleague in exile:

> He [Stark] also has opponents in the Party and among the ministers. He would have been disposed of long ago if he did not have the personal support of Hitler. It is at least good that now as president of the Emergency Association he is bringing *all* the scholars down upon his head. As he does so, we will let him fend for himself.[16]

This prognosis proved quite accurate, and Stark's penchant for making personal enemies soon locked him into conflicts with important figures in the Party and state bureaucracies. His tenure as president of the Emergency Association lasted only two-and-a-half years before he was ousted by Nazi rivals.

In 1936, with the support of Party ideology chief Alfred Rosenberg and the University Teachers League responsible to Rudolf Hess, Lenard and Stark launched their Aryan physics campaign in the popular press.[17] Their goal was to combat Jewish thinking in German academia by discrediting the leaders of the physics community, particularly the practitioners of theoretical physics, and by placing their own followers in positions of influence. Von Laue, Planck, and the young Nobel laureate Werner Heisenberg waged a vigorous countercampaign culminating in a petition that condemned Stark's political machinations and defended theoretical physics. This petition was signed by no fewer than seventy-five scientists—including practically all of German academia's notable theoretical, experimental, and technical physicists.

This appeared to close the issue, but the following year Stark's collaboration with the SS produced an infamous article in *Das Schwarze Korps*, branding Heisenberg and other theoreticians "white Jews" who were Aryan by birth, but Jewish in spirit. Heisenberg became entangled in a long drawn-out effort to become politically "rehabilitated," during which his pending appointment as successor to his teacher Arnold Sommerfeld in Munich was held in abeyance. Although Heinrich Himmler finally repudiated the attack on him in 1938, Heisenberg was denied the Munich position, due to the uproar his candidacy had caused. Instead, an Aryan physics advocate, one Wilhelm Müller, was named to the post in 1939.

The magnitude of this victory was undeniable—which was why it backfired on the followers of Lenard and Stark. The professional community was galvanized into action, and even some physicists within the Party were dismayed at the intrusion of ideology into professional affairs. The Aryan physicists were therefore baited into a face-to-face confrontation with their antagonists in the fall of 1940. Although the meeting was held under the auspices of a Party agency, the followers of Lenard and Stark were forced to talk physics instead of politics and found they had nothing to say. The result was loss of support from the Teachers League, important elements within the Party. Since Rosenberg had already been alienated by the attempt to garner support from his ideological archrivals in the SS, the Aryan physics adherents had ineptly managed to lose their most important bases of political strength. At the same time, the professional physicists were strengthened by the advent of wartime research projects, through which they gained the backing of Göring's *Luftwaffe* and eventually Albert Speer's Ministry of Armaments.

Although the advocates of Aryan physics never constituted more than a small minority of the physics community, their claim to Party orthodoxy and their active contribution to the cultural and intellectual environment of the Holocaust have necessitated a brief exposition of their views and goals. But the virulent, public racism of Lenard and Stark was extremely unusual among scientists during both the Weimar and Nazi periods, and it is important to note that the disaffection of both men from their professional community was an essential factor in their resort to political extremism. Their professed concerns were the establishment of an alternative to mechanistic materialism and the return of German physics to a heroic period prior to its "infection" by the excessive influence of Jews and theoreticians. In the process, they hoped to redress old grievances against the leaders of the physics community.

The Aryan physicists were treated by the professionals as an unpleasant, irritating aberration—at least until the Heisenberg affair. They were regarded purely as a manifestation of politics, not physics, and indeed, it would be difficult to disagree. Yet the question arises whether or not they were a total aberration—a truly unique phenomenon completely unrelated to the professional elite from which they emerged as renegades. With the exception of von Laue, who clashed with the Nazis over basic principles, there was practically no political opposition to National Socialism by physics community leaders. Might there have been some common ground between the professionals and the proponents of politicized physics?

The response of the physicists to National Socialism was generally predicated on a deep-rooted sense of nationalism, which they—like their colleagues and peers elsewhere in the universities—perceived as an apolitical stance above partisan politics.[18] They were as susceptible as other members of the professional elites to the Nazi call for national unity and an end to Party factionalism. This was specifically the case with Planck, whose advice and outlook set the dominant tone in this discipline. Philipp Frank, professor of physics in Prague at the time, has captured that tone:

> Max Planck was one of the German professors who repeatedly asserted that the new rulers were pursuing a great and noble aim. We scientists [Planck held], who do not understand politics, ought not to make any difficulties for them. It is our task to see to it that as far as is possible individual scientists suffer as few hardships as possible, and above all we should do everything in our power to maintain the high level of science in Germany.[19]

The attitude of the physicists toward higher authority—especially among the members of the older generation that had come to maturity before World War I—was to obey and trust the leaders of the state. These persons were regarded as knowledgeable and properly suited to the tasks at hand. As von Laue put it in a letter to Einstein, the scholarly person should not mix into political matters, because, "Political struggle demands other methods and other natures than scholarly research. The scholar as a rule only comes to no good end in it."[20] To Einstein's objection that such reasoning abandoned leadership to the blind and irresponsible, von Laue responded:

> Can you name me a reputable mathematician, a physicist, or chemist who had concerned himself with political successes? These disciplines are—whether one regrets it or not—so alien to the world that they have a pervasive spirit which makes one a stranger to the world when one becomes professionally involved in them. He who works in history, ethics, law stands so close to the workings of the world that he can concern himself with them quite well. He does not need a spiritual change of attitude. But our kind should keep our hands away from such matters.[21]

Among physicists of the younger generation that came to maturity after the war, the prevailing attitude was not an implicit trust in authority, but an effort simply to ignore or minimize all things political. In his memoirs, Heisenberg has lamented how the growth of political unrest in the early 1930's led not only to street battles and demonstrations, but gradually also to intrusion into the scholarly havens:

> Almost imperceptibly the unrest, and with it anxiety, spread also within university life and faculty meetings. For a time, I tried to push the danger away from myself and ignore the incidents on the streets.[22]

In the midst of his efforts to recover from the political attack in *Das Schwarze Korps*, Heisenberg reported to Sommerfeld that a colleague had been politically denounced. "It is really too bad," he observed, "that during a time in which physics is making wonderful advances and it is truly fun to participate in them, one is forced again and again to busy oneself with political matters."[23] The image of science as distinct from and superior to political affairs was unmistakable in his words and quite characteristic of his peers.

The result of the attitudes of both generations was policital ignorance and naïveté. In correspondence with Einstein and on the basis of conservative, moral considerations, von Laue was led by the fall of 1933 into unconcealed opposition to the regime. But in the spring and summer of 1933, he—like Planck, Sommerfeld, Heisenberg, and others—counseled patience and restraint in dealing with the government, especially regarding dismissals and emigration. The primary goal was to preserve the professional autonomy of their discipline by avoiding confrontation and waiting for orderly life and procedures to resume. After all, the upheaval of 1918–19 had been weathered, and at that time the threat had even come from the political Left. Why should the nationalist upheaval of 1933 not gradually subside as well?

I also have the impression—having read accounts and correspondence of these men with each other, and having interviewed some of them—that another factor may have been involved: They had spent the previous three decades in the midst of a fundamental revolution in their own field. The deep and lasting impact of this period has been indicated by such descriptions as "the heroic age of atomic physics," "the golden age of German physics," or simply, "the beautiful years." It seems that the common experiences of these decades had two major effects upon the response of the physics community to the upheavals following 1933. The first was that members of the older generation who had been educated in the world of relatively stable values of the late nineteenth century, had become somewhat more inured to continual upheaval than their contemporaries in other areas of German society. They had learned to adopt a wait-and-see attitude toward the announcement of earth-shaking discoveries and were perhaps less prone to be either swept up or frightened by the prospect of a new order in society. The second was that the younger generation of physicists had been educated and had made their own contributions in a period of intellectual ferment and crisis. Its members had learned to await eagerly the next announcement of discovery and challenge to what had been—often quite recently—accepted as the best word on a subject. They were perhaps at least as likely to expect and accept major change as their contemporaries outside physics or even outside the sciences altogether.

This is merely an impression and may be unverifiable. But it is useful to remember that science is not as dry and unadventuresome as a textbook or high-school class might lead one to believe. The theoretical physicist John Ziman has pointed out that there are distinctly different moods in any scientific discipline. He has argued that "well-established scientific knowledge is academic, a form of orthodoxy, all the more dogmatic for its rationality; in the research phase, science is romantic in its chaos."[24] This distinction certainly applied to science during the romantic "beautiful years" of the quantum revolution.

This was indeed the essence of the charge leveled against Heisenberg by a faction in the Soviet Union which viewed his "uncertainty principle" as aiding the spread of fascist irrationalism in Germany.[25] This principle, which was one of the earth-shaking discoveries of the mid-1920's, holds that when investigating atomic and subatomic scale phenomena there are qualitative limits on what can be measured. The basic problem is that our instruments are made up of atoms, too, and these instruments affect the objects of our interest in fundamental ways. What and how we have *chosen* to measure determines to a large extent what we will find. The ramifications of this principle led Heisenberg, Pascual Jordan, Max Born, and others— mostly of the younger generation—to the view that definitive, causal statements about individual events were not possible; only statistical probabilities could be used to describe occurrences in the atomic realm.

It is revealing that this revolutionary approach was so readily accepted; apparently a significant number of leading professional physicists in Germany was as dissatisfied with mechanistic materialism as the proponents of Aryan physics. In a superb article, the historian of science Paul Forman has convincingly documented a fascination with the crisis milieu of mathematics and physics in the early Weimar period, and has argued that the later abandonment of strict causality entailed in quantum mechanics was basically an attempt to be rid of the onus of determinism. His thesis, as he puts it, is that "the movement to dispense with causality in physics, which sprang up so suddenly and blossomed so luxuriantly in Germany after 1918, was primarily an effort by German physicists to adapt the content of their science to the values of their intellectual enviornment."[26] The statistical interpretation of subatomic events was, of course, an extremely powerful tool of research. But Forman argues that the need for this tool was secondary to the need to deal with the "romantic reaction against exact science," which had undermined the social standing of German physicists following the war.[27]

If Forman's argument is valid, then many of the mainstream German physicists were responding to some of the same concerns voiced by the Aryan physics advocates. If the professionals could adapt their work to a hostile intellectual environment in the Weimar period, could they perhaps adapt to one in the Nazi period as well?

The closest the professional physicists came to this was reflected in a book published in 1936 by Pascual Jordan, one of the co-founders of quantum mechanics. In his book *Die Physik des 20. Jahrhunderts* (Physics of the Twentieth Century),[28] Jordan emphasized pointedly and repeatedly that the positivist insistence on observable quantities, which lay at the heart of the statistical interpretation of quantum mechanics, stood in direct contradiction to outmoded, sterile, mechanistic materialism. Although the book gave full credit to Jews who had contributed to modern physics (including Born, Franck, Hertz, and Einstein) and was thoroughly professional in tone, it was clearly an attempt to make modern physics respectable to the Nazis. It would not be accurate to regard Jordan's exposition as an effort to adapt modern physics to National Socialism. Although the field may have been open to external influences during its formative Weimar years, the time of great ferment was past, the ground rules were firm, and the field had evolved to the status of what the historian of science Thomas Kuhn has called "normal science."[29] But it *would* be appropriate to regard Jordan's book as an attempt to accommodate National Socialism to modern physics, in much the same way the professional physicists later sought to adapt Nazi war-related atomic research funding to their desire to pursue pure academic investigation.[30] The physicists were not prepared to accept National Socialism on its terms, but they were not unwilling to have National Socialism accept them on their terms.

Of course, that was impossible—at least, it was impossible as long as Lenard and Stark were in the picture. With their claim to represent true Aryan orthodoxy, their status as old Party comrades, and their ties to the ideological wing of the Party, they were able to make their presence amply felt until 1940. By then the war demanded results instead of talk, Stark's political enemies within the Nazi apparatus had multiplied, and the professional community had been roused to action over the Heisenberg affair.

It is possible that Lenard and Stark may well have prevailed in their efforts to establish a politically effective Aryan physics, had they incorporated quantum mechanics into their scheme of things. The specific anti-materialist elements of each would have provided common ground. Furthermore, the quantum mechanics' stress on measurable quantities and the role of the observer could have been used to support their claim that the race of a researcher fundamentally affected his work. They would possibly have broadened their appeal among the physicists and would likely have found allies among other Nazi agencies.[31] But Lenard and Stark were unable to overcome personal animosities or to think in terms of broadening their political vision. They were prisoners of their past and of their hatreds.

The leaders of the professional community, for their part were unable to overcome past animosities toward Lenard and Stark. I have suggested that the upheaval in their own discipline predisposed particularly the younger among them to accept a new order at least as readily as other members of German society. And I have indicated some of the tenets of modern physics that could have been areas of common acceptance between the physicists and representatives of that order. But as long as those representatives were Lenard and Stark, the physicists could only find National Socialism unpalatable. When the Aryan physicists threatened the professional control of the discipline, the field's leaders were able to marshal broad support among their colleagues in defense of traditional practices and values. Since they were able to protect their prerogatives by professional opposition to the Nazi ideologues, they perceived no need to go beyond this and engage in political opposition to the regime. Their goal was to remain in full accordance with the unpolitical tradition explained by von Laue to Einstein, which meant that their concerns were to preserve professional autonomy, to stay neutral, and to be involved as little as possible.

NOTES

1. Based on a comparison of the dismissal figures given by Edward Hartshorne, *The German Universities and National Socialism* (London, 1937), pp. 98–99, and the total staff figures provided by Christian von Ferber, *Die Entwicklung des Lehrkörpers der deutschen Universitäten und Hochschulen 1864–1954*, volume 3 of Untersuchungen zur Lage der deutschen Hochschullehrer (Göttingen, 1956), pp. 211–16. See Alan Beyerchen, *Scientists under Hitler: Politics and the Physics Community in the Third Reich* (New Haven and London, 1977), fn. 20, p. 221.
2. An apt phrase suggested by Helge Pross, "Die geistige Enthauptung Deutschlands: Verluste durch Emigration," in Freie Universität Berlin, ed., *Nationalsozialismus und die deutsche Universität* (Berlin, 1966), pp. 143–55.
3. Beyerchen, *Scientists under Hitler*, p. 48.
4. Hartshorne, *German Universities and National Socialism*, pp. 111–12.
5. Georg Hamel, "Jahresversammlung des Mathematischen Reichsverbandes in Würzburg am 20. September 1933," *Jahresbericht der Deutschen Mathematiker-Vereinigung* LXII (1934), 81.
6. Otto Reuter, *Germanische Himmelskunde* (Munich, 1934); Bruno Thüring, "Albert Einstein's Umsturzversuch der Physik und seine inneren Möglichkeiten und Ursachen," *Forschungen zur Judenfrage* IV (1940), 134–61.
7. See Erich Jaensch, *Der Kampf der deutschen Psychologie* (Langensalza, Berlin, Leipzig, 1934); and *Die Lage und Aufgaben der Psychologie: Ihre Sendung in der deutschen Bewegung und an der Kulturwende* (Leipzig, 1933).
8. Ludwig Bieberbach," Stilarten mathematischen Schaffens," *Sitzungsberichte der Preussischen Akademie der Wissenschaften*, physikalisch-mathematische Klasse (1934), 351–60.
9. On the gradual alienation of Lenard and Stark from their professional peers, see Beyerchen, *Scientists under Hitler*, pp. 79–122. The declaration was "Hitlergeist und Wissenschaft," *Grossdeutsche Zeitung*, May 8, 1924, 1.
10. Philipp Lenard, *Grosse Naturforscher: Eine Geschichte der Naturforschung in Lebensbeschreibungen*, second expanded edition (Munich, 1930), p. 93. On nineteenth-century popularizers of mechanistic materialism, see Frederick Gregory, *Scientific Materialism in Nineteenth-Century Germany*, vol. I of Studies in the History of Modern Science (Dordrecht and Boston, 1977).
11. Lenard, "Ein grosser Tag für die Naturforschung," *Völkischer Beobachter*, May 13, 1933, Zweites Beiblatt.

12. This brief discussion follows primarily Lenard, *Deutsche Physik*, vol. 1., *Einleitung und Mechanik* (Munich, 1936), pp. 1–13.
13. Johannes Stark, "Physikalische Wirklichkeit und dogmatische Atomtheorien," *Physikalische Zeitschrift* XXXIX (March 1, 1938): 189–92; also "The Pragmatic and Dogmatic Spirit in Physics," *Nature* CXLI (April 30, 1938), 770–72.
14. In addition to the references given in footnotes 10–13 above, see Stark, *Nationalismus und Wissenschaft* (Munich, 1934); Ludwig Wesch, "Philipp Lenard—Vorbild und Verpflichtung," *Zeitschrift für die gesamte Naturwissenschaft* III (May/June 1937), 42–45; and the collection of speeches in August Becker, ed., *Naturforschung im Aufbruch: Reden und Vorträge zur Einweihungsfeier des Philipp Lenard-Instituts der Universität Heidelberg am 13. und 14. Dezember 1935* (Munich, 1936).
15. Letter from Max von Laue to A. Einstein, October 13, 1933, Einstein Archives, Firestone Library, Princeton University, section 1B1.
16. Letter from Max von Laue to Richard von Mises, September 7, 1934, Harvard University Archives, von Mises Papers, Box 2.
17. The following events have been detailed in Beyerchen, *Scientists under Hitler*, pp. 141–98.
18. Paul Forman, "Scientific Internationalism and the Weimar Physicists: The Ideology and Its Manipulation in Germany after the First World War," *Isis* LXIV (June 1973), 151–80. See also Brigitte Schröder-Gudehns, *Deutsche Wissenschaft und internationale Zusammenarbeit 1914-1928*, Ph.D. dissertation, University of Geneva, 1966 (Geneva, 1966).
19. Philipp Frank, *Einstein: His Life and Times*, trans. George Rosen, edited by Shuichi Kusaka (New York, 1970), p. 236.
20. Letter from Max von Laue to Einstein, May 14, 1933, Einstein Archives, 1B1.
21. Letter from Einstein to von Laue, May 26, 1933 and letter from von Laue to Einstein, May 30, 1933, Einstein Archives, 1B1.
22. Werner Heisenberg, *Der Teil und das Ganze: Gespräche im Umkreis der Atomphysik* (Munich, 1969), p. 174.
23. Letter from Heisenberg to A. Sommerfeld, February 12, 1938, sources for History of Quantum Physics, roll 31, section 5, Archive for History of Quantum Physics, Bancroft Library, University of California, Berkeley.
24. John Ziman, *Public Knowledge: The Social Dimension of Science* (London and New York, 1968), p. 73.
25. See David Joravsky, *Soviet Marxism and Natural Science, 1917–1932* (New York, 1961), p. 293.
26. Paul Forman, "Weimar Culture, Causality, and Quantum Theory, 1918–1927: Adaptation by German Physicists and Mathematicians to a Hostile Intellectual Environment," *Historical Studies in the Physical Sciences*, III (1971), 7.
27. Ibid., 110.
28. Pascual Jordan, *Die Physik des 20. Jahrhunderts: Einführung in den Gedankeninhalt der modernen Physik* (Brunswick, 1936).
29. Thomas Kuhn, in *The Structure of Scientific Revolutions*, 2nd ed. vols. 1 and 2 of the Foundations of the Unity of Science (Chicago and London, 1970), pp. 109–10, 166–70 implies that a discipline is more open to extra-scientific influences in a crisis period than when "normal science" prevails. This is precisely what Forman's work endeavors to show (see fn. 26).
30. As argued by David Irving, *The Virus House: Germany's Atomic Research and Allied Countermeasures* (London, 1967).
31. Beyerchen, *Scientists under Hitler*, pp. 128–29. One ally might have been the Propaganda Ministry of Goebbels; cf. Wilfrid Bade, *Kulturpolitische Aufgabe der deutschen Presse* (Berlin, 1933), p. 30.

THOMAS P. HUGHES

TECHNOLOGY

The public does not associate ideology with the engineering profession. Engineers have usually presented themselves as value-free professionals, rational problem-solvers who do not mix politics and professional activities. Neither the layman nor the engineer expects to find politicians and political parties playing conspicuous roles in engineers' professional meetings. Until recently, few historians have considered the political activities or the ideology motivating or rationalizing the activities of professional engineers and engineering organizations intellectually attractive or significant subjects for study. Nor have the doctrines, myths, and symbols of professional engineers been considered especially interesting by other scholars concerned with twentieth century ideology.[1] In the case of German engineers, the conventional view has portrayed them as models of professionalism and rationality since the late nineteenth century, when they assumed a position of world leadership in professional circles.

It comes as a distinct shock, then, to encounter a 1933 photograph in the professional journal of the *Verein Deutscher Ingenieure* (Association of German Engineers), the most historic, the largest, and the leading German professional engineering society, showing the new head of the organization in a Nazi uniform, on a podium draped with a swastika, in a hall festooned with Nazi banners, asking the assembled engineers to take up the soldier's creed, *Ich dien'* (I serve). Two years later another photograph in the same professional journal showed Rudolf Hess and a host of uniformed Nazis parading into the meeting hall of the engineers' annual convention.[2] These photographs provoke two important questions: What ideological baggage did the Nazi leaders bring to leading professional groups, and was this ideology anti-Semitic? In this short paper, the first question can be given only a general response; the second question, however, can be brought into focus more sharply.

This paper directs attention to two ideological themes that dominated the addresses given before the *Verein Deutscher Ingenieure* (VDI) during the period after the Nazis took power and before the outbreak of World War II. Focus upon principle addresses given at the annual VDI meetings allows consideration of the ideology directed toward the mainstream of a profession, and not a radical fringe of the Left or the Right. Technocracy was the first overarching theme, and variations upon it will be discussed in this paper. The second theme—culture-determined technology—will be explored as well.

In addition to these two themes, two men will be discussed: the first, Gottfried Feder (1883–1941), because he and his ideology were rejected by the VDI; the second, Fritz Todt (1891–1942), because he and his ideology were accepted. The mood of audience or constituency can be judged by the choices they made, both negative and positive. Feder and Todt can be associated with the two major ideological themes that are the subject of this paper; Feder with an extremist technocracy and Todt with culture-determined technology.

The themes of technocracy and of culture-determined technology will be probed, seeking implicit or explicit anti-Semitism. It should be said at the start that I have not found virulent anti-Semitism in speeches and addresses given to large numbers of VDI engineers on public occasions from 1933 to 1939. I should add, however, that the tacit acceptance of the anti-Semitic aspects of Nazi ideological themes by large numbers of rank-and-file German engineers is an insidiously threatening phenomenon. In short, this paper directs attention to the acquiescing witness or, better, the blinkered specialist.

Technocracy, the first of the themes to be considered, has been variously defined by persons who consider themselves technocrats, and by the few historians and social scientists who judge technocratic intellectual and organizational movements worthy of attention. Several organizations in various countries have taken some variation of the word technocracy as a name; numerous persons have expressed ideas that they or others have classified as technocracy. In this way, technocracy has been used as a proper name as well as a general category for a more or less coherent aggregate of ideas. In this paper technocracy is used primarily as a label for a related set of ideas. George Lichtheim has well identified the values and programmatic statements incorporated in most variations upon little "t" technocracy:

> Its [technocracy] principal notions may be summarized as follows: human societies exist for the purpose of developing and for no other; nature having been tamed by science, the task remains, with the help of the "human sciences," to develop the techniques necessary to master human relations; industrial civilization levels the barriers between [sic] classes, races and traditional cultures; the only remaining social stratification is a meritocratic one based on productivity and competence; the ancient political cleavages between the parties, between liberalism and conservatism, capitalism and socialism, are outdated and linked to dead ideologies; the system of boundless wealth-production marks the end of ideology and the de-politicization of society; the age of automation leaves only one opposition: that between the planners and the planned.[3]

In pre-Nazi Germany, technocrats of extreme economic and political persuasion were publicizing their ideas. Influential among them was Heinrich Hardensett who published *Der kapitalistische und der technische Mensch* (1932).[4] The voices of Hardensett and other technocrats were heard more often and attended to more closely as Germany slid into the Depression and experienced the despair of unemployment and the frustration of unused means of production. Hardensett and other technocrats, most of whom were engineers by training or profession, insisted that production technology, unfettered by the irrationalities of the capitalist system, could provide ample employment. Engineers in the VDI also called for a more active political role for engineers. *Technische Menschen*, they believed, could enunciate a theory of technology that would reorder society, politics, and economics and thereby fulfill the desired potential of a technological world. The technocrats were generally neither racist nor nationalistic; they desired a world free of class and group conflict.[5]

It is interesting for the historian to consider the ideological interactions among the technocrats, the Nazi leaders, and the German engineers after the Nazis seized power. There was a high probability of ideological exchange among technocrats, Nazis, and VDI engineers, because organizations involving all three overlapped. The *Technokratische Union*, the organization of German technocrats founded in 1932, was a part of the *Reichsbund Deutscher Technik* (RDT) founded immediately after World War I by VDI engineers dissatisfied with the limited political influence of the VDI.[6] Also, in 1933 Gottfried Feder, a member of the Nazi hierarchy, took over leadership of the RDT.

In the spring of 1933 an obvious prospect was that Feder would impose his racism upon the technocrats, and his technocracy and racism upon the VDI engineers. Therefore, his views and character attract interest. With the exception of his anti-Semitism, Feder's views recall those of the American sociologist and economist Thorstein Veblen, as expressed in an essay entitled *The Engineers and the Price System*. Veblen—and Feder—blamed the profit motivation and the interest-seeking capitalists for the distortions and inefficiencies within the production system. Only when the engineers planned, designed, and operated the means of production would society's material and spiritual needs be fulfilled.[7] Oswald Spengler's *Decline of the West* posited a similar view. The struggle between capitalist and worker, Spengler believed, would pale in comparison to the struggle between the steel-hard men of intellect (the engineers) with their drive for production, and the men of acquisitive drive (the financiers).[8] Spengler also called the "quiet" engineer "the machine's master and destiny. His thought is as possibility what the machine is as actuality."[9]

Gottfried Feder gave technocratic ideology a racist twist. To him, acquisitive capitalists and Jews were synonymous. In the 1920's, Feder, as a Party leader, denigrated acquisitive financiers as exploiters of the creative and productive German managers and engineers. He equated acquisitiveness especially with international Jewish financial circles whose influence, he was convinced, reached deep into the German economy. He believed that "money dominated work and blood" and the world was topsy-turvy.[10] Probably because of a German propensity to idealize the entrepreneurs of industrialization, Feder could not see all capitalist business leaders as enemies. His simple-minded resolution of the threatening contradiction, therefore, singled out some he considered Aryan and constructive, like Henry Ford.[11]

Feder, as well as his anti-Semitic technocracy, arouses interest because he helped to shape Nazi ideology during the early 1920's. Subsequent generations were burdened by his ideological baggage. In addition to making other contributions to Nazism, Feder, who held Party membership six, provided Hitler a model for his brush mustache. Hitler's frustrated drive as an architect-builder was probably relieved by the vicarious satisfaction of association with Feder who had studied engineering at the *Technische Hochschule* in Munich and who had successful construction projects to his credit before he delved into economics and politics in 1917. Later, Hitler found similar satisfaction in his chosen relationships to engineer Fritz Todt and architect Albert Speer. On the same day that Hitler led the abortive putsch in Munich in 1923, Feder's book, *Der deutsche Staat auf nationaler und sozialer Grundlage: Neue Wege in Staat, Finanz und Wirtschaft* appeared with Hitler's introductory remarks. This virtually made it the Party's major statement of principles.

In 1931, Feder headed the engineering technical section (*Ingenieur-Technische Abteilung,* or ITA) of the wing of the Nazi Party assigned responsibility for building up cadres to administer the new order once the Nazis had achieved power. In October 1932, Feder was named head of the state economy section of the Nazi Party; Walter Funk headed the parallel private economy section.[12] Funk's appointment was intended to offset that of the radical Feder, for "acquisitive" businessmen were being canvassed for election campaign funds. Yet, Funk later testified that Feder was responsible for the economic program and philosophy of the Party from its establishment until it came to power.[13] By then Feder probably considered himself—wrongly, as events would show—spokesman for engineers and technocracy; in 1931 he also became head of the Militant Union of German Architects and Engineers (*Kampfbund Deutscher Architekten und Ingenieure,* or KDAI), a left-wing Nazi organization of engineers more interested in political and ideological questions than in scientific or technological ones.[14]

In the years before the Nazis' seizure of power, Feder held the most prominent positions of his career. He used his position as head of the engineering technical section of the Party to proselytize for the implementation of his technocratic views. In the Party platform he helped to write in 1920, he called for large engineering projects such as dams to be constructed with interest-free financing from the state.[15] In this way he intended to break the bonds of what he called interest slavery, which he believed Jewish bankers had imposed on society. His Reichstag bill of 1930 asked for a general limit of interest rates to 4 percent and further demanded that the property of bank and stock exchange magnates and all Eastern Jews be expropriated without compensation.[16] In directives to the engineering technical section he advocated the institution of social-welfare technology to replace prevailing technology designed by the acquisitive and interest-seeking. Agitated because financiers and not engineers dominated the economy, he sought out Nazi engineers throughout Germany who could assume key positions once power was seized. He wanted these engineers to be familiar with natural resources, labor, and other factors that could be marshaled to create socially useful technology. He lamented that such socially useful technology could be introduced only if it were profitable, while profitable technology could be introduced even though it was not socially desirable.[17]

During the period of the *Gleichschaltung*, or coordination, in 1933, Feder attempted to take over the *Verein Deutscher Ingenieure* with its membership of thirty thousand engineers.[18] His abortive efforts to have himself named chairman had comic aspects. In a face-to-face encounter on April 26, 1933, Feder, accompanied by twelve intimidating SA-men and four radical engineers who shared his views, demanded that the VDI name him chairman. He said that the Party considered the leadership of the VDI a Jewish clique that he could best purge and replace.[19] Several politically sensitive VDI leaders, unintimidated by Feder, realized that in the spring of 1933 anyone's assertions about his own status in the fluid Nazi hierarchy were suspect. Hurried telephone calls to Rudolf Hess and Wilhelm Frick confirmed suspicions that Feder acted without a Nazi concensus and so, instead of capitulating to his demands, the VDI ran him as a candidate in a contested election (between Nazis). Feder lost.

Other leading Party members, not all of whom were engineers, struggled for power over engineers in professional engineering organizations during 1933 and 1934. They realized that the German economy and foreign policy depended on technology, and, therefore, the engineering constituency was a strong card in any aspiring politician's suite. Rudolf Hess as chief of the Party's Central Political Commission (*Politische Zentralkommission*), Robert Ley as head of the German Labor Front (*Deutsche Arbeitsfront*), Martin Bormann as head of Hess's staff, Fritz Todt as head of the Reich Union of Technical and Scientific Work (*Reichsgemeinschaft der technisch-wissenschaftlichen Arbeit*, or RTA), an organization intended to coordinate engineering and scientific professional societies, as well as Feder engaged in Byzantine maneuvering. Ley wanted to dissolve existing professional organizations into his embracing Labor Front; Todt intended to maintain professional organizations while subordinating them to the technological, military, and economic goals of the Party; and Feder, remnant of the left wing of the Party, drew upon past pretensions. Ever the rigid ideologist, Feder watched power slip from his grasp into the hands of more opportunistic and flexible men. Todt's power grew as he organized engineers to serve Party ends. Hess and Bormann, using the political power of their Party positions, intervened to tip the scales and formally reinforce settlements that sustained the primacy of politics.[20] Ley, in this case, seems to have been outmaneuvered.

Feder's waning power in the Party and among Nazi and German engineers correlates with the absence of strident anti-Semitism in the technocratic ideas expressed in public addresses and work sessions at the VDI annual conventions in 1934 and 1935. (In late 1934 Feder was "sent off" to become a "harmless professor."[21]) Technocracy was not a dead issue, however. Heinrich Schult, the Nazi engineer who defeated Feder for chairmanship of the VDI, gave a keynote address before thousands of VDI engineers in 1934, demanding that engineers take over from non-technical managers and economists the responsibility for planning and managing the economy.[22] He did not advocate the technocratic ultimate of the displacement of political power by a technocratic administration of things and people, for this would have been a challenge to the Party, a challenge the likes of which had recently brought a Stalinist purge in the Soviet Union.[23] Schult and others wanted a planned, organic, and systematic economy. They insisted that decision making in the economy follow the engineering method. Engineers, Schult believed, should take the key role in solving energy and raw material shortages, unemployment, and urban congestion. It was essential that engineers replace economists in decision-making positions, for the economists, ignorant of technology and engineering, futilely advocated fiscal measures, balance of payment manipulation, and currency reform as solutions to the pressing problems of economy and state.

In 1935, when the annual meeting was convened in June in Breslau, the organic economy theme was enlarged upon. After recalling the prominence given to the question of the preceding year by Schult, the published report on the general meeting of 1935 summarized an address on the subject given by Albert Pietzsch, the commissioner for economic questions on the staff of Rudolf Hess. Pietzsch advocated, like Schult, that National Socialism provide a style of economic leadership that was deeply influenced by the methodology and principles of the engineer, for the engineer was uniquely qualified to observe, measure, and control machines and processes, and to obtain their efficient performance. Furthermore, the engineer was outstandingly qualified to take the systematic and encompassing view of the vital components that make up the living organic economy.[24] Further, Pietzsch called for a quantitative, systematic model of a balanced economy (*Volkswirtschaftsbilanz*), which would provide a firm basis for directing the growth of the economy, related research, and development by engineers.[25] In 1935, attention was also directed to the theme of organic economy (*Organische Wirtschaftsgestaltung*) by designating it the subject of one of the eight major groups (*Fachgruppe*) into which the working sessions were divided during the five-day meeting.[26]

The emphasis in the 1934 and 1935 meetings on the engineer's role in the economy, the insistence that the engineer not simply fetch and carry for technically naïve industrialists and the low-level state administrators, suggests that technocratic objectives and professional status were important to the VDI. Notable, however, is the absence of Feder's racist twist and the challenge to ultimate political authority.

After 1935, neither technocracy nor the related theme of organic economy were part of VDI meetings, which then became dominated by a charismatic personality, Fritz Todt. From 1936 through 1939, he presented major addresses at their meetings, and in June 1938 was elected chairman of the VDI. His presence and his assumption of leadership manifested a change in VDI ideology: the engineers were no longer asked to spread their methods throughout a restructured economy; instead they were told to vitalize the technical skills of a politically compliant profession by the infusion of Nazi values.

The exodus of Feder, the rise of Todt, and the dramatic ideological shift that occurred in 1934 and 1935 were only ripples on the surface of deeply disturbed waters. These surface changes can be related to deeper ones taking place in the power and ideological structure of Nazi Germany. In June 1934 a Hitler purge removed not only Ernst Röhm and the challenge that his SA troops might have posed to the regular army, but also eliminated Gregor Strasser, leader of the left, or socialist, wing of the Nazis with which Feder had associated. In the 1920's Strasser advocated a fascist corporate state and the nationalization of industry. In 1934, Hitler also made clear that there would be no "second revolution," an expression understood to mean an overturn of the industrial and capitalist hierarchy of Germany. Feder's extreme technocratic ideology, therefore, was ruled out as much as Gregor Strasser's socialism. (If Feder had been a stronger force he, too, might have been murdered in June.) Also the more restrained technocracy of Schult and Pietzsch did not survive.[27]

Because Todt was no technocrat and was at ease with the irrational ideology of Mein Kampf, his powerful position and engineering policies were acceptable after Hitler and the Party had discarded the Left and allied themselves with the army and capitalist enterprise. Todt has occasionally been mistakenly protrayed as a technocrat by scholars who confuse technocracy with an enthusiasm for technology and a defense and furtherance of traditional engineering roles and status. As his speeches to the VDI and his energetic engineering management of the Autobahn, West Wall, and armaments projects show, Todt wanted large and rewarding problems for the engineering profession—but technical, not ideological or political ones. Furthermore, Todt's ideological pronouncements reveal that he at least tolerated—and may have been at ease with—the anti-Semitic implications of the theme of culture-determined technology. He was no virulent anti-Semite like Feder; he was, judging by his ideology, the acquiescing auditor.

During the period from 1933 to 1936, Todt's rise was the inverse of Feder's decline. Todt, the bellwether of the ideological shift, took a vantage position in the organizational world of Nazi engineering when Rudolf Hess formally named him head of the RTA in December 1933. In May 1934, Feder had become chief of the newly formed Nazi Party Office of Technology (*Amt für Technik*) and of the National Socialist Union of German Technology (*National-Sozialistischer Bund Deutscher Technik*), which replaced the radical Nazi engineers' and architects' organization Feder had headed when he attempted his VDI coup.[28] In December 1934, however, Frizt Todt took over both positions from Feder, and it was announced that Feder was temporarily retiring (*einstweiliger Ruhestand*).

Todt was a model Nazi engineer. His professional qualifications included a humanistic *Gymnasium* and *Technische Hochschule* education. At the *Technische Hochschulen* of Munich and of Karlsruhe, he concentrated on civil engineering. In the 1920's he served as a field engineer and then as head of the highway construction activities of a Munich engineering firm. He also qualified for leadership as judged by Nazi standards. During World War I he was an officer-observer in military aircraft, was wounded in combat, and won the Iron Cross, First Class. In 1922, when Hitler was harnessing the motive forces of ambition, envy, and resentment prevalent among disillusioned war veterans, Todt joined the Nazi Party. He proved a persuasive Nazi enthusiast in his professional contacts, and prepared papers for the Party on technical subjects. Among the projects that attracted Hitler was the *Autobahn*. With considerable fanfare Hitler named him head of the project in 1933. At the time of his death in an airplane crash on February 8, 1942, he was a Cabinet Minister (Armament and War Production); Plenipotentiary for the Regulation of Building; the Inspector-General for Water and Power; Inspector General of Highway Construction; and head of Organization Todt, which constructed the western defenses of Germany before the war. Albert Speer succeeded him as Cabinet Minister and head of Organization Todt.[29]

Todt assumed ideological positions in major addresses to the VDI membership at their annual meetings. These addresses, including rhetoric tailored to strike responsive chords in the rank and file of engineers, may reveal more about the engineers in the audience than about Todt on the rostrum. Todt's public pronouncements were anti-Semitic by implication, but the implications were clear to anyone familiar with *Mein Kampf*. To

draw out the anti-Semitic implications in Todt's views and to show that his
pronouncements were variations on Hitler's, I have sought roots and
parallels for them in Hitler's *Mein Kampf* and his seminal anti-Semitic
speech of August 13, 1920.

Todt gave an enthusiastically received address to the VDI engineers at
Darmstadt in May 1936, and spoke to four thousand of them again in May
1939 at Dresden. In 1938 he also delivered a speech to a crowd of young
engineers gathered at the annual meeting. In these he dwelt upon the role
of Hitler and the Party in the spiritual regeneration of German engineering.
Because he insisted that culture shaped technology and because he—and
Hitler—denied technological determinism, I call Todt's idealist ideology
"culture-determined technology." We shall learn that when culture is seen
as determining technology, the door is open to nationalism and racism.

Todt insisted that an earlier tradition of excellence in science and
technology did not prevent the decline of the German nation and culture in
the years from 1918 to 1933. Nor did rational expertise provide a base for
the renewal of national strength and the revitalization of the German people
after 1933. "The resurgence of the German people should be attributed,"
Todt said, "to Adolf Hitler and his National Socialist comrades. In their
years of struggle, they established the conditions necessary for the power
seizure in 1933 and by this the conditions for successful professional activity
by men who are active only in the purely scientific or technical realm."[30]
This was clearly an anti-technocratic remark.

In his ideological statements, he also condemned the materialism and
egoism (*materieller Egoismus*) of the Weimar years and those who exploited
technology in their desire for profits and dividends; Todt told his audience
that National Socialism, in contrast, was committed to *"Gemeinnutz vor
Eigennutz"* (common use before selfish possession).[31] Elsewhere he said:
"Who would solve material problems by material means alone will be
dominated by the material. Mastery will come through the spirit. We
idealists will master dead matter through the Nazi spirit of combat and will.
Success comes to those who attack problems as National Socialists."[32]

Todt also followed Hitler in his insistence that Nazi values made
possible the recovery and sustained excellence of German engineering. The
Hitler of *Mein Kampf*, no technological or economic determinist, believed
that culture had a spiritual unity, and that its art, technology, economics,
and other characteristics were manifestations of this unifying spirit. He
wrote that "industry, technology, and commerce can thrive only as long as
an idealistic national community offers the necessary preconditions."[33] For
Hitler, the ideal virtues such as courage, will power, and loyalty made

possible the culture and the form of the culture—the state. The state was an organization of a community of physically and psychologically similar persons united for the purpose of maintaining the species and for race fulfillment. For instance, technology which molded the physical environment emanated from the state. The excellence of the technology depended therefore upon spiritual values, the state, and the race.[34]

Hitler's views on culture, state, and technology were infused by vicious anti-Semitism. He divided mankind into three groups: "the founders of culture, the bearers of culture, and the destroyers of culture."[35] Only Aryans were representative of the first group. The Japanese were considered, for example, the bearers of culture. The Jews were the destroyers of culture and, therefore, of technology. "The Jew," Hitler believed, "is led by nothing but the naked egoism of the individual."[36] The Aryan valued *Gemeinnutz vor Eigennutz*. Hitler's Aryans, bearers of the work ethic and technology, created a habitable environment in the cold north. Jews, Hitler was convinced, placed no positive value on work, seeing it as a punishment inflicted on unwary sinners. Materialism and egoism were explicitly associated by him with the Jews.[37] Todt was obviously using Hitler's views on "culture-determined technology," but Todt left implicit the anti-Semitism in these views.

Todt emphasized the work ethic. In his address of 1939, he recalled the great tradition of German craftsmanship and associated the VDI engineers with it. Hitler, Todt informed his audience, spent his first night in Prague after the occupation of that city, in the Hradschin, a building that was the work of a south German *Baumeister* (master builder). He also told the VDI engineers that they must carry on the proud German tradition of heroic creativity. In reaction against the popular concept of Marxian, or Communist, collectivism, Todt stressed the extraordinary importance of the individual personality in initiating technological innovation, but he qualified his remarks by reminding the engineers that the creations of genius were made available to the people through highly organized cooperative effort.[38]

Again Hitler's and Todt's ideologies run parallel to the point of explicit anti-Semitism. In *Mein Kampf*, Hitler argued that every invention, every discovery, and every organization of elements and forces for production were the work of the individual, and that the more recent the events the clearer and more substantial the supportive historical evidence for this phenomenon. Hitler wanted society to be so organized that the men of genius could rise to positions of power and responsibility by a process of natural selection. He wrote that "a human community appears well organized only if it facilitates the labors of those creative forces in the most helpful way and applies them in a manner beneficial for all."[39] Hitler and Todt also agreed that the German was remarkably creative. In *Mein Kampf,* Hitler wrote that "everything we admire on the earth today—science and art, technology and inventions—is only the creative product of a few peoples and originally perhaps of *one* race."[40] That one race was the Aryan, the culture-creating race. In a darkly prophetic passage, Hitler characterized the Jews and other "lower races" as useful laborers for the culture-building Aryans. "It is no accident," he wrote, "that the first cultures arose in places where the Aryan, in his encounters with lower peoples, subjugated them and bent them to his will. They then became the first technical instrument in the service of a developing culture."[41]

Todt was fulsome in his praise of Hitler. He identified the inculcation of young engineers with his values as a prime problem facing the VDI. His sense of urgency, he explained, arose from his awareness that never before in history had a people been so favored as to have a leader of the stature of Hitler, and that it was unlikely that another of comparable greatness would follow. Therefore, it was imperative not only for the present generation to use to the fullest the time during which "we have our Führer," but also that those so fortunate to have lived with and learned from him and his times should pass on this heritage.[42] In an official biography published shortly after Todt's death, he was quoted as having said, "who lives in the time of Adolf Hitler must deny himself all personal conveniences in order to better fulfill his sacred responsibilities and the objectives set by the Führer."[43] He identified the ultimate purpose of his *Autobahn* project as the honoring of Hitler, "for today, for generations; to this end, all other objectives are means."[44] Against this background of adulation and unquestioning loyalty it is not surprising that Todt instructed the VDI membership that their function was to fulfill, like good soldiers, the goals determined by the Führer and his Party.

Todt's espousal of Hitler's ideology and his public adulation of him was a clear renunciation of technocracy and an assertion of his willingness to fulfill objectives laid down by Hitler and the Party. His promotion of the work ethic and creativity themes showed a determination to solve thoroughly the engineering problems arising from the goals established by the Führer and the Party. Todt was defining a circumscribed world of responsibility for the engineers of the VDI, a world free of messy struggles for political power and even sheltered from the violent language and action of rank anti-Semitism. After Todt's motivating and morale-building addresses, engineers were expected to attend working sessions dedicated to solving the engineering problems of the Four-Year Plan and rapid armament.

Todt did not avoid irrational explanations and nonsensical assertions, but he did draw back from explicit anti-Semitism. Evidence of this is the notable fact that most of the themes he enunciated were taken by him or his speech writers from the chapter "Nation and Race" in *Mein Kampf*, and yet the anti-Semitic assertions interwoven with the other themes in this chapter were expurgated in Todt's presentation. Todt may have found anti-Semitism morally repugnant; it is also possible that he and other engineers considered it a "political" issue and no concern of theirs. Engineers led by Todt were encouraged to be enthusiastic experts focusing on problems that could be solved with their expertise. Todt's attitude toward the role of the engineer probably captured the mood of the rank-and-file VDI members.

The absence of blatant anti-Semitism and of Hitler's more strident assertions about technology and culture in Todt's presentations to the VDI contradicts the belief of the distinguished liberal German historian Friedrich Meinecke, who believed that middle-aged, established engineers were lured into support of the Nazis by the radical and emotional content of Nazi ideology. Meinecke, who lived through the Nazi years, argued that the emotional needs of engineers and technicians were so frustrated by their education and professional life that they turned hungrily to emotion-laden ideology.[45]

Waldemar Hellmich, a director of the VDI before the Nazis seized power, offered, after the war, a persuasive explanation for the Nazis' success in organizing the engineers and professional societies for the fulfillment of their domestic and foreign objectives. His explanation reinforces the conclusion that Todt's ideology captured the engineers' mood and struck responsive chords. Writing in the first emaciated post-World War II and issue of the once vigorous and confident *VDI Zeitschrift*, the principle organ of the society, Hellmich referred to the "spiritual catastrophe" engineering experienced under the Nazis. He made reference to the engineers' eager acceptance of challenging technical projects like *Autobahns* and synthetic fuels, and their easy abandonment of the liberal values to which they had formerly professed allegiance. Hellmich insisted, for example, that before 1933 admission to and advancement in the VDI and the profession depended upon merit, not race or class.[46] This commitment was abandoned by the VDI after 1933 when it accepted the various racial laws affecting the professions.[47]

Assuming that public celebration and festive occasion oratory captured the prevailing mood of VDI engineers, one can conclude, in summary, that the engineers responded positively during the early months of revolutionary Nazism to the proposition that engineers should have more power in managing the economy. However, they drew back from this position when the Party purged its left wing, and eventually the engineers assumed their more traditional role of compliant problem-solvers as Germany embarked on intense rearmament and provided them with an abundance of technically exciting problems.

If this analysis has validity, then the most interesting aspect is the glimpse we catch of engineers revealing—if only briefly and tentatively—their belief that a fundamental problem of modern technological society is governance by the technically naïve. Many Germans, persuaded that the problems of modern Germany could be blamed on the Jews, were diverted from the problems by anti-Semitic ideology; the engineers, in contrast, were diverted from a fundamental twentieth-century issue, technocracy, by the pragmatic appeal to restrict themselves to their traditional role as problem-solvers.*

* For helpful suggestions about earler versions of this paper, I am indebted to Gerald Feldman, John Guse, Oron Hale, Karl-Heinz Ludwig, Kurt Mauel, Reginald Phelps, Reinhard Rürup, and Henry Ashby Turner. Edmund N. Todd of the University of Pennsylvania provided research assistance.

NOTES

1. Recently several historical articles and books that analyze engineers' organizing principles and programs for the well ordered society and, especially, the role of engineers in the governing of it, have appeared. These tend to focus on the technocratic movement. Among these works are Charles Maier, "Between Taylorism and Technocracy: European Ideologies and the Vision of Industrial Productivity in the 1920's," *The Journal of Contemporary History*, V (1970), 27–61; Kendall Bailes, *Technology and Society Under Lenin and Stalin: Origins of the Soviet Technical Intelligentsia, 1917–1941* (Princeton, N.J., 1978); Richard Kuisel, "Technocrats and Public Economic Policy: From the Third to the Fourth Republic," *The Journal of European Economic History*, II (1973), 53–99; Henry Elsner, Jr., *The Technocrats, Prophets of Automation* (Syracuse, N.Y., 1967); Edwin Layton, *The Revolt of the Engineers: Social Responsibility and the American Engineering Profession* (Cleveland, 1971); and William E. Akin, *Technocracy and the American Dream: The Technocrat Movement, 1900–1941* (Berkeley, 1977). A well-documented account of the engineering profession and the armament industry in Hitler's Germany with some attention to the ideology of German engineers is Karl-Heinz Ludwig, *Technik und Ingenieure im Dritten Reich* (Düsseldorf, 1974). Also informative about ideology is Gerd Hortleder, *Das Gesellschaftsbild des Ingenieurs: Zum politischen*

Verhalten der technischen Intelligenz in Deutschland (Frankfurt/Main, 1970). Hortleder concentrates upon the history of the VDI (Verein deutscher Ingenieure); W.H.G. Armytage, *The Rise of the Technocrats: A Social History* (London, 1965) ranges widely over space and time, but overlooks the rise of technocracy in the Nazi movement. Trans. from the French, by Paul Barnes is Jean Meynaud, *Technocracy* (London, 1968).

2. The photograph shows the first annual meeting of the Verein Deutscher Ingenieure after the Nazis took power. *VDI Zeitschrift*, LXXVII (July 8, 1933), 725. In the 1935 photograph, Hess leads Alfred Rosenberg and Fritz Todt into the Breslau meeting hall. *VDI Zeitschrift*, LXXIX (July 6, 1935), 819.

3. George Lichtheim, *Europe in the Twentieth Century* (New York, 1972), p. 335. In his discussion of technocracy Lichtheim draws upon Jean William Lapierre, "Révolution et technocratie" in *Liberté et organisation dans le monde actuel* (Paris, 1969).

4. Edmund Todd, University of Pennsylvania, called my attention to the prominence of Hardensett in his (Todd's) unpublished 1978 paper, "German and American Technocracy: A Comparison."

5. Ludwig, *Technik und Ingenieure*, see especially pp. 35, 50, 56. Hortleder, *Gesellschaftsbild*, discusses the desire of engineers to take a greater role in politics and their anti-capitalist views before 1933, pp. 93–97.

6. Ludwig, *Technik und Ingenieure*, pp. 35–37.

7. Veblen in a chapter entitled "The Captains of Finance and the Engineers" (pp. 71–91), argues that the industrial systems of the twentieth century could not be managed in the best interests of society other than by engineers, inventors, chemists, mineralogists, production managers, soil experts, and other technical specialists. *The Engineers and the Price System* (New York, 1921). See also new edition with introduction by Daniel Bell (New York, 1963).

8. Oswald Spengler, *The Decline of the West* (New York, 1965), pp. 401, 412–14.

9. Ibid., p. 412.

10. Feder, *Der deutsche Staat auf nationaler und sozialer Grundlage: Neue Wege in Staat, Finanz und Wirtschaft* (Munich, 1923), p. 21. Feder's other publications include: *Die Juden* (Munich, 1933); *Kampf gegen die Hochfinanz* (Munich, 1933); *Finanz und Wirtschaft* (Munich, 1923); *Das Manifest zur Brechung der Zinsknechtschaft des Geldes* (1919). In English, see G. Feder, *Hitler's Official Program* (London, 1934). On Feder, see Arthur R. Herrmann, *Gottfried Feder, der Mann und sein Werk* (Leipzig, 1933), an uncritical sketch.

11. Feder, *Hitler's Official Program*, p. 85.

12. Directive *(Anordnung)* No. 1 from Party Organization Control *(Reichsleitung)* to ITA dated Munich, November 2, 1931 and Directive No. 4 dated October 22, 1932, on Microcopy T-580, Roll 52, National Archives, Washington, D.C., Captured German Documents Filmed at Berlin (AHA); and Alan Bullock, *Hitler: A Study in Tyranny* (New York, 1961), p. 110.

13. *International Military Tribunal: Trial of the Major War Criminals: Proceedings* (Nuremberg, 1948), XIII, 91. Funk's statement should be received with reservations, however, because, after 1930, in order to win business support, Hitler reduced Feder's influence as economic adviser. Arthur Schweitzer, *Big Business in the Third Reich* (Bloomington, 1964), p. 100. Alan Bullock, *Hitler*, p. 139.

14. On relationship of ITA and KDAI, see Ludwig, *Technik und Ingenieure*, pp. 91–94.

15. Feder, *Hitler's Official Program*, p. 66.

16. Bullock, *Hitler*, p. 139. Karl Dietrich Bracher, *The German Dictatorship* (New York, 1970), p. 330.

17. ITA directive of October 22, 1932 (see note 12) summarizes Feder's views. Bracher, *German Dictatorship*, p. 89, rightly stresses Feder's anti-Semitism and anti-capitalism, but wrongly labels Feder a reactionary opposed to modern economic development. This completely misses the thrust of Feder's technocratic ideas. On Feder's technocratic views see also Hermann Rauschning, *Men of Chaos* (New York, 1942), pp. 234–37.

18. For an account of behind the scenes events in the VDI in the spring of 1933 *(Vorstand* meeting of April 26–27, and the meeting of May 9), I have relied on A. F. Manning, "Der Verein Deutscher Ingenieure und der Nationalsozialismus," *Acta Historiae Neerlandica*, II (1967), 163–87. Manning had access to source materials in the VDI archive in Düsseldorf. Hereafter cited as Manning, *VDI*.

19. Manning, *VDI*, 171–72. The assertion that the leadership was a Jewish clique is curious. I have been unable to find a breakdown of VDI membership by religious affiliation, but historians with whom I have discussed the question are of the opinion that the number of Jews in the engineering profession in 1933 was small.

20. On the struggle for domination of several technical and engineering organizations by Feder, various other Nazi leaders, and factions, see Ludwig, *Technik und Ingenieure*, pp. 91–96, 111, 118–35.

21. Bracher, *German Dictatorship*, p. 89. In 1934 Feder became an economics professor at the Charlottenburg *Technische Hochschule*. He remained a professor there until his death in 1941. His field was land settlement and utilization, and urban planning.

22. *VDI Zeitschrift*, LXXVIII (June 23, 1934), 762.

23. K. Bailes, "The Politics of Technology: Stalin and Technocratic Thinking Among Soviet Engineers," *American Historical Review*, LXXIX (1974), 445–69.

24. Reference to an organic economy suggests the influence of the Swedish geopolitician Rudolf Kjellén (1864–1922) on Nazi ideology. Kjellén wrote that healthy states grow organically in order to maintain an economic coherence and integrity. Kjellén, *Der Staat als Lebensform*, quoted in A. Dorpalen, *The World of General Haushofer* (New York, 1942), pp. 243–44.

25. *VDI Zeitschrift* LXXIX (July 6, 1935), 823. I am indebted to Professor Henry Ashby Turner for identifying Pietzsch, whose first name was not given.

26. *VDI Zeitschrift* LXXIX (July 6, 1935), 825.

27. There are many accounts of the aborted "second revolution" and the Röhm purge, among them Bullock's in *Hitler*, pp. 238–67 and Bracher's in *German Dictatorship*, pp. 236–47. See also T. W. Mason, "Labor and the Third Reich 1933–1939," *Past and Present*, XXXIII (1966), 112.

28. Records of *Amt für Technik* are on Microcopy T-580, Roll 528, National Archives, Captured German Documents Filmed in Berlin (AHA).

29. *VDI Zeitschrift* LXXX (June 27, 1936), 805; LXXXII (June 11, 1938), 713; and Nazi press release of February 8, 1942 (Berlin) and press clippings on the occasion of Todt's death on Microfilm T-580, Roll 52, National Archives, Captured German Documents Filmed in Berlin (AHA).

30. *VDI Zeitschrift*, LXXXIII (June 10, 1939), 694.

31. Ibid.

32. Eduard Schönleben, *Fritz Todt: Der Mensch, der Ingenieur, der Nationalsozialist* (Oldenburg, 1943), p. 7.

33. Adolf Hitler, *Mein Kampf*, trans. Ralph Manheim (Cambridge, Mass., 1943), p. 423.

34. Ibid., p. 150.

35. Ibid., p. 290.

36. Ibid., p. 302.

37. I am indebted to Dr. Reginald Phelps for calling my attention to relevant passages in Hitler's basic speech on anti-Semitism (*Grundlegende Rede über den Anti-Semitismus*) given on August 13, 1920 in the Hofbraühausfestsaal in Munich.

38. *VDI Zeitschrift*, LXXXIII (June 10, 1939), 693.

39. Hitler, *Mein Kampf*, p. 446.

40. Ibid., p. 288.

41. Ibid., p. 295.

42. *VDI Zeitschrift*, LXXXIII (June 10, 1939), 694.

43. Schönleben, *Todt*, p. 13.

44. Ibid., p. 38–39.

45. Friedrich Meinecke, *The German Catastrophe: Reflections and Recollections* (Cambridge, Mass., 1950), p. 36.

46. Waldemar Hellmich, "Der geistige Aufbruch der deutschen Ingenieure," VDI Zeitschrift, LXXX (January 1, 1948), 2.

47. The *Vorstand* (executive committee) of the VDI in 1935 declared that the VDI accepted the racial principles of Nazism without exception and took these as preconditions for membership of German subjects in the VDI. *VDI Zeitschrift*, LXXIX (October 5, 1935), 1210.

CHRISTOPHER R. BROWNING

THE GOVERNMENT EXPERTS

The interpretation of the Final Solution as a bureaucratic and administrative process has not been seriously challenged since the appearance in 1961 of Raul Hilberg's classic work, *The Destruction of the European Jews*. The German civil service was a major component of what Hilberg termed "the machinery of destruction" and "infused" the other participants with "its sure-footed planning and bureaucratic thoroughness."[1] The fact that the civil service participated in the Final Solution is not in question; what does require further examination is the reason why this part of the German educated elite acted as it did.

The German civil service in the Third Reich was not a monolithic entity, for new government agencies proliferated and existing offices were coordinated and infiltrated by the Nazis with varying degrees of speed and thoroughness. Neither the police, who quickly accommodated themselves to the new police state, nor the new agencies, staffed primarily by men who were Nazis first and only subsequently became civil servants, will be the focus of this paper. Instead I will concentrate on the old ministries which, long before the Nazi seizure of power, had established traditions of independence from party politics, paternalistic responsibility for the German people, and loyalty to the German nation that transcended any particular government of the moment. I will focus in particular on two such ministries which became involved in the Nazi regime's anti-Jewish measures: the Ministry of the Interior and the Foreign Office.

Even the civil servants of the old ministries were not a homogeneous group. At least four elements of the ministerial bureaucracy are discernible below the rank of Cabinet ministers: first, the old guard, an older generation of officials in the upper-echelon positions whose civil service careers began in the Wilhelmian era; second, the young careerists, a later generation of officials in the lower-echelon positions who aspired to move up; third, the Party infiltrators, men who owed their positions to Nazi Party connections; and fourth, the obstructors, a small number of men who utilized their positions to block or mitigate certain measures of the Nazi regime. How, and why, these elements of the ministerial bureaucracy responded to the anti-Semitic impulses of the Nazi regime will be the focus of this paper.

In Hitler's initial Cabinet all the old ministries were headed by non-Nazis, with the exception of Wilhelm Frick of the Interior Ministry. Even when some of the early Cabinet members were edged out in favor of Nazi appointees, the old ministries were still not placed under the strongest Party leaders. Only Hjalmar Schacht, Reich Economics Minister from 1934 to 1937, made serious though ultimately unsuccessful attempts to protect his prerogatives of office. More typical were Frick of the Interior and Konstantin von Neurath of the Foreign Office, who were noted for their indolence. These men were not the practitioners of empire building in the Third Reich, but rather its victims. When Joachim von Ribbentrop replaced Neurath in 1938, he attempted through constant bickering and slavish loyalty to Hitler to defend his position, but he was politically so incompetent that the results scarcely differed from the Neurath regime. Under such ineffective leadership the old ministries, the traditional centers of power in the German government, were bypassed by the growing empires of men like Göring, Himmler, and Goebbels, and subsequently Borman and Speer. Thus the major impulses and initiatives in policy making usually came from the new power centers of the top Nazi leadership and from the Party radicals. The old ministries were cast primarily into a position of response.

Beneath the Cabinet ministers stood the state secretaries. Although they too were political appointees, they were usually non-political experts with a background in ministerial bureaucracy rather than in one of the parties. For them, the position of state secretary thus represented the pinnacle of a civil service career. Of a generation born in Bismarck's Germany, they had passed their formative years in the Wilhelmian era and experienced World War I as men who had already completed their education and begun their careers. Their roots were in another age. They were at home with the conservative authoritarianism and nationalism of Imperial Germany. Defeat, revolution, and the Weimar Republic made them long for a return to the seeming stability and glory of prewar

Germany. Any movement such as the Nazis, which promised to restore internal order and return Germany to the rank of a great power, could not be all wrong in their eyes, no matter how disdainfully they viewed the social origins of the bulk of its adherents. Any group such as the Jews, which could easily be identified with what they perceived to be the major ills of the age—liberalism and Marxism, internationalism and cosmopolitanism, financial speculation and economic disorder—would receive little sympathy from them. Let us examine more closely the roles of two such state secretaries, Hans Pfundtner of the Interior Ministry and Bernhard Wilhelm von Bülow of the Foreign Office.

Hans Pfundtner was typical of the anti-Republican old right in the Weimar Republic. Born in 1881, he was a former official of the Finance Ministry, a frequent contributor to the right-wing press, a confidant of Alfred Hugenberg of the archconservative German National People's Party (DNVP), and deputy president of the National Club—a society of former officials and officers nostalgic for the monarchical era. He distinguished himself from his right-wing colleagues only by virtue of the early date at which he threw in his lot with the Nazis. In March 1932 he resigned from the DNVP, joined the NSDAP, and put himself at the disposal of various Nazi leaders. He boasted of his intimate knowledge of the personnel of the ministerial bureaucracy and proposed plans for the removal of political appointees and leftists as well as for the recruitment of National Socialists to restore a nationally minded officialdom. Pfundtner's plan for a thorough purge of the civil service was only one among many that surfaced in this period, but it was noteworthy in one regard. Despite the pervasive anti-Semitism that afflicted the German right wing in this period, Pfundtner's plan made no explicit mention of Jews as one group to be purged. Like his former mentor Hugenberg, he was more ultra-nationalist and ultra-conservative than anti-Semitic.[2]

The Nazi assumption of power brought Pfundtner the position of state secretary of the Interior Ministry, which had jurisdiction over matters relating to the constitutional guarantees of the vested rights of public officials. In the face of the Nazi onslaught against local government and the growing intervention of Party members against political opponents and Jews in the judicial system, which threatened to spread to other branches of the government as well, Minister of the Interior Frick felt a certain urgency to regularize the disorderly and often violent purging of civil servants. When Vice-Chancellor Franz von Papen put forward the rough draft of a measure, drawn up by the Prussian Finance Minister Johannes Popitz, to govern the dismissal of civil servants, Frick stepped in and took over the legislation. As in the case of Pfundtner's proposal of the previous summer, neither the Popitz draft nor an initial draft produced in the Interior Ministry by Pfundtner's subordinate, Hans Seel, contained any explicit reference to purging officials of Jewish origin.[3] They merely provided for the restoration of the pre-Weimar civil service by permitting the retirement of officials through a temporary suspension of their legal rights. With the crescendo of anti-Semitic propaganda in the last days of March, proclaiming the upcoming boycott of Jewish businesses, the Interior Ministry added provisions to the law explicitly purging officials both of non-Aryan descent and of dubious political reliability. Though the so-called *Arierparagraph* (Aryan Clause) had not been part of his own earlier proposal, Pfundtner subsequently endorsed it as the "most significant" provision of the new Law for the Restoration of the Civil Service.[4]

This law was a double-edged weapon against the German Jews. On the one hand, this first major piece of anti-Jewish legislation excluded Jews from the civil service and provided the model for further measures restricting their participation in other occupations and activities. On the other hand, by providing for the dismissal of officials whose activity "did not offer the guarantee" of loyalty to the new regime, the law intimidated officials, who might otherwise have been hesitant, into displaying enthusiasm for National Socialist goals, one of which was a solution to the Jewish question. Pfundtner mistakenly saw the Nazi movement as a means for reconstituting a civil service free from the influence of political parties. Instead he facilitated legislation laying the foundation for a pliable civil service that would later be manipulated by the Nazis. Early measures such as the "Aryan Clause" were still agreeable to Pfundtner and the old right, but they would later be unable to block more radical measures. Though Pfundtner clung to his post as state secretary until 1943, the Third Reich had long since passed him by.

Unlike Pfundtner, State Secretary Bernhard Wilhelm von Bülow (born in 1885) of the Foreign Office did not welcome Hitler's assumption of power. He was a determined advocate of the revision of the Versailles Treaty and had willingly exploited the rising tide of German ultra-nationalism in 1932 to extract diplomatic concessions from the worried leaders of foreign countries. After January 1933, however, he feared that Hitler's aggressive foreign policy might provoke a preventive war. Though he contemplated resignation, Bülow decided to remain at his post, hoping both to moderate the more dangerous aspects of Hitler's foreign policy and to neutralize growing anti-German feeling by defending the new regime abroad.[5]

Bülow's decision to serve and defend the Nazi regime was based primarily on considerations of foreign policy, but his own inclinations concerning domestic politics did not inhibit him in this regard. An advocate of a corporate, elitist form of government during the 1919 constitutional discussions, Bülow never developed sympathy or understanding for parliamentary government. He was typical of many high officials in the civil service who felt that vital decisions should not be made through a process of give and take between political parties and interest groups, but rather by specialists like himself, devoted solely to the well-being of the state. To foreigners he defended the Nazis' so-called "coordination" process as mere "constitutional reforms" fulfilling the Bismarckian ideal. He belittled the accompanying acts of terror as the understandable discharge of political tensions; over-all, he asserted, the revolution had been carried out entirely through constitutional means. Clearly, the passing of the Weimar Republic and the internal politics of the Nazis did not alarm Bülow in the same way as did Hitler's foreign policy.

Bülow's reaction to Nazi Jewish policy paralleled his over-all reaction to internal developments. He defended this policy not only because he was alarmed by the degree to which Nazi treatment of the Jews contributed to anti-German feeling abroad, but also because he was as unsympathetic to Jews as he was to parliamentary government. His decision to enlist the Foreign Office in defense of Nazi Jewish policy was outlined in a confidential, handwritten letter to his cousin, Vicco von Bülow-Schwante, in late March, before either the boycott or the initial wave of anti-Jewish legislation took place. It is worth quoting at length.

> For the directors and myself, eventually also for the missions [abroad], it would be good as support for conversations with diplomats and foreigners to assemble some material that elucidates the causes of the anti-Semitic movement in Germany. . . . I have always pointed out to diplomats the strong influx of Eastern Jews, as well as their naturalization in mass by the Socialist Prussian government. Numbers pertaining to it must be available. Furthermore, I have stated that, for example, the entire city administration and city hospital [staffs] were swamped with Jews. I believe that that is correct and can also be proved. Furthermore, perhaps a strong percentage of Jews in the Communist caucus of the last Reichstag can be discovered. Certainly there are also blatant examples for the advancement of Jews in law, universities, schools, etc., since 1918.[6]

What emerges from this letter clearly is not only a desire to defuse anti-German feeling abroad, but also the view, shared by many of Bülow's generation in the civil service, that the Jews were an alien group associated with the Socialists and Communists, who in the postwar period had grasped an inordinately influential position in German society. On Bülow's initiative the Foreign Office became the apologist for Nazi Jewish policy.

Under the impact of the foreign boycott of German exports and a barrage of foreign criticism, Bülow and his colleagues in the Foreign Office gradually accepted the Nazi premise that the Jews of the world were Germany's enemies.[7] Any retreat or amelioration in Jewish policy, even any negotiation on the subject, was out of the question. It would indicate a vulnerability to foreign pressure and a weakness of will that would diminish German prestige. Nazi Jewish policy had only to be wrapped in the flag of German patriotism to assure its vigorous defense by the professional diplomats.[8]

The state secretaries and their generation of civil servants were not motivated so much by anti-Semitism as by their desire for a nationalist revival of Germany, conceived primarily in terms of their nostalgic memories of the Imperial era. They were too easily fooled by the charade of Hitler's "national revolution." Even if anti-Semitism was not the driving force behind their actions, they were still not entirely free of this affliction. The Jew was viewed not as an element of society who could trace his German roots back one thousand years, but as an alien from Eastern Europe with left-wing political sympathies who had exploited German weakness after World War I to infiltrate and dominate German life. The Jew was associated with those trends in German life that had to be reversed if a nationalist revival was to take place. The initial anti-Jewish measures of the Nazi regime were viewed as part of this "restoration" process. Even those state secretaries with serious reservations about other aspects of the Nazi movement, like Bülow, sympathized with and defended these measures, provided they were carried out in an orderly manner through the administrative machinery of the state and not in the form of violent "excesses" of Party radicals.

The state secretaries did not initiate the anti-Jewish campaign of the Nazi regime, but they did approve, and in some cases initiate, the participation of their ministries in this campaign. They helped set the bureaucratic machine in motion. On their own the state secretaries would not have proceeded beyond the legislative phase. They may have desired the extirpation of Jewish participation in German life, but not the physical extermination of the Jews themselves. When Nazi Jewish policy went beyond what the state secretaries and the older generation of civil servants desired, they were already morally too compromised to offer any effective opposition, and the ministries whose work they were supposed to supervise

continued to participate. But the driving impulse for continued participation came from elsewhere, not from the old guard. Other factors must be
taken into account to understand the dynamics of this continued civil
service participation.

One of these factors was the establishment and proliferation of the so-
called Jewish experts. Within months of the Nazi assumption of power
almost every branch and agency of the German government had appointed
lower-echelon civil servants to handle all matters related to Jewish policy
that impinged on their jurisdictions. The establishment of a ministry
"Jewish desk" was often a nonchalant and haphazard response to the press
of business. Inquiries poured in concerning how recent Jewish legislation
would affect each ministry's activities, and someone had to be selected to
handle the paperwork. In the Interior Ministry the thirty-two-year-old
Regierungsrat Bernhard Lösener, a Party member since 1931, had been
assigned to citizenship questions. Pfundtner asked him to answer a pile of
letters containing both proposals for and protests against Jewish legislation,
and a *Judenreferat* was born.[9] In the Foreign Office Bülow asked his cousin,
Vicco von Bülow-Schwante, to collect materials to defend German Jewish
policy abroad, and the latter's bureau henceforth handled Jewish affairs at
the Wilhelmstrasse.

However spontaneous its creation, the Jewish desk soon became an
institution. No ministry affected by Nazi Jewish policy could afford to be
without experts to advise it about the impact of Jewish legislation emanating
from other sources, to participate in various inter-ministerial conferences to
defend the ministry's point of view, and of course to prepare the ministry's
own measures. The existence of this corps of Jewish experts explains in part
the bureaucratic momentum behind German Jewish policy. These professional Jewish experts occupied themselves by devising increasingly intensified anti-Jewish measures. Decrees in 1942 prohibiting German Jews
from having pets, getting their hair cut by Aryan barbers, or receiving the
Reich sports badge[10] appear utterly senseless in view of the extermination
process that was taking place at that time, but are further evidence of the
inexorable bureaucratic momentum that had built up. Jewish experts
continued devising anti-Jewish measures even as the objects of their
persecution vanished in the death camps in the East. It did not require
orders from above, merely the existence of the job itself, to insure that the
Jewish experts would keep up the flow of discriminatory measures.

We know all too little about this shadowy collection of young officials
who staffed the Jewish desks of the German bureaucracy. None, unless one
includes Adolf Eichmann, became well-known, and many kept such a low

profile that they easily re-entered the postwar civil service of the Federal Republic. One group of which something is known is the staff of the Foreign Office Jewish desk from 1940 to 1943.[11]

This Jewish desk, known as D III, was headed by one of the authors of the Madagascar Plan, Franz Rademacher. He had in succession three assistants: Herbert Müller, Karl Klingenfuss, and Fritz Gebhardt von Hahn. These four men had much in common. They were all born in the decade between 1901 and 1911. Too young to have fought in World War I, they spent their formative years in the postwar period of political and economic turmoil. Unlike the older generation of civil servants, these men longed for security in a troubled Germany, not the restoration of an unknown past. They were all university graduates specializing in law and intent on a career in the civil service. They all opportunistically joined the NSDAP between March and May 1933, as part of the wave of "bandwagon" Nazis that deluged the Party as soon as it came to power. None became a member of the SS. None actively sought assignment to the Jewish desk. None had a reputation for radical anti-Semitism or expertise on the Jewish question before being assigned to D III. They were four unremarkable, career-minded bureaucrats.

As products of an increasingly right-wing and anti-Semitic university system, and anxious to conform to the standards of both bureaucracy and Party, they were unlikely candidates to oppose anti-Semitic measures exalted by Party ideology and defended by the state secretaries. However, once at the Jewish desk, their reactions differed. While Rademacher and Hahn enthusiastically devoted themselves to the task at hand and took pride in their new-found importance as Jewish experts, Müller and Klingenfuss found the work distasteful and sought reassignment. Both were successful in eventually getting out of D III, but while they were there they performed their duties meticulously. They did not openly object to the job but worked covertly and quietly for their transfers; keeping their records clean was their top priority. Whether zealously or reluctantly, the fact remains that all four worked efficiently. The bureaucratic machine set in motion with the approval of the state secretaries was not going to be stopped by young civil servants concerned primarily with their own personal advancement. On the contrary, they kept the machine moving, and the most ambitious and unscrupulous among them gave it an additional push.

The reliable Jewish experts were prepared to carry out their duties regardless of their personal feelings, but they did not make the major decisions that brought their ministries to the point of participating in an extermination program. They could initiate minor measures implementing existing policy; they could not initiate new policy. As the enthusiasm of the state secretaries slackened and their influence declined, such initiatives had to come from elsewhere. In addition to the state secretaries and the Jewish experts, we now encounter a third element within the ministerial bureaucracy: the Party infiltrators. In contrast to the Nazified civil servants, these men were Party faithfuls before the Nazi seizure of power. They utilized their Party connections to enter the ministerial bureaucracy, and the most dynamic among them received rapid promotion. These men became the political hatchet men and infighters of the bureaucracy; they performed an indispensable function for their ministries in the jungle politics of the Third Reich.

The Party infiltrators led a schizophrenic existence. As Party zealots they were committed to harnessing their ministries to the achievement of Nazi goals. They viewed the conservative-nationalist bureaucracy as insufficiently Nazified and constantly sought to goad it into more radical action. But to preserve their own power bases, they also had to defend the ministries against the constant encroachment and empire building of Himmler, Göring, Bormann, and others. They were viewed by the career civil servants as Party fanatics, and by the Party radicals as defenders of a stodgy, conservative ministerial bureaucracy. The only way to walk this political tightrope was to insure that the ministries played their part in even the most radical of Party policies, including genocide.

Two such Party infiltrators were Wilhelm Stuckart of the Interior Ministry and Martin Luther of the Foreign Office. Stuckart first joined the Party in 1922 at the age of twenty. After a brief and unsuccessful stint in the civil service prior to 1933, Stuckart enjoyed considerable success as state commissioner of Stettin, undersecretary in the Reich Ministry of Science and Education, and finally as the top-ranking department head in the Interior Ministry in 1935. Though subordinate to Pfundtner, he also enjoyed the title of state secretary.[12] In contrast to the weak Frick and the increasingly passive Pfundtner, whose timely conversion to National Socialism had not earned him much respect in the Party, Stuckart was energetic, able, and equipped with solid Party credentials. The ambitious Stuckart soon eclipsed both his superiors and "became the real Minister of the Interior."[13] Though he sought to defend his Ministry's jurisdiction against Party interference, he did join the SS in 1936 and was viewed by Himmler as his contact man in the Interior Ministry.[14] When Himmler took it over in 1943, Stuckart replaced Pfundtner as state secretary.

Though Stuckart felt in 1938 that the mass of racial legislation, to which his Ministry had made no small contribution, was "essentially complete" and comprised a "preliminary solution" to the Jewish question,[15] he was astute enough to continue to move with the times. On several occasions, in fact, he even went beyond what was ultimately decided upon, as when he proposed stripping the German Jews of their citizenship before deportation and making divorce compulsory for mixed marriages.[16] Eichmann recalled that at the Wannsee Conference, "Stuckart had evinced boundless enthusiasm."[17] Indeed Stuckart was a man very concerned with keeping abreast of things. When his Jewish expert, Bernhard Lösener, confronted him with accounts of the massacre of deported German Jews in Riga, Stuckart reproached him for not being "dynamic enough." Lösener, he complained, "had adhered rigidly to the solution of 1935 and had not realized that meanwhile life had gone on."[18] Only in the treatment of half-Jews did Stuckart drag his feet, supporting Lösener in the latter's attempt to preserve a legal category of so-called *Mischlinge* and prevent their deportation and extermination. He was ultimately successful, as Hitler never overruled the Interior Ministry in this regard. For Stuckart, however, such hesitance was the exception, not the rule.

Martin Luther was a prosperous small businessman, and a Party member from 1932, who utilized his intimate connections with the Ribbentrop family to attain a Foreign Office appointment in the fall of 1938.[19] A master of political intrigue and bureaucratic imperialism, Luther reached the rank of undersecretary by 1941 and headed the Foreign Office division for internal affairs known as *Abteilung Deutschland*. The old guard at the Wilhelmstrasse regarded Luther's division as a cancer growing inexorably in its midst, while Ribbentrop's Nazi rivals viewed the contentious undersecretary as an all too zealous defender of Foreign Office interests. That Luther more than held his own against his enemies both inside and outside the Foreign Office is testimony to his driving ambition, unscrupulous methods, and political instinct. However, in February 1943 he overplayed his hand. Impatient with Ribbentrop's incompetence, he attempted to oust his former patron. The intrigue misfired, and Luther passed the remaining years of the Third Reich in the concentration camp Sachsenhausen.

Before his abrupt fall Luther played the key role in arranging for Foreign Office participation in the Final Solution. Until 1941 Luther had shown little interest in the Jewish question, including the Madagascar Plan concocted by his subordinate Rademacher. But Luther was a man with his hand on the political pulse of the Third Reich. Once the *Einsatzgruppen* operations began in Russia, he quickly sensed that a program was underway from which it was politically inexpedient for the Foreign Office to stand aloof. If Jews were being massacred in Russia, where Rosenberg's *Ostministerium* jealousy excluded Ribbentrop's Foreign Office, Luther would see to it that the Foreign Office helped out in Serbia. In cooperation with Himmler's deputy Heydrich, he sent Rademacher to Belgrade to help pave the way for the local extermination of the Serbian Jews.[20] If the Jews were to be deported from other European countries to death camps in Poland, Luther did not want the Foreign Office role in these countries undermined. As the Foreign Office representative at the Wannsee Conference, he arranged with Heydrich for the Foreign Office and SS Jewish experts to confer on all deportations from non-German territory.[21] Both in the Serbian affair and at the Wannsee Conference, Luther was acting on his own initiative, not under instructions from his superiors, Foreign Minister Ribbentrop and state secretary Ernst von Weizsäcker. Like Stuckart in the Interior Ministry, Luther insured that the Foreign Office kept abreast of political developments in the Third Reich despite its incompetent Minister and undynamic state secretary.

There was a fourth and unfortunately very small element within the ministerial bureaucracy that should not be neglected—those who really did use their positions to prevent worse. There was scarcely a civil servant who did not make this claim in postwar de-Nazification hearings; but a quick look at the actions of a few courageous individuals reveals how counterfeit were the claims of the vast majority. The well-known case of Bernhard Lösener of the Interior Ministry has already been alluded to. Though a member of the Nazi Party since 1931, he waged a long and successful struggle to prevent the legal equalization of half-Jews with full Jews, which ultimately saved the former from deportation and death. He was able to persuade Stuckart to share his views on the so-called *Mischlinge* question in 1935, and despite a growing estrangement between the two, as Stuckart strove to keep in step with the evolution of Nazi Jewish policy, the state secretary continued to utilize Lösener's arguments in defense of half-Jews. Upon learning of the first massacres of German Jews at Riga, Lösener openly protested to Stuckart and demanded to be released from his position.[22]

Less well known is the case of Wilhelm Melchers of the Foreign Office Middle East desk.[23] In late 1942 the Foreign Office demanded that European countries with Jews living on German occupied territory had either to recall them or permit their deportation to the East. When confronted with this ultimatum, the Turkish government announced that all Jews of Turkish citizenship who had lived abroad for more than five years were denaturalized. The Turkish consul in Paris submitted a list of 631 Jews there, whose return the Turkish government valued. This left in Paris alone over twenty-four hundred Turkish Jews unprotected. Neither the Turkish ambassador in Berlin nor the government in Ankara expressed interest in the unlisted Jews but would not meet the German request for written confirmation of disinterest. Both the Foreign Office Jewish expert and the local SS-agents in Paris pressed for internment and deportation of the unprotected Turkish Jews, and this proposal eventually crossed the Middle East desk of Wilhelm Melchers.

Melchers' counterparts in the Foreign Office routinely initialed such requests for Foreign Office approval of deportations, but Melchers did not. He had earlier saved Palestinian Jews in German hands by raising the specter of reprisals against German colonists in Palestine. He now intervened for the Turkish Jews who had been abandoned by their own government. In a cogent memorandum he argued that the presence of twenty-four hundred Turkish Jews in France posed no significant security risk, but their deportation would be exploited by enemy propaganda to raise a storm of indignation in the Turkish press. Even though Turkish diplomatic representatives had shown no interest in these Jews, Germany had to be especially cautious to avoid any incident that could bring difficulties with Turkey. In short, he concluded, the disadvantage of twenty-four hundred Jews remaining on German occupied territory was less than the political disadvantage that would arise from their deportation. His superior refused to endorse these views but, afraid of being proved wrong by events, recommended waiting until the situation became clearer.

In the summer of 1943 the Foreign Office Jewish expert and Paris SS-men again urged deportation, but Melchers successfully reiterated his opposition to taking any action that might burden German-Turkish relations. In September 1943 the Turkish government finally permitted the return of all Turkish Jews who so desired. Singlehandedly Wilhelm Melchers had thwarted the SS and Foreign Office Jewish experts, buying time until the Turkish government at last regained its conscience. Such incidents demonstrate that even in the civil service of Nazi Germany, individuals with courage and ingenuity could act to save thousands of lives. Unfortunately, such obstruction was offered by a mere handful, while the vast majority of their colleagues passively or actively abetted the Final Solution.

What tentative conclusions does this small number of examples from two German ministries suggest about the nature of civil service participation in Nazi Jewish policy? Even before the Nazis came to power, the civil service and the social groups from which it was recruited were strongly afflicted by authoritarian and anti-Semitic inclinations, and the Nazi seizure of power intensified both of these characteristics. Yet bureaucratic behavior cannot be understood simply by the standard alibi of obedience to authority or the common accusation of pervasive anti-Semitism. The various elements of the bureaucracy were also affected by their political perceptions, misconceptions, and ambitions.

The upper echelons of the bureaucracy, typified by the state secretaries, were a generation with roots in Imperial Germany. Their longing for a return to the old order made them easy dupes for Hitler's "national revolution," which was couched in the slogans and symbols of restoration. The Jews were not the focal point of their concern, but they were a symbol of all that had gone wrong in Germany—foreign domination, modernistic cultural experimentation, left-wing politics, and the eclipse of the traditional ruling elites by the commercial and professional middle classes. Sympathetic to authoritarian government and insensitive to human rights, the old guard used the bureaucracy to formulate and defend discriminatory legislation as the proper and orderly way to restrict Jewish participation in German life. They wished to discriminate, not exterminate, but once in motion the bureaucratic machine escaped their control, driven onward by the lower-echelon Jewish experts and Party infiltrators. The old guard, hopelessly compromised by its earlier complicity, stood by passively.

The Jewish experts belonged to a generation shaped by the turmoil that gripped postwar Germany. Anxious to conform to the canons of behavior set by university, bureaucracy, and Party, and assaulted by anti-Semitism from all sides, their moral sensitivities were undoubtedly dulled. However, these men were not primarily anti-Semitic crusaders but rather opportunistic careerists seeking security and personal advancement in a world of continual upheaval. Randomly chosen to handle Jewish affairs, some enthusiastically grasped the opportunity. Others sought transfer to a less distasteful task but in the meantime performed their duties all too well. Only a few used their positions to slow the machinery of destruction.

Though the state secretaries created the ministerial Jewish desks, the Jewish experts increasingly received their guidance and inspiration from another source. As events outran the naïve hopes of the disillusioned old guard, it became increasingly passive and ineffectual. Leadership in the bureaucracy passed to Party infiltrators, dynamic and ambitious men who had fought their way into influential positions. Although committed Party men, they nevertheless sought to preserve their own power by defending their ministries against Party encroachment. This was best done by insuring that the ministries stayed abreast of political developments and fully participated in what they perceived to be the essential programs of the Third Reich, which inevitably included the Final Solution.

The German civil service therefore took its initial steps in the destruction process with the approval of the state secretaries in the old guard, received its impetus to the fatal extreme from the Party infiltrators, and was reliably served by the young careerists. The various components of the German civil service—old guard, young careerists, and Party infiltrators—were not free of anti-Semitism and the ingrained habit of obedience to authority. But their actions were also influenced to a significant extent by their naïve delusions, political calculations, and personal ambitions.

NOTES

1. Raul Hilberg, *The Destruction of the European Jews* (Chicago, 1961), p. 39.
2. On Pfundtner, see Gerhard Schulz, "Der 'Nationale Klub von 1919' zu Berlin," in *Das Zeitalter der Gesellschaft* (Munich, 1969), pp. 308–16; and "Die Anfänge des totalitären Massnahmenstaates," in Karl Dietrich Bracher, Wolfgang Sauer, Gerhard Schulz, *Die nationalsozialistische Machtergreifung: Studien zur Errichtung des totalitären Herrschaftssystems in Deutschland 1933–34* (Cologne and Opladen, 1960), pp. 409–11. For a copy of Pfundtner's proposal, see Hans Mommsen, *Beamtentum im Dritten Reich* (Stuttgart, 1966), pp. 127–35. On anti-Semitism and the German Right, see George Mosse, "Die deutsche Rechte und die Juden," in Werner Mosse, ed., *Entscheidungsjahr 1932: Zur Endphase der Weimarer Republik* (Tübingen, 1965), pp. 183–246.
3. Mommsen, *Beamtentum im Dritten Reich*, pp. 40–44; Schulz, "Die Anfänge des totalitären Massnahmenstaates," pp. 495–6.
4. Uwe Dietrich Adam, *Judenpolitik im Dritten Reich* (Düsseldorf, 1972), pp. 61–62.
5. Peter Krüger and Erick J. C. Hahn, "Der Loyalitätskonflikt des Staatssekretärs Bernhard Wilhelm von Bülow im Frühjahr 1933," *Vierteljahrshefte für Zeitgeschichte*, XX (1972), 376–410.
6. Politisches Archiv des Auswärtigen Amtes, Bonn (hereafter cited as PA/AA), Referat Deutschland 42/4, Bülow to Bülow-Schwante, March 23, 1933. Microfilm: T 120/8787/E 612176–7.
7. Eliahu Ben Elissar, *La diplomatie du IIIe Reich et les juifs 1933–1939* (Paris, 1969), p. 139.
8. For various examples, both before and after Bülow's death in 1936, see Christopher R. Browning, "Referat Deutschland, Jewish Policy, and the German Foreign Office, 1933–1940," *Yad Vashem Studies*, XII (1977), 37–73.
9. Bernhard Lösener, "Als Rassenreferent im Reichsministerium des Innern," *Vierteljahrshefte für Zeitgeschichte*, IX (1961), 266.
10. Adam, *Judenpolitik im Dritten Reich*, pp. 339–40.
11. Christopher R. Browning, *The Final Solution and the German Foreign Office: A Study of Referat D III of Abteilung Deutschland 1940–1943* (New York, 1978), pp. 23–34.
12. *Trials of the War Criminals before the Nuremberg Military Tribunals*, 15 vols. (Washington, 1949–53), XIV, 631–2.
13. NG-1944A (Lösener affidavit); unpublished transcript of the "Trials of the War Criminals before the Nuremberg Military Tribunals," Case XI (hereafter cited as TWC, Case XI),

15634–5 (Globke testimony). Both the complete unpublished transcript and the Nuremburg documents cited here are available in the National Archives, the Nuremburg Staatsarchiv, and in some major libraries such as the Law Library of the University of Washington in Seattle.

14. TWC, Case XI, 15636–8 (Globke testimony).
15. *Trials of the War Criminals*, XIV, p. 646.
16. Adam, *Judenpolitik im Dritten Reich*, pp. 295, 323.
17. Raul Hilberg *Documents of Destruction* (Chicago, 1971), p. 101.
18. NG–1944A (Lösener affidavit).
19. On Luther's career, see Christopher R. Browning, "Unterstaatssekretär Martin Luther and the Ribbentrop Foreign Office," *Journal of Contemporary History*, XII (April 1977), 313–44.
20. PA/AA, Inland II g 194; or NG 3354.
21. Hilberg, *Documents of Destruction*, p. 95.
22. Lösener, in *Vierteljahrshefte für Zeitgeschichte*, IX (1961), 264–313; NG–1944A.
23. PA/AA, Inland II A/B 70/3.

JOHN S. CONWAY

THE CHURCHES

In 1927 Otto Dibelius, one of the younger leaders of the Prussian Evangelical Church, published *Das Jahrhundert der Kirche* (The Century of the Church), a book that proved to be a highly popular call for a new beginning in the relations between the Church and the German people.[1] In contrast to the highly conservative older generation of Protestants, who identified the fortunes of the Evangelical Church with the nationalist Empire forged by Bismarck, Dibelius called for a new commitment to a *Volkskirche* (People's Church) which would accept its obligations to promote social reform and be open to new opportunities to serve the whole population. Instead of seeking a restoration of the "good old days" under Kaiser Wilhelm, Dibelius believed that the Church should now look forward to a new era of service to the nation and play a positive role in fostering a social and cultural program touching all areas of life, in a combined effort to counteract the progressive secularization of German society.

In order to understand the readiness with which large segments of the German churches, especially the Evangelical Church, responded to the rise of Nazism, this desire for popular and relevant involvement should be remembered. The Churches, more than other branches of the German *Obrigkeitsstaat*, were aware that their position in society could no longer be defended merely by an appeal to tradition. The loss of faith that was so clearly marked after the disaster of World War I required a vigorous and vibrant social engagement to counteract the danger of atomistic libertarianism and mass materialism. The emergence of the Weimar Republic after the throes of revolution was widely regarded with aversion. Despite the fact that the new constitution gave the churches much greater autonomy over their own affairs, many churchmen called the new republic "religionless," and believed that it would create an immoral state incapable or unwilling to appreciate the public role of religion.[2]

Prominent theologians, such as Reinhold Seeberg, persuasively argued in favor of the maintenance of organically structured *Gemeinschaften* (communities). "Imbued with love of neighbor, the Christian seeks in each *Gemeinschaft* to follow divinely ordained immanent laws designed to check the egoism of natural man."[3] The leading Protestant theologian of Erlangen University in Bavaria was Paul Althaus, whose writings strove to rehabilitate Luther's orders of creation—specifically the family, economic life, political institutions, and, in a broader sense, *das Volk*. It was a part of the larger plan to preserve an essentially Christian society in the absence of a Christian state. But the emphasis on the need for unity, continuity, and nationalistically conditioned conservatism was inimical to the idea of the growth of alternatives. Indeed, strong opposition was raised against the idea of pluralism in society, which was presumed to lead to a false sense of freedom and to encourage immorality. Like other prominent figures in society, the ecclesiastics were wholly convinced of the danger of Bolshevism, which threatened both the institutional and spiritual heritage of German Christianity. Consequently the appeal of a political movement which combined nationalistic devotion to *das Volk*, a popularly relevant social activism, and a strong aversion to Bolshevism achieved rapid growth among wide sections of the Evangelical Churches.

The position of the Roman Catholic Church was no less ambiguous. Its leaders had all grown up during the period of disparagement and oppression of the *Kulturkampf*, Bismarck's attempt to throttle the Roman Catholic Church in the newly formed German Empire. This left a long-lasting impression that Roman Catholics were second-class citizens in Imperial Germany, which was compensated by the attempt to prove themselves loyal—even 200 percent Germans—during the war. The freedoms granted by the Weimar Republic were not enough to remove the sense of discrimination, and led to efforts to secure a legal position through concordats with individual provinces, and at last successfully with the Reich government in 1933. The rise of Nazism in the heart of Catholic Bavaria posed vital questions to the Catholic hierarchy. The Catholic leaders were quick to realize that the racial propaganda of the Nazis was contradictory to Christian principles, and this led to outright prohibitions in various dioceses. But the fear that such a popular movement could result in widespread defections from the Catholic ranks, or to a possible conflation between the Nazi Party and the Evangelical Church, led to the weakening of this opposition. The ban on Catholic membership in the Nazi Party was lifted on March 28, 1933, following Hitler's highly conservative speech in connection with the passing of the Enabling Act. Immediately afterward, the negotiations for a Reich Concordat were quickly completed, apparently granting the Catholic hierarchy the safeguards they had long sought from the Republican governments. Like their Protestant counterparts, the Catholic leaders had no sympathy for a pluralistic society. They looked with favor on a movement that promised national renewal and restoration, and readily indulged in the wishful thinking that the more radical and revolutionary elements of the Nazi creed would be jettisoned once the accession to power brought with it an acceptance of responsibility.

The susceptibility of these church elites to the appeal of a nationalistically oriented authoritarianism was strengthened only to the extent that these attitudes were shared with virtually all their secular counterparts. The fear of revolutionary developments sweeping away the familiar institutions of German society was a uniting factor that ruled out any serious opposition to the Nazi seizure of power from the German elites. Especially the Evangelical Churches had felt profoundly unhappy with their position in the post-1919 state, with its ambiguous world values and its party political allegiances. Although some of the more forward-looking churchmen had recognized the futility of maintaining a stance in favor of a restoration of the monarchy, only a handful were more enthusiastic about the new freedom to experiment which the churches possessed. The vast majority of churchmen were at best *Vernunftrepublikaner* (reluctant republicans); in this they were not alone.

It must be remembered that Hitler deliberately maneuvered for the support of these conservative-minded elites. He consciously claimed to be a friend of the Christian churches, and openly broke with Ludendorff, when the General proposed to form a semi-pagan, semi-mystical Germanic sect. "I need," said Hitler, "Bavarian Catholics as well as Prussian Protestants to build up a great political movement. The rest comes later."[4] Hitler's open disavowal of wanting to be a religious reformer, his playing down such ideologues as Alfred Rosenberg, and his highly conservative statements in the early months of 1933, all contributed to the belief that the churches would be restored to their former positions as guardians of the moral health of German society. Especially at a time when increasing doubt was being cast on the validity of the churches' theological doctrines, there was an undisguised need to reinforce their cultural and social relevance in what seemed to many a unique opportunity for new missionary activities, to recoup the losses of previous decades.

It is undeniable that there was a considerable amount of wishful thinking in such a position. The readiness with which the churches approved the new Nazi regime, thus giving its activities their moral support, made it all the more difficult afterwards to admit that they had been mistaken. None of the churches—with the possible exception of one or two minor sects—were theologically or sociologically prepared to become prophetic or protesting bodies. Even in subsequent years, when the reality of Nazi policy became more apparent, the conflict between the desire to remain an integral part of the state apparatus and the desire to remain true to the Gospel's calling involved severe crises of conscience. Pastor Niemöller, for example, remained a staunch nationalist throughout. The German Catholic bishops never taught their flocks to believe that the regime was one which had to be disobeyed for conscience's sake. The majority continued to hold to the idea that their national and theological loyalties could be reconciled. The excesses of the Nazis were regarded as incidental, or at worst inimical to the true form of German patriotism which the churches still considered their duty to uphold. Even the outbreak of war in 1939, with its foreboding of a still greater catastrophe, did not provoke a large-scale reappraisal. However, it is possible that a number shared the agonizing dilemma so aptly expressed by Dietrich Bonhoeffer in July 1939:

> Christians in Germany will face the terrible alternative of either willing the defeat of their nation in order that Christian civilization may survive, or willing the victory of their nation and thereby destroying our civilization. I know which of these alternatives I must choose; but I cannot make that choice in security.[5]

This susceptibility of the religious elite to the allurements of a nationalistically oriented authoritarianism is undeniable. It precluded open opposition to the destruction of democracy and to the expansionist wars launched by the Nazis in the name of Germany's right to live. Can the same be said of the even more crucial aspects of Nazism: its racial intolerance and its eventual extermination of Jews? Debate still continues to focus on the pre-history of Nazi anti-Semitism, and much remains to be done in this field. "Some Christians and understandably not a few Jews would trace a direct line from the teachings of Chrysostom in the fourth century to the insanity of Buchenwald."[6] Other historians point out that Nazism was just as opposed to Christianity as it was to Judaism. "Consequently, citing Hitler's assault against the Church, some Christians would seek to dissociate Christianity from the evolution of Nazi attitudes and practices."[7] The former group, ably represented by such scholars as Rosemary Ruether, may be called the advocates of the "culmination" theory, whereby the essentially anti-Judaic roots of Christianity can be traced back to the New Testament and forward to the gas chambers. Others wish to differentiate. They point to the very different strain of racial anti-Semitism that arose in the secularist polemical writings of such men as Wilhelm Marr and was supported by pseudo-anthropologists, particularly at the end of the nineteenth century. This form of anti-Christian anti-Semitism has been well analyzed by Uriel Tal in his excellent book *Christians and Jews in Germany 1870–1914*.[8] Tal emphasizes the sharp division between the persistent influence of Christian anti-Semitism and the much more violent and radical racialism of the secularists. Yet he points out how subtly the arguments could be combined, particularly by a sinister blending of Christian vocabulary with more far-reaching concepts of racial segregation and discrimination.

The same point is made with equal force in the most authoritative study by Richard Gutteridge, *Open Thy Mouth for the Dumb: The German Evangelical Church and the Jews 1879–1950*. Because Gutteridge writes more in sorrow than in anger, his observations are all the more forceful. He correctly points out that the "teaching of contempt" as the noted French scholar Jules Isaac rightly described the churches' attitudes toward the Jews, provided successive generations of churchmen with not only the excuse but also the sanction for animosity and persecution.[9] The baleful influence of Adolf Stöcker found a hostile reception in his own rank of society, and a total failure to attract the masses of workers to his own brand of fervent monarchical nationalism. But

> his campaign against the Jews assisted enormously in making the cause respectable and in lending persuasion to the idea that one could without a bad conscience be a Christian and an anti-Semite at the same time. . . . He certainly undermined the future religious and ethical strength of resistance on the part of Protestant Christians to the anti-Jewish battle cries and acts of violence produced by the radical anti-Semites and the Nazis.[10]

No less significant was the influence by Treitschke, whose anti-Semitism was national, not racial, in character, and only incidentally religious. "His chief contribution was the spreading of the type of coarse, brassy, aggressive national pride which did so much to fertilize the German brand of anti-semitism."[11] Because his reputation was so pervasive in the upper echelons of the middle classes who exercised power in the last days of Imperial Germany and during the Weimar Republic, it is perhaps a tragedy that he is now best known for the slogan "The Jews are our misfortune," which was so skillfully exploited by *Der Stürmer*.

Before 1914, the great majority of churchmen abhorred the rabble-rousing techniques of Adolf Stöcker and the polemical attempts to exploit alleged cases of ritual murder, particularly in Austria-Hungary. Nevertheless, it is undeniable that a "polite" anti-Semitism existed, principally because the Jewish presence appeared to question the stability and conservatism of a rapidly changing society. The Jew as "scapegoat" was at first the cry of the lower middle classes, but World War I "saw a change whereby the educated and propertied classes no longer disdained to resort to vulgar anti-Semitic phraseology and proved ready to join with the small man in making a political factor out of anti-Semitism." [12]

The search for a relevant national role for the churches during the Weimar Republic, in place of the monarchical establishment, further encouraged the growth of anti-Semitic attitudes. Here again the subtle transformation of vocabulary and ideology went largely unremarked, except in the rigorous, biblically centered teaching of Karl Barth. Indeed, the principal theologians who attacked Barth for his anti-national, anti-*Kulturprotestantismus* position were men like Paul Althaus, Emanuel Hirsch, Friedrich Gogarten, and Werner Elert, who provided the theoretical framework for the spiritual regeneration of the *Volk* along Germanic-Christian lines, and attacked the cosmopolitan rationalist influences of their day, including the allegedly alien Jew, as *zersetzend* (dis-integrating).

Only a few voices, such as those of Barth, Martin Rade, Friedrich Siegmund-Schultze and Paul Tillich, were raised against this trend. In 1928 they declared

> We are persuaded that the anti-Semitic movement, which in the aftermath of the World War has had so mighty a boom, is irreconcilable with the Christian point of view and is incompatible with our debt of gratitude to the cradle of Christianity. [13]

But after 1933, both Barth and Siegmund-Schultze were forced into exile, Tillich emigrated to the United States, and Rade lapsed into silence. As early as May 1933, Siegmund-Schultze had planned an inter-faith international committee to provide emigration assistance for German Jews, but this proved abortive.

It was concern for the potential disruption of the church's control over its own affairs by the Nazi-inspired plan to prohibit non-Aryans in the service of the church, which led to the founding of the Confessing Church under the direction of Martin Niemöller in the autumn of 1933. His attack on the so-called Aryan paragraph—the proposal by the Nazi-controlled church authorities to prohibit Christians of Jewish descent from holding office in the church—was undoubtedly reluctant; it was based on scriptural and ecclesiastical, rather than ethical or humanitarian concerns. The Confessing Church did not seek to espouse the cause of the Jews as a whole, nor to criticize the secular legislation directed against the German Jews and the Nazi racial philosophy. But it did constitute an undeniable challenge to the Nazi racial outlook and totalitarian system. However weakly their point of view was defended, the Confessing Church provided a rallying point for the opposition which remained intact throughout the Nazi era. The recognition that the Jewish question went to the heart of the Christian Gospel forced at least some church leaders to adopt a different attitude from that of other professional groups among whom no such resistance to Aryanization was found. However, the main statement of the Confessing Church, drawn up at Barmen in May 1934, made no reference to the Jewish question. Defense of purity of doctrine was stressed over concrete Christian action. Later on Barth, the Barmen Confession's principal author, admitted that he had failed to make the Jewish question a decisive issue at that time.

In the ideological field, more was done by Catholic writers to combat insidious Nazi propaganda. Especially in 1935 and 1936 strong attacks were launched against Rosenberg's books, culminating in the famous Papal Encyclical *Mit brennender Sorge* of March 1937. However, most of the Nazi leaders placed little reliance on ideological campaigns against the churches, and soon found that the policies of intimidation and administrative restrictions were more effective. Among the masses, it was less necessary to undertake the time-consuming task of challenging the churches' teachings. Instead, it was more effective to inculcate the masses with an intoxicating, potent brew of racialist, historical, *völkisch*, and nationalistic propaganda which idolized Adolf Hitler, the new Leader.

The dismay of the religious elites at those popular developments, and their attempts to retain the loyalty of their followers, were outclassed by the successfully staged rallies in Nuremberg and elsewhere. According to Gordon Zahn, the German Catholic hierarchy came to the conclusion that they could not count on the loyalty of their "troops" in the event of an open and all-out confrontation with the regime.[14] The same was largely true for those members of the Confessing Church who claimed all along that they were trying to reconcile their allegiances to both the state and the Gospel.

I do not mean to suggest, of course, that the ambivalent attitudes of the churches' milieu, the arrogance and perversity of the Nazi persecution, and the pessimistic assessment of the church leaders were responsible for the triumph of the Nazi challenge. As I have pointed out elsewhere, the reasons for the failure of the churches to resist Nazi oppression were both historically and theologically conditioned.[15] The problem of how to take up arms against injustice and violence in a totalitarian state remains unresolved. If the religious communities still have, or still claim, a special advantage and a special responsibility in this regard, we cannot forget that the moral force of Christianity (as well as Judaism) is no longer the dominant ethical motivator in contemporary society. Any attempt to make the churches a scapegoat for the moral failure of the Germans, especially for the tragedy of the Holocaust, overestimates the effectiveness of the churches' position then and now. The experience of the Nazi era shows that the appeal of nationalism and even totalitarianism can command, or impose, almost total obedience. The triumph of Nazi ideology raises fundamental questions about the ethical norms of every society. Nothing in the history since the fall of Nazism can lead us to assume that the capacity and temptation for such misuse of political and ideological power has been repudiated. The grim prospect is that similar excesses may happen again. If the guardians of the Judeo-Christian heritage betrayed their trust during the Nazi era, let us all beware of following in their footsteps.

NOTES

1. Otto Dibelius, *Das Jahrhundert der Kirche. Geschichte, Betrachtung, Umschau und Ziele* (Berlin, 1927).
2. See Daniel Borg, "*Volkskirche*, 'Christian State' and the Weimar Republic" in *Church History*, XXXV (June 1966), 2, 19 ff.
3. Borg, ibid., 20; R. Seeberg, *System der Ethik* (Leipzig, 1920), p. 97.
4. See the memoirs of Ludendorff's adjutant, W. Breucker, *Die Tragik Ludendorffs* (Oldenburg, 1953), p. 107.
5. Dietrich Bonhoeffer, *The Way to Freedom* (London, 1972), p. 246.
6. R. F. Drinan, *Honor the Promise* (New York, 1977), p. 24.
7. Ibid.
8. Uriel Tal, *Christians and Jews in Germany. Religion, Politics and Ideology in The Second Reich 1870–1914* (Ithaca, N.Y., 1975).
9. Richard Gutteridge, *Open Thy Mouth for the Dumb. The German Evangelical Church and the Jews 1879–1950* (Oxford, 1976), p. 3.
10. Ibid., p. 11.
11. Ibid., p. 17.
12. Ibid., p. 28.
13. Introduction to Eduard Lamparter, *Evangelische Kirche und Judentum*, reprinted in R. Geis and H-J. Kraus, eds., *Versuche des Verstehens. Dokumente jüdisch-christlicher Begegnung, 1918–1933* (Munich, 1966), p. 255.
14. Gordon Zahn, "Catholic Resistance?" in F. Littell and H. Locke, eds., *The German Church Struggle and the Holocaust* (Detroit, 1974), p. 228.
15. John S. Conway, *The Nazi Persecution of the Churches* (New York, 1969), p. 334 ff.

BEATE RUHM VON OPPEN

THE INTELLECTUAL RESISTANCE

The German "educated elite" may not be easy to define. It probably was, however, pretty much what Hitler meant by "the intellectuals," people whose education had sharpened their critical faculty to such an extent that they were not swept off their feet into total faith in the Führer. He said it again and again: how it was the common people he was relying on and with whose unquestioning support and exertions he would redeem the country and give it the greatness that was its due. On confidential occasions, closed meetings of chosen audiences, he would sometimes make it clear that this greatness also meant geographical expansion and the settlement of the added Eastern territories with good German or Germanic stock. Also on such confidential occasions, he would denounce "the intellectuals," people who kept criticizing or questioning his policies; actually, for rhetorical effect, he might mention them even in a public speech, only to dismiss them as quite insignificant, a negligible quantity that could not stop the advance of the people and of history. What, however, he would keep for confidential occasions, closed meetings of chosen audiences, was the off-hand threat of extermination. Even those special audiences could not know how seriously such a remark was to be taken—and obviously it was the kind of thing he could and would utter only off the record. No one could know how seriously he meant it; but he said it. He was capable, for instance, of saying what follows below to an audience of about four hundred journalists and publishers convened on November 10, 1938, to hear from him about the part the press had played and was to continue to play in his foreign policy, his policy of expansion. It is notable that he made his speech the day after the pogrom now known as the *Kristallnacht,* the night of broken glass. But he did not mention that event at all—though the evidence was all around and must have been on the minds of his listeners. Hitler concentrated entirely on foreign policy and domestic policy inasmuch as it was related to it, and on what the press had done and must go on doing to unite the people behind the leader and policy maker. The press had played a particularly important part in the crisis that led up to the Munich settlement and had thus helped to achieve a bloodless victory of enormous dimensions and implications, which dismembered Czechoslovakia and robbed what was left of it of defenses that could be described as the Eastern equivalent of the Maginot Line. There were now no natural defenses left, the system of fortifications was taken over by the Germans with the Sudeten region, that is, the part of the country that was predominantly populated by Germans clamoring for self-determination and "return" to the Reich.

Hitler probably concentrated on the subject of foreign, military, and press policy without even a reference to the pogrom, because he did not want to complicate his message—which was powerful—and because he may have been aware that there might be twinges of doubt and even conscience that had better be left untouched.

The first plot to depose and remove Hitler had formed exactly in the weeks of the Sudeten crisis and had come to naught when Chamberlain decided to come to Hitler and negotiate cessions and concessions to be made by the Czechoslovak government. The plotters had urged the British government to stand firm in the face of Hitler's demands, so that they could expose his recklessness to the people and depose him. But Chamberlain decided otherwise and the plot collapsed. It is hard to say how much of this—and whether, indeed, anything—was known to the four hundred pressmen, though they must have known about the resignation of Ludwig Beck, the chief of general staff, who had been opposed to Hitler's scheme of aggression against Czechoslovakia, whether it turned out to involve the active employment of the German armed forces or the mere threat—which in the rather unexpected event proved to be sufficient. Beck was undoubt-edly what Hitler would describe as an "intellectual"—for all that he was the highest ranking soldier in the Wehrmacht. He was, incidentally, involved in later plots too and designated for the highest military position in the plot that was tried and failed in 1944.

And here is what Hitler said to his four hundred journalists—who presumably could also be described as "educated" or "intellectuals":

> When I look at our intellectual strata—alas, one needs them; otherwise
> one could some day—I don't know—exterminate them or something.
> But unfortunately one needs them. But when I look at these intellectual
> strata and imagine their behavior and examine their attitude to myself
> and to our work, I almost feel afraid.

And then he went on about how they might react to something going
wrong, seeing how critical they were when he had nothing but successes.[1]

In thinking about the response of the professional, intellectual, and
religious communities to the Nazis, one stumbles over the word "communities." It gives me pause. It sounds so American, so un-German, so
inapplicable to the German social configuration—and yet it was Germans
who made so much of *Gemeinschaft,* community, as, for instance, contrasted with *Gesellschaft,* or society. The togetherness of community or
Gemeinschaft was the soulful thing, the thing engaging the inner man, that
could cure or counteract the ills of society, *Gesellschaft.*

Perhaps there's the rub—and a method of access to the subject. If one
proceeds by word association, by listening to overtones and compounds,
one may get into it. The rub seems to be that *Gemeinschaft* or
Gemeinschaftserlebnis, the experience of community, did not, on the
whole, provide the human cohesion that acted as an effective barrier to
inhumanity. No, on the whole not: but what barrier, what resistance there
was, did depend on community or communities, on family, and on
friendship.

The point of difference between America and Germany seems to me to
be that Germany had no professional or intellectual communities, or had at
best some pockets of solidarity in the professions, or some degree of
professional ethos. Community did exist in somewhat higher degree among
co-religionists and that may have been a difference in kind as well as
degree. Christians speak of the communion of saints; and the German word
for that is *Gemeinschaft der Heiligen: Gemeinschaft* here has to do duty for
both communion and community. By "communion of saints" is meant the
community of the faithful. But it is salutary, not just an archaism, that the
sacramental word is kept in English. It may have contributed to the
German perdition that they only had one word for the religious and secular
community, that the word was charged with religious connotation, and that
the Nazis managed to make the notion, slogan, and political and psychological straitjacket of *Volksgemeinschaft* (the community or communion of the
people) more effective, on the whole, than the other communities. Those
they atomized and used the atoms to fill the totalitarian system. That is what
totalitarianism is and does. It absorbs the de-structured or destroyed.

As you know, all parties, unions, and associations but one, the National Socialist, were destroyed, that is, abolished or Nazified. Only the churches remained.

Why did not a sense of danger make a community of opponents and victims? There may be several reasons: Hitler's uncanny gift for timing and deception; an inadequate gift, among his opponents and victims, for seeing where the greatest danger lay; an inadequate gift for appropriate and effective combination; economic insecurity; an almost nationwide resentment of the Treaty of Versailles and the Western powers that had imposed it and were still enforcing it—though they looked like giving to Hitler what they had denied to his predecessors. This was probably Hitler's strongest card in the months and years of his consolidation of power. His promise of removing "the shackles of Versailles," getting rid of reparations and removing unemployment—promises that he seemed, surprisingly, to be able to keep, helped him immensely and hindered the formation of early and effective oppositional groupings. And then, of course, there was a whole series of punitive decrees and laws, brought in with breath-taking speed, which made any banding together and any protest or dissent punishable by savage measures. A legal profession brought up on positive law and without a tradition of natural law, applied these laws, decrees, and regulations—even if many members of the profession did their best to circumvent them or to interpret them in a way favorable to the accused. And then there were the extra-legal means of coercion, concentration camps and, in the summer of 1934, the blood purges ostensibly directed against rebellious Nazis, but in fact also against anti-Nazis, such as the Berlin head of the Catholic Action.

The records of the Gestapo and *Sicherheitsdienst* (Security Service) show where resistance persisted, where fragments of what had been prohibited or *gleichgeschaltet* continued to cohere in some sort of fashion and continued not to conform. They are the chief source on what resistance there was.

While on the subject of sources, the following needs to be said: they have to be read in the original, because the business of wrong translations goes on and seems to be getting worse. Lucy Dawidowicz[2] points out one instance of "egregious mistranslation" from Krausnick's chapter in *The Anatomy of the SS State*,[3] which has now entered the literature, including the *Encyclopedia Judaica*. That chapter was prepared as one of a number of background papers by the Munich *Institut für Zeitgeschichte* for the Auschwitz trial in Frankfurt in the middle 1960's.[4] Lucy Dawidowicz then evidently ceased to rely on or to refer to that translation which, immediately after the example she points to and corrects, has a much worse mistranslation. But by then she had switched from Krausnick's chapter in that book to a later edition by Krausnick and a collaborator of hitherto unpublished speeches by Hitler. It is, to my mind, the most telling and—on the sound track which I have heard—the most frightening utterance by Hitler on the subject of the Jews. Lucy Dawidowicz translates it correctly but calls it a "speech before a regional NSDAP meeting." It was a speech before a gathering of Party *Kreisleiter* or district leaders on April 29, 1937. The point is precisely that it was only the medium-level Party hierarchs who were thus addressed, in confidence, which is why the speech was only found and published long after the war. It was not generally known at the time. The significant paragraph was a response by Hitler to a question in a newspaper why more was not being done against the Jews. Its gist was the inexpediency of uttering a clear and premature challenge to the enemy one means to destroy. Before this audience of Party leaders Hitler explained, in a voice rising with emotion, how he does *not* tell his enemy to fight, but calls on his own inner wisdom so to maneuver him into a corner that he cannot strike back, in order then to deliver the fatal blow. The translators of Krausnick's *Anatomy* chapter have Hitler telling his audience that he shouts louder and louder as he tells his enemy what he has in mind for him.[5] This ultra-egregious mistranslation is due to the translators' insufficient knowledge of the subject and insufficient care with the text itself, notably a failure to notice a pair of square brackets which show clearly that this is an editorial description of a sound track on which Hitler is now shouting louder and louder as he gives his internal dialogue: "and now, wisdom . . .," etc., etc. Actually it would be best, in the case of Hitler certainly, but also in that of Goebbels, if historians could hear the original and not just read a transcript. But in this particular case the punctuation made what happened clear enough.[6]

It is worth giving a little time to this, not in order to add yet another warning to and against translators, but because it shows so precisely what, on the one hand, happened in fact and how, on the other, it can be misrepresented in history. If that speech had been generally known at the time, if it had been published—let alone broadcast—in April 1937, many Jews would not have waited until November 1938 before beleaguering consulates and taking really desperate steps to get out of this now obvious death trap, Germany. It is because they did not know, despite the Nuremberg Laws and everything else that had happened and been written up to then, that it took the post-Munich pogrom to step up the rate of emigration.

And what applies to the victims also applies to the bystanders, including the "educated elite." They did not know about the possibility or probability of physical extinction. I had read *Mein Kampf,* secretly (because of its obscenity), as a teenager, had taken it seriously, and left the country in the summer of 1934—and I could only do that because it was made relatively easy for me. But put yourselves in the position of fathers of families, perhaps aging fathers with unexportable professions, in the midst of a worldwide economic crisis and unemployment everywhere and restrictions on immigration not only to the Western democracies but also to mandated Palestine, and you will see why so many stayed so long and many too long. As for Hitler's old book—few people seemed to know how seriously to take it.

You will also see why friendly and decent Gentiles did not think of removing Hitler by force until 1938, and why the final plot did not happen, and miscarry, until 1944.

But to turn more specifically to the educated elite in Germany, let me start with the professional academics—or rather with the leading luminaries in the politically and ethically most relevant disciplines. Ernst Nolte once wrote an essay on "The Typology of the Behavior of Academic Teachers in the Third Reich."[7] He displayed quite a spectrum, from instant and continuing collaboration to instant and persistent recalcitrance and resistance. In some cases there was more than instant collaboration, there was anticipation. And remember, the student organizations were Nazified before the Nazis came to power. Academic youth, inasmuch as it was political, was in the vanguard of the Nazi movement and exercised pressure on the professors. Not that there were not many spontaneous nationalists and even some Nazis in the faculties; but the organized student body was far more advanced in Nazism. This may have had something to do with the economic crisis and academic unemployment as well as with the restlessness of youth. So, speedy faculty adaptation to the new regime was in fact enforced from below as well as from above, from the students as well as the Party and government. German professors are civil servants. Some, many of them, were responsive to pressures, including at times physical violence, from the students as well as the younger faculty.

Nolte, who later turned historian and became a great authority on fascism, put his former teacher Martin Heidegger in the middle of his article and roughly in the middle of his spectrum. He did not think that Heidegger was so lamentably subject to the prevailing mental climate of 1933 because of his philosophy.[8] I wonder about that. But I am fairly sure that Heidegger's relationship with language was his temporary undoing, when he made that Nazi speech as new Rector of Freiburg and when he fulsomely endorsed the Nazi government later that year—as did the leading theologian Emanuel Hirsch—when that government had flounced out of the League of Nations and put its decision to a plebiscite. His philosophical language was so deep, his spirit dwelt on such heights, that he could be badly mistaken on what happened on the middle ground where politics take place and people's livelihoods and lives are at stake. I would say that he had a tin ear for the language of that level; and he had never read *Mein Kampf*. This was, admittedly, a nasty thing to have to do; but I still think it was a duty—certainly for anyone who took any part in the political dialogue.

There was a general weakening of the sense of language among the educated; not only because nationalist emotions were inflamed and the language in which they were expressed tended to extremes, but also because nineteenth-century philosophers, from Hegel to Nietzsche, had disdained common comprehensibility and played their own games with language which, in Nietzsche's case, was often aphoristic or poetic. But in a nation as musical as the German, the chief corrupter came by the vehicle of music. His name was Richard Wagner.

In all the discussion of Wagner's contribution to Nazism (and we know what a Wagner addict Hitler was ever since his attendance, in his teens, at a performance of *Rienzi* in Linz) and in all the discussion of Wagner's anti-Semitism, too little attention has been paid, so far, to his destruction of the sense of language (and of shame) among his compatriots. Whatever he served up as language (written, remember, by himself—he did not employ librettists) with its compulsive alliterations and hypnotic music, cast its spell, its destructive spell, on the music-loving educated elite—to the extent that it went to the opera and did not avoid Wagner. Remember Mime in the *Ring*? He is the excessively unattractive foster father of Siegfried. He has also been interpreted as an incarnation of heartless capitalism. Remember the terms and manner of Siegfried's rejection of him before he storms out, free at last, into the world? Take Mime himself. His language and music are the exact operatic equivalent of "the Jew" who, in Wagner's article on "The Jew in Music" is said to be incapable of human speech and therefore also of music. Everyone knows about Beckmesser in *Die Meistersinger*, that sunny work (when compared with the gloom of the others): he was meant to represent Eduard Hanslick, Wagner's half-Jewish critic. What people do not seem to realize or to have, so-to-speak, any gut-reaction against, is the frightening text of Beckmesser's garbled version of the Prize Song in Act III. I do not see how any solid citizen, *Bildungsbürger*, or opera buff can sit through that scene of the good people of Nuremberg all turning against the limping plagiarist who delivers a nonsense text full of frightening metaphors, among other things about hanging and deprivation of air. True, few people really hear or know the text—but that is what Wagner, as always, wrote first, read to others, and published separately. What no one can help noticing in this scene of "radiant joy" and apotheosis of peoplehood is the all-against-one scenario on the sun-drenched *Festwiese* outside Nuremberg. It seems to me it is not so much Hans Sachs's aria about the survival of "holy German art" even if the wicked and shallow West were to make the German people and Holy Roman Empire fall apart, or the patriotic and anti-Eastern harangue of King Heinrich (Henry the Fowler) in *Lohengrin* that are the most objectionable. What strikes me as bound to be either acutely uncomfortable or dangerously desensitizing is the combination of massive rejection of single figures in the image of Wagner's Jew and the incestuous narcissism of the rejectors, the heroes and heroines, whether human or divine, or half-and-half. And then the language in which all this is transacted is itself a desensitizing factor, leaving those who submit to the experience with their linguistic judgment impaired.

I seriously think that whoever sits through a work by Wagner without at least some reservation or revulsion is bound to be brutalized by the exposure. Can opera or music drama really have such an effect? Yes, but of course mainly on people whose German is up to understanding the language of the work. That is the only mitigating circumstance about the Anglo-American and Jungian new wave of Wagnerism. Its followers and *afficionados* know not what they hear.

The Berlin opera celebrated Hitler's arrival in power with a Wagner opera. I got most of my operatic education in my remaining months in Berlin and I am grateful for the experience. It included quite a dose of Wagner.

After leaving the country, and while finishing high school in Holland, I noticed that other intellectual young German refugees, including especially Jewish Germans, were reading not only Thomas Mann, with whom I was acquainted, but also Stefan George, with whom I was not. For me it was the beginning of an interest in George that was both philological and political. Before that, I had not got much beyond Christian Morgenstern in German poetry.

Since the subject of this paper is the educated elite, let me now talk briefly about what Peter Gay, in a chapter on "The Secret Germany: Poetry as Power," has referred to as "an elitist program pushed to the very limits of elitism." He was right in that; he was also on to a true thing in his subtitle:

George's poetry had power and I'd be prepared to argue that it helped to keep the language truthful and forceful—even if it strikes many as somewhat forced. The George Circle was elitist and it included Jews. Gay is not comprehensive enough in his account of what happened to its members in the Nazi years. George himself evaded Nazi claims on him by going to Switzerland in 1933, where he died in December of that year. His chief disciple, Friedrich Gundolf, had died in 1931, "but," says Gay, "most of the others survived him, some as Nazis, some as the victims of the Nazis, some in sullen silence, some in exile."[9] There is no mention of Claus Stauffenberg who broke the silence with a loud bang on July 20, 1944. The bomb he planted beside Hitler did not kill him, and the plot failed. But no one else had got so close to killing Hitler and removing the regime as Stauffenberg and his fellow conspirators. It is, surely, significant that it was two younger members of the inner George circle, the brothers Stauffenberg, who were also central in the July plot. They had defended the dying and dead George against German government attempts to lay late and posthumous claim to him as their poet laureate. The Stauffenbergs were his literary executors until their execution.

The other significant feature of the George-Stauffenberg connection is that despite the hellenic streak in George's poetry and ways, it was his poem "The Antichrist" with recitals of which Claus Stauffenberg denounced the regime and rallied opponents. And more: This was not just the case of an appropriate poem, but Stauffenberg made it his business to brief himself on the theology of resistance and tyrannicide, both Catholic and Protestant, in order to overcome conscientious scruples in the pious men he recruited for the conspiracy. It may sound strange that this needed doing. But it is not strange if you put yourselves in the shoes of a Catholic or Calvinist or Lutheran. The last had the greatest difficulties of conscience.[10] Nor is it surprising that Gestapo interrogators always asked those they questioned about church connections and religious ties.[11]

It was the turn or return of so many men of conscience to their faith that made Helmuth von Moltke—a landowner and lawyer far removed from George and his circle, though acquainted with the lawyer Berthold Stauffenberg—work quite systematically to bring Catholics into his own group of planners for a better Germany. He may not have been so far from the truth in a letter to his wife written during and after the trial that sentenced him to death: he commented sardonically that he was dying as a martyr for St. Ignatius of Loyola, as a Protestant who had the temerity to bridge the denominational gap and to bring three Jesuits into his circle. One of them, Alfred Delp, was sentenced to death in the same trial. And it was not just the judge's, Roland Freisler's, personal aversion to Jesuits that caused his diatribes and death sentences. Hitler himself had, on the one hand, officially deplored and, on the other, energetically exploited the religious schism in Germany. To oppose him effectively, one had to overcome the division between Protestants and Catholics. [12]

I am inclined to say, after what I have seen and heard of the surprisingly pervasive presence of Christian faith among those who did resist, among the educated elite as well as among common folk, that Bonhoeffer was right in his statement in his *Ethics* [13] and elsewhere about the rediscovery of the Christian foundation of Western culture brought about by the attack of the neopagan barbarians.

It is therefore surprising that cultural historians—be they Stern or Gay—have paid so little attention to the factor of religious faith and theological foundation, and only little more to its attenuation or perversion. An Israeli, Uriel Tal, seems to be the notable and laudable exception. [14] He limits himself to the Second Reich, but within those limits he traces, with great seriousness and subtlety, the differences between Christian and anti-Christian anti-Semitism, and shows the deadly danger of the replacement of the one by the other. Fritz Stern seems less clear about the danger of idealism which replaces biblical faith (though he likes his idealist villains), [15] J. P. Stern adds little to the clarification [16] and Peter Gay does not believe in belief. [17]

It may be a matter of generations and personal experience. The generation of Thomas Mann and Max Horkheimer saw the significance of religion in the lives of those who had it, in times of pressure and persecution. The younger generation that stayed in Germany and did not succumb to the National Socialist pseudo-religion saw it too.

The small group of student rebels who were executed in Munich in 1943 for a campaign of anti-Nazi leaflets, deplored the failure, the sins of omission, of the educated majority. They pleaded for a recognition of guilt and an uncompromising struggle against Hitler and his all too many helpers. In their indictment of the most detestable tyranny the German people had ever put up with, they mentioned the misguidance, the uniforming, revolutionizing, and anaesthetizing of a whole young generation, to make it into godless, shameless, and conscienceless exploiters and murderers. Their—at first cautious or at least circumspect, and finally quite reckless—campaign against the regime ended in a proud and willing expiation on the guillotine. One professor died with them. It was he who had undertaken to help them to get something like a real education—both in his classes and in extramural meetings involving some of the leading

figures of Munich's displaced intelligentsia, such as Theodor Haecker and
Carl Muth, the former editor of the Catholic monthly *Hochland*. Among
these students, too, there was the realization that an education without a
metaphysical and religious dimension was making their academic generation into tools of the regime. They made up the deficiency as best they
could and were fortunate in finding older mentors to help them.[18]

Elites are apt to be faithless. The part of the German educated elite
which resisted the Nazis found its faith again in surprising measure. And I
think there are enough records left, if one knows how to read them, to show
the role not only of a proper education but of faith in a person's ability to
resist the devil and his works.

Perhaps I should not end without saying that these conclusions were
reached by an agnostic observer.

NOTES

1. *"Es spricht der Führer": 7 exemplarische Hitler-Reden.* Herausgegeben und erläutert
    von Hildegard von Kotze und Helmut Krausnick, unter Mitwirkung von F. A.
    Krummacher. (Gütersloh, 1966), pp. 281–82. My translation.

2. Lucy S. Dawidowicz, *The War Against the Jews 1933–1945* (New York, 1976), p. 550.

3. Helmut Krausnick and Martin Broszat, *Anatomy of the SS State*, trans. Richard Barry,
    Dorothy Long, and Marian Jackson (London, 1970), p. 51.

4. Hans Buchheim, Martin Broszat, Hans-Adolf Jacobsen, Helmut Krausnick, *Anatomie des
    SS-Staates.* Gutachten des Instituts für Zeitgeschichte. (Olten and Freiburg im Breisgau,
    1965). Vol. I: Hans Buchheim, "Die SS—Herrschaftsinstrument" and "Befehl und
    Gehorsam"; vol. II: Martin Broszat, "Nationalsozialistische Konzentrationslager
    1933–1945"; Hans-Adolf Jacobsen, "Kommissarbefehl und Massenexekutionen sow-
    jetischer Kriegsgefangener"; Helmut Krausnick, "Judenverfolgung."

5. Krausnick and Broszat, *Anatomy*, pp. 51–52.

6. *"Es spricht der Führer,"* p. 148.

7. Ernst Nolte, "Zur Typologie des Verhaltens der Hochschullehrer im Dritten Reich." *Aus
    Politik und Geschichte, Beilage zur Wochenzeitung "Das Parlament"*, B 46/65 (November
    17, 1965).

8. Ibid., p. 11.

9. Peter Gay, *Weimar Culture: The Outsider as Insider* (New York, 1968), pp. 47, 48.

10. Beate Ruhm von Oppen, *Religion and Resistance to Nazism* (Princeton, N.J., 1971),
    p. 70, and Beate Ruhm von Oppen, "Revisionism and Counterrevisionism in the
    Historiography of the Church Struggle." In Franklin H. Littell and Hubert G. Locke,
    eds., *The German Church Struggle and the Holocaust* (Detroit, 1974), p. 58

11. This is borne out by interrogation report after interrogation report in *Spiegelbild einer
    Verschwörung. Die Kaltenbrunner-Berichte an Bormann und Hitler über das Attentat
    vom 20. Juli 1944.* Geheime Dokumente aus dem ehemaligen Reichssicherheitshaupt-
    amt, herausgegeben vom Archiv Peter für historische und zeitgeschichtliche Dokumenta-
    tion (Stuttgart, 1961). These reports are also available on microfilm from the National
    Archives.

12. Beate Ruhm von Oppen, "Trial in Berlin," *The College*, January 1977, pp. 13–20.

13. Dietrich Bonhoeffer, *Ethics*, ed. Eberhard Bethge (New York, 1965), p. 55–56.

14. Uriel Tal, *Christians and Jews in Germany. Religion, Politics, and Ideology in the Second Reich, 1870–1914*, trans. Noah Jonathan Jacobs (Ithaca, N.Y., 1975).

15. Fritz Stern, *The Politics of Cultural Despair. A Study in the Rise of the Germanic Ideology* (New York, 1965), p. 125, where he does pinpoint the problem: "In this distortion of Christianity and in the mass desertion from the Christian faith—one of the most obscure and most important aspects of the rise of national socialism—Lagarde's thought played a central role." It is the obscurity and the importance of this aspect that still need stressing and, as far as possible, elucidating.

16. J. P. Stern, *Hitler: The Führer and the People* (London, 1975).

17. Peter Gay, *Freud, Jews and Other Germans: Masters and Victims in Modernist Culture* (New York, 1978), does not add anything, in this respect, to his earlier *Weimar Culture* (see Note 9).

18. See Inge Scholl, *Students Against Tyranny. The Resistance of the White Rose, Munich, 1942–1943*, trans. Arthur R. Schultz (Middletown, Conn., 1970) and Christian Petry, *Studenten aufs Schafott: Die Weisse Rose und ihr Scheitern* (Munich, 1968).

IV.
ANTI-NAZI ELITES
IN OCCUPIED
EUROPE, 1939-1945

LUCJAN DOBROSZYCKI

JEWISH ELITES
UNDER GERMAN RULE

The question of Jewish response to the German policy of destruction has been a matter of constant concern. But debate has focused almost exclusively on the role of the Jewish Councils, the passivity of the Jewish masses, and the incidence of Jewish resistance. The discussion, however, has somehow failed to pay proper attention to the way in which German rule or influence in a particular region of occupied Europe determined Jewish behavior and fate. This paper attempts to delineate the limits of Jewish response by focusing on the situation of the Jewish leadership within the framework of the status of a given country in the German scheme.

Every nation and every people is represented, at home and abroad, by its most prominent and accomplished members, i.e., its elite. The Jews of prewar Europe had in their elite a worthy representative. A representative in a more literal sense of the word than it might be thought, for among the Jews the gap between the highest and lowest social classes was smaller than in most other societies. Jewish society had never experienced the stratification of the medieval feudal system. Indeed, there was always much upward mobility among the Jews, and often a man's elite status was a matter of one generation or two. This was true especially in Eastern Europe.

The Jewish elite differed from place to place, and within a single country it was by no means a homogeneous group. The elite was often criticized; its failures were widely discussed and its decisions publicly challenged. Yet its stature as well as the importance of its role in leading the Jewish community was always and everywhere beyond question. The Jewish elite also influenced the political, social, economic, and cultural life of the host countries to a greater or lesser extent; and it was among the influential, the wealthy, and the educated that the greatest amount of contact and interaction between Jews and non-Jews took place.

Thus it could have been thought that after the German occupation of Europe, the Jewish elite—as is true of any leadership whenever there is a state of emergency—would assume a role that was more significant than ever. No one but the elite could even have attempted to arrange compromises, take protective measures, and organize and command resistance. Indeed, all this was done, and has since become a subject of polemics, rationalizations, and legends. However, one thing is certain: the elite acted in such a way, amid such extraordinary circumstances, and with such unpredictable results, that even the keenest mind and the wildest imagination could not have foreseen what would happen.

Even before the unthinkable mass killings took place in 1941–42, the position of the Jewish elite had been greatly undermined. Shortly before and immediately after the German invasion of Poland in September 1939, the Jewish elite was reduced in size and quality. Those able to escape at the outbreak of the war and during the first months of the occupation were mostly people with names, means, and connections. Those of the elite who remained behind lost all the independence and self-sufficiency they ever had. They were deprived of almost everything that, before the war, had defined their position in society. They were stripped of their property and banned from their professions; they were forced from their houses, their businesses, their clubs and associations. They were subjected to extreme isolation—not only from their non-Jewish colleagues but also from fellow Jews in other cities. In Eastern Europe this was accomplished with the creation of ghettos; in Western Europe with restrictions imposed on residence and travel. Everywhere the prohibition of all free communications—newspapers, radio, letters—made joint action nearly impossible. In addition, the Germans imposed collective responsibility on the Jewish communities, making the leaders hostages for the behavior of the masses. The most terrifying example was the case of the Vilna ghetto. There, under the threat of total destruction, the resistance surrendered its leader to the Gestapo.[1]

Strange as it may seem, members of the elite retained their illusions the longest. More than other Jews, they were deceived by their confidence in the strength of international conventions, in the power of law, and in the supremacy of civilization. More than anything else, however, they believed that no matter what might happen, there was no place for barbarity in the middle of the twentieth century and in the middle of Europe.

Two stories, each from a different stage of the Holocaust, may serve as examples.

It was at the time of innocent beginnings. On one and the same day, shortly before Hitler's seizure of power, Stanislaw Vincenz, a Polish writer and ethnographer, had two conversations. The first was with Mendel, a young Jewish waiter at a restaurant in the city of Lvov in Galicia. Struck by Mendel's worried appearance, Vincenz asked: "What happened to you today Mendel?" After a considerable silence Mendel replied: "I cannot take these Jews, that entire family of mine, any longer. In our little street in the Zamarstynów quarter they behave, without reason, as if the world were coming to an end. Sometimes, when I get away from them and see healthy people like you, I think they must have gone crazy. They lament, cry, and scream that in Germany there is this Hitler, that he is after the Jews. And who is saying these things? One grandpa, another grandpa, one uncle, another uncle, father, the neighbors too."—Several hours later, while having tea with a group of mathematicians, Vincenz quoted Mendel and expressed his own concern. His words were received with laughter. Professor Blumenfeld, the mathematician, said: "My dear fellow, you have a way of 'poking fun' at Russell and Freud, but you also have a way of listening to every cowherd, *Yid*, and *shleper* as if he were revealing the greatest wisdom. I recognize and respect your independent spirit, but don't you see that this anti-Jewish business is no longer a burning issue?"[2]

Some ten years later, in another part of Europe—in Holland—when the first reports of the mass killings in Poland were broadcast over the BBC and Radio Oranje, Abraham Asscher, the President of the Jewish Council, commented: "As far as I am concerned, the reports are nothing but English propaganda, with the sole intention of inciting the world against Germany." And the other President of the Council, David Cohen, a distinguished historian and classical scholar, later described his own reaction to the same news: "The fact that the Germans had perpetrated atrocities against Polish Jews was no reason for thinking that they would behave in the same way toward Dutch Jews, firstly because the Germans had always held Polish Jews in disrepute, and secondly because in the Netherlands, unlike Poland, they had to sit up and take notice of public opinion."[3] One year later, people from Amsterdam, Paris, Brussels, Prague, and Warsaw, arrived in Auschwitz with musical instruments, finished and unfinished manuscripts of their work, and their most valuable books in their suitcases.

It is true that there were illusions from beginning to end. But with each year, with each consecutive stage of the Holocaust, it mattered less and less whether the elite was deceived or not. Nor did it make any difference that it had been weakened by reduction in ranks, by loss of status, by isolation. Under other conditions, all this could have been compensated for, and surmounted. But the reason for the elite's inability to fulfill its role must be sought not in the elite itself, but rather in the nature of the Holocaust.

After extensive planning and preparation, and with the same force and determination that they put into their military effort, the Germans embarked upon the methodical destruction of the Jews. The totality of their aim—the annihilation of an entire people—left no room for exceptions. Had it been their purpose to enslave the Jews, the Germans might indeed have made the Jewish elite the first victim. That is what the Germans did with the elites of nations they conquered and wanted to keep in submission—as was the case in Poland and the occupied territories of the Soviet Union. The fate of the Jewish elite, however, was in no way different from that of other Jews. In fact, no special steps were planned or taken that the elite as a group should perish either earlier or later than the rest of the community. The German approach was pragmatic: sometimes members of the elite were killed to ensure compliance; sometimes they were given positions of authority to ensure pacification. While some became victims during random arrests, deportations, and killings, others received protection—or "preferential" deportation to the "model" ghetto of Theresienstadt—as members of Jewish Councils or as needed professionals such as physicians.

Before the mass extermination took place, there was a period of preparation. At this stage the Jews were marked with the yellow star, forced to live under different rules from everyone else, and physically shut off, separated from the rest of the country's population. To make the whole process smoother, more convenient, and more efficient, the Germans set up Jewish Councils (*Judenräte*) to act as intermediaries between themselves and the Jews. The people who were given posts in the Councils were for the most part prewar communal leaders, intellectuals, and professionals. Besides transmitting and enforcing orders from above—which they did with greater or lesser reluctance—the Jewish Councils provided social, religious, cultural, and health services.

Under conditions of mass starvation, forced labor, and shortages of living space and fuel, the Councils went on with their everyday work. They even evolved a routine, and believed that they had reached some kind of stabilization that would allow the Jews to cope with—and survive—the hard times.

There was also activity on the part of those members of the elite who were not connected with the Councils. With extreme effort and self-sacrifice, they established charitable and self-help organizations, and organized cultural and educational activities: work that was both legal and clandestine. In addition, they also engaged in underground political and military activities. All this was not only done to make the intolerable less so, or to partially relieve the current situation, but also with thought for the future: to make sure that when liberation came, they would have something to start with again.

The Germans, seeing through all this and aware of everything, often did not even deem it necessary to interfere. At times they even encouraged cultural and religious activities. From the beginning in 1933 until the deportations in 1942, the Nazis pursued a policy of de-assimilation: while driving the Jews from European society they encouraged the practice of traditional Jewish culture. In Germany, they had encouraged Zionists against the assimilationists. In occupied Poland, they persecuted and humiliated Jews in traditional garb on the streets or in houses of prayer. Yet at the same time, they regarded Jewish religious observances as a necessary proof that Jews were different and inferior. Hence, in many Polish ghettos they permitted houses of prayer, the observance of Jewish holidays, including even the baking of *matzoth* for Passover, as long as these activities did not interfere with their aims of exploitation and pacification. Pursuing the same policy, the Germans gave permission to open schools where Yiddish, Hebrew, Yiddish literature, and Jewish history were taught. There was even a legal newspaper published for the ghettos in the *Generalgouvernement*, which provided classical Jewish literature (including stories by Mendele Moykher Sforim, Sholom Aleikhem, and Isaac Leib Peretz), religious calendars, and stories about Jewish achievements in Palestine.[4]

The Germans treated this period as a transitory episode of Jewish isolation. The Jews viewed it as a sign of some kind of stabilization. Since Raul Hilberg published *The Destruction of the European Jews*, we know that for the perpetrators the annihilation of the Jews was a step-by-step process. But we do not always realize that the victims also went through different consecutive stages. They, however, did not know beforehand what each next stage would be.

The following may serve as illustrations:

In the first weeks of World War II some Jews fled from German-occupied Western and Central Poland to Eastern Poland, which was occupied by the Russians in accordance with the Molotov-Ribbentrop agreement of August 23, 1939. During the winter of 1939–40 many returned—of their own free will, though not without difficulties—from

Russian-occupied Poland to Warsaw, Lodz, Lublin, Cracow, and other towns, because life under Soviet rule seemed unbearable to them. At that time they did not realize that under Nazi rule one stage of the Holocaust was coming to an end and another stage was about to begin.

During the early months of the occupation, Jews were constantly abused and harassed by German soldiers, German policemen, Nazi youths, and both German and non-German civilians. Thus, when the Germans established ghettos, many Jews entered them with a feeling of relief, because they saw this as an escape from random acts of violence. But they did not suspect the fate awaiting them in the ghettos during the next stage of the Holocaust.

In the same way, when the Germans dismantled the ghettos, some of the inhabitants, having been starved for years, could not know what they were doing when they willingly reported for deportation, because as a reward they had been promised a whole loaf of bread.

When we speak of hunger in the ghettos, we may assume that everything is well known; we have detailed records of how much food was supplied to the ghettos, what the daily rations consisted of, how many calories they contained, and also how many people died of hunger. In the Warsaw ghetto one hundred thousand starved to death, and in the Lodz ghetto forty-two thousand perished. We could go on in this way, citing numbers and figures from one ghetto after another, and there were more than two hundred ghettos in Poland alone. But from experience in classrooms we know that students are not able to go beyond these numbers and figures, because they think of hunger, thank God, in terms of a time-span separating one meal from another during the day.

The behavior of the Jews, their reactions, and their policies, either good or bad, did not have any impact on the German plans—at least not from the time the Germans occupied any given territory. Disregarding for the moment the ethical side of the problem, there was no difference in the fate of the Jews, between the attitude of Adam Czerniakow of the Warsaw ghetto, who commited suicide to escape compliance; Chaim Rumkowski of the Lodz ghetto, who cooperated to the end; and Ephraim Barasz of the Bialystok ghetto, who supported the Jewish resistance.

In occupied Europe there was hardly anything the Jews and their elite could do to deter the Germans from reaching their aim, or even to alter the German procedure. Even when the Jews and their elite did accomplish something, they did so only by taking advantage of external factors. One such factor was the geographic and topographic setting of a given country.

Thus Denmark's and Norway's proximity to Sweden—and Croatia's proximity to the Italian Zone on the Dalmation coast—made escape possible. In
Byelorussia the existence of extensive forest regions made concealment and
partisan activities possible.

Another factor was the nature of relations between Jews and non-Jews
in a particular country. In general, the attitude toward the Jews in occupied
Europe depended on the tradition of relations between the Jewish and non-
Jewish population; the sociopolitical maturity of the entire population, or
the well understood national self-interest; and the degree of integration of
the Jews, i.e., their knowledge of the language of the country in which they
lived, their everyday contacts with their neighbors, and the level of their
knowledge of the customs of the country and its religion.

But the most decisive factor—perhaps overriding all others—was the
status of a given country in the German scheme for occupied Europe, which
had been set up in accordance with Nazi strategic aims. In the territories
under German rule or influence—extending from the front line deep in the
Soviet Union to the frontier at the Pyrenees—there were no two systems of
occupation or domination that were exactly alike. They ranged all the way
from direct incorporation into the Third Reich—as was the case of the
Warthegau, Polish Upper Silesia, and West Prussia in the East; Luxem-
burg, Alsace-Lorraine, and Eupen-Malmédy in the West; and parts of
Slovenia in the South—to the creation of satellite states, as in the case of
Hungary, Romania, Slovakia, Croatia, and Bulgaria. Between these two
extremes there were several other forms of control: an outright and severe
form of occupation that resulted in the liquidation of the prewar central and
local government apparatus, as well as all political, social, and cultural
institutions, such as in the occupied territories of Poland and the Soviet
Union; a combination of military and civilian occupation under which the
prewar central governments were abolished while the local governments
were left intact under German supervision, as was the case in the
Netherlands under *Reichskommissar* Arthur Seyss-Inquart; a military
takeover with the preservation of some aspects of sovereignty, as was the
case in Denmark prior to August 28, 1943; a military occupation—as in
Belgium and Northern France; and, finally, an occupation through a
collaborating government, as was a case in Norway under *Reichskommissar*
Joseph Terboven and head of state Vidkun Quisling, and in Southern
France under the Vichy government of Marshal Pétain.

The fate of the Jews—and thus the margin of action left for the Jewish
elite—depended largely on the status of their country in the German

scheme. Moreover, there seems to be a close relationship between the percentage of Jews who survived the Holocaust and the status of a given country.

Thus, it remains an undeniable fact, regardless of what one may think of the position taken by the Vichy regime regarding both Frenchmen and Jews, that as a result of the special status given to the Vichy government, a sizable part of the Jewish population in southern and northern France escaped destruction. And this did not happen without special effort on the part of the Jewish elite. Only in France was it possible for such Jewish organizations as the *Consistoire Général des Israélites de France,* the *Colonie Scholaire,* and others to remain legal and retain their prewar status and functions to some extent. They even refused to form a Jewish Council, although they were pressured to do so; and after an official Jewish representation was established by German order anyway, they were able to oppose and criticize this openly. It must be added that this representation, the *Union Générale des Israélites de France* (UGIF), was quite unlike the Jewish Councils set up in Eastern European cities. One may in fact doubt whether there was any basis for comparison, since the UGIF did not operate within a closed quarter or a ghetto, did not have its own police force, and was not involved in deportations. It came to be defined as "primarily" a relief and welfare organization—and that only after its leaders had fought a losing battle over the word "primarily," for which the Jews wanted to substitute the word "exclusively."[5]

If we move from West to East, from France to Romania—a country with entirely different historical and cultural traditions—we see that there too it was the country's status that largely determined the situation of the Jews. The Jewish elite in Romania is known to have done the most to save the Jews from destruction. But this elite had been able to accomplish practically nothing, in spite of all its efforts and connections, as long as the government of Marshal Antonescu, notorious for its anti-Semitism, remained faithful to Germany. It was only after the Romanian government realized that Hitler would lose the war—and after it started to move toward independence and began to seek an understanding with the anti-Nazi coalition—that the Jewish leadership could play its role with any success.

It is not uncommon to contrast the stand and action of the Jewish elite in Romania with the alleged failure of the leadership of the Hungarian Jews.[6] While we can admire the accomplishments of the chief Jewish personalities in Romania (Rabbi Alexander Safran, Dr. Wilhelm Filderman, and Dr. M. Benvenisti), we must nevertheless realize that the Jewish community in Hungary had remained intact until the spring of 1944, when the German police, soon followed by the German army, seized Hungary. Then, in the few months before the liberation of the country, two hundred thousand Jews were deported to Auschwitz.

The fact that virtually the entire Jewish population of Bulgaria survived the war cannot be attributed to the efforts or abilities of the Bulgarian Jewish elite. In the same way, the huge losses among the Jewish population of Holland, which was almost as high a percentage as in Poland, cannot be blamed on the failures of the Dutch Jewish elite. In Holland, it was the Nazi authorities that planned and carried out the deportations to the killing centers; in Bulgaria, the most independent of the German satellites, it was the king and the government that influenced the fate of the Jews. Thus the differences in status were more important than the geographic differences between West and East. Of course, these differences between West and East, strongly emphasized in most analyses of the Holocaust, did exist. Often, however, they were a matter of appearances. In Holland, for example, David Cohen, one of the two presidents of the Jewish Council in Amsterdam, considered it rude treatment when F. H. aus der Fünten of the Security Police failed to offer him a seat.[7] In Poland, on the other hand, Adam Czerniakow, the Chairman of the Jewish Council in Warsaw, and Chaim Rumkowski, the Elder of the Jews in Lodz, often returned from their visits to the Gestapo beaten and bleeding.[8]

Basically, the confrontation between Germans and Jews took place within three settings:

First, Germans dealt with the Jews directly, without the employment of Jewish Councils or non-German local governments as intermediaries. This happened in the German occupied territories of the Soviet Union, where *Einsatzgruppen* shot the Jews in mass executions.

Second, Germans confronted the Jews and transmitted their orders to them via the Jewish Councils. This was the case in Germany and in countries that were either annexed by the Third Reich or put under German occupation, such as Poland or Holland. There the Germans made use of the Jewish Councils to deport the Jews to the killing centers.

Third, Germans confronted the Jewish masses and the Jewish representatives via local governments, as in Romania and France. There the Germans needed the consent and cooperation of the non-German authorities before they could deport the Jews.

Only in the third setting could the Jewish elites attempt to influence events. Only in that setting could—and often did—cooperation between Jewish organizations and non-German local governments frustrate German plans. The setting for the confrontation between Germans and Jews derived from the status of a territory in the German scheme. Thus, this status largely determined the fate of the Jews. The wider the margin of sovereignty of an occupied or a satellite country, the more favorable were the conditions for survival of the Jewish community.

NOTES

1. Isaiah Trunk, *Judenrat. The Jewish Councils in Eastern Europe under Nazi Occupation* (New York, 1972), p. 470; Betti Ajzensztajn, ed., *Ruch podziemny w ghettach i obozach (Materiały i dokumenty)* (Lodz, 1946), p. 122; Isaac Kowalski, *A Secret Press in Nazi Europe* (New York, 1969), pp. 191–97. In Vilna, when the Gestapo threatened to destroy the ghetto if the leader of the Jewish resistance, Itzik Wittenberg, were not surrendered to them, the Jewish Council with the support of the Jewish masses and the acquiescence of the Jewish resistance turned him over to the Germans. Wittenberg submitted to the orders of the resistance and surrendered without the need of force, but with the understanding that he would be supplied with poison to end his own life.
2. Stanisław Vincenz, *Tematy żydowskie* (London, 1977), p. 57–58. My translation.
3. Cited in Louis de Jong, "The Netherlands and Auschwitz: Why were the Reports of Mass Killings so widely Disbelieved," in *Imposed Jewish Governing Bodies under Nazi Rule. YIVO Colloquium December 2–5, 1967* (New York, 1972), pp. 17–18.
4. *Gazeta żydowska* (published in Cracow two, later three times a week, from Spring 1940 to July 1942).
5. Zosa Szajkowski, *Analytical Franco-Jewish Gazetteer, 1939–1945* (New York, 1966), p. 47; Vicki Caron, *The UGIF. The Failure of the Nazis to Establish a Judenrat on the Eastern European Model*. Columbia University, Center for Israel and Jewish Studies, Working Papers (New York, 1977).
6. For a more detailed account of that problem, see Bela Vago, "Jewish Leadership Groups in Hungary and Rumania during the Holocaust," International Scholars Conference on the Holocaust—A Generation After, New York, 1975 (copy at the YIVO Institute, New York).
7. Jacob Presser, *The Destruction of the Dutch Jews* (New York, 1969), p. 123.
8. On Czerniakow, see Emanuel Ringelblum, *Togbukh fun varshever geto (1939–1942)*, ed. A. Eisenbach, T. Berenstein, B. Mark, and A. Rutkowski (Warsaw, 1961), p. 245 (entry of April 10, 1941). On Rumkowski, see my forthcoming study of the Lodz ghetto.

ALLAN MITCHELL

POLISH, DUTCH, AND FRENCH ELITES UNDER THE GERMAN OCCUPATION

The reaction of European elites to Nazism and the Holocaust is a theme so diffuse and so daunting that one may well question whether it is at all susceptible to coherent analysis. The available historical literature is of course quite extensive, but also, as a rule, highly specialized. Scholarly studies tend to be of two types: Either they concentrate on the general ideological and institutional bases of the German decision-making process after 1933;[1] or they deal in a monographic fashion with the experience of a single European people under the impact of Nazi domination.[2] One type regards the periphery of the Third Reich from its center; the other reverses the perspective and treats the problem exclusively from a specific vantage point on that periphery. It may be useful, therefore, to see what conclusion can be drawn from a simultaneous consideration of both views. Given the present state of the art, such an enterprise can have only a provisional character. Yet a brief survey will serve its purpose well enough if it assists in transcending narrative detail and in conceptualizing the topic at hand.

This already suggests an opening premise: Nazism was not a uniform phenomenon throughout Europe. The response of elites depended in the first instance on the kind of pressure to which they were responding. Nazi Germany may not have been all things to all men, but it did present different aspects to different nations. Consequently, one cannot begin with

Reproduced with permission of *The Wiener Library Bulletin.*

the assumption that the essential variable was the attitude of the conquered peoples. In some cases they had a wide latitude of choice as to a *modus vivendi* within the New Order; in other cases, they had virtually no choice whatsoever. The limits of their accommodation to German hegemony were therefore set not primarily by their desire to cooperate, or the lack of it, but by the economic needs and racial predispositions of the Nazi state. "In the long run," as Robert Paxton has observed, "Hitler's victims suffered in proportion to his need for their goods or his ethnic feelings about them, not in proportion to their eagerness to please."[3]

POLAND: The fate of the Polish nation was, alas, all too characteristic of its unhappy history. In 1939 Poland was yet again partitioned. The German acquisitions, aside from the Baltic and border areas annexed by Russia, were divided into two zones. One was composed of the two provinces of West Prussia and Posen that were officially designated as "Incorporated Eastern Territories" and marked for Germanization. The rest was called the "Government General for the Occupied Polish Territories," a long euphemism that implied little more than the creation of a German colony, a buffer zone between the Greater German Reich and the Soviet Union, which would serve as a dumping ground for racial undesirables.

Initially, German interest centered on the newly acquired provinces; and the attitude toward Polish elites there was, in sum, to seal them off or ship them out. Germanization meant the export of as many Poles as possible to the outer reaches and the import of German stock from the Baltic and elsewhere.[4] This frank exercise in demographic engineering required the practical elimination of Polish officials, politicians, business leaders, professional men, and intellectuals. With them, of course, went the Jews. Thereby the first hint was given of a principle that would, in a complex manner, apply throughout Europe: the treatment of indigenous elites by the Nazis was inseparable from the treatment of Jews. To this we must return later. Suffice it here to observe that in the incorporated territories of Poland no one was consulted, no one was offered a perplexing choice. Higher education was taken over and Germanized, the press was strictly censored or closed, Polish churches were isolated from German churches, place names and signs were altered, German and Prussian law was introduced, a four-year economic plan was enforced, state property and much private property were confiscated, and concentration camps were put into operation.

If this list seems depressing enough, the situation in the unincorporated areas in the East was worse. The descriptive words that come to mind are plunder, congestion, and brutality. There was no question of Germanization but of elminiation of all elites, closing of schools and universities, arrests and internments, and finally the beginning of group liquidations. Hitler's subalterns, chief among them Reinhard Heydrich, were true to the Führer's promise: the Polish nobility and clergy, along with Jews and other *Gesindel* (riffraff), were to be exterminated in the name of ethnic purity. To be a member of the Polish elite meant, at best, to live in mortal danger. By April 1943, only sixty thousand of the half million Jews that had once huddled in the Warsaw ghetto remained. Whatever its moral importance, the uprising caused only a temporary delay in the grim proceedings.[5] It will never be precisely established how many Poles were eliminated, along with the Jews, after 1939. Their resistance too was condemned to futility.

In the end, the Nazis were utterly consistent. Poland had no claim to be a nation, and consequently its inferior people deserved no right to their own leadership. Indeed, the notion of a "Polish elite" became a contradiction in terms. To be unexceptional and subservient was perhaps to survive; to be extraordinary in any way meant, more often than not, to perish. The common experience of Polish elites and Jews was unfortunately defined by the ugliest word in the German language: *Ausrottung* (extermination).

THE NETHERLANDS: The distinction between Poland and Holland was put accurately, if imprecisely, by Reichskommissar Arthur Seyss-Inquart, just before his transfer from one country to the other: "In the East we have a National Socialist mission," he said, "over there in the West we have a function. Therein lies something of a difference!"[6] That function was to bring the Netherlands, like his native Austria, *heim ins Reich*. As kindred Aryan brothers, the Dutch people were to be coaxed and cajoled into cooperation with the Greater German Reich in which they were to be privileged partners. "There is nothing," Seyss-Inquart assured them, "that should prevent us from meeting each other on a plane of mutual respect."[7]

But the Dutch had other ideas. The Queen and her government went into exile, thereby depriving any future regime of the pretense of legal continuity. More important, the German occupation forces were generally received with cold formality, something less than the delirious enthusiasm of the Austrians over whom Seyss-Inquart had presided two years before, when Hitler made his triumphal entry into Vienna. Therefore, one cannot speak of a honeymoon but only of a brief truce, during which few Dutch were imprisoned and few anti-Semitic measures were taken. Once again, in an inverse sense, the treatment of elites and of Jews initially seemed not far different. But, of course, the process of singling out the Jews began; and the authentic countenance of German policy was soon to be revealed in all of its impeccable logic. If the Netherlands were to be incorporated into the German Reich and the Dutch people embraced as fellow Aryans, then Holland, like the fatherland itself, must be made *judenrein*. This was all the more feasible since there was scarcely anywhere for the Jews to hide. They found themselves, as Raul Hilberg has said, caught in "a natural trap."[8]

Meanwhile, the truce could not last, and it did not after the Amsterdam transportation and labor strike in February 1941 provoked a new severity of repression: more stringent rationing, the compulsory registration of workers, the arrest of more hostages, the first deportation of Jews to the unincorporated areas of Poland, and the beginnings of more thoroughgoing Germanization.

Nazi procedures in Holland can be defined in fairly simple terms: when in doubt, organize. Virtually every public activity and profession was regimented into groups, guilds, or "chambers," making them all the easier to control. This included journalists, artists, musicians, architects, veterinarians, dentists, pharmacists, physicians, teachers, and so on.[9] The parliament and local assemblies were dissolved, while mayors and bureaucrats were kept on. The machinery of administration thus continued to function, with a German command apparatus superimposed on it.[10] Ostensibly, the one sector left unmolested was business; free enterprise was to continue. But the reality of strict regulation proved to be much the same. The Germans simply placed orders or signed contracts with local Dutch firms. Once the initial period of truce had passed, however, requests became requisitions. Dutch businessmen quickly learned that Germanization meant exploitation. This realization resulted in a gradual slowdown of the economy, particularly as the Germans began to increase pressure for the forced draft of labor. In the crunch, some Dutch officials and business leaders chose to resign rather than submit, but most stayed on to hinder the application of harsher measures. In retrospect, it is easy to be cynical about those who, in effect, remained to collaborate, but in the circumstances of the Netherlands such a choice was not only plausible but sometimes demonstrably effective.[11]

Special mention should be made of the universities, which proved to be greenhouses of resistance, probably because of the substantial number of Jewish professors who taught there before the war. Their dismissal in 1940 brought protests and, in turn, a retaliatory closing of the university at Leiden and the technical institute at Delft. The ensuing unrest prompted the requirement of a loyalty oath for all students, which only about

15 percent of them signed. Let it be added that the Church hierarchy, both Reformed and Roman Catholic, also moved hesitantly toward more open defiance, and that they did so notably in protest over the deportation of Jews. Except for the Danes and possibly the Bulgarians, the Dutch came as close as any other nation in Europe to effective passive resistance.[12]

Yet nowhere, not even in the Netherlands, did the story have a remotely happy ending. There, as in Poland, Nazism was implacable. As far as elites were concerned, Holland proved to be a land of small compromises and painful accommodations, of slight risks and delicate choices that were never offered to the Poles. This may have delayed, but finally did not prevent, the seizure and destruction of the Dutch Jews. After the liquidation or Aryanization of Jewish firms, the requirement of yellow stars was imposed in May 1942. The Dutch tried to ease the embarrassment by donning yellow flowers and by making light of the "wearing of the orange." The same weak humor made the rounds of Amsterdam and of Warsaw in those days: the Jewish quarter of the city was called Hollywood because there were so many stars.[13] There were concealments and there was some sabotage; but also, "there was, in fact, a great deal of administrative cooperation."[14] By 1944, well over one hundred thousand Jews were deported. For them the reluctance of Dutch elites to join with their Germanic brethren had not mattered. It is nonetheless remarkable, and to their enduring honor, that a people that might more easily have assumed the guise of racial fraternity with the Nazis finally preferred to be treated as an occupied enemy country.

FRANCE: As always, the French case was an anomaly. The principal reason is clear. If it is true that Nazi racial attitudes determined German policy toward occupied territories, the problem was that the French were neither subhuman nor Aryan. For Adolf Hitler they were just an uncongenial people beyond the Vosges: alien, weak, and eminently exploitable. Hence there was an apparent uncertainty about the status of French elites in the New Order; and hence also, a certain ambiguity about the treatment of French Jews.

From the German perspective, the zonal demarcation of France after the glorious summer of 1940 was not a matter of great importance. Indeed, the Vichy government was in some regards a convenience, particularly insofar as this meant that fewer German personnel would be required to administer France. Politically it seemed a relatively minor nuisance, since the existence of Marshal Pétain's regime in the South required only an extra step or two in the chain of command. Vichy meant much active collaboration, a little passive resistance, and a barely tolerable measure of French inefficiency. This is how it appeared at the time to the Nazis, and so it should strike the critical historian now.[15]

Initially the border between the occupied and unoccupied zones was to be tightly sealed. That this proved to be impracticable can be attributed mainly to economic necessities imposed by the German war effort. Most of French industry was, of course, located in the northern occupied zone, and the boundaries had been carefully drawn to incorporate everything from the port of Bordeaux to the metal works at Creusot. But the economic infrastructure of France, including agricultural production and raw materials, could not be so neatly divided. As in Holland, the Germans at first intended to leave industry in private hands and place orders with individual French firms. From the standpoint of some capitalists, this promised to be a bonanza. They might actually welcome German "reforms" as a means to rid themselves of French government controls accrued during the decades of the Third Republic; and, if anything, the industrialists of France could suppose themselves more firmly in charge of the economy than before.[16] Yet this was soon revealed to be another delusion. German requisitions of everything from bauxite and coal to textiles and aircraft became increasingly pre-emptive. Well before the Allied invasion of North Africa in November 1942 and the resulting German occupation of southern France, the economic distinction between the two zones was disappearing. Total war meant total exploitation. Arrangements that had originally appeared as a boost to French capitalists proved to be only a prelude to their economic *Gleichschaltung* into the New Order. By the autumn of 1943, virtually 50 percent of French production was going directly into German hands. Too little and too late came the protest of Pierre Laval: "It is no longer a matter of a policy of collaboration," he complained, "but on the French side of a policy of sacrifice and on the German side of a policy of compulsion."[17]

Generalizations do not come easily for France, but the foregoing may serve fairly well as a paradigm. One cannot overlook how quickly and how completely French elites adjusted to German domination. As they saw things, this was not so much to maintain normalcy, but to recover it. Above all, Pétain represented a restoration of the French notability after a long season of republican government during which their economic and social grip had been loosened. *Travail, famille, patrie*—for the notables those were the good old virtues of bygone days. And to rescue them could seem downright honorable. Hence, collaboration could be espoused not only as realistic but even as salutary. However that may now appear, at the time it was unquestionably the prevailing attitude of French elites. Those who can genuinely be counted as resisters from the outset were very few; and most of them—some military personnel, several administrators and journalists, a university professor or two—happened to be caught outside of metropolitan France when the war began.[18]

Both the myth and the anti-myth of the French Resistance have had their vigorous advocates. In one version nearly every Frenchman resisted, if only to utter some clever obscenity as the local Gestapo chief passed by. In the other, France emerges as a nation of cowards and hypocrites.[19] Even if one assumes, as surely one must, that the truth lies somewhere within the broad spectrum of possibilities, it does not necessarily lie midway. Neither statistically nor morally were the French equally divided. In most regards Vichy was not a compromise; it was, after all, a capitulation.

Still, the situation was not without ambiguity; and that was nowhere more evident than in the treatment of Jews in France. In the earliest German conception, France lay outside the area to be made *judenrein* and was, in fact, like the unannexed portion of Poland, originally used as a refugee camp for racial outcasts. This proved to be a stimulus for French anti-Semitism: the Vichy government set about to establish its own system of quotas and purges "long before the Germans began to apply any pressure" to require such measures.[20] Starting in October 1940, without German prodding, discriminatory legislation was enacted that removed Jews from elite roles in legislatures, civil service, the judiciary, education, editorial and business functions. Not until late 1941 did the Germans order the first mass arrest of Jews and, a few months later, the deportation of aliens. In June 1942 Heinrich Himmler announced a quota for further deportations to Eastern Europe: fifteen thousand from Holland, ten thousand from Belgium, and one hundred thousand from France, "including the unoccupied zones."[21] One month later, about thirteen thousand Jews were herded into the Vélodrome d'Hiver in Paris, prior to their "evacuation" to the East. Thereafter the familiar pattern of dispossession, dehumanization, deportation, and destruction was to be repeated.

But in one crucial regard the French case was different. The quota was never entirely fulfilled. Probably as many as 90 percent of French Jews survived. They did so, however, at the expense of foreign Jews who were abandoned while the native Jews were protected. "To no small extent," one historian has concluded, "that Vichy strategy met with success. By giving up a part, most of the whole was saved."[22] Approximately sixty-five thousand Jews in all were deported from France, of which the foreign-born outnumbered the French at a ratio of perhaps ten to one.[23]

It is a gruesome judgment indeed when such statistics are described as a "success." Can we, in fact, give credit to Marshal Pétain, Pierre Laval, and the Vichy elites for saving the lives of thousands of French Jews? On a number of counts that proposition is dubious. Several factors other than the response of French elites to Nazism could explain the survival of some two hundred thousand Jews there.

In the first place, unlike Holland, France was a large country with a variety and topography well suited for concealment. No less important, a substantial portion of the French Jewish population had been highly assimilated and frequently intermarried, making them often invisible to German officials trained to make categorical distinctions between Aryan type and Jewish stereotype. To render matters more difficult, the Church insisted that any Frenchman was a Roman Catholic who had been baptized as such, and the episcopate refused to cooperate in sorting out the flock. Such complications would have been of little consequence had the Germans not found it necessary to rely on French bureaucrats for the implementation of policy. By German standards this was, as noted, an annoyingly inefficient solution, but to administer a nation so vast and populous left them little choice short of committing an enormous quantity of their own personnel to the task. The method upon which they settled was the surest but also the slowest: quotas of Jews were assigned to French police officials who were told to fill them as they saw fit; otherwise the Germans themselves would do so without regard to nationality. This helps to explain the low percentage of French citizens among the victims but also the large number of non-French Jewish children deported from France to Auschwitz. If the choice was agonizing for French authorities, it does in any event seem problematical again to qualify the result as a "success."

To these considerations must be added the tentative and erratic course of German attitudes toward France altogether. As we saw, the initial role assigned to French territory was that of a huge racial dumping ground to which Jews from Baden and the Saar were expelled. Others entered from Belgium and Holland. By the time that phase had passed, the Germans had already developed administrative problems of their own. The enforcement of any policy whatever was confused by the competing prerogatives of Army Chief Heinrich von Stülpnagel, Ambassador Otto Abetz, SS leader Karl Oberg, and the various liaisons with Pétain's regime at Vichy, all of which caused further delays well into 1943. By that time the military conflict had irrevocably turned against the Germans, whose undermanned forces in France became increasingly preoccupied by the threat of an Allied invasion. The circumstances of war, the difficulties of transportation across the continent of Europe, the specter of defeat—these and not the opposition of

French elites cut short the systematic destruction of French Jews, which had begun to take a mounting toll by 1944.

Pierre Laval later claimed that all his efforts had been directed toward preventing France from becoming another Poland. If in a certain sense he did "succeed" in that objective, it was not primarily for the reason he claimed, namely, the intransigence of the Vichy regime.[24] More fundamental were the ambiguities of German racial policy toward France from the beginning, administrative inefficiency, internecine rivalry, and the encroachment of the war before a Final Solution could be effected. Were it not for these, can we really doubt what the outcome for the French Jews would have been?

We have proceeded from a central theorem that Nazism did not present itself in an identical fashion everywhere in Europe, but that its appearance varied according to German racial posture toward the various conquered peoples. Thus the effects of the incursion by the German army in 1939 were devastating for the Polish elites. Written off as unworthy and inferior, they were soon hounded out of existence by Nazi administrators for whom all Slavs were *Untermenschen* (subhumans) by definition, regardless of their status, wealth, or talent. In the Netherlands, by contrast, the Germans made elaborate efforts to treat the populace as racial equals and to encourage Dutch elites into cooperation and assimilation with the Greater German Reich. Although reality fell far short of theory in Holland, at least the structure and personnel of elites remained largely unchanged, if not totally uncompromised. France hovered somewhere between the Polish and Dutch examples. Unable to classify them conveniently into one unambiguous racial category or another, German officials approached French elites with an irresolute mixture of authoritarian civility and faintly disguised contempt. For the most part the French responded with a collaboration born of fear, humiliation, self-interest, and repressed distaste for the conqueror. Each of these three models was quite different, and the differences essentially had more to do with the options afforded by German racial policy than with the willingness of the subdued elites to court the favor of their masters.

From this basic axiom we have deduced a corollary which is neither self-evident nor simple: that the fate of European Jews was a concomitant function of the relationship between German Nazis and the national elites.[25] From the incorporated portions of Poland, Jews were immediately expelled along with the Polish elites in the name of Germanization. To the East, in the unannexed Government General, the Jews were at first crowded and then, for the most part, pitilessly eliminated. The ruthless assertion of German racial superiority in Poland required that all other ethnic groups be forced, in one way or another, into submission. The rationale for the thorough purge of Dutch Jews was curiously inverse. Since the elites there were to be awarded a favored status and indeed equal citizenship in the New Order, by a certain logic it followed that the Netherlands must be totally cleansed of Jews in order to make the nation racially fit for such a supreme honor. Only in France did ambiguity abound; and as the Germans groped for a coherent policy toward French elites, both in the Vichy south and in the occupied north, so were they also dilatory in ordering and executing drastic measures against French Jews. In acting to benefit themselves, the French notability in Vichy also managed to salvage some of their Jewish compatriots. Such were the perverse circumstances of the early 1940's that a partial genocide might almost appear as a moral victory. We are led to conclude that ambiguity has its virtues.

NOTES

1. Among these see especially Hans-Adolf Jacobsen, *Nationalsozialistische Aussenpolitik, 1933–1938* (Frankfurt/M, 1968); Gerhard L. Weinberg, *The Foreign Policy of Hitler's Germany* (Chicago, 1970); Klaus Hildebrand, *Deutsche Aussenpolitik, 1933–1945*, 2nd ed. (Stuttgart, 1973); and Norman Rich, *Hitler's War Aims*, 2 vols. (New York, 1973–1974).
2. Most useful in the preparation of this essay have been Martin Broszat, *Nationalsozialistische Polenpolitik, 1939–1945* (Stuttgart, 1961); Hans Roos, *A History of Modern Poland* (New York, 1966); Werner Warmbruun, *The Dutch under the German Occupation, 1940–1945* (Stanford, 1963); Jacob Presser, *The Destruction of the Dutch Jews* (New York, 1969); Eberhard Jäckel, *Frankreich in Hitlers Europa* (Stuttgart, 1966); Alan S. Milward, *The New Order and the French Economy* (Oxford, 1970); and Robert O. Paxton, *Vichy France. Old Guard and New Order, 1940–1944*, 2nd ed. (New York, 1975).
3. Paxton, *Vichy France*, p. 372.
4. The ratio of Poles to Germans in the annexed provinces dropped from 13:1 (August 1939) to 4:1 (January 1944). Roos, *Modern Poland*, p. 189. See Broszat, *Nationalsozialistische Polenpolitik*, pp. 118–37.
5. Rich, *Hitler's War Aims*, vol. 2, p. 104. See Raul Hilberg, *The Destruction of the European Jews* (Chicago, 1961), pp. 125–74, 309–45.
6. Quoted by Rich, *Hitler's War Aims*, vol. 1, p. 151.
7. Ibid., vol. 2, p. 145.
8. Hilberg, *The Destruction of the European Jews*, pp. 365–82.
9. Warmbruun, *The Dutch under German Occupation*, pp. 34–47.
10. Rich, *Hitler's War Aims*, vol. 2, pp. 146–48.
11. Warmbruun, *The Dutch under German Occupation*, pp. 121–27.
12. Ibid., pp. 146–64.
13. Presser, *The Destruction of the Dutch Jews*, pp. 124–26.
14. Hilberg, *The Destruction of the European Jews*, p. 381.

15. The Pétain government "enjoyed mass support and elite participation." Paxton, *Vichy France*, p. 5.

16. Milward, *The New Order*, p. 68.

17. Quoted by Milward, ibid., p. 119.

18. Paxton, *Vichy France*, pp. 42–44.

19. An intelligent example of the former is Henri Michel, *Histoire de la Résistance en France, 1940–1944*, 7th ed. (Paris, 1975); and of the latter, the transcript of the brilliant documentary film by Marcel Ophuls, *The Sorrow and the Pity* (New York, 1972).

20. Paxton, *Vichy France*, p. 174. See Hilberg, *The Destruction of the European Jews*, pp. 389–421.

21. Quoted by Paxton, *Vichy France*, p. 181.

22. Hilberg, *The Destruction of the European Jews*, p. 389.

23. Gerald Reitlinger, *The Final Solution*, 2nd ed. (London, 1968), pp. 327–51, 538. See Jäckel, *Frankreich in Hitlers Europa*, pp. 311–15.

24. Paxton, *Vichy France*, pp. 184–85, 359–72. For a reasoned defense of Vichy policy see Geoffrey Warner, *Pierre Laval and the Eclipse of France, 1931–1945* (New York, 1969), pp. 304–307, 374–77.

25. No discussion of non-German Nazis has been attempted here, since in general they neither constituted an elite nor were they relied upon as such by officials of the German occupation.

V.
THE UNITED
STATES
AND THE
HOLOCAUST

HENRY L. FEINGOLD

THE GOVERNMENT RESPONSE

For the historian of the Holocaust, the role of witness poses the greatest problems. The witness is assumed to have had options: He could resist, he could be indifferent, or he could even collaborate. The assumption that there was a choice gives the moralist his entree. He demands to know why Roosevelt, the Pope, the neutral nations, and the International Red Cross did not do more to save the Jews. Since there can never be an adequate answer to this question, a series of pseudo-historical works have appeared, which are in reality thinly veiled indictments.[1] What I would like to demonstrate in this paper is that the model of conspiratorial indifference hardly encompasses the complexity of motives behind the inaction of the witness. That is especially true of Roosevelt's America to which other witnessing nations and agencies looked for an example. A blanket indictment conceals more than it reveals about the problem of rescue itself, about the fairly broad spectrum of opinion on what ought to be done, about the intractability of the credibility problem, and about the difficulty of assigning humanitarian objectives to nations at war.

I will focus primarily on decision-making elites in the United States. The Roosevelt Administration played the classic role of the witness, but from what we know, the complexity of motivation, the gap between intent and policy were no less manifest in London and Vatican City. Let us turn first to a fuller examination of the problem of the witness.

For the historian anxious to avoid the morass of moral fulminations—the natural stomping ground of the theologian—the primary question is not why more was not done but what was done, and what was possible. We are well on the way to answering the first question but the second continues to pose difficulties.[2] The researcher soon discovers that it is nearly impossible to determine possibilities of rescue, and that in examining the Final Solution we are faced with a catastrophe of such enormous magnitude that no matter what was done to rescue the victims, it would never have been enough. Indeed, the question of rescue possibilities actually reverts to the bitter debate of the Holocaust years, which revolved precisely around what was possible. We are not much closer to resolving that conflict today. Given Nazi fanaticism, how possible was it for witnessing nations to rescue Jews in the death camps in 1943? The problem can be seen clearly when one considers the Hungarian episode in 1944. There the rescue effort reached its apogee. Led by the War Refugee Board, all the components for rescue were in place. The witnessing nations had enlarged their diplomatic legations, a sustained psychological warfare campaign suggested by the World Jewish Congress was aimed at the Hungarians, money was funneled to underground sources, and the Vatican and the International Committee of the Red Cross (ICRC) were encouraged to play a more active role.[3] Yet it hardly balanced Berlin's zeal to win this last battle against the Jews. In full view of a world that now understood what the Final Solution meant, and even though Nazi decision makers knew that the war was lost, the cattle cars nevertheless rolled to Auschwitz as if they had a momentum of their own. More than half of Hungary's Jews were gassed. Those who controlled the actual slaughter determined possibilities for rescue even at this late date. Until there is some agreement on rescue possibilities, the tendency to assign witnesses a responsibility their power to influence events did not match will remain strong, and the gap between polemics and history will remain wide.

It seems clear today that the greatest possibilities for rescue existed during the first phase of the crisis, from November 1938 to June 1941. During that phase the Nazi leadership was uncertain about the ultimate disposition of the Jews. While much of the murderous rhetoric emanating from Berlin openly suggested mass murder, the bureaucracy actually worked within the context of emigration and forced extrusion to achieve the much desired goal of making the Reich judenrein.[4] That policy is best symbolized by a remarkable "statement of agreement" that resulted from the secret negotiations between George Rublee, an old Groton school friend of Roosevelt's who served as director of the Intergovernmental Committee on Political Refugees (IGC), Robert Pell, Rublee's technical adviser assigned by the State Department, Hjalmar Schacht, president of the Reichsbank, and Helmut Wohlthat, an official of the Ministry of Economic Affairs. It called for the phased ransoming of German Jewry over a period of three to five years by "outside" Jews, and the finding of a resettlement haven. It is possible to make certain judgments regarding rescue during this phase. Clearly, had there been a will among receiving nations to take in the penniless refugees from the Reich, more might have been saved. But that was enormously difficult and it required considerable good will. Germany had only five hundred thousand Jews, but in the wings stood Poland and Romania with four million. The situation seemed impossible for the receiving nations, and the ground rules of indifference and moral obtuseness were established during that first phase. They were not changed again until 1944 when it was all but too late.

It is neither necessary nor possible to recount here the now well-known story of the Roosevelt Administration's action and inaction in relation to the Holocaust. What I want to illustrate is the existence of a broad spectrum of opinion on the issue among decision makers (broader among political leaders than the public at large), and the complex intertwining of personalities, domestic politics, and conflicting views of the world, which fed into the policy-making arena on the question of the Holocaust. A case study of three leading personalities will best illustrate these points. I have selected Henry Morgenthau, Jr., Secretary of the Treasury and Roosevelt's close friend, who became the most powerful advocate of rescue in the Administration; Breckinridge Long, director of the State Department's Special Problems Division who became the most adamant foe of rescuing the Jews; and finally Roosevelt himself, perhaps the only political leader alive at the time whose actions might have drastically changed the course of events.

Breckinridge Long made his debut in the State Department during the Wilson Administration.[5] In the 1920's he gained a considerable reputation as an attorney specializing in international law. He returned to the State Department during the New Deal. As in the case of Laurence Steinhardt, it was a political appointment; he had made a considerable monetary contribution to Roosevelt's campaign. Steinhardt ended up as minister to Switzerland, and Long ultimately became ambassador to Italy. Long loved the glamour of the position but a series of bad decisions led to his removal and to what may have been a nervous breakdown. Long was extremely ambitious, a careerist who poured out his frustrations—and there were many—into his diary at night. He felt that he deserved at least to be Undersecretary and, failing that, perhaps ambassador to the Court of St. James. Instead, he was made head of a potpourri of operations assembled under the newly organized Special Problems Division. Little did he understand that his appointment to a position that would make him responsible for visa policy implementation was as unfortunate for rescue advocates as he felt it was for his career.

For historians the crucial question about Long is to what degree his blocking activity was motivated by anti-Semitism. Despite revealing passages in his diary, it is difficult to answer this question with certainty. Long was typical of those bureaucrats who resented the intrusion of Jews into the upper echelons of the civil service, which occurred at an accelerated pace during the New Deal.[6] But Long rarely spoke about Jews as such. He preferred code words such as "New York liberals." His attitude confirms what every Jewish aspirant sensed about the State Department: Jews were not welcome. Long wrote about his attendance during the oral part of the foreign service examination.[7] He frankly stated that he preferred the boys from his Princeton alma mater to the "pushy" candidates from the city colleges. But for Long it was a matter of gentility and class. One rarely sees evidence of strident anti-Semitism. He missed the character, the social ambiance, and the grace of the Department under the Wilson Administration, when it was a playground for the sons of the rich established families of America.[8] His resentment of the "new men" who had made their debut under Roosevelt knew no bounds, although only a small proportion of these were Jewish. Ironically, he recognized in Roosevelt a fellow patrician, and throughout the crisis successfully gained the President's consent to administratively block the inflow of refugees. To build what the historian David Wyman called a "paper wall" to keep refugees out, Long capitalized on what I have called a security psychosis, an intense fear that Germany had infiltrated the refugee stream with agents. During the crucial years between 1939 and 1941, increasingly stringent security procedures were employed so that by June 1940 it was no longer possible to issue a visa to anyone with a "close relative" under Nazi control. This meant that a good number of the refugees was subject to rejection. Indeed so successful were Long's gambits that only in 1939 was the combined quota for Austria and Germany filled. The security procedures of a neutral United States were as rigid as those of wartime Britain, and one historian maintains that, considering comparative absorptive capacities, Britain's refugee admission policy before September 1939 was more generous.[9] Yet while one can safely say that the congressional rejection of the Wagner-Rogers Bill which would have allowed the entry of ten thousand mainly Jewish children in 1939 and 1940—while the admittance of thousands of British children, non-Jewish victims of the 1940 blitz, was greeted with enthusiasm—was anti-Semitic, one can have some doubts that the security screening was simply anti-Semitism translated into policy. Long was genuinely convinced—as was his friend Martin Dies—that there was a conspiracy to breach American security and that there were spies in the refugee stream. There were magazine stories to support such a belief, and of course the FBI had files. When Stephen Wise pointed out to him after the SS *Struma* episode that German intelligence could surely find a safer means to transport their agents to America, Long thought he was being facetious. Even Roosevelt spoke about fifth columns and Trojan-Horse techniques which must be guarded against. Indeed, so effective was Long's strategy that it was practically impossible for any political leader to oppose the measures without calling his own loyalty into question. And that was the last thing Roosevelt wanted to do after the unsuccessful radical left turn taken by his Administration after 1936. When combined with the dislocation caused by the Depression, and the popular opposition to refugees at a time of unemployment at home, Long's use of the security gambit was virtually irresistible. Keeping refugees out had not only a popular mandate, but it seemed to be in consonance with the national security interest as well. It was a combination few decision makers cared to oppose.

A second policy, that of suppressing news of the Final Solution, is not so easily rationalized. The story of cable no. 354, which instructed Leland Harrison to cease forwarding reports of mass murder, is well known. Suffice it to say that the Department not only conspired to conceal news of the Final Solution, but attempted to cut off at the source any additional news emanating from Harrison in Berne. According to one source, this went a long way in creating the "wall of silence" which rescue advocates found almost impossible to penetrate.[10] The paucity of authenticated information on the implementation of the Final Solution, when combined with the incredibility of the story, is one of the key factors used to rationalize the inactivity of all witnessing nations and agencies. Long doubted the stories and attributed them to atrocity mongering by the Jewish leadership.[11] However, it is important to note that he was hardly alone in his skepticism. Some Jewish leaders could not believe it either. In the American context there was a special reason for such doubts. One of the principal arguments of the revisionist school of history during the 1930's was that the United States had been duped into entering World War I by the skillful atrocity mongering of the British.[12] It was believed that Lord Bryce, Wilson's favored scholar, had sacrificed his academic career to further the British interest in the United States.[13] For those who saw World War II as merely a recapitulation of World War I, and for congressmen who in the 1930's had legislated a series of neutrality laws designed to prevent a situation like that of the pre-World-War-I period from arising, the idea of atrocity mongering was not so far fetched. Even the Jewish leader Stephen Wise, who had been the recipient of the message from Gerhard Riegner (agent of the World Jewish Congress in Switzerland) giving the first confirmed gruesome details of the slaughter and the use of prussic acid, feared that such a story would not be believed. For confirmation, he gave the message to Undersecretary of State Sumner Welles, who was considered friendly to the Jewish cause. Indeed, the question of credibility deserves a book in itself. It plagued even those stationed in the listening posts around the periphery of occupied Europe, who found it difficult to believe such stories. It plagued the victims, who did not want to believe it, and the witnesses, who found it too incredible to believe. A poll taken in December 1944 showed that most Americans estimated Jewish losses at about one hundred thousand.[14]

The label "Roosevelt Administration" with its implication of collectivity and unity also poses certain problems for the researcher. There were in fact men in the Administration who recognized the problem and wanted to do more. Harold Ickes, the Secretary of the Interior, put up a strong fight to get Alaska considered as a refugee haven. Attorney General Francis Biddle fought Long at every turn, also over the question of the internment of the Japanese, which Long predictably favored. Long wondered how a man with so "much courage and determination" could place himself in the camp of those with "tender hearts."[15] James McDonald, who headed the President's Advisory Committee on Political Refugees (PACPR), a quasi-official agency whose task it was to monitor the crisis, compiled special visa lists, and investigated resettlement suggestions. His conflict with Long over visa lists even reached the Oval Office. But Long had little difficulty convincing the President that McDonald's plea for refugees was "sob stuff." McDonald lost his battle despite the strong support of Eleanor Roosevelt, who put herself at the service of rescue advocates and acted as a direct line to her husband.[16] Among the Catholic hierarchy the strongest advocate for rescue was Archbishop Joseph Rummel of New Orleans.[17] His stance was directly opposed by men like Archbishop Michael Curly of Baltimore, who refused to make a judgment on Nazi Germany because it was three thousand miles away. But most decision makers were simply indifferent to the issue, and in that stance they reflected general American public opinion. We tend to forget that during the refugee phase the Jewish question was a small side issue in the great debate between isolationists and interventionists, and after the United States entered the war the rescue issue was subsumed by the overriding objective of winning the war. Jewish leaders were told that the fastest way to save their brethren was by victory, and nothing must be allowed to interfere with that—not even the rescue of their brethren.

The case of Henry Morgenthau, Jr., has a special irony.[18] Roosevelt sometimes tried to use Morgenthau as a liaison to the Jewish community. He was asked to head the PACPR but rejected the idea, informing the White House that he was not interested in philanthropy. Morgenthau was rather taken aback when in the early months of 1939 he was asked to compile a list of the richest Jews in America to finance a visionary resettlement project favored by the President—the United States of Africa scheme. The President slipped easily into notions that there were rich Jews who might actually fund such a proposal. Morgenthau came rather late to the question of rescue. In 1940 he brought Isaiah Bowman, a noted geographer and resettlement expert, to Roosevelt's attention but after that we hear little of his activities. When he finally did take an interest in the final months of 1943, it was caused as much by a spin-off from his long standing rivalry with the State Department as it was by news of the fate of his co-religionists in Europe. But his involvement changed when he learned from his non-Jewish assistants—Randolph Paul, the general counsel of the Department; Josiah Du Bois, his assistant; and John Pehle, head of the Foreign Funds Control Division—that the State Department had deliberately suppressed news of the Final Solution. Then Eleanor Roosevelt observed that he began to play a new role in the inner circle of the Administration: the President's conscience.[19]

On January 13, 1944, Morgenthau's assistants had ready a report on the State Department's blocking role entitled "A Report to the Secretary on the Acquiescence of this Government in the Murder of the Jews." Morgenthau felt the title was too strong and changed it to read "A Personal Report to the President." He delivered it on January 16.[20] Possibly, it had the desired effect for two reasons: its contents were political dynamite and 1944 was an election year. It set in motion a new effort to save the Jews. The War Refugee Board was established with seed money from Roosevelt's slush fund and it initiated a new and somewhat imaginative program to save those Jews who might still be saved. A few months later, in April, a second breakthrough occurred when rescue advocates convinced Roosevelt to circumvent the immigration laws by establishing a temporary refugee haven in Oswego, New York. It was the high point of the Administration's rescue program.

We should note that Morgenthau became active rather late, and that he paid dearly for his open action in favor of his co-religionists. Accusations that his loyalties were ethnic rather than American were soon heard, and were partly responsible for bringing his political career to an abrupt end.[21] Once involved, Morgenthau sustained his interest. Undoubtedly it was his knowledge of what the Germans had done to Jews that led to his conception of the Morgenthau Plan for the treatment of postwar Germany. It was a "hard" plan, calling for the pastoralization of that country, and the Secretary convinced Roosevelt to make it America's official policy. But there was opposition from the State and War departments. When it was pointed out to him that fifteen million German workers would likely starve to death if his plan were ever implemented, Morgenthau's response was bitter: "Why the Hell should I worry about what happens to their people? . . . We didn't ask for war, we didn't put millions of people through gas chambers, we didn't do any of these things. They have asked for it."[22] After leaving office in July 1945, he wrote *Germany is Our Problem*. It was published at that historical juncture when many Washington decision makers were becoming convinced that "our problem" lay further to the east, in the Kremlin.

We come finally to the case of Roosevelt himself, who throughout the crisis hovered somewhere between the positions of Long and Morgenthau. What emerges from the growing record is that the President, so beloved by American Jewry, did not have the spiritual depth to fathom the crucible being experienced by European Jewry, the historical insight and intelligence to understand the meaning of Auschwitz for our time, or the political courage to bring his Administration to a more active rescue policy. It was at once a failure of mind, spirit, and will.

We must attribute the vacillating, contradictory character of America's rescue activity to Roosevelt himself. The State Department, which he never trusted and bypassed at every opportunity, was used as a foil to absorb the ire of the Jews as well as other components of the liberal urban ethnic coalition which sometimes helped to amplify the Jewish voice. There developed a "policy of gestures," composed of the rhetoric of humanitarianism and an occasional insignificant step while at the same time the State Department conceived and implemented increasingly restrictive measures to curtail the influx of refugees. After the *Anschluss*, Roosevelt announced dramatically that he was combining the German and Austrian quotas in order to prevent the loss of the latter. (The step entailed an indirect recognition of the annexation.) Other such steps were the extension of visitor's visas and the calling of the Refugee Conference at Evian with the clear stipulation that none of the participants would be required to alter their immigration regulations. That meant of course that the conference would accomplish little to mitigate the refugee chaos. Meanwhile the State

Department was carrying out a policy candidly articulated by Long: "We can delay and effectively stop for a temporary period of indefinite length the number of immigrants into the United States. We could do this by simply advising our consuls to put every obstacle in the way and to resort to various administrative advices which would postpone and postpone the granting of visas." [23] That was precisely what was done. By September 1940 we hear him gloating over his success on the granting of special visas. "The list of Rabbis has been closed and the list of labor leaders has been closed and now it remains for the President's Committee to be curbed." [24] The Department went on to rule out the possibility of Alaska as a resettlement haven; finally it even concealed news of the Final Solution.

In the case of rescue Roosevelt was clearly more of a fox than a lion. Undoubtedly he wanted to do more, but doing so would have entailed a price he was unwilling to pay. It meant thwarting a very clear political consensus that Jewish refugees were not welcome. Paradoxically, Washington's failure in the crucial first phase of the Holocaust was a classic example of democracy at work. [25] Public opinion was adamantly opposed to tampering with the restrictive immigration laws so that a distinction between immigrants and refugees *in extremis* could be made. To be sure, he was impressed with the caliber of refugees coming from the Third Reich. [26] One of his most farsighted acts was to heed the advice of Albert Einstein and Leo Szilard concerning the potential for building an atomic bomb. [27] But he did not allow that positive impression to interfere with political reality. He rejected the idea of a refuge in Alaska, and he did nothing to support the Wagner-Rogers Bill to bring twenty thousand Jewish refugee children to the United States. Instead he turned to a strategy that would avoid both political conflict at home and confrontation with London. He proposed visionary and grandiose resettlement schemes in Africa and Latin America. (The British used much the same gambit when they proposed settling the Jews in British Guiana with American financing. [28]) At the same time Roosevelt seemed anxious to conceal the Jewish character of the crisis. Thus while Berlin spoke incessantly about Jews, and converted all enemies including Roosevelt to that faith, his State Department reconverted them to a bland category called "political refugees" and insistently stuck to that classification as late as the Bermuda Conference. The President was dismayed when George Rublee mentioned Jews directly in his agreement with Schacht.

The reasons for his distress are not difficult to discern. The Depression had released intense inter-group tensions. The anti-Semitic right pictured Jews in Nazi images. They considered them a "paramount menace to

American values and tradition." They prattled about "Judeo-Bolshevik conspiracies." This was not exactly new, it merely re-echoed the nativist restrictionist line of the 1920's, but something new had been added on the political scene. The aberrant right, men like Charles E. Coughlin, Gerald L. K. Smith, William Palley, and Fritz Kuhn, had been successful in linking themselves to the tide of isolationism which amplified their voice and cloaked them with the mantle of legitimacy.[29] The link between anti-Semitism and isolationism was sealed with a golden spike by no less an American hero than Charles Lindbergh, who in September 1941 warned America that Jews and Anglophiles were pushing the nation toward war with Germany, a war he was convinced would be catastrophic for the national interest.[30] Roosevelt, the supreme politician, would not risk the consequences of having his administration labeled a "Jew Deal." He had appointed Felix Frankfurter to the Supreme Court, he had surrounded himself with Jewish advisers, and Jews were flooding the enlarged Federal Civil Service. To push for Jewish refugees against popular opposition required him to run the political risk of overly close association with an American Jewry that was not winning medals for popularity.[31] That kind of political courage was simply not in the Roosevelt arsenal. The Jewish voting bloc had moved closer to him after 1936 while other hyphenates had cooled their ardor. The Jewish "love affair" with Roosevelt was unrequited.

Politically, Roosevelt—like Stalin—wanted to avoid making World War II a war to save the Jews. That was true despite the fact that Nazi cosmology pictured it in precisely those terms.[32] Yet political considerations only partly explain Roosevelt's indifferent showing. Oliver Wendel Holmes once described him as possessing a third-rate intellect but a first-rate temperament.[33] In the case of the Holocaust, that observation is borne out by the President's failure of mind. He never remotely understood the meaning of Auschwitz. His thinking on the rescue question had an above-the-battle quality. A refugee conference is proposed without any serious effort for a solution or follow up, and the British soon dismiss it as "intuitive."[34] Resettlement havens of immense proportions are sought without any serious consideration of the enormous difficulties involved in such nation-building schemes. In October 1939 he proposes a massive refugee absorption plan to delegates of the IGC meeting in Washington who feared above all that they would soon become refugees themselves. Roosevelt was a visionary who knew what he wanted to do in the abstract, even while his State Department was implementing quite another policy on the administrative level. That accounts for the duality of Washington's policy on the Holocaust which some less kind observers have labeled duplicitous. There is always a gap between a policy and its administration. But in the case of rescue policy, its administration actually refuted the ostensible humanitarian intentions of the Administration. That is perhaps what Roosevelt desired, a policy which made political points at home but risked very little. The bitter irony is that every other witnessing nation soon understood the game being played by the Roosevelt Administration and planned its own actions accordingly. But, with only a few distinct exceptions, American Jewry seems never to have understood that it was being manipulated.

For Roosevelt it was politics as usual. In other areas, New Deal rhetoric was also a far cry from performance. The gap between policy and implementation on the rescue question was therefore not atypical. But the saving of lives is qualitatively different from such issues as unemployment or rural electrification. Ultimately the yawning gaps and contradictions between the rhetoric of humanitarian concern and actual policy may have to be explained by an examination of Roosevelt's psyche. Some of the required data is already available. It speaks of Roosevelt's emotional superficiality. The historian Paul Conkin observes that "few men were more attuned to people and less attuned to ideas," but he actually loved people only in groups and rarely fathomed the travail and agony of any single person. "He loved the adoration and attention of people, even when elementary privacy was violated. With consummate art he played for his audience and won their plaudits. Some grew to love him and projected onto him their hopes and joys and deepest longings. They invested so much in the relationship; he invested so little and invested so broadly."[35] That is the way it seems to have been between the Jews and the Roosevelt Administration.

Finally, one cannot escape the conclusion that the will and mind-set required to save the lives of the victims was simply not present among the witnesses who might have acted. Decision makers never had the support of an aroused public opinion which might have compelled them to take more active steps. Yet we should note that in the case of the Roosevelt Administration, and in the case of London and the Vatican as well, there were always notable exceptions, leaders who realized what was happening and were anxious to do more. Although they did not often succeed, they might serve today to redeem our fallen image of humankind, for those who need such an image. If one had to give a primary reason for the failure of the witnesses to act, then the inability of rescue advocates to gain credibility and to pierce the "wall of silence" would have to be placed close to the top.

Linked to the problem of credibility one can identify a certain failure of mind. Roosevelt shared with the general public the sense that what Berlin was doing to Jews was merely another atrocity in a particularly cruel war. He never remotely fathomed the meaning of Auschwitz and the centrality of the Jewish question to the war. Most leaders did not. We are just now, more than thirty years after the event, beginning to understand the centrality of the Holocaust to the enigma of what World War II was all about. It is true that Hitler began and ended the war with statements about the need to destroy the Jews, but Allied leaders at the time were convinced that the Jewish question was peripheral and ordered their priorities accordingly. Rescue of the Jews had a low priority because that was not what they thought the war was about. Even today, few historians go as far as Lucy Dawidowicz in viewing the war as one against the Jews. In that context the conflict over rescue was really a conflict over priorities. Policy makers felt that the first order of business should be to win the war. Saving the Jews would be accommodated only as it fit into that priority. It usually didn't. It is likely that no amount of pressure—whether on London with regard to the White Paper or on Roosevelt with regard to admission of refugees—could have changed that. The historical problem of the role of witness cannot be resolved until we find an answer to the larger problem of what World War II was all about. Yet even today most historians do not recognize the destruction of the Jews as a central event in that war.

Lastly one should note that even had Washington's priorities been successfully reordered there would still have been almost insurmountable roadblocks. The mass slaughter of the Jews was focused and coordinated by Nazi authorities who possessed total power and a bureaucracy noted for its efficiency. The effort at mass rescue, on the other hand, could not be coordinated because it involved various witnessing nations and agencies, each of which retained its own conception of its priorities on the Holocaust question. Latin American nations, for example, rejected exhortations to be more generous about accepting Jewish refugees and offering havens for mass resettlement. Roosevelt's private emissary to the Vatican, Myron C. Taylor, could not convince the Pope to speak out. Salazar, the dictator of Portugal, could not be convinced that Angola was ideally suited to accept Jewish refugees.[36] Most British Commonwealth nations were as reluctant as the United States when it came to opening their gates.[37] Britain would not abandon her White Paper policy which limited immigration to Palestine, since she viewed her interest in the Middle East and the exigencies of the war as having a far higher priority than the rescue of Jews. The International Red Cross felt it would lose its effectiveness as an absolutely neutral agency if it were overly bold in interpreting its role vis-à-vis the incarcerated Jews.[38] So it went. Ironically, the Intergovernmental Committee on Refugees, whose purpose it was to coordinate the refugee effort, and after the Bermuda Conference, also the effort at rescuing Jews, became itself an early casualty of this fragmentation and general lack of will. The early international effort, like the national efforts, was strangled in a sea of red tape, which in itself reflected the lack of will. Collective responsibility, like collective guilt, has an allure of its own. When everyone is responsible or guilty—no one is. Throughout the crisis the Nazis were in physical control of the slaughter. Given their fanaticism on the Jewish question, it probably would have required a physical intrusion to remove their hand from the throats of the victims. Such an intrustion was not in the power of the witnessing policy makers who were, at least for the first years of the war, concerned with their own survival. The suggestion to bomb the camps and the rail links to them came rather late in the crisis and could not be achieved until advanced air bases in Italy were secured. Moreover, allied leaders feared that it would lead to an escalation of terror such as the retributive slaughter of war prisoners and hostages.[39] The Allies, it was felt, could never match the Germans in their ability to implement such steps of escalating terror.

One comes away from the examination of the role of witness with some skepticism regarding the assigning of humanitarian roles to nation states who bear witness to man-made catastrophes like the Holocaust. The instrument of slaughter was, after all, the nation-state itself. Nation-states are man-made institutions, not man himself. They possess no souls, no conscience, and are not the containers of the spirit of civilization. When they act at all it usually is to assure little else than their own continuance. Can we assign to them a humanitarian mission? One wonders if the assumption that we can is warranted by the history of the twentieth century.

NOTES

1. See for example Rolf Hochhuth, *The Deputy* (New York, 1964); Arthur D. Morse, *While Six Million Died: A Chronicle of American Apathy* (New York, 1967); Saul S. Friedman, *No Haven For the Oppressed: United States Policy Toward Jewish Refugees, 1938–1945* (Detroit, 1973).

2. Besides the works cited above, see also Henry L. Feingold, *The Politics of Rescue: The Roosevelt Administration and the Holocaust* (New Brunswick, N.J., 1970); David Wyman, *Paper Walls: America and the Refugee Crisis, 1938–1941* (Boston, 1968). A second volume will appear shortly. On the role of Great Britain, see A. J. Sherman, *Island Refuge: Britain and Refugees From the Third Reich 1933–1939* (Berkeley, Cal., 1973) and Bernard Wasserstein, *Britain and the Jews of Europe 1939–1945* (New York, 1979). The works focusing on the White Paper and policy toward the Yishuv are too

numerous to list here. The most objective work on the Vatican continues to be Günter
Lewy, *The Catholic Church and Nazi Germany* (New York, 1964). Others include Carlo
Falconi, *The Silence of Pius XII* (Boston, 1965); Anthony Rhodes, *The Vatican in the Age
of the Dictators, 1922–1945* (New York, 1973); Saul Friedländer, *Pius XII and the Third
Reich* (New York, 1966). The best work detailing the activities of the Red Cross and other
agencies remains *Unity in Dispersion, A History of the World Jewish Congress* (New
York, 1948). The most complete anthology of relevant articles is *Rescue Attempts During
the Holocaust: Proceedings of the Second Yad Vashem International Historical Conference* (Jerusalem, April 8–11, 1974; Jerusalem, 1977).

3. See Henry L. Feingold, "The Roosevelt Administration and the Effort to Save the Jews of
   Hungary," in Randolph Braham, ed., *Hungarian Jewish Studies* (New York, 1969).
4. For an elaboration of this point, see Karl A. Schleunes, *The Twisted Road to Auschwitz
   1933–1939* (Urbana, Ill., 1970); also, Feingold, *Politics of Rescue*.
5. A biographical sketch of "Breck" Long is included in Fred L. Israel, ed., *The War Diary
   of Breckinridge Long: Selections from the Years 1939–1944* (Lincoln, Neb., 1966),
   pp. xi–xxv. Hereafter cited as: *Long Diary*.
6. See Jerold A. Auerbach, "From Rags to Robes: The Legal Profession, Social Mobility and
   the American Jewish Experience," *American Jewish Historical Quarterly*, LXVI (December 1976), 265 ff.
7. *Long Diary*, January 23, 1940.
8. Ibid., April 22, 1942.
9. Sherman, *Island Refuge*, pp. 264–65.
10. This phrase was first used by A. L. Kubowitzki, *Unity in Dispersion*, p. 160.
11. Long MSS, Manuscript Division, Library of Congress, Intradepartmental Memorandum,
    May 14, 1943.
12. See, for instance, the revisionist work by H. C. Peterson, *Propaganda for War: The
    Campaign Against American Neutrality, 1914–1917* (Norman, Okla., 1939).
13. Ernest R. May, *The World War and American Isolation 1914–1917* (Chicago, 1966),
    pp. 180 ff.
14. Charles Stember, ed., *Jews in the Mind of America* (New York, 1966), p. 141.
15. "Long Diary," January 20, 1942 (unpublished section, Manuscript Division, Library of
    Congress).
16. The helpful role of Eleanor Roosevelt is examined by Jason Burger in Chapter III of an
    unpublished doctoral dissertation now being completed at the Graduate Center of the
    University of the City of New York.
17. Haim Genizi, "American Catholic Attitude Toward Catholic Refugees from Nazis,
    1933–1945," Bar Ilan University, August 1977 (unpublished). Genizi's research finds that
    the record of the Catholic Church in relation to its refugees was characterized by less
    interest and less effectiveness than that of the American Jewish community toward Jewish
    refugees.
18. John M. Blum, *Roosevelt and Morgenthau: A Revision and Condensation of From the
    Morgenthau Diaries* (Boston, 1970). Probably the best single source for Morgenthau's
    relationship to the Holocaust.
19. Henry L. Feingold, Review of John M. Blum, *Roosevelt and Morgenthau, American
    Jewish Historical Quarterly*, LX (December 1970), 207.
20. Morgenthau Diaries, Book 693, pp. 212–29, and Book 694, pp. 194–202, Franklin D.
    Roosevelt Library (Hyde Park, N.Y.).
21. See, for example, Cordell Hull, *The Memoirs of Cordell Hull* (New York, 1948), vol. II, p.
    471. Morgenthau denied the ethnic source of his bitterness toward Germany. He claimed
    it stemmed from World War I, when he observed the behavior of German officers in
    Turkey while acting as his father's assistant.

22. Blum, *Roosevelt and Morgenthau*, pp. 582–83.

23. Long MSS, Memorandum from Long to Adolf Berle and James C. Dunn, June 26, 1940. Manuscript Division, Library of Congress.

24. *Long Diary*, September 18, 1940.

25. That is the underlying theme of Wyman, *Paper Walls*, and is also prominent in Feingold, *Politics of Rescue*.

26. Frances Perkins, *The Roosevelt I Knew* (New York, 1946), p. 95.

27. Leo Szilard, "A Personal History of the Bomb," in *The University of Chicago Roundtable*, (Chicago, 1949), pp. 3–7.

28. Henry L. Feingold, "Roosevelt and the Resettlement Question," *Rescue Attempts During the Holocaust* (Jerusalem, 1977), pp. 123–80.

29. See Geoffrey Smith, *To Save a Nation: American Countersubversives, The New Deal and the Coming of World War II* (New York, 1973).

30. *New York Times*, September 12, 1941. Lindbergh's threat was reminiscent of those emanating from Berlin: "Instead of agitating for war the Jewish groups in this country should be opposing it in every possible way, for they will be among the first to feel its consequences."

31. Stember, *Jews in the Mind of America*, pp. 128, 129, 133–34. See also, November 1938 and Opinion Research Corporation, May 1938 through November 1939 on various aspects of fear, dislike, or distaste of the Jews.

32. See, for instance, Lucy S. Dawidowicz, *The War Against the Jews, 1933–1945* (New York, 1975), ch. 5; also, Eberhard Jäckel, *Hitler's Weltanschauung: A Blueprint for Power* (Middletown, Conn., 1972).

33. Frank Freidel, *FDR, Launching the New Deal* (Boston, 1973), p. 274.

34. Sherman, *Island Refuge*, pp. 100, 113.

35. Paul C. Conkin, *The New Deal* (New York, 1967), p. 5.

36. Feingold, *Politics of Rescue*, p. 105.

37. Sherman, *Island Refuge*, p. 103.

38. Meir Dworcezki, "The International Red Cross and Its Policy Vis-á-Vis the Jews in the Ghettos and Concentration Camps in Nazi-Occupied Europe," *Rescue Attempts During the Holocaust* (Jerusalem, 1977), pp. 71–110. See also the unpublished paper by Monty N. Penkower, "The World Jewish Congress Confronts the International Red Cross During the Holocaust Years," Touro College, New York, 1978.

39. Feingold, *Politics of Rescue*, p. 168.

JOHN FELSTINER

THE POPULAR RESPONSE

I was eight when World War II ended—old enough to feel but not to
understand its force. For me, the act of memory, the reconstructive act of
bearing witness to the obliteration of a millennium-old Jewish existence,
seems to have a double hold. I am carried back to what happened then and
there, yet at the same time confronted with what we are here and now.
How do individuals, how do institutions, deal with moral choices? This
question points to the years from 1933 through 1945, but in its present
tense, it also touches the late 1960's and early 1970's that we have lived
through.

For Eberhard Bethge and his Church there are not two questions but
one, originating in 1933 and still in force today. I wonder whether the same
holds true for most of us in America. In imagining that we can use the
Holocaust as a paradigm, an example of moral choices, or that we can hold it
up as a case study in genocide, we are distancing the event, and saying: It
happened *then*, this is something else. I know that examples and case
studies make for effective teaching. Yet did not the Holocaust—*does* it not,
once and for all, radically condition our own existence? In naming other
historical events, such as the French Revolution, the Civil War, we do not
have that sense of ongoing presentness we have in speaking of "the
Holocaust."

To begin with, I want to offer a familiar saying which I believe can
speak for both Jews and non-Jews, a saying of Rabbi Hillel, who taught in
Jerusalem just before Christ: "If I am not for myself, who is for me? And if I
am for myself alone, what am I? And if not now, when?" These words
concern the victim as well as the onlooker; they apply now as well as then;

and they have a particular bearing upon Jews in America today, who are relatively secure and yet carry the Holocaust within them. Hillel's saying challenges human beings to stand up for themselves while staying responsive to others.

As a complement to Dr. Bethge's German experience, I mean to recall the prewar and war years in the United States, when currents of immigration, anti-Semitism, nativism, and patriotism affected American attitudes toward potential refugees. Those attitudes were, in turn, linked to lack of knowledge, suppression of facts, disbelief, governmental inertia, and to the Jews' own disunity—all of which tragically marked America's response to the Final Solution. Having sketched in this history, I will try to reorient the question of moral choices toward ourselves in the present.

I might begin by recalling one quite typical response to Jewish refugees: A small boatload fleeing persecution arrived on the East Coast and was at first refused entry. Why? Out of fear that they would compete economically, or else that they would become a public charge; out of intolerance of their religious difference, and habitual repugnance of them as Jews. As it happens, that boat, containing twenty-three refugees from Portuguese Brazil, was greeted at New Amsterdam in 1654 by Peter Stuyvesant. But the instance is typical.

Between 1881 and World War I, driven by oppressive restrictions, pogroms, and poverty, well over two million Jews came to the United States from eastern Europe. Existing immigration laws were inadequate to preserve the country's Anglo-Saxon character in face of this massive non-Nordic infusion; consequently, in 1921 the Johnson Act was passed, restricting annual immigration to 3 percent of the number of each European nationality in the United States in 1910. But that wasn't strict enough, so in 1924 Congress passed a second law, basing the quota on 1890 and setting it at 2 percent. Hardest hit by it were southern and eastern Europeans, or, as one Congressman then put it, "Bolshevik Wops, Dagoes, Kikes and Hunkies."[1]

The 1924 National Origins Act was still in force in 1945. What sustained it was the same feelings as three centuries earlier, now intensified by the specter of Bolshevism and by unemployment during the Great Depression. In addition, restrictive immigration policy was indebted to the racist, eugenicist theories of men such as Stanford University's Ellwood Cubberley and David Starr Jordan.[2] Whatever economic, political, religious, or social axe you had to grind, "the Jew" was alien and corruptive. Anti-Semitism grew throughout the 1930's; and though a flagrant list of anti-Semitic organizations makes them seem more significant than they were— Silver Shirts, Christian Mobilizers, Crusaders, Defenders, Knights of the

White Camelia, and the like—anti-Jewish feeling in this country was also buttressed by the rise of Nazism. By 1938 Father Coughlin had three-and-a-half million regular radio listeners for his Sunday diatribes against the Jews, who were at once job stealers, Communists, and plutocratic manipulators.

From 1933 on, this xenophobic, racist vein helped stiffen American opinion against admitting those whom Hitler persecuted. What's more, many Jews in this country were themselves timid, uninsistent. An older friend of mine remembers meeting the Jewish leader Stephen Wise in 1934. He was clamoring for Christians and Jews alike to demonstrate and to boycott German goods, and she, as a Jew, felt offended by him—his clamoring might cause anti-Semitic reprisal here and in Germany. Besides, most Americans, Jews included, were far from seeing the outright danger of Nazism, much less its central anti-Jewish animus. Most people did not recognize, in Hitler's Nuremberg Laws, the methodical degradation of German Jewry. When Hitler annexed Austria in March 1938, and immediately terrorized his Jewish and Christian enemies, President Roosevelt would not consider suspending the quotas. Sentiment was against it, mainly because of a 20 percent unemployment rate, although immigrants of the 1930's did not seriously threaten the economy.

Roosevelt did, however, call the Evian Conference, which met in July 1938 but only exposed the reluctance of all but Holland and Denmark to take in more Jewish refugees. Since his coming to office in 1933, Roosevelt's humanitarian policies had gained increasing support from American Jews. In fact, it was his closeness to the Jewish community—the New Deal was sometimes labeled a "Jew Deal"—that made him wary of singling out Europe's Jews for special attention. At the same time, he found that Jewish voters were not alienated—not in 1940, not in 1944—by his inaction on the rescue issue.

Witness *Kristallnacht*. The whole country was shocked, scores of Christian spokesmen deplored it, as did the American Legion and William Randolph Hearst. The once outspoken anti-Semite Henry Ford said the United States could not now fail to act as a "haven for the oppressed."[3] Roosevelt said he could scarcely believe the Nazi barbarism, but when asked about getting masses of Jews out of Germany he said, "The time is not ripe for that." Asked about relaxing immigration restrictions: "That is not in contemplation; we have the quota system."[4] And nothing was done, because one high-placed observer could say, in January 1939: "It is . . . shameful . . . how the entire democratic world dissolves in tears of pity, but then, in spite of its obvious duty to help, closes its heart to the poor, tortured people." It was Adolf Hitler who made this observation, thus he could with impunity predict, in the same speech, "the annihilation of the Jewish race in Europe." Within months, a British White Paper had restricted immigration to Palestine, and a U.S. bill to admit twenty thousand German refugee children (not named as Jews, as usual, though most of them were), a bill with widespread non-sectarian support, had died in committee.

Why were quotas rigidly maintained and so few people saved, when through 1941 there was still a good chance? Liberal agitators feared stimulating even greater restrictionist opposition, and Jews feared that special pleading would bring on the age-old charge of dual loyalty. At bottom, the populace did not want aliens, and made them the scapegoat for social and economic ills. In 1939 and 1940 came the fanatic scare of a Nazi fifth column here at home. All these currents flowed through Congress and through U.S. consulates in Europe. Some vestiges of American isolationism remained, even while Czechoslovakia and Poland were occupied in 1939, France, Belgium, and Holland in 1940, and Russia invaded in 1941, gradually sealing the fate of millions of Jews. Then, after our own declaration of war, the patriotic cry became "rescue through victory," and immigration plummeted. That same cry continued through 1944, as refugee boats were turned back from America, and ransoms, exchanges, and plans to bomb the railway to Auschwitz fell through.[5]

Other factors kept the United States from a wholehearted rescue mission. One was the state of its Jewish community, broken up into Zionist versus non-Zionist groups, or those urging extreme versus moderate action. Even if these groups had acted in concert, the U.S. effort to save Jews could scarcely have matched the Nazi effort to destroy them, which was going on six thousand miles away, in countless isolated locations, with the single-minded, unstinted backing of a regime that put extermination ahead of the war effort.

There was disunity, helplessness, and unadorned disinclination. The journalist I. F. Stone discovered a 1943 British Embassy memo to the State Department, expressing fear lest the Germans "change over from the policy of extermination to one of extrusion, and aim as they did before the war at embarrassing other countries by flooding them with alien immigrants."[6] "Embarrassing?" we want to ask, and "alien immigrants?" Most tragic of all, there was a stubborn disbelief, strangely akin to that of the victims themselves, that genocide was actually occurring. News of the greatly intensified persecution had emerged since 1940, in fact even before then, if you read the *Contemporary Jewish Record* or the inside pages of the *New York Times*. Then definitive reports of the Nazi program finally reached the United States in mid-1942—reports of wholesale deportation, massacre, and gassing at Chelmno, Treblinka, Auschwitz. Yet leading Jewish publicists, acute men and women such as Haim Greenberg and Marie Syrkin, at first rejected these reports as monstrous imaginings.[7] Stephen Wise, in agony, let the State Department suppress the facts and check on them further. Apparently the opportunity to fuel anti-Nazi feeling was less compelling than the awkwardness of telling G.I. Joe he was fighting to save the Jews.

In December 1942, government and press formally acknowledged the mass killings. But there was no hysteria. The public at large took on the mantle of disbelief. In 1944 Arthur Koestler said that nine out of ten Americans considered the Nazi atrocity stories to be propaganda.[8] And at war's end, people who were asked how many Jews the Nazis murdered in the camps estimated about one hundred thousand.

Elie Wiesel has questioned the American Jewish leadership of those years. Why no hunger strikes to the end? Why no daily marches on the White House? "They should have shaken heaven and earth, echoing the agony of their doomed brethren."[9] Wiesel and others have asked: Why did Jews in this country not go mad? Well, perhaps some did. Anyway, countless Jews and their children, and not only Jews, live now with the blank, black fact of the Holocaust somewhere within them.

During the last few years there has been a surge of interest, not only in World War II but in the Jewish catastrophe. One can go back farther, to 1960, when both Wiesel's *Night* and Bruno Bettelheim's *The Informed Heart* appeared.[10] Or to 1961, to the Eichmann trial, surrounded by controversy yet for most people a form of awakening. In 1963 Rolf Hochhuth's play *The Deputy* aroused a storm and raised many questions still debated today.[11] In recent years, though, the spate of books, movies, documentaries, and conferences has had a broader impact than could have been predicted.

Why? Perhaps it takes decades before something so unconscionable can come to full consciousness—something that so threatens human measure. The annihilation of European Jewry was submerged at first in this country by wartime exigencies, then by grief at FDR's death, and relief at the war's end. Afterwards, the Cold War and Civil Rights seized our political imagination. Why are people now attending to the Holocaust? I think the general urge toward ethnic identification in recent years, and the recovery of their history by Afro-Americans, Mexican-Americans, Native Americans, Asian-Americans, has also helped make American Jews rediscover what connects them to the past. What's more, as the largest Jewish population in the world, they have been profoundly troubled by Israel's insecurity—by the sense that not only her neighbors but much of the world's intolerance threatens her. And it was, after all, the destruction of European Jewry that precipitated the statehood of Israel.

Finally, and less obviously, I suspect that many minds, in settling on the Holocaust, are bypassing the Vietnam war. In 1961, as people were listening horrified to the witnesses against Eichmann, U.S. intervention in Vietnam increased decisively. Almost no one noticed it, and from start to finish our country's leaders reassured us about the war, by a mixture of euphemism, suppression, and lies. Now, few people actively sustain a memory of the decade of senseless biologic degradation that ended in 1975. Almost no one notices the thousands of veterans in our midst who are jobless, drug-ridden, disabled, or estranged from friends, family, and society.

It seems to me that Americans are engaged in a private and collective amnesia about Vietnam. The war was physically distant, its victims utterly alien, its instant news packaged for television. One was not compelled to take the human fact of the war to heart. As this nation strays into the future, people are silting over the images of human carnage which, during the war, burned too deeply too quickly to be dealt with. Thirty years from now, we may have to listen to Vietnamese voices, as we now hear survivors of the war in Europe. Yet Vietnam is a part of America now, as the Holocaust is of the whole Western world—not to be repressed.

Nations are in this like individuals: they must keep on bearing witness to their past, so as to move more honestly into their future. (What a twist it was, that after *Kristallnacht* the Nazis should have burned the works of Freud!) Recently the U.S. government has found it possible to ban Vietnam from the United Nations for not being "humanitarian" enough, not "peace-loving" enough. Telford Taylor, a prosecutor at Nuremberg, said some years ago that with Vietnam, America failed to learn the lessons it taught at Nuremberg.[12] I am afraid that too much malaise and misunderstanding and cynicism now attach to the Vietnam war for the American public at large even to begin acknowledging it fully.

Returning to my question: Why this attention to the Holocaust? I feel it is partly because Americans are baffled by Vietnam, and are in some sense looking back past it at World War II. That war at least we won, we punished the criminals. I suppose I am even suggesting that a certain human craving for moral absolutes and irreducible truths is answered by the Holocaust. Out of the moral hollowness of post-Vietnam America and the falsities of Watergate, there is a need to reach toward something absolute, even though it be wholly negative—something that does not fade and buckle the way the Vietnam era does when one looks back on it. Maybe a deep, continuous engagement with the Holocaust can keep men and women alert to disbelief, inertia, incurious obedience, callousness, euphemism—the human constants that take some spirit to overcome.

There is an old Yiddish proverb that runs like this: "'Thou hast chosen us from among the nations'—why did you have to pick on the Jews?" It reflects an acquaintance with suffering, yes, but also a sense that suffering is temporal, even temporary. Sholom Aleichem might have uttered that proverb but not Elie Wiesel. For the Final Solution put an end to the consolations of irony, and the Holocaust finally demanded too much of the chosen people. Yet the demand for moral responsibility persists, and it generates a dilemma that sensitive Jews share with other sensitive people.

A friend of mine at Stanford University, a man whose liberal commitment I respect, asked me why I was involved in the Holocaust when so much present misery and injustice cry out to us. I could have replied with the saying of Rabbi Hillel I quoted at the beginning. But does that saying justify my friend or me? "If I am not for myself, who is for me? And if I am for myself alone, what am I? And if not now, when?"

My friend may have meant that Jews should leave the Holocaust behind them. I hope I never do. The Holocaust asks almost annihilating questions, but by a mysterious paradox, it thereby asks of Jews and Christians their most humanly fulfilling response: a passionate understanding that is the heart of moral responsibility.

NOTES

1. Congressman J. M. Tincher (Kansas), quoted in Saul S. Friedman, *No Haven for the Oppressed: United States Policy Toward Jewish Refugees, 1938–1945* (Detroit, 1973), p. 21.
2. Ellwood Cubberly (1886–1941), distinguished educator, founded Stanford's School of Education. David Starr Jordan (1851–1931), educator, philosopher, was the first president of Stanford.
3. Friedman, *No Haven for the Oppressed*, p. 85.
4. Ibid., p. 87. See also Henry L. Feingold, *The Politics of Rescue: The Roosevelt Administration and the Holocaust* (New Brunswick, N.J., 1970), chapter 6; David S. Wyman, *Paper Walls: America and the Refugee Crisis, 1938–1941* (Amherst, Mass., 1969); Arthur D. Morse, *While Six Million Died: A Chronicle of American Apathy* (New York, 1968).
5. David S. Wyman, "Why Auschwitz Was Never Bombed," *Commentary*, LXV, 5 (May 1978), 37–46.
6. Eric Bentley, ed., *The Storm Over the Deputy* (New York, 1964), p. 235.
7. Marie Syrkin, Letter to the Editor, *Midstream* (May 1968), 62. See also Yehuda Bauer, *The Holocaust in Historical Perspective* (Seattle, 1978), chapter 1.
8. Arthur Koestler, "The Nightmare that is a Reality," *New York Times*, January 9, 1944. For this reference and other information, I am indebted to Professor Deborah Lipstadt's article (in manuscript), "The American Media and the Holocaust: A Case Study" (November 1976).

9. Friedman, *No Haven for the Oppressed*, p. 143.
10. Elie Wiesel, *Night*, trans. Stella Rodway (New York, 1960). Bruno Bettelheim, *The Informed Heart: Autonomy in a Mass Age* (Glencoe, Ill., 1960).
11. Rolf Hochhuth, *Der Stellvertreter* (Reinbek bei Hamburg, 1963). American version, *The Deputy*, trans. Richard and Clara Winston (New York, 1964). See also Bentley, *The Storm Over The Deputy*.
12. Telford Taylor, *Nuremberg and Vietnam: An American Tragedy* (Chicago, 1970), p. 207.

VI.
AFTER THE
HOLOCAUST

FRANKLIN H. LITTELL

THE CREDIBILITY CRISIS
OF THE MODERN UNIVERSITY[1]

As the years have gone by, those most deeply involved in the study of the Holocaust—of which study the conduct and misconduct of the churches and their leaders is an important aspect—have become increasingly aware that not only the pathology of the event must be studied but also the implications for the present and future must be drawn. More and more, we are teaching not only the brute facts of the Holocaust but also the lessons of the Holocaust.

Here the university has a fundamental contribution to make. That contribution is not merely to foster research and publication about the event and its implications: it is—and this is much more difficult—to undertake that level of self-examination and reorientation that the memory of the Holocaust compels of the live conscience.

The question concerning the pathology of the Holocaust is this: What kind of theological faculties, law faculties, medical faculties, teachers' colleges, etc., produced those who made the Holocaust possible?

The lesson yet to be learned by the modern university runs like this: How do we structure the university in its relation to society and internally that its graduates function as men and women of conscience and wisdom with a commitment to life—and not as mere cogs in genocidal machines?

In sum, the problem I call to your attention is the fact that among university teachers and students and alumni the conviction is spreading that higher education is caught in an ever more acute loss of inner self-confidence and public credibility. Although the problem is in one sense part of a larger malaise of Western civilization, which used to be called

"Christendom," it is not geographically confined. Not only the multi-national corporations and cartels, with their own discourse and personnel and structures, have exploded far beyond the control of any single national government. In a very real sense, the associations of academics in the many specialties cross national and linguistic boundaries with remarkable freedom. Mathematics, which has created its own language—and has achieved what the Russian physician Lazarus Ludwig Zamenhof hoped of Esperanto—is of course the best example. But there are others.

A new university like that of Kuwait hopes to become like the California Institute of Technology, which in turn reflects earlier developments at MIT and the University of Chicago, which in turn were founded, like Johns Hopkins University and Cornell University, to appropriate perspectives on higher education learned from the University of Berlin. We academics not only run into each other in the study of the history of ideas: it is our common experience to meet colleagues of our own institution more frequently in Ann Arbor, or New Haven, or Jerusalem, or even Prague than on the home campus.

The question of where the modern university is going, and what we are producing in the way of new products and persons, has become a global issue. In the United States it has surfaced with increasing frequency during and since the Vietnam adventure. In candor, we American professors must admit that for some years it was easier to be articulate about the Nazi abuse and misuse of the sciences (Wissenschaften) during the Third Reich than to face the questions raised about our own universities' service to Dow Chemical, Minneapolis Honeywell, or Boeing Aircraft under Presidents Johnson and Nixon, or to ITT in the re-establishment of fascism in Chile.

It now seems clear, however, that the lessons learned from the period of the Nazi assault on the traditional creeds of Christendom (the story of Christianity and Kirchenkampf, of the Jewish people and the Shoah), are paradigmatic for the general malaise of the twentieth century. American and German scholars, in cooperation with individual colleagues from other countries (including, especially, Israel), have worked together for years on the pathology of the Third Reich. Today we are working very closely together in examining and expounding the lessons we can learn from the "alpine" event of the Holocaust, lessons which if appropriated can improve the life chances and the life of our children and children's children.

In studying the Book of History, as in examining the Book of Nature, we shall not progress unless we pose the right questions. Thousands of laboratory experiments have produced no results because the wrong questions were asked: the protagonist failed to push nature at the right point, until it pushed back. The same generalization can be made for conducting the dialogue with the past. What then is the question?

Let us take two questions put by writers from the people most savagely assaulted during this century. In his book *The Holocaust Kingdom*, Alexander Donat—a survivor of the Holocaust—put one question: "How can Christianity survive the discovery that after a thousand years of its being Europe's official religion, Europe remains pagan at heart?"[2]

The second question was put by Lucy Dawidowicz in her history, *The War Against the Jews, 1933–1945:* "How was it possible for a modern state to carry out systematic murder of a whole people for no reason other than that they were Jews?"[3]

The first question points toward the credibility crisis of Christianity. The second points to the credibility crisis of the modern university.

Concerning the credibility crisis of Christianity, consider these facts: The most powerful ideologies and substitute religions *(Ersatzreligionen)* of the modern age were not spawned by other religions or cultures— Hinduism, Buddhism, Jainism, for example. No: they arose in Moscow— the "Third Rome" of Eastern Orthodoxy, in the shadow of St. Peter's, and in the heartland of the Protestant Reformation. And the slaughter of six million Jews was not accomplished by superstitious savages out in the bush somewhere; it was done in Christendom by baptized Christians. Adolf Hitler died a Roman Catholic—never rebuked, let alone excommunicated, and an annual Mass is said in his memory in Madrid. Hermann Göring died a Protestant, never rebuked, let alone handled according to the requirements of church law. Of the inner circle, only Walther Darré and Martin Bormann had left the church (were *ausgetreten*), in the formal sense, "not of us."

How then shall we speak of the Messianic age, which the church fathers believed to have been inaugurated with the coming of Jesus, the Christ of God? Was Jesus a "false Messiah," of the kind the Jewish people has produced a number of times—not, of course, for what he taught but because of the conduct of those who claim his name? As Elie Wiesel has said, "No one can be a true Messiah whose followers feel they must torment and kill other men."[4] The question is not rhetorical, but of concrete historical import.

With the emergence of a new triumphalism in Christendom, the words are heard: "Yes, the Jews suffered . . . but the Christians suffered too." And the obscene question is even raised why we should be especially concerned for the six million Jewish martyrs when approximately eleven million died in concentration camps and approximately fifty-two million perished in

World War II. The question is abstract, based upon abstract generalizations of the kind popular among the educated since the Enlightenment.

If the generalization is this: "All life is sacred," then, to be sure, there is no difference between a murder, a fatal automobile accident, and a successful hunt in the Taunus. Common sense usually protects us from such absurdities. But when we turn to the deadly programs of the criminals who ran the Third Reich, it is astonishing how eagerly the Gentiles blur distinctions. The philosophers willingly talk about "man's inhumanity to man." The theologians address their minds to "theodicy." The sociologists talk fluently about "racism." For those who live in history, however, and think about discrete events, there is a basic difference between outdoor prisons that are run so brutally that people die, and camps that are constructed to serve as killing centers, deaths that occur in the clash of hostile forces and deaths that are planned, targeted, and accomplished upon the helpless.

The Holocaust—like the Exodus, Sinai, the first Return from Exile, the destruction of the Second Temple—is a discrete, indeed theologically and morally unique, event. It may function as a "plumbline"—to use the expression of the prophet Amos—in reference to other cases of mass murder, but it cannot be handled simply as one case of genocide among many.

The generalization that although the Jews suffered, the Christians suffered too, is false. To state the issue that way is simply to express Christian triumphalism, unrepentance, in a new set of words. There were, to be sure, eleven thousand to twelve thousand genuine Christian martyrs of the classical type—Paul Schneider of the Hunsrück, the Jesuit Father Alfred Delp, Dietrich Bonhoeffer, Probst Bernhard Lichtenberg, and others—and a larger group of unnumbered and unsung "righteous among the Gentiles." But the sign over this period of church history is not persecution: it is apostasy.

The church has not yet figured out how to deal theologically with apostasy, although it has a vast library of essays, hymns, and litanies on persecution. One of the reasons the observance of Yom HaShoah (the memorial day to the six million) by several hundred Christian congregations in the U.S.A. in 1979 is so important is precisely that it begins the necessary process of what the therapists call "grief-work," of working through our shame and grief for the season when so many of the baptized betrayed their calling.

Until that grief-work is completed, until by corrected teaching and fraternal acts we shall have re-established our Christian relationship to the

Jewish people on a sound basis, Christianity will have to continue to struggle through the greatest credibility crisis of its two millennia of history. It is important that our theological faculties teach seminars on the Holocaust and its meaning. It is even more important that Christian people remember, for to have faith is to remember.

More than forty years ago Julien Benda published a book entitled *The Treason of the Intellectuals*.[5] He was dealing with the decline of the educated leadership of the West into ethical relativism and moral bankruptcy. The awfulness of that "treason," however, was first spelled out for higher education in a book by Max Weinreich of the Yiddish Scientific Institute (YIVO).[6] In his classic work, published immediately after the collapse of the Third Reich, Dr. Weinreich reviewed the contribution of professors of great reputation to the growth of the Nazi ideology and system. He discussed the activities of men like Philipp Lenard and Johannes Stark (physicists and Nobel Prize winners), professors Emanuel Hirsch, F. K. Schumann, and Gerhard Kittel (theologians), the historian Walter Frank (of the *Institut zur Erforschung des jüdischen Einflusses auf das deutsche kirchliche Leben*), Professor Ernst Bergmann of Leipzig, Professor Walter Grundmann of Jena, and many others. He then gave major attention to the work of scientists in the extermination centers.

The credibility crisis of the modern university arises from the fact that the death camps were not planned and built, and their operational scheme devised by illiterates, by ignorant and unschooled savages. The killing centers were, like their inventors, products of what had been for generations one of the best university systems in the world. Himmler was always proud of the high percentage of Ph.D's in his officer corps!

How did the modern university—today in America as well as earlier in the universities of the Weimar Republic—an institution which was once called *universitas magistrorum ac scholarium*, even *universitas fidelium*—become great engines for turning out thousands upon thousands of technically competent barbarians? This is the question that will not die down, a question that arises when we relate the Holocaust to the German universities of the Weimar Republic and the Third Reich—but equally relevant to the universities that trained the university men who performed the "White House horrors," symbolized by "Watergate" and the American adventure in Vietnam.

It is only fair to point out that by 1936 some fifteen hundred professors had been expelled from their posts in the German universities—deemed uncooperative and unsuitable for the adventures of the Third Reich. And in the period from 1966 to 1970, a considerable number of teachers and students in the American universities raised vigorous opposition to the collaboration of those institutions with the CIA, the Pentagon, the FBI, and the other tools of the "military-industrial complex" which so damaged American society internally and American status and influence abroad.[7] Nevertheless, the American universities have changed very little as a result of those protests, and the recovery of corporate integrity then demanded of the university by the protestors is far from being accomplished.[8]

By and large, the process of rethinking and reshaping the university in America is just beginning, in good part as a result of recent study of the lessons of the Holocaust. In America we are, as it were, backing into attention to the conditions of our peace by way of initial reflection on the corruption of science and the debasement of the universities which attended the implementation of the "Final Solution to the Jewish question" by university men during the Third Reich.

Although we shall certainly not return, even if it were desirable, to the original model of the modern university, it might be well to remind ourselves of where *alma mater* began. In the first charters extant, those of Paris of 1219 and 1226, the *universitas* was not a place, a building, nor— remembering the modality of the present American scene—was it centered in a semi-professional basketball team. "Universitas" was a word inter- changeable with "community," "corps," and "college."[9] And the *studium generale*, contrary to the illusions of many contemporary humanists, was not a place where everything dealing with the human dimension was taught: it was a school of general resort, where students of many specializations were received.[10]

Arising out of the training of novices in the monasteries and the work of the cathedral schools, the university was the training field (the *campus*), where young men learned the subjects—and also a style of life, were equipped with technical competence—and launched in a lifelong pursuit of wisdom. The dormitory, the refectory, and the infirmary were but three of the structural expressions of a view of education that we find today in the Indian *ashram* and the Jewish *havura*—but very seldom in the large modern university.[11] Significantly, our student protests of recent years have centered on two points: first, a demand that the university recover the internal integrity of a community (*Gemeinschaft*); second, a demand that the university establish its own self-definition, and cease to be a mere adjunct to government or corporation interests.

Although devoted to producing skilled technicians, the kind of technicians that presumably have a future in the market place, the modern university no longer even turns out the skilled persons needed—in human terms. All questions of wisdom and ethics aside, we have an acute shortage in society of the doctors, nurses, legal counselors, teachers, etc., that the people really need.[12] Those who have the skills have followed the example of the university: they concentrate where government and the corporations can use them, rather than where the common good requires their services. In a world of multi-nationals, autonomous and sovereign powers controlled by no national government, in economies controlled by the profit motive alone, the technicians have become cogs in the machine. Our graduates work without serious internal conflict for social democratic Chile or fascist Chile, for the Greek junta or the Greek republic, for Franco Spain or republican Spain, for Russia, for China, for the Kuwaitis or the Israelis, for America, England, Indonesia or Pakistan—as long as the price is right. This summarizes, if harshly, the historical role of trained technicians, those who have been "educated" to skills in the moral and ethical and religious indifference of the modern university.

We are discussing the role of the university in society. To be sure that we have a common understanding of the social and economic setting, let me quickly summarize the major modes of human society.

In primitive society, "community" (Gemein/Gemeinschaft) depended upon blood relationships. Even separated by distance, different branches of the same extended family (Sippe) tribal group considered consanguinity the primary loyalty. With the development of an agricultural economy and settled villages, "community" (Gemein/Gemeinde) became a geographic reality with physical boundaries. The idea of "neighborhood" emerged. With the rise of modern industrialized society and the nation-state, the family and the neighborhood have left center stage. Some writers, considering the high divorce rate and the extreme mobility of personnel associated with the military and the corporations, have concluded that "community" is a vanishing phenomenon. But in fact a new kind of identity of interest, and of conscious identification (Wir-Gefühl) has appeared, based on economic function and social role.

In sum, a doctor in Los Angeles has more in common with a doctor in Boston than he has with the history teacher—whose name he probably doesn't even know—who lives in the apartment next door. And if we review the political activities of the American Medical Association, we learn how that community of interest among doctors affects the rest of society. A truck driver for a Boeing supplier in Seattle has more in common with a bus driver for SEPTA (Southwestern Pennsylvania Transit Authority) in Philadelphia than he has with the druggist who lives next door. And if we follow the politics of the Teamsters Union, we discover what that means for the rest of us. The taxi drivers know the taxi drivers, the lawyers know the lawyers, the bankers know the bankers. Even the spies know the spies.

The industrialized and specialized society at large depends for its life on the professional and vocational ethics and integrity of technicians, from milk testers to policemen to hospital administrators. If any one of them degenerates into a merely predatory, self-seeking association, with no commitment except to technical competence and group interest, the commonwealth suffers and will eventually collapse.

The modern university is structured like the modern society, and, in fact, to a large extent created it. For advanced society today is not a simple *Gemeinschaft*, in spite of the desperate effort of some political ideologies and systems to resurrect the archaic model. And the up-to-date university is no longer a *universitas fidelium*, in spite of the desperate effort of some religious groups to hold their colleges to the primitive familial model. Yale was founded in 1707 to produce educated Christian gentlemen. At the time there was a prevailing opinion as to the meaning of the terms "educated," "Christian," and "gentlemen." It was a former chaplain (*Universitätspredi-ger*) at Yale who defined the religious effort to preserve the archaic model, saying that today "a small Christian college" is an institution that produces small Christians. We cannot go back. But is the university now so tied to the necrophiliac machines and power structures of the modern nation-state that it cannot recover internal integrity and discipline?

When the university at Marburg (the first Protestant university) was founded, it was possible for such a signal event to be conceived as part of a program for the religious transformation of a whole people (*Reformatio Hassiae*).[13] Certain themes of contemporary importance were present even then, such as the devotion to ecumenism. But the real turning point in the history of the modern university may be symbolized by the founding of the University of Berlin (1809) and the triumph of the von Humboldt schemata of learning. In the United States the turning point came with the Morrill Land Act of 1862 and the launching of Johns Hopkins University and Cornell University on the German model. Daniel Coit Gilman of Johns Hopkins, Andrew Dickson White of Cornell University, William Rainey Harper of Chicago—these were among the great American educators who turned our institutions away from the familial, monochromatic model of a Christian *universitas* toward the specialized, research-centered "multi-versity."

The new model worked rather well as long as the cultural momentum of Christendom continued, as long as the technicians—including those trained in new academic disciplines such as anthropology, economics, sociology, political science, textual criticism—were still shaped in life style and restrained in professional conduct by a prevailing Christian ideology. With the contemporary collapse of that ideology and culture, however, and with the powerful claims of other ideologies and systems of being, usually in the service of the nation-state and its power elite, the university entered a state of crisis. It no longer has the internal consensus and integrity, nor the independent economic base, nor the strong sustaining support of other social institutions, to maintain its critical independence and coherent impact. A quick review of the list of research contracts at Temple University gives the picture, as it stands today. When, a decade ago, the revolting students broke into the administrative files of Columbia University and the University of Wisconsin (inter alia), they published the information on how those institutions had become adjuncts to government and corporation enterprises. Seldom did those who condemned the students for their destruction of office doors and pillaging of filing cabinets think to condemn also those who had destroyed the university itself.

We are brought back to the basic question put to the modern university by the Holocaust—and by subsequent necrophiliac actions by university-educated men and women, in America as well as elsewhere, taken in disregard of professional ethics and in contempt for the sacredness of human life. Is scientific expertise (*techne*) the only concern of the university—whether the discipline be theology, or journalism, or nuclear physics—or is it possible to reclaim and reassert the importance of the pursuit of wisdom (*Sophia*, even *Logos*)?

Here the paths of the postwar *academe* of West Germany and America diverge radically. In Germany, much of the basic educational work of the campus was taken up by the Evangelical Academies. From the founding of Bad Boll Evangelical Academy in October of 1945, and later in a number of strong centers, for two decades major attention was given to professional and vocational conferences and the rehabilitation of the specialized communities shattered by the experiences of the Third Reich and the war.

Dozens of conferences were held, and dozens of books[14] and reports were produced to help lawyers, school teachers, civil servants, apprentices, farmers, factory workers, surgeons, nurses, dance instructors, policemen, corporation executives, labor union leaders, engineers, journalists, etc., to rethink and rework their stewardship of power.

Two questions were always present, whether explicit or implicit: Where did we go wrong? What is our responsibility now, in "Germany's second chance at democracy?" It is not too much to say that the much-heralded "German miracle" is not only economic. It is rather more. One generation after the collapse, the police of Stuttgart are better disciplined servants of the public order than the police of Philadelphia, and the health services in the Federal Republic are greatly superior to those available to most citizens of the United States of America.

In America, because the universities are more accessible to the general public, and because every major institution of higher education has a considerable extension program, work like that of the Evangelical Academies has remained by and large a function of the university itself. In principle, it should be easier for questions affecting the public to be reflected in America in the improvement of higher education. In point of fact, however, the kinds of issues that arise when we consider the role of the university in twentieth-century genocide and potential apocalypse are just now coming to the fore.

The reason for this is difficult to find. In Germany, after the war, everyone was aware that something basic had gone wrong. There was not always agreement as to how to describe it or explain it, but the fundamental point was clear. At least a discussion of fundamentals could begin. In America, we still carry the awful burden of an easy conscience.

From Konrad Adenauer to Helmut Schmidt the representative leaders of public policy in West Germany have been strong to emphasize those policies which have given the society a measure of morale within and credibility without: maintenance of the delicate balance between individual liberties and popular sovereignty, rejection of totalitarian ideologies and programs, restitution to the Jewish people and friendship with Israel, loyalty to the alliance and common interests of the free countries. And, it might be added, this has been done in the face of the most severe provocations by terrorists and spies, and on one of the most dangerous frontiers in the world. The only country in the world that has maintained republican principles at greater risk has been Israel. In the Federal Republic, some of the lessons of the Holocaust have been learned.

In the United States, the delay in effecting reforms of the university, in raising in the professions and vocations the questions that can lead to a consensus and discipline of higher ethical level, has been due to the easy conscience and moral complacency that are so widespread. And nowhere is the easy conscience and complacency about its own record more thoroughly rooted than on the campus. Widespread moral revulsion finally stopped the adventure in Vietnam, but those who deceived the American people and betrayed the high trust of their posts have not been punished. Only when another massive betrayal of the stewardship of power occurred, symbolized by the term "Watergate," did some people begin to sense that there was something fundamentally wrong in the structures and direction of American society and government. And then some wrongdoers were punished, although the arousal of a general public concern has been sidetracked by a sentimental, subjective epidemic of individualistic religiousness (*Geistigkeit*).

In the last decade we have had a few important developments in professional and vocational training and ethics: bioethics programs at the Kennedy Center at Georgetown University and at Harvard University, Theology and Law seminars at Southern Methodist University and the University of Texas, a new center for the Life Sciences at Hastings-on-Hudson. And in 1978 the American Bar Association recommended that all law schools teach at least a single course in "professional ethics." Each of these programs owes its existence to the vision of a single person or a small group, and there is no connection between them. Only very recently has a more widespread uneasiness become evident, resulting in conferences and seminars and a few seminal articles in professional journals. To this latter development study of the Holocaust has made a considerable contribution. To a growing number of religious teachers in America, Christians as well as Jews, the Holocaust is coming to be viewed as a unique and shaping event in human history.[15]

For research purposes of humanists and atheists as well as professors of religious conviction, it is an event that gathers up the major pathological forces of Western civilization. The theoretical hypothesis runs as follows: Every good medical school has a department or division of pathology, for the study of decayed and dead bodies gives important clues to the nature of human health. Similarly, the study of pathological social and political situations, of which the Holocaust remains Exhibit A, can produce new and deeper understandings of what a good society is like.

I set up the first graduate seminar to deal with the Holocaust at Emory University in 1959. Ten years later we held the first academic conference on the Church Struggle and the Holocaust, at Wayne State University.[16] This conference was international, interfaith, and interdisciplinary, and the number participating annually has grown to approximately three hundred and fifty scholars and religious leaders. There have been dozens of "spin-offs" in state, university, and city conferences across the country—more yet since the showing of the Holocaust series on television. The Annual Scholars Conference is now held in New York City every March, under the auspices of the National Conference of Christians and Jews, but it is worth noting that when it started the host and co-founder was an American black professor, Hubert Locke, now Vice-Provost at the University of Washington in Seattle. Just last November Dr. Locke arranged an International

Scholars Symposium in Seattle, on the occasion of the fortieth anniversary of *Kristallnacht*.

In 1975 we founded in Philadelphia an Annual Conference on Teaching the Holocaust.[17] Out of this conference series have come several independent but cooperating institutions.[18]

As the work has grown over two decades, the volume of public as well as academic participation has expanded tremendously. At the time of the first Scholars Conference in 1970, there were perhaps a dozen university courses on the Holocaust. A count last year came to an estimated seven hundred courses, chiefly in religion, literature, and history.

The question is sometimes asked why, a generation later, so much attention is concentrated on the Holocaust. The real question is why it took so long for all but a few poets and novelists to get to work on it. The answer to the question comes, however, with reflection: a generation with the immediate experience of trauma and shame had to pass before anyone dared approach the data scientifically. Here, at least, we must be sure that the technical competence in handling materials is matched by sensitivity and wisdom in interpreting their meaning. In this sense, too, the university is challenged to be a genuine community of learning, embodying both *Techne* and *Sophia*.

NOTES

1. As delivered at Philips University, Marburg, June 19, 1979, this paper is an expanded version of the paper read at the San Jose Conference.
2. Alexander Donat, *The Holocaust Kingdom* (New York, 1965), p. 230.
3. Lucy S. Dawidowicz, *The War Against the Jews, 1933–1945* (New York, 1975), p. xiii.
4. Personal conversation with the author.
5. Julien Benda, *La trahison des clercs* (Paris, 1926). American edition: *The Treason of the Intellectuals* (New York, 1969).
6. Max Weinreich, *Hitler's Professors: The Part of Scholarship in Germany's Crimes Against the Jewish People* (New York, 1946), pp. 11 f, 195 ff.
7. See Immanuel Wallerstein and Paul Stern, eds., *The University Crisis Reader*, vol. II, *Confrontation and Counterattack* (New York, 1971).
8. Cf. a representative article by Warren Bryan Martin of the Danforth Foundation (which, however, is confined to the American experience): "The Ethical Crisis in Education," *Change*, VI (1974), 28–33.
9. F. M. Powicke and A. B. Emden, eds., *The Universities of Europe in the Middle Ages* (Oxford, 1936), vol. I, pp. 4–5.
10. Ibid., pp. 6–7.
11. A recent article by Myron S. Bloy, Jr., describes the confusion on our campuses this way: "every student must master a mass of unstated norms—which have enormous socializing effect, often exactly the opposite of the stated goals. . . . What the hidden curriculum teaches is competition, not communality." "Academic Values and Prophetic Discernment," *The Christian Century*, XCIII (1976), 889–94.

12. Ivan Illich, *Deschooling Society* (New York, 1972), p. 129.
13. Cf. Franklin H. Littell, *Landgraf Philipp und die Toleranz* (Bad Nauheim and Berlin, 1957).
14. See especially Eberhard Mueller, *Bekehrung der Strukturen* (Zurich and Hamburg, 1973).
15. See Franklin H. Littell, *The Crucifixion of the Jews* (New York, 1975).
16. See the conference report, Franklin H. Littell and Hubert G. Locke, eds., *The German Church Struggle and the Holocaust* (Detroit, 1974); see also Franklin H. Littell, "Ethics After Auschwitz," *Worldview*, XVIII (1975), 22–26.
17. Conference Reports (1975, 1976, 1977, 1978), as well as other materials, are available from the National Institute on the Holocaust, P. O. Box 2147, Philadelphia, Pa., 19103.
18. *a*. The Philadelphia Coordinating Council on the Holocaust, comprised of persons associated with the Roman Catholic Cardinal's Commission on Human Relations, the ecumenical Metropolitan Christian Council, and the Jewish Community Relations Council. The Coordinating Council has its primary work in planning and funding the annual teaching conference, and it also serves as a public forum for sharing information on work in high schools, colleges and universities, Christian and Jewish congregations, and developments in other American cities, in Israel and in the Federal Republic of Germany.
b. The first American system-wide teaching of the Holocaust at high-school level, with a syllabus and resources prepared under Philadelphia's metropolitan Board of Education. This program is now being replicated in a number of other American cities.
c. The National Institute on the Holocaust. This Institute is not primarily for conducting research or collecting archival material. It is a public service agency to universities, high schools, congregations, and concerned individuals throughout the United States and Canada.
d. A Ph.D program in Holocaust Studies at Temple University. This program started in the fall of 1977 and is conducted in cooperation with the Department of Holocaust Studies at the Institute of Contemporary Jewry, Hebrew University (Jerusalem).

PAUL M. VAN BUREN

CHANGES IN
CHRISTIAN THEOLOGY

Are there reverberations of the Holocaust in contemporary Christian theology? They can be heard, if you listen with care. What is to be heard does not sound like a band wagon. It is perhaps similar to what King David heard, "a rustling sound in the treetops" (II Sam. 5:24), not noisy, but not to be ignored. I should like to suggest an interpretation of what is happening and offer an outline of the consequences for the church's theology.

The facts are out in the open for anyone who cares to see them. From the Vatican to the World Council of Churches, in many branches of the church, something literally unheard of in the whole long history of the church is beginning to be said, namely, that the Jewish people have survived, that the people of God are alive, and that Judaism is to be affirmed, not denied. It is being said by councils of bishops, official study commissions, ecclesiastical bodies of standing, not just by individuals. In fact, a recently published collection of such pronouncements runs to some 150 pages.[1]

If you are familiar with the history of the church and its theology, you may see that what is now being said is not only new. It is a repudiation, a flat contradiction of what the church has said and taught from the second century until the twentieth. With these pronouncements, which have been appearing with increasing frequency and with increasing urgency over the past dozen or so years, the church appears to be turning away from its age-old teaching of contempt for the Jews and beginning to repent its age-old persecution of the Jewish people. This reversal on the part of one major religious tradition's attitude toward another is a matter of note in the history of religion.

How are we to assess this reversal? Admittedly, this change appears primarily in official documents; it expresses the views of the elite, the most reflective, or those in positions of responsibility. It has by no means become a majority sentiment among the rank and file of those who call themselves Christians, and it is not a "grass-roots" change. Still, it is not an insignificant shift for those holding positions of responsibility. But how shall we assess it? Is the church, or are its spokesmen, becoming tolerant under pressure of the liberal, humanistic, and culturally relativistic spirit of the age? That is one possible interpretation. However, I think it is more reasonable to see behind this shift the workings of Christianity's original hermeneutic of history, whereby historical events force themselves on the attention of the church and help to reorient its thought and action. If, in fact, the church is acknowledging the continuity of the Jewish people as providential and affirming the continuing validity of Judaism, this move entails major theological consequences and seems highly unlikely to be the result of the weak spirit of liberal toleration.

It seems that the change that is beginning to take place in the church's assessment of Judaism is a result of two twentieth-century events that have forced it to look directly at the Jews. These events are the Holocaust and the existence of the state of Israel. My guess is that neither of these two events standing alone could have caused such a change. Some of the earliest ecclesiastical responses to the Holocaust reflect the traditional, long-standing, negative assessment of Judaism by the church. Only when the shock of the horror of the Holocaust was coupled with the other, even greater, theological shock of the existence of a Jewish state, do we begin to see the first reversals of the church's teaching about the Jews.

These two events force themselves on the attention of the church, not because of the horror of the one or the novelty of the other. They present themselves as unavoidable events to the church because they have occurred in the history of that very people whose ancestors were the authors, compilers, and preservers of the Scriptures that the church holds to be Sacred Writ, and because they also were the protagonists of these Scriptures. He who reads the Scriptures reads of Israel. And if ever a people had a claim to continuity of identity, then Israel of old, the Jewish people down through their long, complex history, and the Jews of today are that people. By biological descent, language and practice, literature and religion, Israel and the Jews of today are one people. And it is concerning that people, what it did and what was done to it, what it had to say and what was said to it, that the Scriptures tell. Considering the respect and attention the church pays to those Scriptures, it is not out of place that it study the recent history of the Jewish people. At last the church is just beginning to learn about and respect the long history of the Jews, with a fresh awareness of the extent to which the church itself contributed so much to what has been unhappy in that history. The church, contrary to its fixed tradition, is slowly becoming aware of the fact that the Jews and their history did not come to an end in the first century of the Common Era.

I now want to turn to some of the consequences and implications that must logically follow this change in the church's thinking. I am not a prophet, and I do not know whether what has begun will continue. If it does, I think we will be witnesses to a change in the history of the church, compared to which those that occurred in the sixteenth century will seem insignificant.

Let us begin with the matter of identity. If the Jewish people are recognized to be God's Israel, the people of God, still worshipping the God of Israel, still trusting in God's promises, still holding true to the Torah, and, indeed once more re-established in the land God had promised them—then who are we of the church? I am, of course, aware that many Jews, maybe even the vast majority, do not so consider themselves. If they consider themselves Jews at all—and many of them do—then they think of themselves not as the people of God, but rather as the descendants of those who did so consider themselves. Nevertheless, they remain Jews by rabbinic definition, and also by self-understanding. And as for their faith and faithfulness, when was it not the case that many, if not most, fell far short of the intentions of Moses? If one's apprehension of reality is such as to focus on a God who created just this world, and who is concerned with such beings as we are, and therefore involved in just such a history as the sort we live, one will not be put off by the fact that many Jews want to have no part of Judaism. Suffice it now, as it has always sufficed, that some are faithful and others are not. The grounds for recognizing the Jewish people as God's people, called to hallow His Name in the world, are no weaker today—and of course no stronger—than they were before the beginning of our Era.

Who, then, are the Christians? Surely not the Jews, not the Israel of God. Christians are Gentiles, and the church is a Gentile enterprise, which may be distinguished from all other Gentile entities by the single fact that it worships the God of Israel, the God of the Jews. The church is not the people of God; it is, just as it has always said, the church of God, and that is something different. The first consequence that must follow from a new awareness of the Jewish people must be a fresh self-understanding of the church as of Gentiles who worship the God of the Jews.

From this there must follow a new understanding of the origins of this Gentile movement, and indeed, this area is receiving much attention these days from scholars and teachers of the church. Students of Christian Origins are becoming increasingly aware of the rich diversity and vitality of Judaism during the first century of the Common Era and through several following centuries. The Jesus-movement of that first century is now presented by scholars as a movement within Judaism, at first made up exclusively of Jews, and forming its self-understanding exclusively with the help of Jewish concepts. Those Jews who were loyal to the Jew Jesus understood him and responded to events in their history in a thoroughly Jewish way. Following Jesus first as a prophet of the End-time, they were then confronted by utterly unexpected events: his arrest and execution by the Gentile Pilate on the charge of having pretended to be a Messiah—one of many so treated by Pilate. Following this unheard of situation of finding their leader defined as a crucified Messiah, they were faced with something even more unexpected: whatever it was that happened at Easter, which left them convinced that God had acknowledged and ratified the Gentile Pilate's intrusion into whatever His divine plan had been for Jesus. As the Jews had done from the beginning, they understood these events as part of God's further dealings with them, further signs of the hand of the living God of history.

They did what the authors of the various Scriptures had done before them. They set out to reinterpret their Jewish tradition in such a way as to make it clear that these latest events were indeed the latest steps in the story, the latest chapters to which the story had been moving from the beginning. As their forebears had reinterpreted the tradition to take into account every major event in Israel's continuing history, so did the Jews of the young Jesus-movement. Nor did the story stop there, for two more events also proved to have this reorienting power of further shaping their Midrash (their way of telling the tradition). The first, which was to be decisive for the future, was the fact that although some of their fellow Jews accepted their Midrash, more and more Gentiles, already attracted to Judaism and frequenters of the synagogues, sought to join the Jesus-movement. This too was an astonishing, an unsettling, unexpected development. But this too was an event that led them to reinterpret their tradition in such a way as to include this new fact as the latest in God's holy history with His creation. Finally, the last event to be mentioned was the destruction of Jerusalem and the Temple by Titus. They took this as a sign, a confirmation by God of all that had happened so far, especially in the movement's openness to the Gentiles entering into their midst. By then, the movement had broken off relations with the rest of Judaism, and each proceeded to develop its own Midrash in its own way. In effect, both the young church and the developing rabbinic Judaism closed their canons, and neither felt free to take note of further historical events as potentially reorienting.

The church regarded the story as complete. It saw itself as having recognized the fulfillment of the purposes of Israel. It therefore assumed Israel's name and tradition, and regarded the vast body of the Jewish people as if they no longer had any significance. I shall not pursue the dark course of the development of this hostile attitude. Instead—in the light of events of our own time, which hold some claim to being reorienting and which, in fact, appear to be effecting some degree of reorientation in the church's mind—let me draw your attention to two further facts the church had completely ignored and which, had they been noticed, would surely have called into question that negative view of Judaism that had been so well established by the end of the first century.

The first of these facts was that during the period of the church's own formative development, from the end of the first to the end of the fifth century, in which all its major teachings and the form of its life and structure came to be established, during precisely that period, Judaism underwent a major renaissance, a formative period without parallel in its history, a flowering of Jewish spirituality and vitality to which we owe the Talmud in its entirety. Contrary to the developing theology of the church, Judaism was as far removed from withering away and decaying as it could possibly have been. History proved that part of the church's Midrash to be simply wrong.

The other fact that passed unrecognized was that by the end of the second century, the church, which had begun as a purely Jewish movement and had developed into that new society of Jews and Gentiles together of which as we read in the New Testament documents, had become an overwhelmingly Gentile enterprise. Gentile—99 and $\frac{44}{100}$ percent pure Gentile—yet worshipping the God of the Jews! No one put it that way, of course. No one has even thought about this transformation of the church until our own day, that is, until recent major events in the history of God's Israel began to reorient our thinking. Once we allow that to happen to us, however, we need to consider anew those earlier events which the church had ignored: the flourishing of Judaism and the Gentilization of the church. What is the meaning of these events? What does the Lord of history have up His sleeve that He wills to revive and cleanse His eternal people again and again, and that He means to have this strange new company of Gentiles who also call upon His name?

Fresh thinking on these matters is leading some in the church to set about the task of rethinking the meaning of its originating events. Without presuming to predict the outcome of all this, let me share with you some preliminary reflections. Historical scholarship has more or less reached at least one consensus: Jesus of Nazareth was a figure in no respect outside of the rich diversity of first-century Palestinian Judaism. I referred to him as a prophet of the End-time—a general term with which to place him in his time and context. Pilate's mocking title for him was "King of the Jews," which played on some aspects of some kinds of first-century Messianism. It tells us next to nothing if we say that his disciples called Jesus Messiah, because at that time there were a great many different conceptions of the Messiah. In any case, as the church rapidly became inundated by Gentiles, its language was Greek, not Hebrew or Aramaic; so it used the Greek term "Christ," and used it as a proper name, not as a title.

What seems to lie at the heart of everything the early church thought and said about Jesus was its conviction that in this man, and in his history—including his grim death—God, Israel's God, the God of history was at work. They were convinced that this faithful Jew was a servant of the living God, who was using His servant to accomplish something radically new. They were sure that God Himself was planning something, that He was as present and active as He had been when the Jews, under Moses' leadership, escaped from Egypt and camped before Mount Sinai. All the language reflects this conviction, and nothing could have been more Jewish. Indeed, who but a Jew could have dreamed of saying that these events and God's purpose were one. If you grasp these events, then you have grasped God's purpose, they were saying.

It seems likely that the first idea of the disciples—as it had been of Jesus himself—was that God was bringing about a new age, the age of redemption. This new age was about to begin at any moment, certainly within the lifetime of that generation. History has proved this expectation to have remained unfulfilled. After nineteen centuries—and especially after the events of our own century—there can be no doubt that the age of redemption has not yet come. The disciples thought that whatever it was that happened at Easter, the appearance of Jesus alive after his death, was the first sign of the beginning new age. Easter became for them the sure sign of total victory, and the Easter hymns and the Easter liturgy of the church continue to reflect that conviction. But surely, after all that I have referred to, we must see that Easter was only a hint, a token of that which we and Israel may and must hope for, but hardly the beginning of the age of redemption. We may say of Easter, as Churchill said of the victory at El Alamain during World War II: "This is not the end. It is not even the beginning to the end. But it is, perhaps, the end of the beginning."[2]

What, then, was that new thing God was doing in those strange events that centered on that Jew, Jesus of Nazareth? I have already said it: He was beginning something new, something unheard of, something that cannot possibly mean as much for a Jew as it does for a Christian. He was paving a way for Gentiles, those who, as one New Testament writer put it, were "alienated from the commonwealth of Israel, strangers to the covenants of promise, having no hope and without God" (Eph. 2:12), to call upon Him and to call Him what every Jew is free to call Him: Father.

No Jew has need of a mediator between him or her and God: of course not, for God is the God of Israel, the God of the Jews. But how, and by what right, can Gentiles come to know the love of the God of the Jews? How can they come to claim Him as their God too? The answer of the church is that we can do so because God has provided a way for us to do so, holding up to us this one Jew who claims us as his adopted sons and daughters. He is the one who teaches us to say, along with him, "Our Father." It is therefore no mere liturgical flourish when Christians conclude each prayer to the God of the Jews with the words, "through Jesus Christ, Our Lord."

With the perspective that new, reorienting events are making possible, it is now becoming clear that that most misunderstood doctrine of the church, its own most characteristic teaching, is by no means the confusing speculation it has seemed to many. Rather, the doctrine of the Trinity is a direct expression of the concrete, historical experience of the Gentile church. The one God, the God of Israel, who is ever and only one, has reached out and drawn us Gentiles to His service. When we confess God as Holy Spirit, we are acknowledging this fact of God's dealing with us: He has drawn us to himself, and this is truly His own doing. And God has drawn us to Himself by drawing us to one of His sons, as the people of Israel are so often called in the Scriptures. This one son is the one among His sons to and through whom He has drawn us, so that we may find our way out of Gentile darkness into His light by holding onto the hem of the garment of this one Jew who guides and teaches us. This too is God's own doing. God is fully and completely Himself in doing what He has done with and through Jesus of Nazareth. From our Gentile perspective, this one son of God stands alone for us, the Jew above all Jews, for it is through him that we may come to know the love of the God of Israel. Drawn by the Spirit, through Jesus Christ, we dare to call God our Father. That is how it has always been for Gentile Christians. The doctrine of the Trinity simply expresses this peculiarly Gentile apprehension of the One God of Israel.

I have only touched on some of the major areas of Christian theology, in which reverberations of the Holocaust can be detected. I have said nothing about the more important question of the effects on the life of the Christian church. I must mention at least one, because it is so closely connected with the church's theology. What will the consequences be of such new reflections on the understanding of the church's mission? Sooner or later, that mission will have to be seen as inseparably related to Israel's mission, the mission or purpose of the Jews. From the theological perspective that I have outlined, it is clear that the church will have to ponder anew the mystery of Israel, God's purpose for his beloved people. The church's mission—whatever it may be—will have to be worked out anew in the light of rethinking what God's purpose may be for His own people. Tentative beginnings suggest that we see the Holocaust and the state of Israel as God's way of putting us on notice that He expects us to shoulder far more of the burden of history than we thought He required of us. It is evidently not His will to pull us out of the mess we make of things, and if we are to come closer to the days of the Messiah, then it will be importantly up to us how we get there.

In conclusion, I want to offer two further observations. The first has to do with the church's traditional concern with converting Jews to Christianity. There are signs of a change here. As the church comes to see more clearly and more commonly the implications of its developing affirmation of Judaism, the more clearly it will come to see that it cannot wish to convert Jews. To what or to whom should the Jew convert, when he or she is already with the Father, and already one of God's people? To ask the Jews to be other than themselves would be to deny the election, the purpose of God. The first signs of this recognition, the growing hesitation to seek Jewish converts, are the first reverberations of the Holocaust that are just beginning to be felt.

Finally, I want to qualify all I have said by reminding you of what I mentioned at the beginning. What we are witnessing may be an important turning point for the church, but the turn is only beginning to be made. Since this turn, as I have outlined it, would be a response to the impact of historical events, it is not surprising that those branches of the church least attuned to historical thinking and least inclined to apply the methods of historical analysis that seem to be most fruitful in our age, show the fewest signs of taking part in the changes I have been discussing. What that suggests is that we will see the Catholic and Protestant wings of the church moving faster along these lines than the Eastern Orthodox branch; those least willing to see the biblical texts as historical products will be the slowest to make the turn I have been discussing.

Nevertheless, from many quarters and from persons and bodies of ever more authority, things are being said which may mark the beginnings of a whole new history in the relationship between the church and the Jewish people. I see no other way to account for this fact than to say it is one of the consequences of the Holocaust. This does not justify one single moment of that horrible event—even less could such a consequence compensate for the death of a single Jew. But I believe we should thank God that at least something positive is beginning to come out of it.

NOTES

1. H. Croner, ed., *Stepping Stones to Further Jewish-Christian Relations; an Unabridged Collection of Christian Documents* (London and New York, 1977).
2. Speech delivered at a dinner for the Lord Mayor of London, November 10, 1942. Reproduced in *Vital Speeches of the Day*, IX, 3 (New York, 1942).

JOHN T. PAWLIKOWSKI

CHRISTIAN PERSPECTIVE
AND MORAL IMPLICATIONS

It is not easy to grapple with the many dimensions of the Holocaust experience. It is especially difficult for sensitive Christians, considering that classic Christian anti-Judaism provided the seedbed for the ideology of the Nazis. Yet to ignore the questions raised by this experience would be to place ourselves in even greater danger. For the Holocaust was not an isolated example of insane human brutality. Rather, it marked the coming together of many of the major forces shaping contemporary Western society: bureaucracy, technology, and the loss of transcendent morality.

While the attempt to liquidate the Jewish people had everything to do with the legacy of Christian anti-Semitism, the Nazi "Final Solution" was not aimed at the Jews alone. As the Israeli historian Uriel Tal strongly maintains, it was meant to answer a universal crisis of the human person. Its stated goal was the complete transformation of human values. It was to liberate humankind from what were considered the "shackles" imposed by traditional ideas about God, moral responsibility, redemption, sin, and revelation. It attempted to restate classic theological notions in purely anthropological and political categories.[1] The Holocaust has shattered not only Christianity's moral basis, but that of Western liberal society as well, a point Irving Greenberg has so correctly insisted upon in his writings on the significance of Auschwitz:

> One of the most striking things about the *Einsatzgruppen* leadership makeup is the prevalence of educated people, professionals, especially lawyers, Ph.D.'s, and yes, even a clergyman. How naïve the nine-teenth-century polemic with religion appears to be in retrospect; how

simple Feuerbach, Nietzsche, and many others. The entire structure of autonomous logic and sovereign human reason now takes on a sinister character. . . . All the talk in the world about "atavism" cannot obscure the way in which such behavior is the outgrowth of democratic and modern values, as well as the pagan gods. . . . This responsibility must be shared not only by Christianity, but by the Enlightenment and democratic cultures as well. Their apathy and encouragement strengthened the will and capacity of the murderers to carry out the genocide, even as moral resistance and condemnation weakened that capacity.[2]

Thus the Holocaust not only poses a God-problem; it also raises the question of whether it is any longer possible to construct a hopeful image of the human person. For it was humanity in one of its most developed forms that perpetrated the Holocaust. It was a carefully planned and executed event, conceived by people who seemed to have attained the ultimate in human rationality and understanding. It also amounted to a deliberate decision on the part of the Nazi leadership to live within the condition of finitude while arrogating to themselves total power within this condition. As Michael Ryan has put it, Hitler's "world view amounted to the deliberate decision on the part of mass man to live within the limits of finitude without either the moral restraints or the hopes of traditional religion—in this case, Christianity."[3] Thus the most basic moral question that emerges from a study of the Holocaust is how we today grapple with a new sense of freedom within humankind in the context of a highly sophisticated technological capability with the capacity for massive destruction. The Nazis were perceptive in at least one area. They correctly sensed that a fundamental transformation was slowly taking place in the realm of human consciousness. Under the impact of the new science and technology, made more efficient by the concomitant sophistication in bureaucratic organization, humankind was undergoing a "Prometheus Unbound" experience on a much more massive scale than ever before in human history. More than just a few of the elite began to recognize a greater sense of personal dignity and autonomy than most of Western Christian theology had thought possible. Basic theological notions such as divine punishment, Hell, the wrath of God, divine providence, and the like, which had sustained a popular morality among the believing masses for centuries, were beginning to lose the hold they had had on people virtually since the biblical period. Hence a central task for Christian theological ethics today must be the discovery of a way to affirm the new sense of human freedom that continues to develop, while at the same time constructing the kind of meaningful norms that will channel this freedom into positive actions in behalf of humankind and the earth it inhabits. Any Christian morality that tries to deny the reality of this freedom will simply be exposing itself to irrelevance. Christian ethics will need to welcome the development of the sense of human liberation and elevation as a positive, crucial, and central part of the process of human salvation. It must come to appreciate the wisdom of Richard Rubenstein's insight about Nietzsche: he was the first among the modern thinkers to grasp the tremendous creative power inherent in the human person and to try to spell out the full implications of this discovery.[4]

In light of the Nazi experience, however, it would prove a grave mistake for Christian theological ethics to embrace this new sense of human liberation without qualification. The ethical philosopher Hans Jonas has written of the post-Holocaust period as a time in which "we shiver in the nakedness of a nihilism in which near-omnipotence is paired with near-emptiness, greater capacity with knowing least what for."[5]

Can post-Holocaust theological ethics overcome this impasse, this spirit of nihilism? Can it express an understanding of God and religion that will prevent the creative powers of the human person from being transformed into the forces of destruction that were horridly made visible in the Auschwitz era? That is the moral challenge facing the Christian churches today. I would agree with Irving Greenberg that the challenge is also one that besets contemporary Judaism, although in a somewhat different manner. But it is up to Jewish thinkers to wrestle with the problem in its Jewish context.

In his perceptive, albeit controversial, writings on the Holocaust, Richard Rubenstein has advocated "paganism" as the only adequate moral response to the dilemma posed by the Holocaust. Only a commitment to paganism can insure that human creativity will not turn on a massive scale into the destructiveness that the world witnessed during the Nazi period. By "paganism" Rubenstein means the willingness of men and women to rediscover their roots as "children of the earth," to perceive their existence as a

> wholly and totally earthly existence. It means once again to understand that for mankind the true divinities are the gods of earth, not the high gods of the sky; the gods of space and place, not the gods of time; the gods of home and hearth, not the gods of wandering, though wanderers we must be.[6]

He underscores the need for the human community once again to plant its feet firmly in the earth. Only thus can it save itself from further destruction.

While the new "earthliness" Rubenstein calls for must be part of any authentic morality after the Holocaust, his position by itself constitutes an insufficient response to the event. Accompanying that new earthliness must be the recovery of a sense of transcendence. If human life continues at a one-dimensional level, the utilization of the powerful new dimensions of human creativity, which we have stumbled across during the past two centuries, will undoubtedly result in a new manifestation of the hideousness revealed by Auschwitz.

Any in-depth analysis of modern attempts to create new societies based on ideologies that suppress or at least ignore any notion of transcendence will reveal frequent efforts to eliminate diversity and individuality in the name of creating the "universal person," and in many cases the unprecedented destruction of human life. We see some of this in the societies fathered by the Enlightenment which, in their European versions, could not fit Jewish self-identity into their universalizing scheme[7] and which, in their American version with its melting-pot concept tried to force Blacks, Jews, White ethnics, Native Americans, and Hispanics into a basically Northern European cultural pattern. Thus modern Western thought resulted in cultural dissolution and, for some groups such as Blacks and Native Americans, physical death, because their origins did not permit their self-respecting entry into a preconceived mold.[8]

Western liberal thought also played at least an indirect role in preparing the ground for the Holocaust by shattering the tight grip the God-concept and its attendant moral norms exercised on previous generations. In so doing it opened the doors to far greater human freedom and self-sufficiency minus any real understanding of the destructive potential that continued within human consciousness. It was this potential which eventually perverted authentic human freedom into Nazi cruelty. The Holocaust has in fact seriously tarnished much of the grandeur attached by many to Western liberal thought. It has clearly revealed the dangers inherent in building a society deemed capable of moral excellence without any reference to transcendent ethical norms.

The ultimate effect of the attempt to create the "new person" on the basis of an explicit rejection of transcendence is even more clearly revealed in the emergence of the so-called "new societies" in the U.S.S.R. and the People's Republic of China. Without blindness to the corruption and inhumanity of the regimes they replaced, and cognizant of some of their positive social accomplishments, we still cannot overlook the fact that millions died in the struggle to establish a so-called "heaven upon earth." An identical pattern is being played out at the present time in certain parts of the Third World, for instance in Cambodia.

However, a strong word of caution is in order to people dealing with this issue from a religious perspective. We must be completely honest. Past history has shown that many people have lost their lives at the hands of religious groups that clearly affirmed a sense of transcendence. The Crusades, the extermination of perhaps ten million Jews since the birth of Christianity, and the annihilation of tens of thousands of Native Americans as the colonists built the "new Zion" on these shores are clear illustrations of this. Yet this legacy cannot permit religiously motivated people from condemning the suffering and death inflicted upon millions by modern non- or anti-transcendence philosophies. There is no prospect of a return to the era of the Crusades and the Inquisition, at least not in the Western world. While a knowledge of this history is important for a proper focus today, the threat hanging over humankind is rather more ovens and gas chambers manned by proponents of ideological systems that aim to replace the religious vision.

Thus an approach to the problem of morality and the Holocaust such as that advocated by Richard Rubenstein is not wholly satisfying. It fails to come to grips with the tremendous potential for human destructiveness that remains an integral part of the new power and freedom residing in humanity, a potential so tragically realized during the Nazi era. Any theological ethic that avoids a serious confrontation with this phenomenon of destructiveness will prove of little worth in the creation of values for the post-Holocaust society.

To put it positively, a primary task facing contemporary theological ethics is the development of a sense of transcendence, which can counterbalance the potential for destructiveness to be found in the present-day human condition. It must be a sense of transcendence that will help guide human freedom toward the creation of societal patterns marked by dignity and diversity, and imbued with a profound sense of communal responsibility.

Theological ethics, however, cannot develop this new sense of transcendence in a vacuum. It can only emerge from the creation of meaningful religious encounters in which men and women begin genuinely to experience contact with a personal power beyond themselves. It will have to be an experience that heals the destructive tendencies which continue to lurk in the deepest recesses of human consciousness. Out of necessity, people must rediscover a loving presence in their midst which draws them beyond themselves, and in so doing provides a moral norm greater than humankind for guiding and judging human conduct. For the newly liberated person to be able to work continually toward the building and maintaining of a just, humane society there needs to emerge a deep awareness that there is a judgment on people's endeavors that transcends mere human judgment.

However, this sense of judgment will not be rooted primarily in fear of divine punishment, as was the case in past civilizations. Such an appeal will not work, for it is the modern human experience that people can perpetrate the worst atrocities with apparent impunity. While certain individuals may be capable of sustaining a high degree of moral commitment purely on the basis of a non-transcendent personal philosophy, the Holocaust has convinced me that on the level of mass morality the only norm that can curb further examples of the human degradation that was Auschwitz is one that is rooted in an experience of a love and unity beyond the narrow dimensions of this earth, together with the clear understanding that the use of power and freedom in the manner of the Nazis directly blocks the ultimate realization of such love and unity. Until this realization moves from the level of ethical ideas to a deeply felt perception within the human community, the dangers of another Auschwitz will remain high.

It is the task of theological ethics to express the reality of this experience; to speak to the human community of God; to describe their mutual relationship in a way that is faithful to the new understanding of human freedom and creativity which Nietzsche so dramatically brought to modern consciousness, and which was so brutally misused during the Nazi era. If theological ethics fails in this task, then we can expect continued repetitions of human degradation on a worldwide scale. Though some anti-transcendence philosophies such as Marxism and Western liberalism have without question bettered the quality of human living conditions in many areas, the abuses we have seen in both, as well as the potential for even greater destructiveness that has been shockingly revealed in the Holocaust, cannot be stopped without some continued belief in a transcendent God who is a loving, moral judge. Our generation needs to come to know this transcendent God in an intimate, personal way through meditation, liturgy, and poetry. The moral problem after Auschwitz is the recovery of some sense of God's judging presence as a guide for human freedom and power. Without such a recovery, we will continue to shiver in the moral nakedness of which Hans Jonas speaks.

At this point I must make it clear that the above description of the primary moral challenge stemming from the Holocaust is in no way intended to exonerate the complicity of the Christian churches in the event. In this respect, the remarks of Father Edward Flannery have to be taken with the utmost seriousness. While fully aware of the multicausal nature of the Holocaust, Flannery insists that in the final analysis, some degree of the charge (against the church) must be validated. Great or small, the apathy or silence was excessive. The fact remains that in the twentieth century of Christian civilization a genocide of six million innocent people was perpetrated in countries with many centuries of Christian traditions and by hands that were in many cases Christian. This fact in itself stands, however vaguely, as an indictment of the Christian conscience. The absence of reaction by those most directly implicated in the genocide only aggravates this broader indictment.[9]

Flannery goes on to say that even if we accept the position that the roots of Nazism are to be found in theories developed by modern secular thinkers, we cannot escape the fact that the architects of these racist philosophies were greatly aided in selling their ideas to the masses by the centuries of Christian anti-Semitism:

> The degraded state of the Jews, brought about by centuries of opprobrium and oppression, gave support to the invidious comparisons with which the racists built their theories. And in their evil design they were able to draw moral support from traditional Christian views of Jews and Judaism.[10]

It is clear that Hitler would not have achieved such widespread cooperation and support for the Final Solution if there had not already existed an anti-Semitic seedbed in much of European Christianity. This fact definitely creates a moral imperative for Christian churches to rid themselves of all anti-Semitic outlooks in theology, religious education, and liturgy. We cannot go into this question in great depth at this point, but it must be said without any qualification that the Christian churches cannot recover their moral integrity unless they seriously and honestly confront this issue. After all, a great many of the anti-Jewish laws devised by Hitler closely parallel the anti-Jewish laws enacted for centuries in Christian-dominated societies. Any attempt to sweep the problem under the carpet will only add to the serious moral failure on the part of the churches, which Flannery has so correctly brought to the forefront with respect to the Holocaust.

Certainly the churches have taken some important steps in virtually eliminating the historic charge of deicide from their Gospel proclamation, and in a sweeping overhaul of educational materials. However, serious problems still remain in systematic theology, liturgy, and even in the New Testament itself. These problems must continue to be discussed and resolved before the churches can truly return to a post-Auschwitz state of moral health.[11]

There is another major issue for theological ethics that arises from the ashes of Auschwitz. Historians and popular writers have debated at length the morality or immorality of Pope Pius XII's handling of the extermination of the Jews of Europe. Could he have done more? Could he have been more effective in saving Jewish lives if he had gone more public in his opposition to the Nazis? To some extent this issue may never be answered satisfactorily, for how does one accurately assess the impact of what might have been?

Beyond any personal evaluation of the moral quality of Pius XII's stance, it is important for Christian ethics to explore the theological framework that conditioned his mentality and guided his decision making during this critical period of human history. Professor Nora Levin is near the truth when she writes the following about Pius's papacy:

> In the years of fateful concern to European Jews this institution [i.e., the Vatican] was entrusted to a man who undoubtedly believed he was being scrupulously neutral in his appraisal of world-shattering events but who, admittedly, believed that National Socialism was a lesser evil than Communism. In this context alone, could Jews be viewed other than as unfortunate expendables? After all, it was the Nazis, not the Bolsheviks, who were destroying them.[12]

An evaluation of Pius XII and the Jews that moves in a similar vein is offered by the Catholic sociologist Gordon Zahn, in his various writings on the Nazi period.[13]

One aspect of Pius XII's papacy that needs further probing by ethicists is his ecclesiology, which largely defined the church in its essence as the institution through which the vital ingredients of human salvation—the Mass and the sacraments—become available to the human community. Since the continued existence of the Church was of the very highest priority, the goal had to be to keep the Church alive, no matter what the costs in non-Catholic lives. As one Vatican spokesman remarked, "you can conclude a concordat with the Nazis but not with Moscow." This ecclesiology did not directly intend to be callous with respect to the rights and very existence of non-Catholics. Rather, it envisioned the Church and its value for human beings in such a way that in crisis situations, when hardnosed decisions had to be made regarding the very survival of the institution, the destruction of non-Catholics could become an unfortunate by-product because non-Catholics had no central role in the definition of ecclesiology within Catholicism.

It seems to me that one can never underestimate the link between ecclesiological vision and moral questions. The theological presuppositions of Pius XII without doubt determined his attitude toward the Jewish question during the Nazi period. And the ecclesiological questions that emerged in Pius's time remain very much with us as the Church confronts totalitarian oppression in various parts of the world. We cannot change the decisions made by Pius XII. But from an analysis of the Holocaust the Church can alter its own self-understanding, relative to the role of outsiders, so that their continued survival becomes a central concern of the Church in a way unlike the ecclesiological vision that predominated in Pius's day. The ecclesiology that must direct moral decision-making in the Church today is one that sees the survival of non-Catholics as integral to the authentic survival of the Church itself. There is no way for Catholicism to survive meaningfully if it continues to allow the death of other peoples to be a by-product of its efforts at self-preservation.

Another major issue facing post-Auschwitz ethics concerns the image of the human person. Is there any basis for building an ethics upon a hopeful image of the human person after the Holocaust? While Elie Wiesel may have been speaking primarily in a personal context when writing the following at the conclusion of his volume *Night*, his words also take on a wider meaning:

> One day I was able to get up, after gathering all my strength. I wanted to see myself in the mirror hanging on the opposite wall. I had not seen myself since the ghetto. From the depth of the mirror a corpse gazed back at me. The look in his eyes, as they stared into mine, has never left me.[14]

Wiesel himself hinted at a wider meaning in response to a question presented to him at a symposium on the Holocaust. After reading his paper, Wiesel was bitterly attacked by a young Jewish scholar who finally demanded of him, "Wiesel, after six million Jewish dead, after Belsen and Dachau and Auschwitz, how can you ask us to believe in God? How can you or anyone believe in God?" To this attack Wiesel responded, "The question, my friend, is not how can I believe in God. The question after the Holocaust is, how can I believe in man?"

Any theological ethic that wishes to be authentic in light of the Holocaust experience must deal with this question. Is it possible, how is it possible, to rebuild a hopeful image of the human person in terms of working for a just and humane society in our world? The Holocaust has shattered much of the grandeur accorded the human person by both liberal rationalism and Marxist humanism. I think it is possible to rebuild, and so, ultimately, does Wiesel. But it will have to be a careful and painful process with a clear willingness to make theological and practical provision for the evil powers that remain in the human psyche. No theological ethic today can glibly assume a positive image of the human person. Such an image will be valid only if it has emerged from a profound and honest confrontation with the forces of destruction that showed their ugly faces in the Nazi leadership. For the Holocaust was not devised by raving idiots. It co-opted many of the best minds in the society of its time into its organization and development. And it depended, in part at least, on philosophies coming from thinkers many still consider to be giants of Western liberal thought. Rebuilding a hopeful image of the human person after Auschwitz is a preliminary step in ethical construction that no serious Christian can bypass.

Part of this rebuilding program will involve a rekindling of a sense of hope within the post-Holocaust generation. Unless we can reacquire a deeply felt sense of hope that is both realistic and optimistic, there is little chance that civilization will respond to an increasing number of social problems in a just fashion. In one of his more recent volumes, *The Oath,* Elie Wiesel alludes to the predicament in which men and women of the post-Auschwitz generation find themselves:

> To dream is to invite a future, if not to justify it, and to deny death, which denies dreams. Not so simple. Today's young people are choked by the sterile world that is theirs. For them there are no more distances, everything is made easy; they no longer need their imagination, and so it atrophies. The past is too far removed, the future not far enough. What need is there to imagine distant places when they are within your reach? And how is one to worship a heaven splattered with mud? What is the good of prolonging a civilization wallowing in ashes?[15]

The noted American ethicist Max Stackhouse confirms this prevailing mood among young Westerners, victims directly or indirectly of Auschwitz's destruction of fundamental human values, whom he interviewed as part of a team evaluation applicants for grants. These were people who in the not too distant future would be the decisive "bearers of culture." Stackhouse says that he felt in these young men and women an anguish that approach the tragic. While they held to certain personal ideals, they knew not why. Over-all, he says, "they held a fundamental doubt that anything was objectively valid in ethics, that there was a verifiable theoretical touchstone of cultural interpretation, that there was anything real about the life of the mind." A young American poet, whom Stackhouse does not name, has, in his view, captured the fundamental ethos he found prevalent among these students:

And the world turns:
> Crimes are legal now
> Shades of Eichmann and Calley watch
> over us like over-protective fathers,
And age-old Wars are today's Peace.

Pasts are forgotten
> or ignored;
Futures are only tentative figments of
> our collective imaginations;
And the Present swells its belly,
> Belching out poverty and hate.

And the world turns;
> Sins are moral now,
> or the word is extracted from our wizened minds.
We are victims of mass psychosurgery.
In our self-centered ambitions
> and our personal awareness,
> we all perform our own gay lobotomies
> with nimble, curious fingers.
Our steady, inpracticed hands are eager to transplant
> our hearts to our minds.
And together we chant: "I am truly a world."[16]

There cannot be any authentic moral commitment in the world that lies ahead until this malaise of the Holocaust is overcome.

In the area of hope, the post-Holocaust Church will also need to face the question raised by the Catholic philosopher Friedrich Heer. For him, Catholicism's failure to adequately confront the Holocaust is symptomatic of Catholicism's reaction to all other evils, especially to war and the possibility of a nuclear holocaust. For him, the main problem springs from the Church's withdrawal from history:

> The withdrawal of the church from history has created that specifically Christian and ecclesiastical irresponsibility toward the world, the Jew, the other person, even the Christian himself, considered as a human being—which was the ultimate cause of past catastrophies and may be the cause of a final catastrophe in the future.[17]

Heer attributes this fatalistic tendency primarily to the dominance of the "Augustinian principle" in Western Christian thought, which views the world essentially under the category of sin. This led to Auschwitz and may bring about a nuclear holocaust in the future unless the sense of despair about the world is seriously undercut. The only cure for this centuries-long moral cancer in Christianity, according to Heer, is for the Church to liberate itself from the dominance of the "Augustinian principle" and return to the Jewish roots of Jesus's own piety, to the original vision of the Hebrew Bible in which the human person felt the call to be both God's creature and his responsible moral partner in the world.

There are many other practical moral questions that need to be debated by Christians in the light of the Holocaust experience. They can be mentioned here only briefly. They include the need to reconsider how religion is legitimately to influence the shaping of public values in our pluralistic society. Has the emphasis on church-state separation resulted in an overprivitization of religion in American life, as Massachusetts Congressman Robert Drinan has charged? Do we need major readjustments in the way we think about religion's role in public life in the light of events like the Holocaust, as Pastor John Neuhaus has been saying recently? Auschwitz, I am convinced, has made some of our former theories of church-state separation obsolete.

On the other hand, we must also be sensitive to the warning issued by Gordon Zahn that one of the lessons of the Holocaust is the need for "preserving the purity and independence of the spiritual community and its teachings from domination by the national state with its definitions of situational needs and priorities."[18] The proper balance will obviously not be easy to strike. But it must be a new balance if Western society is to be characterized by a high moral purpose in its public life.

Consideration will also have to be given to the use of power. Both Richard Rubenstein[19] and Irving Greenberg have insisted that the use of power becomes a moral imperative for human survival after Auschwitz. This conclusion must be taken seriously by Christians. Yet a dialogue needs to take place about necessary curbs on power, a dialogue that is not yet adequately present in their writings. Here is an area where the moral tradition of Christianity may prove of some value.

Finally, there are such questions as the use of language by the Nazis, and the total depersonalization of the official description of their activities, which some see as the forerunner of the type of reporting employed by the United States government during the Vietnam War. And there is the southern border problem facing the United States, caused by poverty and the population explosion in Mexico. Here Rubenstein, for example, sees the potential for another holocaust.

One postscript: A proper understanding of the Holocaust will of necessity force us to recommit ourselves to ecumenism and interreligious dialogue. The Holocaust has clearly demonstrated that our respective covenants are not automatic guarantees of happiness and safety on the earth. It has shown how totally interrelated we are, both with each other and with all humanity. If some part of the human community decides to misuse the creative powers that human freedom gives them, all may suffer. God will not intervene to spare any special group. Our mission is to bring the knowledge and the experience of the loving transcendent God to all humankind as the only effective curb against the violence of Auschwitz. But if we Christians and Jews refuse to cooperate, if we take Auschwitz to mean we must remain silent and separate from one another, this opposition will be an obstacle to the humanization of the world and will create the potential for even greater destruction and suffering. As a popular television slogan put it: "We are all in this together." The Holocaust has elevated interreligious cooperation to the level of a moral imperative for both Christians and Jews.

NOTES

1. Uriel Tal, "Forms of Pseudo-Religion in the German *Kulturbereich* prior to the Holocaust," *Immanuel*, III (Winter, 1973–74), 68–73.
2. Irving Greenberg, "Cloud of Smoke, Pillar of Fire: Judaism, Christianity, and Modernity after the Holocaust," in Eva Fleischner, ed., *Auschwitz: Beginning of a New Era? Reflections on the Holocaust* (New York, 1977), p. 17.
3. Michael D. Ryan, "Hitler's Challenge to the Churches: A Theological Political Analysis of *Mein Kampf*," in Franklin H. Littell and Hubert G. Locke, eds., *The German Church Struggle and the Holocaust* (Detroit, 1974), pp. 160–61.
4. Richard L. Rubenstein, *After Auschwitz* (Indianapolis, 1966), p. 124.
5. Hans Jonas, *Philosophical Essays* (Boston, 1974), p. 124.
6. Richard L. Rubenstein, "Some Perspectives on Religious Faith after Auschwitz," in Littell and Locke, eds., *The German Church Struggle*, p. 267.
7. See Arther Hertzberg, *The French Enlightenment and the Jews* (New York, 1968).
8. Protestant and Catholic textbook studies give good evidence of this. See Bernhard E. Olson, *Faith and Prejudice* (New Haven, 1963); John T. Pawlikowski, *Catechetics and Prejudice* (New York, 1973); Eugene Fisher, *Faith Without Prejudice* (New York, 1977).
9. Edward Flannery, "Anti-Zionism and the Christian Psyche," *Journal of Ecumenical Studies*, VI, 2 (Spring 1969), 174–75.
10. Ibid.
11. See, for example, Eva Fleischner, *Judaism in German Christian Theology since 1945* (Metuchen, N.J., 1975); Charlotte Klein, *Anti-Judaism in Christian Theology* (Philadelphia, 1975); Rosemary Ruether, *Faith and Fratricide* (New York, 1974); Alan T. Davies, ed., *Anti-Semitism and the Foundation of Christianity* (New York, 1979); John T. Pawlikowski, "Judaism in Christian Education and Liturgy," in Eva Fleischner, ed., *Auschwitz: Beginning of a New Era?*, pp. 155–78; see also the "Response" by Claire Huchet-Bishop, ibid., pp. 179–90.
12. Nora Levin, *The Holocaust* (New York, 1973), p. 693.
13. See Gordon C. Zahn, "Catholic Resistance? A Yes and a No," in *The German Church Struggle*, pp. 203–37.

14. Elie Wiesel, *Night* (New York, 1969), p. 127.

15. Elie Wiesel, *The Oath* (New York, 1973), p. 64.

16. "Peace, Civilization and Culture," *Comprendre* (1976), No. 41–42, 152–54.

17. Friedrich Heer, *God's First Love*, trans. Geoffrey Skelton (New York, 1967), p. 406.

18. Zahn, "Catholic Resistance? A Yes and a No," in *The German Church Struggle*, p. 235.

19. See, for example, *The Cunning of History* (New York, 1978).

LAWRENCE L. LANGER

THE WRITER AND
THE HOLOCAUST EXPERIENCE[1]

All art requires a collaboration between the artist and his audience, since they presumably share certain common assumptions about the nature of reality and imagined experience. Holocaust art likewise requires a collaboration, but the demands on the audience are infinitely more complex. We do not and cannot share with the victims, in imagination or fact, the experience of extermination. Except for survivors of the death camps, who themselves sometimes admit that they find their recollections unreal, we cannot identify with the fate of so many millions consumed in the gas chambers and crematoria. And these are the images that ultimately dominate all accounts of the Holocaust, though often they are implicit rather than explicit. Whatever impact Anne Frank's *Diary* has on us today derives from our knowledge of what happened to her, in Auschwitz and Bergen-Belsen, after she was taken from the secret annex in Amsterdam. Similarly, a major source of the impact of films like *The Shop on Main Street* and *The Garden of the Finzi-Continis*, both of which end with roundups for deportation, is our foreknowledge of where those deportations will lead. The Holocaust moves beyond harassment, anti-Semitic legislation, pogroms, and emigration to the supreme unthinkable horror of our time: the annihilation of European Jewry. The constant pressure of this fact on our minds, as we witness films and read tales about the event, makes us vital collaborators with such art; if, whether through indifference or the passage of time, the moment ever arrives when an audience will have grown unmindful of this fact, Holocaust art will fail—precisely because it depends for its effect on memory as well as on imagination.

Films like *The Shop on Main Street* and *The Garden of the Finzi-Continis* (like Anne Frank's *Diary*) present illusions as realities, though we are usually the ones aware of the distinctions. The characters in these films believe that by clinging together as families, or neighbors, or lovers, or friends, they can make a difference in their eventual fate. Abnormal circumstances drive them to depend on old loyalties, whose values strengthen human ties even as their doom closes in on them. One test of these films is their creators' ability to convey the presence of this doom, to the audience if not to the characters, so that future disaster hovers on the edge of our imagination even as we are consoled by the familiar feelings of fellowship that united the potential victims and those who still show sympathy for them. One of the most unmanageable truths of the Holocaust is the failure of familiar sympathies to forestall the fate of the victims. Once the machinery of destruction was underway, nothing—not negotiation (for the Hungarian Jews), not international protest (weak as it was), not military reverses or the certainty that Germany would lose the war—could stop it. Films like these testify to the impotence of the humanistic vision in an age of atrocity, when the agents of atrocity, the Nazis, are utterly contemptuous of the values on which that vision is based.

This is one of the Holocaust's most painful truths, and we still have trouble accepting it. Neither the Jews, nor the nations of the world that refused to accept those who could escape while there was still time, believed that the Final Solution was literally what it proposed to be: the obliteration of all Jewish men, women, and children caught within the Nazi net. When viewing these films, we need to watch carefully for evidence—or the lack of evidence—of what these victims are soon to suffer. One of the great unsettled questions of the Holocaust era is who knew what—and when. The German people, of course, knew nothing of the death camps! Ordinary German soldiers were too busy fighting the war to learn of them. A distinguished historian has recently written a thick volume to prove that not even Hitler knew of the Final Solution or, at least, was not responsible for it.[2] And the Jews, as they climbed into boxcars all over Europe, were told that they were being resettled, not sent to their deaths. We shall never know what the victims thought as they were forced into the gas chambers which, they were told, were showers or disinfection rooms. None returned to tell us. The Allied refusal to bomb Auschwitz, or even the tracks leading to it, was surely based in part on the inability of officials to believe that the main purpose of the camp was the extermination of innocent human beings. We also have volumes, written by Frenchmen and Americans, proclaiming that the Holocaust was the hoax of the twentieth century: the Jews were never killed at all!

Behind much of this disbelief lies the failure of the humanistic vision to accept what we might call the inhumanistic vision, which includes the Nazi view of Jews as creatures less than human. Most of the characters in these films are victims of this failure—to their credit, in the sense that they remain human themselves by refusing to embrace the possibility of Nazi monstrosity; but simultaneously to their discredit, since their naïveté made them more vulnerable. We have a graphic example of this dilemma in the recently translated *Warsaw Diary* of Adam Czerniakow, first chairman of the Warsaw Jewish Council.[3] Two days before the deportations to Treblinka began, the ghetto was full of frightening rumors. Czerniakow asked for, received, and apparently believed an official Nazi denial of the impending event, then blithely issued a public proclamation to that effect. He expected from his oppressors the same good will that he exhibited toward them. Although his faith in human nature is appealing (as is the faith expressed by many of the characters in these films), we cannot escape a sense of the irrelevance of such moral and spiritual earnestness in a world that mocked his (and their) belief. If Czerniakow's fate—he committed suicide the day after the deportations began—and the fate of the Jews in these films persuade us of anything, it is of the vanity of trying to oppose decent values to the murderous ambitions of indecent men.

Although we like to read and hear about the connection between dignity and survival, the fact is that more than 90 percent of trapped European Jewry perished despite their innocence, their humanity, their faith in community values, and their belief in all those traditions that normally support civilized living. They perished in part because the world could not imagine, while there was still time to prevent it, the disaster that threatened to consume them; and in part, because they did not understand that in an age of atrocity, power knows no limits when it is in the hands of men like the leaders of Nazi Germany. As we watch the normal lives of the people in these films edge closer to disaster, we need to fill in the abnormal destiny that follows, as if their lives were incompleted paintings, abandoned by the artist when he realized the horror toward which his vision was drawing him. Unless we immerse ourselves in the worst of that horror, and not only the bearable pain that precedes it, we will be guilty of the same naïveté that made the victims so vulnerable, and delinquent in our reverence for the dead.

That reverence requires a grim piety; the doom that stifled their breath suffocates our spirit, leaving us gasping in despair. If one purpose of art, whether cinematic or literary, is to celebrate the moral vitality of man in the midst of tragedy, what are we to make of the Holocaust, which in the death camps denied the individual the moral space to choose his destiny? We cannot find analogies in earlier literature: Dante's damned were guilty of sin, and merited their punishment; the Jews were innocent. We do not recognize the features of an Oedipus or an Othello, whose destinies at least in part follow from their deeds, in the faces of the victims on the way to the gas chamber: the Jews have done nothing to deserve their fate. Unlike the tragic figure, their doom is unconnected to their previous lives. We must penetrate the traditional notions of character, which join act to consequence, to reach the unprecedented view that governs the lives of the elderly Jewish shopkeeper in *The Shop on Main Street* and the aristocratic Jewish family in *The Garden of the Finzi-Continis:* they are deported and will die because they are Jews, and for no other reason. Their deaths will not be linked to their lives in any way: our perception of this invariably affects our response to their stories.

One of the great merits of these films is their fidelity to the gradualness of the Nazi program of genocide. Extermination was the culmination of a long, slow process which began with irritating but manageable deprivations: Jewish merchants lost the right to own their shops; Jewish students were excluded from the public libraries; Jewish officials were banned from the Fascist Party in Italy. The Finzi-Continis, sheltered by their wealth, do not display alarm at the rising anti-Semitism. They withdraw a little further into the mausoleum of the family mansion, and continue their academic pursuits, their dinners, their ingrown devotion to a faded ideal. Today, we may look back and wonder why they did not act more vigorously in their own defense, take precautions to ensure their safety; but the benefit of hindsight is our luxury, not theirs. The anti-Semitism that was part of their tradition did not prepare them or anyone else for the ruthlessness of the Final Solution, though some historians still charge the victims with collaborating in their own destruction by complying too readily with orders for resettlement. If those victims could have imagined the atrocity that lay before them, they might have behaved differently; but since so many of us more than thirty years later still have trouble imagining the atroctiy that lies behind us, how can we blame the victims for not foreseeing the manner of their extinction, or for not accepting the rumors about it that filtered through to them?

The challenge of imagining the Holocaust—not the anti-Semitic tactics which led up to it, but its apocalyptic end in the gas chambers and crematoria of the death camps—is a permanent one, and will indeed grow more difficult for future generations who will lack the advantage of hearing living voices confirm the details of the ordeal they survived. The only evidence we will have available then is the kind we depend on increasingly today: verbal and visual accounts which inspire the imagination to conjure up an unimaginable world. The most convincing and effective are documentary films like *Night and Fog* or *The Eighty-First Blow* and survivor memoirs like Elie Wiesel's *Night* and Primo Levi's *Survival in Auschwitz*. Although there is not universal agreement on this point, my own conviction is that any student of the Holocaust must begin (though not end) here, confronting the unthinkable in its most naked form. Because of the nakedness of the horror in these films and books, however, many audiences turn away from their content as too awful, preferring more manageable experiences like *The Shop on Main Street* and *The Garden of the Finzi-Continis* where the unfocused threat of the death camps still hovers on the perimeters of the story. And this can create a dilemma, especially for members of future generations who will bring no direct memories of the Holocaust to the viewing of these films, deriving their response only from what is given. The imaginative film, unlike the frank documentary, is limited by certain aesthetic restrictions, and with rare exceptions has not yet solved the problem of bringing the death camp to the screen. The television extravaganza on the Holocaust sanitized the gas chamber episode, making of that humiliating chaos the modest march of clean naked bodies single file to their deaths. When Lina Wertmüller tried to convey the utter degradation of the experience in *Seven Beauties,* she roused a whirlwind of controversy and abuse for her unconventional views. But she was far closer to the horror of the event.

The "unthinkable in its most naked form,"—my own words are inadequate to convey what they are trying to say. Films like *The Shop on Main Street* and *The Garden of the Finzi-Continis* anticipate but do not reproduce the unthinkable; hence audiences can diminish the blood-chilling fear of the future by enjoying the heartwarming atmosphere of the present. Compare, for example, the generosity of spirit prevailing in these films with the views of character proposed by Salmen Lewental, a member of the last Jewish *Sonderkommando* in the Auschwitz gas chambers, who perished with the other victims, but left behind a buried manuscript dug up in the ruins in 1962: "There was a time in this camp," says Lewental, "in the years 1941–42, when each man, really each one who lived longer than two weeks, lived at the cost of lives of other people or on what they had taken from them."[4] It is virtually impossible to imagine the gentle protagonists of these films transformed by the mere instinct to stay alive into the kind of predatory creatures Lewental describes; yet this is one of the truths of the death camps that we must bring to a viewing of these films if we are to appreciate them as one kind of imaginative experience of the Holocaust.

The world of the death camp often mocks the hope and good will motivating the behavior of prospective victims before they entered that world: out of this conflict grows the vision of the Holocaust writer who is caught between old fidelities and new and unspeakable horrors as sources for his inspiration.

What literature has gained from the Holocaust, then, is a heritage that literature might well have done without; but it is inescapable now, and we have no choice except to confront it. The Holocaust has bequeathed to us a double vision, a knowledge of the intolerable and a desire to disbelieve it: the challenge of maintaining a tension between them raises some perplexing questions for the literary imagination. If one cannot imagine events that have actually happened, how are they to be presented to a curious but unprepared audience? Listen to the voice of an adolescent survivor of the camps, trapped between the knowledge of the intolerable and the desire to disbelieve: "One cannot forget what one has lost. I don't believe that my parents were shoved into the oven, although I saw it with my own eyes. When the war was over, I went back home hoping to find them."[5] On the one hand, the experience of unspeakable atrocity; on the other, the instinctive longing for reconciliation and renewal, the desperate hope that total disruption of human life has been only an illusion. There is simply no place in familiar moral reality for a line like: "my parents were shoved into the oven"; where then in the traditional landscape of death is the writer to locate it?

"Dying" is only one of the ideas that has been altered by the Holocaust. An entire literary vocabulary, which for generations furnished a sanctuary for motive and character, has been corrupted by that event. How, after Auschwitz, is the writer to conceive of the individual in conflict with his environment and his society? We think of Hamlet, wrestling with the awful responsibility of vengeance; of Oedipus, resolutely pursuing his identity, gaining insight though the price is terrible; of Anna Karenina, whose miserable fate does not destroy the sublimity of the grand passion that preceded it. Then we listen to another child's voice, contemplating her destiny with a confusion that admits no resolution, and we wonder what conventional motives like "vengeance," "insight," and "passion" could possibly have to do with her: "Maybe it would have been real lucky if I had gone toward the left with my mother and the others when the Nazis in the camp separated the prisoners for gassing and for working. They are at peace, they have no struggles. Is it lucky to have had to live in concentration camps and DP camps like I did? Not to know whether I would live or die from day to day? And to come out of it alone, and not to be with my family? I have often wondered if it would not have been better to have been taken care of by the Nazis, as my mother was. But here I am and I have to live; what for?"[6] Sometimes one wonders whether any art form can do justice to such lucid despair, or evoke a world in which men and women are divided into those "for gassing" and those "for working." Without such bizarre options from the past, the barren austerity of a writer like Samuel Beckett would be paranoiac melodrama; but his work is made luminous by the futility of the question raised by this young girl about survival in a post-Holocaust era: what for?

There are many reasons to live, one might hastily add, but none of them meaningful if they exclude the reality that orphaned this child. The paradox is this: Normally, the act of recollection unites one with moments in his past and offers the imagination the reassurance of a continuous flow in time; but the recollections of these children widen the gulf between the dead and the living, the past and the present, creating a void which memory cannot fill and which makes new beginnings impossible. We have no rituals of mourning to provide consolation long after the fact, especially after the fact of death by extermination. Dr. Joost Meerloo, a psychiatrist who worked with Dutch survivors after their liberation, reported that for many of them every "future is denied, any gratification is forsaken, and a withdrawal into persistent unhappiness takes place. . . . There are certain psychic wounds that prevent the utilization of the new-found freedom. These victims continue to live under the enemy's death verdict."[7]

The current interest in coping with death may be a manageable diversion from the more unmanageable task of confronting atrocity. The new concern with life after death may be a compensation for our inability to face life before death, the kind of death for which the Holocaust remains our starkest illustration. The longing for continued existence in infinite space reverses the situation of the victim in the camps who saw the boundaries of his fate shrink from the boxcar to the barracks to gas chamber to crematorium to chimney itself. Out of such unpromising material it was virtually impossible to create a literature that would celebrate the growth of the human spirit. An epic of genocide is a contradiction in terms. Any attempt to celebrate the dignity of the human spirit during the Holocaust would falsify the event if it did not first portray the humiliation of the human body. Only then would we discover how little nourishment such humiliation left the human spirit to feed on.

The implications of this truth for literature are enormous. For ever since the time of classical antiquity, the tragic vision has left men room to balance physical suffering with moral grandeur. The hero has a voice, up to the moment of his death, and through noble resignation or defiance can transcend the limits of his mortality. Hamlet's dying words to Horatio assure him of a future:

> If thou didst ever hold me in thy heart,
> Absent thee from felicity awhile,
> And in this harsh world draw thy
>   breath in pain,
> To tell my story.

And indeed, we still have Hamlet's story before us. But what narrative form, what literary art can tell the story of six million anonymous victims who left no voice behind? And how is a child, who saw his parents "shoved into the oven," to play Horatio in a world far harsher than any dreamt of in Hamlet's philosophy?

Yet someone must try, and many have. So far, it is easier to discover which literary traditions do not lend artistic support to imaginative expressions of the Holocaust, than those that do. Clearly the usual notion of tragedy, with a hero caught between difficult choices but free to embrace an attitude toward the consequences, and hence to preserve his moral stature, does not apply to men dying in the gas chamber. We need a new name for the art form that will portray the reputed dilemma of the Greek mother of three children who was told by the Nazis that she might save one of them from execution. She was free to "choose," but what civilized mind could consider this an example of moral choice? The alternatives are not difficult, they are impossible, and we are left with the terrifying revelation that life is sometimes reduced to impossible alternatives like these. How is literature to unearth a satisfactory solution for this inhuman dilemma? How is character to survive any decision in such a situation, and retain a semblance of human dignity? What can one do but echo the weary refrain of the young girl who was the sole survivor of her family: "but here I am and I have to live; what for?"

Heroic defiance, growing into tragic insight, needs a vision of moral order to nourish it, and this is precisely what the Holocaust universe lacks. The Holocaust is a saga without a controlling myth, opening out into an unending vista of chaos. Consider the protest of a survivor of a related sort, a woman worker in Solzhenitsyn's *Cancer Ward*, who one day was commanded (like the Jews) to leave her home with her family within twenty-four hours, only to see her daughter die in exile and her husband swallowed up by one of Stalin's labor camps. "These literary tragedies are just laughable," she says, "compared with ones we live through. Aida was allowed to join her loved one in the tomb and to die with him. But we aren't even allowed to know what's happening to them." Art can no longer transfigure a love that life so brutally discards; narratives of love's tragedy cannot illuminate the despair of the victims of atrocity. "Children write essays in school," this woman complains, "about the unhappy, tragic, doomed and I-don't-know-what-else life of Anna Karenina. But was Anna really unhappy? She chose passion and she paid for her passion—that's happiness! She was a free, proud human being." In fact, Anna was humiliated by her society and, in the end, by her uncontrollable jealousy, but she is the agent of her love and of her death, which distinguishes her from the helpless, innocent victims of the Holocaust universe. "So why should I read *Anna Karenina* again?" asks Solzhenitsyn's character. "Maybe it's enough—what I've experienced. Where can people read about us? *Us?* Only in a hundred years' time."[8]

The consequences of atrocity cannot be undone, nor can the lessons learned from it be transmitted as a ritual of rebirth to surviving generations. The Holocaust world lacks tragic energy because the contempt for the human which permeates it has combined with the terrors of the gas chamber to drown the protest of the individual will. And the fault lies not with the individual will, despite the contrary view of figures like Viktor Frankl and Bruno Bettelheim who suffer from a failure of imagination when faced with the dilemma of admitting what atrocity can do to the faculty of human choice.[9] I think of the survivor who told me what happened when she, like most of the women deported to Auschwitz with her, contracted typhus; a Polish doctor who befriended her and who had access to medicines brought in on prisoner transports, gave her a supply of tablets and instructed her to take one a day and not to share them with the other women in her barracks, because only a few for each would help none of them. So she kept them to herself, and survived the epidemic; many of her friends did not. Now how do we measure "dignified" behavior under such circumstances? Was her refusal to share the pills a courageous act, or a cowardly one? Where is the moral framework for dramatizing such conduct? Traditional values fail in the kind of world inhabited by the victim, and the traditional ideas of will and choice fail with them. They fail most significantly in moments of atrocity, when meaningless death imposes impossible choices and erases the options of possible ones that are our heritage from a meaningful life.

To anticipate heroism in such moments is to misunderstand both heroism and the essential nature of the moments. We inherit our comprehension of heroic choice less from life than from literature and allied art forms, so nothing is more natural than to expect responses based on our prior reading of apparently similar situations. But nothing is more inappropriate either, as I have been trying to suggest. Perhaps an illustration from a visual rather than a verbal art form will clarify the distinction between a character faced with impossible options in a moment of atrocity and possible options that enable the individual to retain that core of dignity, whatever the consequences, that makes life worth living, and death worth dying. The illustration is from Lina Wertmüller's much-praised and much-maligned film, *Seven Beauties,* when Pasqualino is ordered by the camp commandant to shoot his friend Francesco, who, having reached the limits of his endurance, had verbally insulted his Nazi captors. Miss Wertmüller uses her lens to capture a seminal moment of atrocity, as the camera pauses on Pasqualino's hesitating arm with the gun pointed at his friend's head. Viewers like Bruno Bettelheim who insist on the moral simplicity of this challenge—turn the gun on the SS guard—betray a sublime indifference to how the human will functions when threatened by the prospect of meaningless death. The confrontation is between Pasqualino and Francesco as they to work out their destiny in a hopeless situation while retaining some shred of human dignity. "Be brave and shoot," pleads Francesco; "If you don't someone else will, and I'd rather a friend did it. . . ." *"Francesco lifts up his head and looks at his friend pleadingly,"* read the directions in the printed text. *"Pasqualino isn't able to pull the trigger."* "This is torture," cries Francesco; "come on, hurry, I can't play the hero for much longer." And this is the point: the Holocaust does not permit its victims to play the hero. No triumphant gesture exists because neither death nor survival can rescue the human spirit from the physical humiliation to which the victims have been reduced. "If you wait any longer I'll pee in my pants," Francesco exclaims (in the printed text; the film version translation speaks of defecation); and Pasqualino shoots, perhaps to prevent this final degradation, a futile attempt to limit the unbearable for his friend in the absence of any means of affirming his humanity at the last instant of his life.[10]

Francesco dies for nothing, and Pasqualino lives for nothing, despite his haste to get married and raise a large family. "Don't think about the past," his mother urges him, using the familiar language of reassurance that blocks out the intolerable; "You're alive, Pasqualino . . . alive!"[11] Anyone who looks closely at his ravaged face as he stares blankly at his reflection in the mirror will recognize how atrocity has transformed a vain and ambitious petty criminal not into an image of moral grandeur but into a diminished human creature whose closing words—"yeah . . . I'm alive"—only stress the urgency of redefining the meaning of survival in a post-Holocaust era.

How different after all is his bitter, futile tone from the sentiment of the young Jewish girl who was the sole survivor of her family: "But here I am and I have to live; what for?"

We long for transfiguration, for some moral miracle that will change the victim of the Holocaust into a creature of heroic dimensions. After all, polluted Oedipus, that incestuous parricide, eventually regained the favor of the gods and ascended to heaven. But we lack a myth to restore man to the transcendent possibilities of a pre-Holocaust world, and we lack one precisely because, unlike Oedipus, the victim shared no responsibility for his destruction. Perhaps this explains why some historians and psychologists, among others, insist that the Jews were collaborators in their own extermination. If this were true, then a myth would exist to restore them to the normal flow of time: through prolonged suffering, or some act of expiation, they might purge themselves of guilt and gain redemption. The careful observer will note how I have lapsed into the familiar vocabulary of the tragic sensibility and the religious vision: "suffering," "expiation," "guilt," and "redemption." But the price we pay is to ignore how the Holocaust has radically disrupted the equilibrium of our moral and spiritual universe, by pretending that a logic of cause and effect, including the participation of the victim, led from the ghettos of Europe to the gas chambers of Auschwitz.

Atrocity is a merciless master, and will not allow us to escape along such well-worn paths. The essential challenge of the Holocaust was not spiritual but physical, not the purification of the soul through suffering but the disfiguration of the human body, the annihilation of the human form, the fragmentation of the human self. A new vision of character is necessary to dramatize this unsettling and unappealing proposition. A writer like Charlotte Delbo, herself an Auschwitz survivor, is one of the few to devise an idiom compatible with the experience of atrocity; the very rhythm of her language expresses the agony of the body struggling against the physical assault on its integrity. Long accustomed to sky, men finally learn to know the earth. Accustomed to earth, they must now learn to know the mud, the mud of the marshes about Auschwitz, where Delbo and her fellow prisoners dig daily, until their bodies merge with the very soil they seek to exhume.

As a result of this experience, nightmare displaces dream as a reflection of the human condition in *None of Us Will Return*, the first volume of Delbo's Auschwitz trilogy. Instead of character development, we get a vision like the following, a macabre ballet of human limbs and organs in mortal combat with the unimaginable:

The octopi were strangling us with their viscous muscles, and we freed
an arm only to be checked by a tentacle that wrapped itself around our
necks, squeezed the vertebrae, squeezed them until they snapped. . . .
We had to free our throats and in order to save ourselves from
strangulation, we had to sacrifice our arms, our legs, our waists to the
clasping intruding tentacles that multiplied endlessly, sprang up
everywhere, so innumerable that we were tempted to give up the
struggle and the exhausting vigilance.[12]

The progress from nightmare to recognition, the connection between
dream strangulation and the real suffocation that lay poised above them as a
common fate—indeed, the allusions to "our throats . . . our arms, our
legs"—all combine to emphasize the absence of differentiation among the
victims, preventing the emergence of a heroic prototype. This monster with
its tentacles, faceless and undefined, is to an age of atrocity what the demon
frozen in ice in the lowest depths of Dante's *Inferno* was to his Christian
contemporaries, though that demon was a concrete embodiment of evil
confirming a meaningful opposition between sin and repentance.

In Charlotte Delbo's concentration camp world, character succumbs to
anatomy. Crowded in restless sleep with her friends on a narrow wooden
bunk, the narrator merges with them and loses her definition of self:
"Everything vanishes into a shadow in which the leg that is moving belongs
to Lulu, the arm belongs to Yvonne, the head on my chest is Viva's head,
and awakened by the sensation that I am at the edge of the tier, on the
verge of falling out into the corridor, I plunge again into another
nightmare. . . ."[13] Albert Camus, with a restraint that seems optimistic in
comparison, had challenged his contemporaries to live within the limits of
the possible; in Charlotte Delbo's universe, women are forced to die within
those limits, when their lives were merely a reflection of their impending,
meaningless deaths and the imagination is left no room to breathe, the will
little space to hope. The tentacles of atrocity strangle the future, for victim
and survivor.

They strangle the future for the writer too, at least for the one who
tries to adapt traditional values to the Holocaust experience. In a vision of
reality reformulated by this experience, the writer must develop a kind of
choking and gasping idiom, reflecting the encounter with extermination
that lies at the heart of the Holocaust world. Pierre Gascar, whose *Season of
the Dead* narrates the response of a French prisoner of war in the Ukraine
to the discovery that the Nazis are systematically massacring the local
Jewish population, understands this need for a new idiom: "A language," he
writes, "does not always remain intact; when it has been forced to express
monstrous orders, bitter curses and the mutterings of murderers, it retains

for a long time those insidious distortions, those sheer slopes of speech from the top of which one looks down dizzily." Gascar goes further than most in his recognition of how the Holocaust has ruptured the rhythm of renewal that once characterized the literary view of human experience. His metaphors generate insight into a universe palsied by the heritage of genocide:

> Summer drew to a close. In the darkened countryside all life was slowed down; even the great convoys of death became more infrequent—those harvests, too, had been gathered in. But the dawn of a new season was less like the morning after a bad dream or the lucid astonishment of life than the final draining away of all blood, the last stage of a slow hemorrhage behind which a few tears of lymph trickle, like mourners at life's funeral. Autumn brought a prospect of exhausted silence, of a world pruned of living sounds, of the reign of total death.[14]

Nature itself, which can tolerate the tragedy of man dying, has been blighted by the atrocity of mass extermination. Holocaust literature must contend with a kingdom of diminished splendor, and Gascar provides a solid reason why: "Nothing makes you feel so impoverished as the death of strangers; dying, they testify to death without yielding anything of their lives that might compensate for the enhanced importance of darkness." It is an epitaph for all those anonymous millions, but an epigraph for the imaginative work that will be written in their behalf.

Imagining atrocity means imagining a disaster without consolation for those who must contemplate it. When Elie Wiesel asked the distinguished American critic Alfred Kazin whether he thought the Holocaust had any meaning, the critic replied: "I hope not."[15] Though accustomed to search for meaning in human experience, as in literature, we must be content to find none here. The paradox of Holocaust art is that creative energy must be used to evoke a destructive vision. Reading books and watching films about the Holocaust, we know in advance that there can *never* be a happy ending; even if a few survive, we dare not celebrate, since the fate of the others casts a shadow over our joy. Verbal and visual images may mediate between man and that fate, but they cannot duplicate it: they remind us, they prevent us from forgetting, and as the Holocaust fades into history, this in itself—keeping it vivid in people's minds—will be an overwhelming challenge. Wherever the journey of inquiry begins, it always ends in the same place—the gas chamber and crematorium.

Insofar as we acknowledge Holocaust art, we participate in this ceremony of remembering. All we can ask of ourselves is that, since the victims died in such terror, we should have the courage to live through it, if not with our flesh, then through the shared imaginative vision of the artist.

But the ultimate focus, the one requiring our constant collaboration, must be unambiguous—such art is deceptive and unfaithful if it does not bring us closer to the worst, and beyond the worst—to the unthinkable. Not in tribute to the dead, not to redeem them—but in agonizing confirmation of the catastrophe that consumed them.

NOTES

1. This is an expanded version of the paper read at the San Jose Conference. It appeared in *Congress Monthly,* 46, Nos. 4 and 5 (May and June 1979).
2. David Irving, *Hitler's War* (New York, 1977) and *Hitler, the War Path and Germany* (New York, 1978).
3. Raul Hilberg, Stanislaw Staron, and Joseph Kermisz, eds., *The Warsaw Diary of Adam Czerniakow* (New York, 1979).
4. Jadwiga Rezwínska, ed., *Amidst a Nightmare of Crime: Manuscripts of Members of Sonderkommando,* trans. Krystyna Michalik (Oświęcim, 1973), p. 147.
5. Editha Sterba, "The Effect of Persecution on Adolescents," in Henry Krystal, ed., *Massive Psychic Trauma* (New York, 1968), p. 55.
6. Ibid.
7. Joost A. M. Meerloo, "Neurologism and Denial of Psychic Trauma in Extermination Camp Survivors," in *Massive Psychic Trauma,* p. 73.
8. Alexander Solzhenitsyn, *Cancer Ward,* trans. Nicholas Bethell and David Burg (New York, 1969), p. 479.
9. See Viktor Frankl, *Man's Search for Meaning* (Boston, 1959), and Bruno Bettelheim, *The Informed Heart* (New York, 1960).
10. *The Screenplays of Lina Wertmüller,* trans. Steven Wagner (New York, 1977), p. 332.
11. Ibid., p. 334.
12. Charlotte Delbo, *None of Us Will Return,* trans. John Githen (Boston, 1978), p. 61.
13. Ibid., p. 62.
14. Pierre Gascar, *Beasts and Men and the Seed,* trans. Jean Stewart and Merloyd Lawrence (New York, 1960), pp. 215, 247, 248.
15. Elie Wiesel, "The Guilt We Share," in *Legends of Our Time* (New York, 1968), p. 201.

HENRY FRIEDLANDER

POSTCRIPT: TOWARD A METHODOLOGY OF TEACHING ABOUT THE HOLOCAUST

The Holocaust—a term that has come to describe the Nazi extermination of the European Jews—had until recently a special meaning only for a small circle of experts. This has changed during the past decade of debate on torture, terrorism, and human rights. The increasing number of books, films, documentaries, and newspaper stories dealing with the Holocaust indicates that it has slowly begun to enter the mainstream of public discourse. It was inevitable that with instant popularity the Holocaust would also become a subject taught in schools and colleges.

Recently the *New York Times* editorialized that "the annihilation of European Jewry should be a mandatory subject" in our public schools. The editors refused to express an opinion on method and content; they asked the schools to make all curricular decisions.[1] But as colleges and school systems rush to implement the popular mandate, they have no clear idea about the nature, limits, and implications of the Holocaust as a subject. It is therefore essential that we discuss the methodological basis for instruction on the Holocaust. This essay attempts to do so. It does not present a lesson plan or course outline; it does not concern itself with the question of technique. Instead, it attempts, for purposes of discussion, to present arguments on why, how, and to whom the Holocaust ought to be taught.

In the two decades that followed the end of World War II, the Jewish

---

Reprinted, with permission, from *Teachers College Record*, Vol. 80, No. 3 (February, 1979).

catastrophe in Europe remained a hidden and buried subject. Yet, this repression was not total. There was much publicity concerning the camps, the Nuremberg trials, the rescue of the survivors, and the creation of Israel. This period also saw the publication of many memoirs, the collection of documents, and the appearance of the first substantial monographs. Nevertheless, the Holocaust remained a special case, a kind of curiosity. My study of university textbooks in the late 1960's clearly shows this.[2] The Holocaust did not become part of our historical consciousness.

The refusal to overcome and integrate the past (what the Germans have called the *Bewältigung der Vergangenheit*) left psychological scars and, more important, made it impossible to view historical events accurately. The need to consider the Holocaust is of course obvious when we attempt to analyze the historical trends closely connected with it. Thus any interpretation of modern German or modern Jewish history must deal with the problems posed by the Nazi murder of the Jews. But it is not as well understood that the study of the Holocaust also has wider application. Nazi genocide forces us to re-examine our traditional interpretations of modern history and present-day society. Since the eighteenth century we have largely accepted the ideas of the Enlightenment, including the idea of progress. Even after two world wars we still tend to believe that the condition of modern man is improving, or at least moving in the direction predicted by the optimists of the nineteenth century. Historians and social scientists have made adjustments, but they have not abandoned this viewpoint.[3] And here a serious consideration of the Holocaust would necessitate a re-evaluation.

Recently there has been a change. In the 1970's the Holocaust became a subject of general interest. We now have more research and more publications. We also have a growing number of conferences to explore the subject and discuss its implications. Most important, we are also starting to teach about it.[4] This is an improvement. But at the same time there have also been two other, far more ambivalent, effects: proliferation and popularization.

The problem with too much being taught by too many without focus is that this poses the danger of destroying the subject through dilettantism. It is not enough for well-meaning teachers to feel a commitment to teach about genocide; they must also know the subject. It is ludicrous for large school systems, like New York's, to mandate teaching about the Holocaust without proper teacher training; even a curriculum guide and a few in-service hours will not be sufficient. For this reason small systems, like that of Brookline, Massachusets, have been more successful.[5] But even in the universities, dilettantism poses a problem. Because so few departments of history, the social sciences, or the humanities have integrated the Holocaust into their curriculum, teaching it has remained a matter of chance. Unless someone already tenured in the department happens to know the subject and undertakes to teach it, the Holocaust has been offered as a subject only under pressure and without serious intent. The faculty involved has tended to reflect this lack of departmental commitment: often they are volunteers interested in experimentation and attracted by novel subjects; sometimes they are junior members drafted from vaguely related areas like Judaica or German literature; frequently they are local rabbis recruited as adjuncts.

Popularization poses a similar problem. Though distasteful to scholars and many others, there is nothing intrinsically wrong with the popularity of a subject. It shows that the subject has been accepted. But unfortunately it can also mean sensationalism and exploitation. The semi-pornographic film *The Night Porter* is a rather crass example of exploitation. The Holocaust demands treatment with taste and sensitivity; it is not likely to receive this if it becomes a media fad. A good example is Gerald Green's *Holocaust,* an NBC-TV extravaganza and a Bantam mass market paperback. This soap opera was poor history and bad drama.[6] It could be argued that this is simply poor taste, and not a pedagogical problem. However, this product has been peddled as history by NBC and various Jewish agencies. This can be dangerous, especially if this kitsch is seen by millions. Supporters have argued that because millions who had never heard of the Holocaust saw this production, it performed an educational function. But while all might agree that it is important for us to understand the events of the Holocaust and their implications, no one has yet explained why it is valuable for many millions simply to know that genocide occurred. There is a difference between education and mass culture; it is an error to confuse the two.[7] Popularization is particularly dangerous for new and complicated subjects not yet fully understood or academically accepted.

The problems of popularization and proliferation should make us careful about how we introduce the Holocaust into the curriculum; it does not mean that we should stop teaching it. But we must try to define the subject of the Holocaust. Even if we do not agree about the content of the subject, we must agree on its goals and on its limitations.

First we must ask why we should teach the Holocaust. There are a number of reasons. One of them is our need to understand the past so that we can explain the present. While this might be a truism that could apply to all kinds of past events, it applies particularly to those of major importance.

The Holocaust is such a major historical event. It is not simply an aberration or a footnote to the history of the twentieth century; its various aspects—political, ideological, administrative, technological, sociological, moral, etc.—symbolize the problems and dilemmas of the contemporary world. Like the fall of Rome or the French Revolution, the Holocaust is one of those historical events that represent an age.

But how does a study of the past illuminate the present? The obvious lessons are often simplistic and cannot be applied; usually they are introduced for current political reasons. (In this way the lessons of the Holocaust have been misused in the current debate about abortion and affirmative action.[8]) One way to avoid such pitfalls is to see how scholars have approached the subject. Thus in 1944 Paul Farmer analyzed the historiography of the French Revolution, and discussed those French historians who wrote about the Revolution in the late nineteenth and early twentieth centuries. By doing this he not only illuminated the historical controversies about the Revolution, but also the political and social complexities of the troubled Third Republic.[9]

Tentatively, this method can already be applied to the Holocaust. Although there are numerous exceptions, we can place publications on the Holocaust into several large categories; each reflects different contemporary concerns. Thus Israelis write about the Holocaust from the vantage point of Israeli experiences and anxieties. Confronted with problems of security and survival, they tend to emphasize resistance; concerned with questions of national identity, they tend to focus on judeophobia.[10] East European and other Marxist authors tend to stress class structure and economic motives.[11] Theologians and moralists—both Jewish and Christian—emphasize heroism, compassion, and ethical dilemmas, as well as the Christian responsibility for anti-Semitism, when they deal with the Holocaust. For them these questions have been most applicable, particularly during the years of Vietnam and the Civil Rights struggle.[12] Sociologists, psychologists, and scholars from the humanities have tended to focus on the behavior of individuals. While the first two groups have usually emphasized the mechanical and passive behavior of victims in extreme situations, the third group has usually stressed their victory over adversity.[13] Historians, political scientists, and others concerned with public policy have concentrated on the bureaucratic and technological dimensions of the Holocaust. There they seek solutions to the problems of our mass society, where the individual seems powerless when confronted by the coercion of a faceless state.[14] It is not a question of the truth; all these approaches explain a portion of the truth. It is a question of different interpretations—different emphases—to shed light on different aspects, selected because of different present-day concerns.

But this attempt to use the Holocaust to illuminate the concerns of our age poses problems, because to do so means that the Holocaust must become a subject of legitimate public debate and scholarly controversy. For many, this has been terribly difficult to accept. And there have been attempts to impose serious restrictions on discussions of the Holocaust by those who wish to elevate the subject to the level of sacred history and who denounce opponents for sacrilege. Thus at the very start of the study of the Holocaust, the legitimate intellectual and academic analyses by Hannah Arendt, Bruno Bettelheim, and Raul Hilberg were denounced in a mindless way. Norman Podhoretz's "Study in the Perversity of Brilliance," Jacob Robinson's "Psychoanalysis in a Vacuum," and Nathan Eck's "Historical Research or Slander?" are particularly stark examples.[15]

And this attempt to stifle discussion continues. At a conference in Jerusalem in 1970, Emil Fackenheim lifted the discussion of the Holocaust to a sacred level: "A Jew knows about memory and uniqueness. He knows that the unique crime of the Nazi Holocaust must never be forgotten—and, above all, that the rescuing for memory of even a single innocent tear is a *holy task*."[16] In 1977, at the first San Jose Conference, Fackenheim argued that those who disagree with him about the uniqueness of the Holocaust, "insult" and "betray" the dead. At the same conference, and also in print, Bruno Bettelheim, once a victim of these arguments, denounced Terence Des Pres, accusing him by implication of spurious scholarship and aid to fascism; as a psychoanalyst he compounded the attack by stating that Des Pres was doing it unconsciously.[17]

But the Holocaust is not sacred history; it is a public event. Not only scholars in their histories, but also victims in their diaries and survivors in their memoirs, have treated the Holocaust as a public event that deserves thorough analysis. The imposition of restrictions on the study of the Holocaust by those who wish to elevate it to sacred history limits serious discussion of the Holocaust as a historical topic and does so unjustly and to the disadvantage of knowledge. (Of course, there is room and need for commemoration. But this must not be confused with discussion and analysis; the tendency to mingle the two diminishes both. In addition, there are related theological concerns that deserve, and have received, attention.[18])

As far as the study and teaching of the Holocaust is concerned, the problem is that one cannot have it both ways. One cannot treat the Holocaust as sacred history and also insist that it become a lesson and a warning for public discussion as well as an integrated part of our school curriculum. And throughout much of the debate about the Holocaust there is this attempt to have it both ways: to have it unique, and yet to have it as only the last example of two thousand years of persecution; to teach it as a moral lesson, and yet to make it so particular that no one else can use it. These are contradictions that must be resolved.

I must agree that it is difficult to accept a truly open discussion of the Holocaust, but there is no escape, and we must welcome viewpoints different from our own. Of course, there are limits. Legitimate controversy excludes authors like Butz, who argue that the Nazis never killed the Jews. But like crackpots who maintain that the earth is flat or that man did not evolve, one must simply disregard them. This is not possible when dealing with more respectable, but politically tendentious authors like David Irving. They must be refuted thoroughly and dispassionately.[19]

One reason we study the Holocaust is to understand the present; another is to understand man and his society. Like few other subjects, the Holocaust permits us to glimpse human behavior in extreme situations. Much work has already been done in this area by psychiatrists and others: Bruno Bettelheim, Elie Cohen, Robert Jay Lifton, and Terence Des Pres.[20] But the best way to study this is to consult the memoir literature as an original source; the best of the memoirs about life in the Nazi and Stalinist camps give us unusual insight into human behavior under extraordinary stress. Primo Levi's *If This Is a Man* is probably the best memoir of Auschwitz: detached and clinical, it tells us something about daily existence and human perseverance. (I also recommend the sequel, *The Reawakening*, which tells with humor and pathos of his liberation and his sojourn in Poland and Russia prior to his return to Italy.[21]) Equally revealing are the short stories of Tadeusz Borowski. These terrible tales about Auschwitz haunt the reader with their stark simplicity.[22] (The best literature of the Holocaust has tended to imitate Borowski's style; but such stories transform simplicity into surrealism as authors like Jakov Lind apply the experiences of Auschwitz to the everyday world.[23]) Memoirs of life in the Stalinist camps provide insights similar to those about the Nazi camps. Here the literature is also extensive. Susanne Leonhard's *Gestohlenes Leben* is the story of a highly educated Central European Communist; she spent years as a prisoner in the Vorkuta camp system of the Northern Polar region and as an exile in the Altai district of Central Asia, and her account, one of the best available, reflects the perceptions and sensibilities of a cultured and politically sophisticated European woman.[24] We even have memoirs that record experiences in both camp systems: Margarete Buber-Neumann recounts life in both Soviet and Nazi camps in vivid, journalistic language.[25]

To understand man and his society as revealed by the Holocaust, we must also study the intellectual mileu that made genocide possible. We must attempt to understand the totalitarian ideology. Much has been written about Hitler's ideological obsessions; the student can choose from a large number of interpretations.[26] But even more important, we want to know how leaders can motivate their followers to commit acts of inhumanity on a vast scale; how a worldview can create a society where gas chambers for human beings are considered normal. We want to understand the psychology of the perpetrators, of the SS-men, bureaucrats and butchers, who did the deed. There is plenty of documentation: biographies and autobiographies, descriptions and interpretations, interrogations and rationalizations, and a vast number of documents.[27] But it is still difficult to understand the killers.

In this context we want to understand the causes, the limitations, and the dynamics of anti-Semitism.[28] Unfortunately, this subject is steeped in mythology. Popular understanding tends to link it to bigotry without differentiating sufficiently between ideological hatreds and everyday prejudices.[29] Traditional histories lump together judeophobia in various ages, from antiquity to modern times, treating anti-Semitism as a permanent and unvaried phenomenon. This analysis, which sees only quantitative differences between the anti-Semitism of medieval Christianity and that of modern anti-Christian ideologies, is not a very convincing explanation when applied to the Holocaust.[30] Studies of modern anti-Semitism are more useful. They analyze the social roots and political uses of modern anti-Semitism; they trace the birth of the anti-Semitic parties and of their transformation into totalitarian movements. They show how the new anti-Semitism based on race differed qualitatively from the preceding type based on religion. Thus they delineate the radical nature of modern anti-Semitism.[31] But because they usually do not include the demonic, they fail to provide a fully satisfying explanation of how this ideology could lead to genocide.

A different approach, provocative and promising, is Norman Cohn's investigation of "how the impulse to persecute or exterminate is generated." In his first study he traced this impulse back to the Middle Ages and beyond. Analyzing the "apocalyptic fanaticism" directed against Jews as well as others by medieval millennial movements, he pointed out the similarity between their "militant, revolutionary chiliasm" and the totalitarian ideologies espoused by Nazis and Communists.[32] In his latest study he has continued this investigation of how genocide is possible. But this time he analyzed a "collective fantasy" not directed specifically against Jews, but against what medieval and early modern man, the educated as much as the ignorant, imagined as a society of witches. By investigating the background of the great witch-hunt, Cohn reveals the "inner demon" that can cause mass killings.[33] In a third study Cohn applied his investigation of historical psychopathology to the modern period. He analyzed a "fantasy at work in history" as exemplified by the modern forgery known as "The Protocols of the Elders of Zion"; he thus tried to show how the myth of the Jewish world conspiracy was a modern fantasy that provided the justification for the Holocaust.[34]

Complementing Cohn's studies are investigations into the social and psychological roots of twentieth-century unreason. The best of these is George Mosse's analysis of how nineteenth-century public festivals created the mythology and symbolism of a secular religion that culminated in the twentieth century in the mass pageantry of the Nazi revolution.[35] Related to this approach is the investigation of Nazi language. Here the best work, unfortunately not yet translated, is Viktor Klemperer's study of the *Lingua Tertii Imperii*. Klemperer was a Jewish professor who, though isolated and harassed, survived in Germany and evaded deportation. As a linguist he spent his years of inactivity observing the use and perversion of Nazi language. After the war he published his results in a fascinating book, part analysis and part personal memoir. He showed how Nazi language, devoid of reason, became a kind of exorcism, transforming clichés into realities. He dissected the exaggerations of this boastful language, indicating how words like "synchronize," "organize," "fanaticism," and "idealism" came to symbolize its poverty. His study remains the most successful attempt to analyze the political manipulation of culture and language under totalitarian rule.[36] In addition to the Nazi language analyzed by Klemperer, there is the specific language of the Holocaust. The former was the language of the propagandists, and it became the Nazis' linguistic milieu. The latter was the special bureaucratic language used by the technician who implemented the regime's terror. It contained those terrible euphemisms—*Aktion*, special treatment, *selekzya*, etc.—used by both perpetrators and victims.[37]

Technology is as important as ideology if we want to understand man and his society. We want to know how technology as system and as tool fits into the Holocaust. The futurists have seen this most clearly. The prototype of many futuristic stories, including George Orwell's *1984*, was the work of the Russian emigré Eugene Zamiatin. He wrote *We* in France during the 1920's, based on his experiences in Lenin's Russia. Unlike *1984*, the futuristic society of *We* did not have to coerce its citizens; they coerced each other. They lived as numbers in cubicles whose sides, floors, and ceilings were composed of glass, so that all could watch each other. For procreation, couples could obtain tickets permitting them to lower the shades for a few minutes. Apart from that, privacy did not exist.[38]

As we have seen, mass murder is nothing new; but the technological dimensions of the Holocaust are *sui generis*. Technological efficiency made Nazi genocide possible. The Nazis rationalized the killings and built factories for mass murder. In their killing centers they processed human beings on the assembly line; they operated their installations on the basis of productivity, cost accounting, and space utilization. The technology of the Holocaust does not only mean that the Nazis had the ability to use modern wares, such as guns and gas, to kill large numbers of people rapidly. More important, they possessed the capability to organize genocide. This required a know-how unavailable to earlier generations. Like modern warfare, genocide required bureaucracy and logistics. Millions of Jews residing throughout Europe had to be identified, registered, isolated, and moved before they could be killed. Only modern technology could accomplish this. It required the collaboration of a large bureaucracy in government, the army, and industry. Civil servants far removed from the killing centers had to help. Technicians, not ideologues, were needed to make genocide work. Raul Hilberg has recently shown how even the apolitical experts who ran the railroads participated; their technical knowledge was needed to move the victims to the death camps.[39]

A number of excellent studies have explored the technological dimensions of the Holocaust. They provide us with the best information we possess about what the Nazis called the "Final Solution." Of these, Raul Hilberg's investigation of the "process of destruction" is still the classical work on the subject. This massive study describes in minute detail the conception and execution of the Nazi program of extermination.[40] In recent years two other works treating the technological dimensions have appeared. A Tübingen dissertation by Uwe Adam explains in great detail and with unusual sophistication the official German policy vis-à-vis the Jews during the period that preceded and led to the decision to kill them. Adam shows how the civil service, including the police bureaucracy, approached their collective task; like Hilberg, he describes how they identified, excluded, despoiled, and removed them. He describes the process of removal: first by forced emigration, then by deportation, and finally by extermination. His study ends with the decision to kill the Jews. Unlike others, who have maintained that this decision became final just before the war with Russia, he has placed it in the late fall of 1941 when the plan to dump Europe's Jews beyond the Urals in a defeated Russia proved no longer feasible.[41] H. G. Adler's exhaustive study fills the gaps in our knowledge of the ways used by the Nazis to accomplish mass murder. With infinite detail he treats the deportations of the German Jews and the bureaucracy that managed them. Mingling theoretical analysis, narrative descriptions, and case studies, he delineates the process that placed the Jews in Germany on the trains to the killing centers; using surviving Gestapo files, he traces specific decisions and the fate of individuals.[42]

As it is our aim to study man and society, we cannot escape searching for parallels. Those who argue for the uniqueness of the Holocaust find comparisons objectionable. But even if their position were correct, comparisons are essential if we are to learn the lessons posed by the Holocaust. However, we have seen that the impulse to exterminate is old and pervasive; we only have to read the newspapers to know that it still exists. In intent and performance Nazi genocide was not unique; in technological efficiency it was *sui generis:* for the first time a modern industrial state implemented a calculated policy of extermination. Of course, no single historical event duplicates the Nazi deed, but many share different aspects of the process that led to the death camps.

Norman Cohn has shown how mass murder was practiced in medieval Europe, and there are no doubt numerous other historical examples. In modern times the obvious comparison is the attempt to exterminate the Armenians. Without the capabilities of the German state, the Turks uprooted and killed a people that had long lived amongst them. Their process was an innovation later imitated and improved by the Germans.[43] Another comparison is the treatment of the American Indians by the U.S. Government during the nineteenth century. Although the massacres of Indian men, women, and children occurred on a lawless frontier where the victims dared to strike back, the intent and the execution were to uproot and kill an entire group.[44] Almost a century later, while waging a war to liberate Europe from the Nazi yoke, the U.S. Government applied modern technological means to uproot native-born Japanese-Americans; it followed the process of destruction—registration, deportation, incarceration—but without the final step of extermination.[45]

In 1959 Stanley Elkins pointed out the parallels between the black slaves in America and the inmates in the Nazi camps. Although the aims of slavery were perpetual exploitation, not murder, many experiences were similar. The fate of the African slaves in the ships transporting them to the New World was not different from the tortures suffered by millions on the trains that brought them to the Nazi camps. The dehumanization of the black slaves strongly resembles that of the inmates in the Nazi and Stalinist camp systems.[46]

A very recent parallel was the war in Vietnam. Franklin Littell has argued that "the death camps were built by Ph.D.'s," and the Holocaust does shake our faith in formal education. Similarly, the barbarism of the Vietnam war, including its body counts so reminiscent of SS statistics, was directed by men and women highly educated in the sophisticated uses of technology, from computer war games to the logistics of aerial combat.[47]

Comparisons, though essential, should not be used indiscriminately. Unfortunately, there are those who dredge up a large number of apparent parallels to prove that Nazi genocide was not extraordinary; contending that as a subject the Holocaust is "too narrow,"[48] they can avoid dealing with the murder of the Jews. But comparisons are designed to make us understand and learn from the Holocaust; they must not be used to trivialize it.

A final reason for teaching the Holocaust is that its lessons can help us teach civic virtue. Purists may frown on this practice, but to a large degree this has always been part of education. Of course, I do not mean that the Holocaust should simply be used to teach conventional patriotism and accepted moral values; instead, its lessons must be used to demonstrate the need for what the Germans have called *Zivilcourage*. We need to teach the importance of responsible citizenship and mature iconoclasm. We must show that the only defense against persecution and extermination are citizens prepared to oppose the power of the state and to face the hostility of their neighbors to aid the intended victim.

But if we wish to teach the Holocaust in order to teach civic virtue, we are forced to universalize it. A good example of this is Peter Weiss' *The Investigation*, a play about the Auschwitz trial that does not mention Jews.[49] I can understand why some consider such treatment offensive; they remember the 1930's and 1940's, when the democratic West refused to recognize the existence of a Jewish people at a time when the Nazis were killing them because they were Jews. But Weiss transforms Jews into mankind, not into Poles or Czechs, to universalize the lessons and the meaning of the Holocaust.

For some, any attempt to universalize the lessons of the Holocaust is anathema. As we have seen, they consider the Holocaust so unique that they view all comparisons to parallel situations as a debasement, rejecting all analogies to past and current racial conflicts as inappropriate. But perhaps we can agree with the late Arthur Morse in his reply to Emil Fackenheim at the Jerusalem conference cited earlier: "It is not necessary that the analogy be perfect for a young person to hurl himself into peaceful combat against what he regards as barbarism. For him that war in Vietnam or that instance of racial injustice is his Holocaust of the moment."[50] A few take an even more extreme position. Thus Lucy Dawidowicz has argued that the Holocaust is a subject that only Jews can understand and teach.[51] But only in a closed group—Jews teaching Jews—can the Holocaust retain the particular alone. Certainly this ought not to be our aim. For this reason it ought to be taught in the major humanistic disciplines; exile to departments of Judaica spells ghettoization for the Holocaust as a subject. The *New York Times* said it succinctly: "Just as the subject of slavery must not be consigned to black studies, so the gas ovens ought not to be consigned to Jewish studies."[52]

We have seen why we should teach about the Holocaust; we now have to decide what ought to be taught when dealing with it. Of course, the preceding discussion of "why" has already shown us the dimensions of "what." And teachers will construct their own curricula to meet their particular goals. Here we simply need to delineate the essential topics and thus define the circumference of the Holocaust as a subject.

The first topic must be the German historical setting that produced Hitler and the Nazi movement.[53] German and Nazi history is well known and the literature is voluminous. Early interpretations went far back into the German past, to Arminius and Luther, to explain Nazism.[54] Most historians have rejected this sweeping indictment. Some have traced the roots of the Nazi phenomenon to the political, intellectual, and cultural trends in the nineteenth century; others have looked for answers in the political and economic turmoil of the Weimar Republic.[55] The events of 1918–19 were crucial. The trauma of defeat, the failure of revolution, and the armed struggle between factions doomed the democratic experiment and made the triumph of fascism almost inevitable.[56] In this atmosphere the Nazi movement could grow, prosper, and seize the state. Once in power, Hitler and his cronies transformed Prussian authoritarianism into German totalitarianism.[57]

A second topic must be totalitarianism. There have been many theories to explain the totalitarian phenomenon. They cover the spectrum: from Hannah Arendt, who saw it as *sui generis* in our times, to Karl Wittfogel, who saw it as the last in a line of human despotisms.[58] To explain the origins we must understand the major trends in modern history that led to the triumph of a new kind of authoritarianism of both the right and the left. Nazism was only one manifestation. Like Communism, it was an international ideology. But while Communism, tied to the doctrine of international egalitarianism, became national only with difficulty, Nazism—and fascism in general—was tied to a racial and national doctrine, and thus found it difficult to be international. It attracted not only Germans; many different nationals marched under the swastika. The Nazi leaders considered themselves the vanguard of a European movement, but they usually assumed the roles of leaders of the German Reich. The soldiers and bureaucrats who fought and worked for them only paid lip service to National Socialist doctrine; they continued to serve because they continued to equate Nazism with the Fatherland. Thus we can equate German and Nazi, something usually done in the study of the Holocaust, only with reservations.

Nazi ideology reflected this polarity. Their racial theory—what Hannah Arendt has called the biological interpretation of history—contained contradictions that were never resolved. Although less elegant and far less respectable than Marxism, racialism fulfilled the same function for the Nazis that Marxism did for the Communists (or that any religion, secular or not, has done for others). Anti-Semitism was only one aspect, though a central one, of this ideology (we must remember that gypsies were also killed in Auschwitz). The racial theory reflected the conflict between Nazi nationalism and internationalism. Ideology demanded that the Nazis prefer the nordic race but their world view required that they recruit others. Thus, while they tended to exclude non-Germans from policy decisions, they allied themselves with the Japanese and raised SS units in every European country. Similar contradictions existed in their views of the Jews. On one level they denounced them as totally inferior "vermin," who were to be exterminated by gas. On another level they saw them as "devils," a group with extraordinary power who, if not exterminated, would wreak terrible vengeance. But perhaps these contradictions did not matter; Nazism was not a rational ideological system that demanded consistency.

A third topic must be Jewish history, so that we can understand the victims and their response. Although it is probably not necessary to become familiar with the long course of Jewish history, some knowledge of the Jewish experience in post-biblical times is desirable. However, to understand why the Jews became the target of Nazi hatred, we must examine the Jewish condition in the modern world.[59] This should not be confused with the investigation of anti-Semitism, which concentrates on the fantasies of the judeophobes; their vision of the Jewish situation had little to do with reality. But a study of Jewish post-Emancipation history will reveal the exposed position of the Jews in European society. To grasp this we must try to understand the struggle over Emancipation, the process of acculturation, and the Jewish participation in cultural and economic life.[60]

Modern Jewish history will also help us to understand Jewish response to Nazi persecution. The Jewish historical experience and the structure of

Jewish communal life influenced that response; without knowing this we will never fully understand the life in the Jewish ghettos, the behavior of the Jewish Councils, or the nature of Jewish resistance.[61] Of course, answers cannot be monolithic: Jewish experience and Jewish response differed from country to country. Here we can agree with Lucjan Dobroszycki's argument that the Jews in Nazi-dominated Europe could do nothing to alter events; conditions external to their control—the German timetable, the status of the territory, the attitudes of the local population, and the physical geography—determined their fate.[62]

A fourth topic must be the behavior of the bystanders, the reaction of the outside world to the fate of the Jews. Much has been written about this; works by Henry Feingold, Saul Friedländer, Alfred Häsler, Arthur Morse, David Wyman, and Leni Yahil are good examples.[63] Some studies record successful efforts to save Jewish lives; most, however, describe the failure to rescue Jews before and during the war. And there is evidence that some bystanders, particularly in Eastern Europe, applauded and aided the murder of the Jews. Even the Western democracies refused to intervene. Recently David Wyman analyzed "why the United States rejected requests to bomb the gas chambers and crematoria at Auschwitz, or the railroads leading to Auschwitz." He proved that in the summer of 1944 the Allies had the capability and the opportunity to disrupt the process of destruction; their refusal to do so, at a time when the flames in Birkenau were consuming the Jews from Hungary and the Lodz ghetto, was not based on valid military considerations. Wyman concluded: "That the terrible plight of the Jews did not merit any active response remains a source of wonder, and a lesson, even today."[64]

The fifth and last topic must deal with the Nazi concentration camps, the arena for the Holocaust. This is the "other kingdom" the memoirs describe. But while their names and their most gruesome secrets are now widely known, specific facts about them are still not common knowledge. Confusion about their origin, their history, and their function is widespread; students cannot distinguish between them and usually confuse the various types of camps. Most assume that all were killing centers, and that the methods used at Auschwitz and Treblinka applied also at Dachau and Buchenwald. Although the memoir literature is enormous, few analyses are available; there is still no satisfying history of the Nazi concentration camp system.[65]

The best general accounts are still the semi-memoirs by Kogon and Kautsky. Eugen Kogon was imprisoned in Buchenwald for six years as an Austrian anti-Nazi. He originally wrote his analysis for the U.S. Army after liberation; although Buchenwald-centered, it provides a good survey of the camp system. As the partly Jewish son of Karl Kautsky, the famous Marxist theoretician, Benedikt Kautsky was incarcerated as a Jew in Buchenwald for four years, but was "reclassified" as a non-Jew after his transfer to Auschwitz. His analysis of the camps treats the system, the SS, and the inmates.[66] In addition, there are scholarly studies of individual camps; reports and memoirs about almost all camps; analyses of camp economics; and investigations of the behavior of the inmates.[67]

Almost immediately after the seizure of power in January 1933, the Nazis created the concentration camps (*Konzentrationslager,* officially abbreviated as KL and unofficially as KZ). The earliest camps were *ad hoc* creations by the brown-shirted SA stormtroopers. Located in jails, offices, factories, and other makeshift locations, they were places where the Nazis settled accounts with their political enemies. All were dissolved after several years. The first permanent camp, established by the SS in 1933, was Dachau near Munich. After the SS seized control of all camps and moved to regularize the system, Dachau became the model for all other camps, the training ground for generations of camp commanders. At first, expansion was slow: Sachsenhausen was established near Berlin in 1936, Buchenwald near Weimar in 1937. During 1938–39 more were added: Mauthausen in annexed Austria, Flossenbürg in Bavaria, Neuengamme near Hamburg (during 1938–40, as a Sachsenhausen subsidiary), and for women Ravensbrück near Berlin. Early in the war, more camps were established: in 1941–42 Gross-Rosen in Silesia, Stutthof in West Prussia, Natzweiler in Alsace, and Vught in Holland; in 1944 Dora-Mittelbau in Saxony. These were the main concentration camps, the so-called *Stammlager*.

At first the camps contained only the political enemies of the regime; to these were soon added non-political groups: professional criminals, homosexuals, religious dissenters, and other so-called asocial elements. Jews were incarcerated only if they also belonged to one of these groups; as Jews they entered the camps in large numbers only after *Kristallnacht* in 1938, but most of these were eventually released and forced to leave Germany. The Gestapo and the Criminal Police (later part of the Central Office for National Security, the RSHA) delivered the prisoners to the camps; the administration of the camps was under the Inspectorate of the Concentration Camps, and the guards came from the SS death-head units. Theodor Eicke, the first Dachau commander, served as Inspector and developed the system. Its aim was punishment and "re-education"; labor was used as a form of torture. The system was based on extreme brutality and a total disregard of human life. Each national camp system reflects its own traditions; unlike the Russian system, the German camps used military discipline as a form of control and torture. They were a caricature of a noncom's view of army life: the symmetry of barracks, flowers and trees, music and singing, marching and roll-call, standing at attention. For punishment and torture the SS preferred physical activity: calisthenics, beatings, exhausting labor.

During the war this changed. Political opponents and resistance fighters from all European countries swelled the camp population; Jews who at first were confined to the ghettos, labor camps, and killing centers of the East, later also flooded the camp system. While the size made the camps less manageable, the needs of the war economy made the labor of the inmates more valuable. The camps came to resemble the Soviet model where malnutrition, exposure, and death through labor took the place of capricious torture. Under Eicke's successor Richard Glücks, the Inspectorate became part of Oswald Pohl's economic empire, the SS Central Office for Economy and Administration, or WVHA. Still, the old structure—roll-calls, beatings, etc.—was always retained. Each *Stammlager* eventually headed numerous subsidiary camps; these covered Germany and a simple list fills a massive volume.[68] The camps became a world apart; the French called them *l'univers concentrationnaire*.

This system spawned the killing centers.[69] At first, the death camps were not run by the Inspectorate and were not staffed by Eicke's students; but eventually the killing centers were absorbed into the concentration camp system. The three death camps in eastern Poland—Belzec, Treblinka, Sobibor—were operated by the local SS and Police Leader Odilo Globocnik as part of Operation Reinhard; the one in western Poland—Chelmno (Kulmhof)—was run by a special *Einsatzkommando*. The techniques they used came from the experiences of the mobile killing units that murdered the Jews in Russia and from the commandos that killed the ill in the so–called Euthanasia Program.[70] These death camps were surrounded by many smaller camps that were *ad hoc* installations where conditions varied; some were labor camps and some smaller killing centers: the Janowska camp in Lemberg and camp Trawniki near Lublin are good examples.[71] No such camps existed in the West. There the Nazis established transfer camps, antechambers for the killing centers: Westerbork in Holland; Malines in Belgium; Drancy and Pithiviers in occupied France. The worst conditions obtained in the camps operated by the French authorities in Vichy France at Les Milles, Rivesaltes, and Gurs.[72]

Two death camps—Auschwitz-Birkenau and Lublin-Maidanek—were administered by the Inspectorate and became an integrated part of the concentration camp system, combining in perfect balance the methods of total control with the procedures of mass murder. The most important of these, the largest of all extermination and concentration camps, was Auschwitz in Upper Silesia. Established as a concentration camp in 1940 with the function of killing center added in 1941, it eventually became a huge enterprise, the center of many subsidiary camps. Divided into three parts, it swallowed millions of victims. Camp I was the *Stammlager* at Auschwitz; camp II was the killing center at Birkenau; camp III was the BUNA industrial complex at Monowitz.[73]

We have discussed the reasons for teaching the Holocaust and have attempted to outline the topics any treatment ought to include. But while teachers must master the materials, not all students should or could profit from an intensive study of the Holocaust. A detailed investigation along the lines indicated above is obviously designed only for those who have a professional interest in the Holocaust or one of its facets. College students majoring in history or one of the social sciences ought to become familiar with the details; graduate and professional education should also include appropriate aspects of the Holocaust. Thus medical students can investigate it as part of their concern for questions of bio-medical ethics; law students can study it to understand bureaucracy, administrative law, and the perversion of justice.

Most students are not professionally interested in the Holocaust. If they care about it at all, they come to it for various reasons: self-identity, moral commitment, concern with contemporary issues, etc. For them a specialized approach might not be appropriate. Here the problems and topics we have outlined could be covered in a less systematic fashion. Thus a study of the literature of the Holocaust could serve as a springboard for analysis. Using various readings—memoirs, novels, plays, essays—students can engage in a semi-structured discussion of the issues raised by the Holocaust. The growing number of books containing art from and about the Holocaust can serve as a visual supplement to the readings.[74] And as with literature and art, films about the Holocaust can become the focus for discussion and analysis. Films add immediacy for a generation born after 1945. Of course, one must be careful about the films one shows; too much visual horror can obscure understanding. A film like *Night and Fog* ought to be screened after careful preparation to students who have already obtained some information; it must not be used as a shock treatment to arouse interest.[75] In addition to the excellent documentaries, like the BBC films *Genocide* and *The Warsaw Ghetto*, there is also a growing number of superior commercial films: De Sica's *Garden of the Finzi-Continis* is a sensitive study of human response, while Costa-Gavras' *Special Sections* is a penetrating study of bureaucracy and the process of destruction.

NOTES

1. "Teaching the Holocaust," *New York Times*, 11 September 1977.
2. Henry Friedlander, "Publications on the Holocaust," in Franklin H. Littell and Hubert G. Locke, eds., *The German Church Struggle and the Holocaust* (Detroit, 1974), pp. 69–94, 296–303.
3. George G. Iggers, "The Idea of Progress: A Critical Reassessment," *American Historical Review*, (LXXI) (October 1965), 1–17. For an optimistic view, see Peter Gay, *The Enlightenment: An Interpretation* (New York, 1968), and for a pessimistic view, see Arthur Hertzberg, *The French Enlightenment and the Jews* (New York, 1970).
4. See *The Chronicle of Higher Education*, XVI, 10 (May 1, 1978).
5. Compare *The Holocaust: A Study of Genocide*, 2 vols., Curriculum Project Report No. 4042 by the Division of Educational Planning and Support, Board of Education of the City of New York, September 1977, and the Brookline, Mass. guide: Margot Stern Strom and William S. Parsons, *Facing History and Ourselves; Holocaust and Human Behavior*, 1977. For a college guide, see *Thinking about the Unthinkable: An Encounter with the Holocaust* (Hampshire College) Amherst, Mass., 1972.
6. Gerald Green, *Holocaust* (New York, 1978). For the controversy surrounding the TV play and book, see the *New York Times*, drama sections, April 14, 16, and 23, 1978; book review, April 16, 1978; and letters, April 30 and May 4, 1978. For the publicity blurb touting the TV drama, see the glossy, five-part package entitled "Holocaust," an Educational Guide to the NBC Television Special, a National Jewish Interagency Project, coordinated by Barry Shrage and introduced by Rabbi Irving Greenberg, 1978.
7. These comments do not apply to the show seen overseas, particularly in West Germany. There, unlike in the United States, the mass audience was personally involved and did not learn something entirely new. The show thus served to uncover a past long repressed and made it possible for the generations to confront each other in private and in public. See Peter Märthesheimer and Ivo Frenzel, eds., *Im Kreuzfeuer: Der Fernsehfilm "Holocaust." Eine Nation ist betroffen* (Frankfurt/Main, 1979). That this could be accomplished only by a TV soap opera and not by the excellent documentaries long available, tells us a great deal about the nature of mass communication and the mentality of the mass audience in all industrial countries. See Heinz Höhne, "Schwarzer Freitag für die Historiker," *Der Spiegel*, January 29, 1979, 22–23.
8. Some of those opposed to abortion on religious grounds have argued that it compares to Nazi genocide. They have pointed to the murder of the Jews as comparable to the prevention of birth after conception. But the killing of the Jews was centrally directed, ideologically determined, and brutally enforced; it cannot be compared to a medical procedure chosen by individual volunteers. It is also interesting to note, though rarely mentioned, that the Nazis themselves prohibited abortion, imposing on its practitioners draconic punishments. The truth, if any, of the anti-abortionist argument must be determined on its own merits; the Holocaust cannot be used to validate political positions. In the Bakke Case well-meaning people lined up on each side. In the creation of racial and sexual quotas some saw parallels to Nazi methods, while others argued that failure to assure sufficient representation for the underprivileged would perpetuate and increase the kind of exploitation practiced by the Nazis.
9. Paul Farmer, *France Reviews its Revolutionary Origins* (New York, 1944).

10. See Henry Feingold, "Some Thoughts on the Resistance Question," *Reconstructionist*, XLIV, 4 (May 1978), 7–11, who has described this as the "Bauer-Suhl approach"; Yehuda Bauer, *They Chose Life* (New York and Jerusalem, 1973); and Yuri Suhl, ed., *They Fought Back* (New York, 1967). For a scholarly and exhaustive study of Jewish resistance, see Reuben Ainsztein, *Jewish Resistance in Nazi-Occupied Europe* (New York, 1974). Some Israeli historians, like Leni Yahil, do not share this approach, and some non-Israeli historians do: a good example, combining resistance and identity is Lucy Dawidowicz, *The War Against the Jews* (New York, 1975), who, however, treats only the Polish Jews, consigning all others to an appendix.
11. See Ota Kraus and Erich Kulka, *Massenmord und Profit: Die faschistiche Ausrottungspolitik und ihre ökonomischen Hintergründe*, trans. Hanna Tichy (East Berlin, 1963); Tatiana Berenstein, Artur Eisenbach, Bernard Mark, Adam Rutkowski, eds., *Faschismus—Getto—Massenmord: Dokumentation über Ausrottung und Widerstand der Juden in Polen während des zweiten Weltkrieges*, issued by the Jewish Historical Institute Warsaw, translated from the Polish and Yiddish into German by Danuta Dabrowska (East Berlin, 1961).
12. Eva Fleischner, ed., *Auschwitz: Beginning of a New Era? Reflections on the Holocaust* (New York, 1974); Franklin H. Littell, *The Crucifixion of the Jews* (New York, 1975), A. Roy Eckardt, *Christianity and the Children of Israel* (New York, 1948); and *Elder and Younger Brother: The Encounter of Jews and Christians* (New York, 1967); Alice and Roy Eckardt, Studying the Holocaust's Impact Today, *Judaism*, Spring 1978, 222–32.
13. Bruno Bettelheim, *The Informed Heart: Autonomy in a Mass Age* (New York, 1971); Robert Jay Lifton, *History and Human Survival* (New York, 1970). For a book from the humanities, see Terence Des Pres, *The Survivor* (New York, 1976).
14. Raul Hilberg, *The Destruction of the European Jews* (Chicago, 1961); Uwe Dietrich Adam, *Judenpolitik im Dritten Reich*, Tübinger Schriften zur Sozial- und Zeitgeschichte (Düsseldorf, 1972); H. G. Adler, *Der verwaltete Mensch: Studien zur Deportation der Juden aus Deutschland* (Tübingen, 1974).
15. Norman Podhoretz, "Hannah Arendt on Eichmann: A Study in the Perversity of Brilliance," *Commentary*, XXXIV (November, 1962), 201–8; Jacob Robinson, *Psychoanalysis in a Vacuum: Bruno Bettelheim and the Holocaust* (New York, 1970); Nathan Eck, "Historical Research or Slander?" *Yad Vashem Studies*, VI (Jerusalem, 1967), 385–430. For a detailed and bibliographically valuable attack on Arendt, see Jacob Robinson, *And the Crooked shall be made straight* (New York, 1965). For Hilberg's and Bettelheim's works, see above, notes 13 and 14; For Hannah Arendt, see her *Eichmann in Jerusalem: A Report on the Banality of Evil* (New York, 1964).
16. Emil L. Fackenheim, *From Bergen-Belsen to Jerusalem* (Jerusalem, 1975), p. 10.
17. Presented at the First Western Regional Conference on the Holocaust, San Jose, California, February 1977. See also Bruno Bettelheim, "Reflections (Concentration Camp Survival)," *The New Yorker*, August 2, 1976, 31–52.
18. Some theological works are: Richard Rubenstein, *After Auschwitz: Radical Theology and Contemporary Judaism* (Indianapolis, 1966); Emil L. Fackenheim, *God's Presence in History: Jewish Affirmation and Philosophic Reflections* (New York, 1972); and *Encounters between Judaism and Modern Philosophy* (New York, 1973); Irving Greenberg, "Cloud of Smoke, Pillar of Fire: Judaism, Christianity, and Modernity after the Holocaust," in Fleischner, ed., *Auschwitz*, pp. 7–55. For a critique of Fackenheim's and Greenberg's theology, see Michael Wyschogrod, "Faith and the Holocaust," *Judaism*, XX, 3 (Summer 1971), 286–94 and "Auschwitz: Beginning of a New Era?" *Tradition*, XVII, 1 (Fall 1977), 63–78. For an extreme form of commemoration, see Irving Greenberg, "The Holocaust: The Need to Remember," Council of Jewish Federations, *General Assembly Papers*, 1977. For a solid treatment from the position of traditional Judaism, see Irving J. Rosenbaum, *The Holocaust and Halakha* (New York, 1976).

19. David Irving, *Hitler's War* (New York, 1977). For a sober review that demolishes Irving's thesis, see Martin Broszat, "Hitler und die Genesis der 'Endlösung'; Aus Anlass der Thesen von David Irving," *Vierteljahrshefte für Zeitgeschichte*, XXV (1977), 739–75.

20. For Bettelheim, Lifton, and Des Pres, see note 13. For Elie Cohen, see his *Human Behavior in the Concentration Camp*, translated from the Dutch by M. H. Braaksma (New York, n.d.).

21. Primo Levi, *If this is a Man* (New York, 1969; paperback ed.: *Survival in Auschwitz*, New York, 1973); and *The Reawakening* (Boston, 1965; publ. in Great Britain as *The Truce*).

22. Tadeusz Borowski, *This Way for the Gas, Ladies and Gentlemen* (New York, 1976).

23. Jakov Lind, *Soul of Wood and Other Stories*, translated Ralph Manheim (New York, 1966).

24. Susanne Leonhard, *Gestohlenes Leben* (Frankfurt/Main, 1956).

25. Margarete Buber-Neumann, *Als Gefangene bei Stalin und Hitler* (Zurich, 1949).

26. For traditional historical biographies, see Konrad Heiden, *Der Fuehrer: Hitler's Rise to Power*, trans. Ralph Manheim (Boston, 1944); Alan Bullock, *Hitler: A Study in Tyranny* (New York, 1964); Hugh R. Trevor-Roper, *The Last Days of Hitler* (New York, 1966). For psycho-historical biographies, see Rudolf Binion, *Hitler Among the Germans* (New York, Oxford, Amsterdam, 1976); Walter C. Langer, *The Mind of Adolf Hitler* (New York, 1972); Robert G. L. Waite, *The Psychopathic God: Adolf Hitler* (New York, 1977); Erich Fromm, *The Anatomy of Human Destructiveness* (New York, 1973).

27. Gerald Reitlinger, *The SS: Alibi of a Nation, 1922–1945* (New York, 1957); Heinz Höhne, *The Order of the Death's Head: The Story of Hitler's SS*, trans. Richard Barry (New York, 1971); Helmut Krausnick, et al., *Anatomy of the SS State*, translated from the German (London, 1968). For biographies and autobiographies, see Hannah Arendt, *Eichmann in Jerusalem* (see note 15); Henry V. Dicks, *Licensed Mass Murder: A Socio-Psychological Study of Some SS Killers* (New York, 1972); Gitta Sereny, *Into That Darkness* (New York, 1974); *Commandant of Auschwitz: The Autobiography of Rudolf Hoess* (New York, 1972). For interrogations and documents, see Robert M.W. Kempner, *SS im Kreuzverhör* (Munich, 1964); *Reichsführer: Briefe an und von Himmler*, Helmut Heiber, ed. (Munich, 1968); *The Stroop Report: "The Jewish Quarter of Warsaw Is No More!"* facsimile edition with translation by Sybil Milton (New York, 1979).

28. For one attempt to define terms and concepts, see Gavin I. Langmuir, "Prolegomena to any present analysis of hostility against Jews," *Social Science Information*, XV (1976), 689–727.

29. This is most obvious in the publications of defense agencies like the Anti-Defamation League, the American Jewish Committee, and the World Jewish Congress. See also Lucy Dawidowicz, *The Jewish Presence* (New York, 1977), Chapter 13.

30. *Anti-Semitism* (Jerusalem, 1974); Malcolm Hay, *The Foot of Pride* (Boston, 1950; paperback ed. as *Europe and the Jews*); E. H. Flannery, *The Anguish of the Jews* (New York, 1965). The best general history is Leon Poliakov, *The History of Anti-Semitism*, 3 vols., trans. from the French (New York, 1964–75).

31. Eva Reichmann, *Hostages of Civilization* (Westport, Conn., 1971); Peter Pulzer, *The Rise of Political Anti-Semitism in Germany and Austria* (New York, 1964); Paul Massing, *Rehearsal for Destruction: A Study of Political Antisemitism in Imperial Germany* (New York, 1967); Robert Byrnes, *Anti-Semitism in Modern France* (New York, 1969); Andrew Whiteside, *The Socialism of Fools* (Berkeley, Cal., 1975); Richard S. Levy, *The Downfall of the Anti-Semitic Political Parties in Imperial Germany* (New Haven, 1975); and Uriel Tal, *Christians and Jews in Germany*, trans. from the Hebrew (Ithaca, N.Y., 1975).

32. Norman Cohn, *The Pursuit of the Millennium: Revolutionary Messianism in Medieval and Reformation Europe and its Bearing on Modern Totalitarian Movements* (New York, 1961).

33. Norman Cohn, *Europe's Inner Demons: An Enquiry Inspired by the Great Witch-Hunt* (New York, 1975).

34. Norman Cohn, *Warrant for Genocide: The Myth of the Jewish World-Conspiracy and the "Protocols of the Elders of Zion"* (New York, 1969).

35. George L. Mosse, *The Nationalization of the Masses: Political Symbolism and Mass Movements in Germany from the Napoleonic Wars through the Third Reich* (New York, 1975). See also his *Toward the Final Solution* (New York, 1978).

36. Viktor Klemperer, *LTI: Notizbuch eines Philologen* (East Berlin, 1946; West German ed. as *Die unbewältigte Sprache* Munich, 1969).

37. See Friedlander, "The Manipulation of Language," p. 103 this vol. Also Cornelia Berning, *Vom "Abstammungsnachweis" zum "Zuchtwart." Vokabular des Nationalsozialismus* (Berlin, 1964); Dolf Sternberger, Gerhard Storz, W. E. Süskind, *Aus dem Wörterbuch des Unmenschen* (Munich, 1962); Joseph Wulf, *Aus dem Lexicon der Mörder* (Gütersloh, 1963).

38. Eugene Zamiatin, *We* (New York, 1952).

39. Raul Hilberg, "German Railroads—Jewish Souls," *Society*, November-December, 1976, 60–74.

40. Raul Hilberg, *The Destruction of the European Jews* (see note 14). For an earlier attempt, see Gerald Reitlinger, *The Final Solution* (New York, 1953).

41. Uwe Adam, *Judenpolitik im Dritten Reich* (see note 14).

42. H. G. Adler, *Der verwaltete Mensch* (see note 14).

43. For an introduction, see Franz Werfel, *The Forty Days of Musa Dagh*, trans. Jeoffrey Dunlop (New York, 1935), and Abraham H. Hartunian, *Neither to Laugh nor to Weep. A Memoir of the Armenian Genocide*, trans. Vartan Hartunian (Boston, 1976).

44. For an Introduction, see Dee Brown, *Bury My Heart at Wounded Knee* (New York, 1970). For a broad historical treatment, tracing attitudes and practices from Spain to the New World, see Ronald Sander, *Lost Tribes and Promised Lands: The Origins of American Racism* (Boston, 1978).

45. See Michi Weglyn, *Years of Infamy: The Untold Story of America's Concentration Camps* (New York, 1976); John Modell, ed., *The Kikuchi Diary: Chronicle from an American Concentration Camp* (Urbana, Ill., 1973); Miné Okubo, *Citizen 13660* (New York, 1946).

46. Stanley M. Elkins, *Slavery*, 2nd ed. (Chicago, 1968).

47. Littell quote from conference on the Holocaust at Arizona State University, Tempe, Arizona, 1978. See also Telford Taylor, *Nuremberg and Vietnam* (Chicago, 1970).

48. This was the phrase used by the editor, Albie Burke, of the journal *The History Teacher* (letter of 23 Feb. 1978) rejecting an earlier version of this article.

49. Peter Weiss, *The Investigation: Oratorio in 11 Cantos* (London, 1965).

50. Arthur Morse in Fackenheim, *From Bergen–Belsen to Jerusalem*, p. 23 (see note 16).

51. At the meeting of the Modern Language Association, New York, 1976.

52. September 11, 1977 (see note 1).

53. Some textbooks: Marshall Dill, *Germany: A Modern History* (Ann Arbor, 1970); Koppel Pinson, *Modern Germany* (New York, 1966); Golo Mann, *The History of Germany Since 1789*, trans. Marian Jackson (New York, 1968); Hajo Holborn, *A History of Modern Germany*, 3 vols. (New York, 1959–69).

54. Rohan D'o Butler, *The Roots of National Socialism* (London, 1941).

55. For the nineteenth century, see Peter Viereck, *Metapolitics: The Roots of the Nazi Mind* (New York, 1961); Fritz Stern, *The Politics of Cultural Despair* (Garden City, N.Y., 1965); George L. Mosse, *The Crisis of German Ideology* (New York, 1964); A. J. P. Taylor, *The Course of German History* (London, 1961). For the Weimar Republic, see Arthur Rosenberg, *The Birth of the German Republic*, trans. Ian D. Morrow (New York, 1931) and *A History of the German Republic*, trans. from the German (London, 1936); William Halperin, *Germany Tried Democracy* (New York, 1965); Erich Eyck, *A History of the Weimar Republic*, 2 vols. (Cambridge, Mass., 1962–64); Francis Carsten, *The Reichswehr in Politics* (Oxford, 1966); Karl Dietrich Bracher, *Die Auflösung der Weimarer Republik* (Villingen, 1960).

56. See Henry Friedlander, *The German Revolution, 1918–1919* (Ann Arbor, Univ. Microfilms, 1968). Also Rudolf Schlesinger, *Central European Democracy and its Background* (London, 1953).

57. For the Third Reich, see Karl Dietrich Bracher, *The German Dictatorship*, trans. Jean Steinberg (New York, 1970); Karl Dietrich Bracher, Wolfgang Sauer, Gerhard Schulz, *Die nationalsozialistische Machtergreifung* (Cologne and Opladen, 1962); Franz Neumann, *Behemoth* (New York, 1966). Also Edward Peterson, *The Limits of Hitler's Power* (Princeton, 1969).

58. On totalitarianism, see Hannah Arendt, *The Origins of Totalitarianism*, 2nd. rev. ed. (New York, 1958); Karl A. Wittfogel, *Oriental Despotism: A Comparative Study of Total Power* (New Haven, 1957); Carl J. Friedrich, ed., *Totalitarianism* (New York, 1964). On Fascism, see Ernst Nolte, *Three Faces of Fascism*, trans. from the German (New York, 1966); Walter Laqueur and George L. Mosse, eds., *International Fascism* (New York, 1966); Hans Rogger and Eugen Weber, eds., *The European Right: A Historical Profile*, (Berkeley, Cal., 1965).

59. A good textbook is Howard M. Sachar, *The Course of Modern Jewish History* (New York, 1968). For a massive history from ancient times, see Salo Baron, *A Social and Religious History of the Jews*, many vols. and still in progress (Philadelphia, 1937). For an excellent study of how the Jews were perceived in Christian medieval Europe, see Joshua Trachtenberg, *The Devil and the Jews* (New York, 1961); for the modern period, see George L. Mosse, *Germans and Jews* (New York, 1970).

60. See Jacob Katz, *Out of the Ghetto* (Cambridge, Mass., 1973); Reinhard Rürup, "Kontinuität und Diskontinuität der 'Judenfrage' im 19. Jahrhundert," in *Sozialgeschichte Heute*, Festschrift für Hans Rosenberg (Göttingen, 1974), pp. 387–415; Michael R. Marrus, *The Politics of Assimilation* (New York, 1971); Monika Richarz, ed., *Jüdisches Leben in Deutschland: Selbstzeugnisse zur Sozialgeschichte 1780–1871* (Stuttgart, 1976); Werner E. Mosse, ed., *Deutsches Judentum in Krieg und Revolution, 1916–1923* (Tübingen, 1971); Werner E. Mosse, ed., *Entscheidungsjahr 1932* (Tübingen, 1966); Ismar Schorsch, *Jewish Reactions to German Anti-Semitism* (Philadelphia, 1972); Walter Laqueur, *A History of Zionism* (New York, 1972).

61. Isaiah Trunk, *Judenrat: The Jewish Councils in Eastern Europe under Nazi Occupation* (New York, 1972). For a specific ghetto, see the excellent study by H. G. Adler, *Theresienstadt 1941–1945: Das Antlitz einer Zwangsgemeinschaft* (Tübingen, 1955). For the history of one of the eastern ghettos, see Isaiah Trunk, *Lodzer geto* [Yiddish] (New York, 1962); for the history in one specific country, see Jacob Presser, *The Destruction of the Dutch Jews*, trans. Arnold Pomerans (New York, 1969).

62. See Dobroszycki, "Jewish Elites under German Rule," p. 221 this vol.

63. Henry Feingold, *The Politics of Rescue* (New Brunswick, N.J., 1970); Saul Friedländer, *Pius XII and the Third Reich: A Documentation*, trans. from the French and German (New York, 1966); Alfred Häsler, *The Lifeboat is Full*, trans. C. L. Markmann (New York, 1969); Arthur Morse, *While Six Million Died* (New York, 1967); David Wyman, *Paper Walls: America and the Refugee Crisis, 1938–1941* (Amherst, Mass., 1968); Leni Yahil, *The Rescue of Danish Jewry*, trans. from the Hebrew (Philadelphia, 1969).

64. David Wyman, "Why Auschwitz Was Never Bombed," *Commentary*, LXV, 5 (May 1978) 37–46.

65. For a survey, see Martin Broszat, "Nationalsozialistische Konzentrationslager 1933–1945," in Helmut Krausnick et al., *Anatomie des SS-Staates*, Vol. II (Munich, 1967; for English translation, see note 27).

66. Eugen Kogon, *Der SS Staat: Das System der deutschen Konzentrationslager* (Frankfurt/Main, 1946), English translation as *The Theory and Practice of Hell* (New York, 1950); Benedikt Kautsky, *Teufel und Verdammte* (Vienna, n.d.), English translation as *Devils and the Damned* (London, 1960).

67. *Studien zur Geschichte der Konzentrationslager*, Schriftenreihe der Vierteljahrshefte für Zeitgeschichte, No. 21 (Stuttgart, 1970); Eberhard Kolb, *Bergen-Belsen: Geschichte des "Aufenthaltslagers" 1943–1945* (Hanover, 1962); Elie Cohen, *Human Behavior in the Concentration Camps* (see note 20); Joseph Billig, *L'Hitlerisme et le système concentrationnaire* (Paris, 1967); *De l'Université aux camps de concentration: Témoignages Strasbourgeois* (Paris, 1947); Enno Georg, *Die wirtschaftlichen Unternehmungen der SS* (Stuttgart, 1963); Joseph Billig, *Les camps de concentration dans l'économie du Reich Hitlerien* (Paris, 1973).

68. Comité International de la Croix-Rouge, International Tracing Service, *Vorläufiges Verzeichnis der Konzentrationslager und deren Aussenkommandos, sowie anderer Haftstätten unter dem RF-SS in Deutschland und deutsch besetzten Gebieten, 1933–1945* (Arolsen, February 1969).

69. Ino Arndt and Wolfgang Scheffler, "Organisierter Massenmord an Juden in nationalsozialistischen Vernichtungslagern," *Vierteljahrshefte für Zeitgeschichte*, XXIV (1976), 105–35, and Adalbert Rückerl, ed., *NS-Vernichtungslager im Spiegel deutscher Strafprozesse* (Munich, 1977). See also Central Commission for Investigation of German Crimes in Poland, *German Crimes in Poland*, vol. I (Warsaw, 1946). "Killing Center" is Raul Hilberg's term.

70. Rückerl, *NS-Vernichtungslager;* Raul Hilberg, *The Destruction of the European Jews*, Chapter 7; Joseph Tenenbaum, "The Einsatzgruppen," *Jewish Social Studies*, XVII (1955), 43–64; Helmut Ehrhardt, *Euthanasie und Vernichtung "lebensunwerten" Lebens* (Stuttgart, 1965); Klaus Dörner, "Nationalsozialismus und Lebensvernichtung," *Vierteljahrshefte für Zeitgeschichte*, XV (1967), 121–52; Lothar Gruchmann, "Euthanasie und Justiz im Dritten Reich," ibid., XX (1972), 235–79.

71. Arnold Hindls, *Einer kehrte zurück: Bericht eines Deportierten*. Publication of the Leo Baeck Institute (Stuttgart, 1965); Leon Weliczker Wells, *The Janowska Road* (New York, 1963).

72. Georges Wellers, *De Drancy à Auschwitz* (Paris, 1946); Joseph Weill, *Contribution à l'histoire des camps d'internement dans l'Anti-France* (Paris, 1946); Hanna Schramm, *Menschen in Gurs: Erinnerungen an ein französisches Internierungslager, 1940–1941*, mit einem dokumentarischen Beitrag zur französischen Emigrantenpolitik, 1933–1944, von Barbara Vormeier (Worms, 1977).

73. Bernd Naumann, *Auschwitz: Bericht über die Strafsache gegen Mulka u.a. vor dem Schwurgericht Frankfurt* (Frankfurt/Main, 1968); Hermann Langbein, *Der Auschwitz Prozess: Eine Dokumentation*, 2 vols. (Frankfurt/Main, 1965).

74. For literature see Lawrence Langer, *The Holocaust and the Literary Imagination* (New Haven, 1975); for art, see Sybil Milton, "Artists in the Third Reich," p. 115 this vol.

75. For an example of this unfortunate approach, see Roselle Chartock, "A Holocaust Unit for Classroom Teachers," *Social Education*, XLII (April 1978), 278–85.

CONTRIBUTORS

Werner T. ANGRESS was born in Berlin in 1920, served in the U.S. Army during World War II, and was educated at Wesleyan University and the University of California in Berkeley. He is currently Professor of History at the State University of New York at Stony Brook. He is the author of *Stillborn Revolution. The Communist Bid for Power in Germany, 1921–1923* (1963); "Juden im politischen Leben der Revolutionszeit," in *Deutsches Judentum in Krieg und Revolution 1916–1923* (1971); and numerous articles in American and German scholarly journals. He is a Fellow and Member of the Board of the Leo Baeck Institute, New York.

Alan BEYERCHEN was born in Michigan in 1945, and studied science and German history at the University of California in Santa Barbara and the Georg August Universität in Göttingen. He is currently Associate Professor of History at the Ohio State University in Columbus. He is the author of *Scientists under Hitler: Politics and the Physics Community in the Third Reich* (1977), and various scholarly articles. He is currently doing research on the post-World War II reconstruction of German science and on a biography of the physicist James Franck.

Gert H. BRIEGER, M.D., Ph.D., was born in Hamburg in 1932, and is currently Professor and Chairman of the Department of History of Health Sciences at the University of California in San Francisco. He has written widely about medicine in America in the nineteenth and twentieth centuries.

Christopher R. BROWNING was born in 1944, received his A.B. from Oberlin College, his Ph.D. from the University of Wisconsin in Madison, and is currently Associate Professor of History at Pacific Lutheran University in Tacoma, Washington. He is the author of *The Final Solution and the German Foreign Office: A Study of Referat D III of Abteilung Deutschland 1940–43* (1978), and articles in *Yad Vashem Studies* and the *Journal of Contemporary History*.

Paul M. van BUREN was educated at Harvard College, The Episcopal Theological School, and the University of Basel. He is currently Professor in the Religion Department of Temple University. He has published five books and a number of articles, held a Guggenheim Fellowship, and served as Fulbright Senior Lecturer at Oxford University. For the past five years he has been working on a theology of the Jewish-Christian reality; the first volume, *Discerning the Way, A Theology of the Jewish/Christian Reality*, was published in 1980.

John S. CONWAY was born in London in 1929, received his B.A., M.A., and Ph.D. from St. John's College, Cambridge, taught at the University of Manitoba, and is currently Professor of History at the University of British Columbia. He is the author of *The Nazi Prosecution of the Churches 1933–1943* (1969), and of numerous articles on the Vatican's policies in World War II, the German churches in the twentieth century, and the rise of European anti-Semitism. He is Director of the Tibetan Refugee Aid Society of Canada, and has long been involved in international work on behalf of refugees.

Lucjan DOBROSZYCKI was born in Lodz in 1925, and was interned in the Lodz ghetto, 1939–44, and in Auschwitz, Buchenwald, and Theresienstadt, 1944–45. After completing his M.A. at the University of Leningrad, he received his Ph.D. in Warsaw at the Institute of History of the Polish Academy of Science, where he held the position of Assistant and Associate Professor of History, 1954–69. He came to the U.S. in 1970, and is currently Research Associate at the YIVO Institute for Jewish Research, and a faculty member of the Max Weinreich Center for Advanced Jewish Studies and the Columbia University Continuing Education Program. He is the author of numerous monographs in Polish, and of *Image Before My Eyes: A Photographic History of Jewish Life in Poland, 1864–1939* (1977), and *Die legale polnische Presse im Generalgouvernement 1939–1945* (published by The Munich Institut für Zeitpeschichte in 1977).

Henry L. FEINGOLD was born in Ludwigshafen, Germany, in 1931, and received his Ph.D. from New York University in 1966. He is currently Professor of History at Baruch College and the Graduate Center of the City

University of New York, and has also taught at the Reconstructionist Rabbinical Academy and the Jewish Theological Seminary. He is the author of *Politics of Rescue: The Roosevelt Administration and the Holocaust 1938–1945* (1970); *Zion in America: The Jewish Experience from Colonial Times to the Present* (1974); and numerous articles on American Jewry and the Holocaust.

John FELSTINER was born in Mt. Vernon, New York, in 1936, and was educated at Harvard University, receiving his Ph.D. in 1965. He is currently Professor of English at Stanford University. He is the author of *The Lies of Art: Max Beerbohm's Parody and Caricature* (1972); *Translating Neruda: The Way to Macchu Picchu* (1980); and numerous scholarly articles. He is currently studying Holocaust poetry.

Henry FRIEDLANDER was born in Berlin in 1930, and was deported to the Lodz ghetto in 1941, and to Auschwitz, Neuengamme, and Ravensbrück in 1944. He came to the U.S. in 1947, and received his Ph.D. in German history from the University of Pennsylvania. He served on the Captured German Documents Project of the National Archives in Alexandria, Va.; taught history at the Louisiana State University, McMaster University (Hamilton, Ont.), the University of Missouri, and the City College of New York; and is currently Associate Professor of Judaic Studies at Brooklyn College of the City University of New York. He is the co-editor of *Détente in Historical Perspective* (1975), and the author of several *Guides to German Records* (1958 ff.); *On the Holocaust* (1973); and scholarly articles on the German Revolution of 1918, the historiography of the Holocaust, the Nazi concentration camps, and German war crimes trials.

Raul HILBERG was born in Vienna, served in the U.S. Army during World War II, and received his doctorate in Public Law and Government from Columbia University in 1955. In 1951–52 he was employed in the War Documentation Project at Alexandria, Va. Since 1956, he has taught at the University of Vermont, where he is currently John G. McCullough Professor of Political Science. He is the author of *The Destruction of the European Jews* (1961), the editor of *Documents of Destruction* (1971), and an editor (with Stanislaw Staron and Josef Kermisz) of the *Warsaw Diary of Adam Czerniakow* (1979). He is a member of the United States Holocaust Memorial Council.

Thomas Parke HUGHES was born in Virginia in 1923. He received his Bachelor of Mechanical Engineering and his Ph.D. in Modern European History from the University of Virginia. He has taught at M.I.T., Johns Hopkins University, and S.M.U., and is currently Professor of History of

Technology, and Chairman of the Department of History and Sociology of Science at the University of Pennsylvania. He is the author of *Elmer Ambrose Sperry: Inventor and Engineer* (1971), and numerous articles in American, British, and German scholarly journals. He is President of the Society for the History of Technology, Council Member of the History of Science Society, and former Chairman of the U.S. National Committee for the History and Philosophy of Science.

Lawrence L. LANGER was born in New York in 1929, received his B.A. from the City College of New York, his Ph.D. from Harvard University, and is currently Professor of English at Simmons College in Boston. He is the author of *The Holocaust and the Literary Imagination* (1975); *The Age of Atrocity: Death in Modern Literature* (1978); and the forthcoming *Versions of Survival: The Holocaust and the Human Spirit*. In 1963–64 he was Fulbright Professor of American Literature at the University of Graz, Austria.

Gavin I. LANGMUIR was born in Toronto in 1924, and served in the Canadian Army during World War II. He was educated at the University of Toronto and Harvard University. He is currently Professor of History at Stanford University, specializing in medieval history. He is the author of numerous articles and monographs on medieval French and English political institutions and on the formation of anti-Semitism.

Franklin H. LITTELL was born in Syracuse, New York, in 1917, educated at Cornell College, Iowa, and the Union Theological Seminary, and received his Ph.D. from Yale University in 1946. He is currently Professor of Religion at Temple University; Adjunct at the Institute of Contemporary Jewry of the Hebrew University; and Chairman of the National Institute on the Holocaust, Philadelphia. He is the author of *The German Phoenix* (1960); *The Crucifixion of the Jews* (1975); and co-editor of *The German Church Struggle and the Holocaust* (1974). He has been founder and Chairman of the Annual Scholars Conference on the Church Struggle and the Holocaust, 1970–76; founder and honorary chairman of the Annual Conference on Teaching the Holocaust, 1975 ff.; consultant on religion in higher education to the National Conference of Christians and Jews; and co-chairman of the Public Advisory Group of the President's Commission on the Holocaust.

Peter H. MERKL was born in Munich in 1932, educated in Germany and the United States, and received his Ph.D. from the University of California in Berkeley. He is currently Professor of Political Science at the University of California in Santa Barbara. He is the author of *The Origin of the West German Republic* (1963); *Germany: Yesterday and Tomorrow* (1965); *Political Continuity and Change* (1972); *Political Violence under the Swastika: 581 Early Nazis* (1975); *Modern Comparative Politics* (1977); the forthcoming *The Making of a Stormtrooper* and *Western European Party Systems;* and numerous articles for American, German, and Italian political science journals.

Sybil MILTON was born in 1941, and educated at Barnard College, the University of Munich, and Stanford University. She served on the Historical Commission in Berlin and the Commission for Parliamentary History in Bonn; taught at Stanford University; and is currently Chief Archivist at the Leo Baeck Institute, New York. She is the author of numerous scholarly and bibliographical articles about Czechoslovakian history, German labor and socialist politics, captured German documents, Jewish archives, and art of the Holocaust. She is co-author of the text for the National Albert Einstein Centennial Exhibit by the American Institute of Physics (1979); editor and translator of *White Flags of Surrender: Memoirs of a Half-Jew in Frankfort on the Main, 1933–1945* (1974) and *The Stroop Report* (1979); and co-author of the forthcoming *Artists of the Holocaust, 1933–1945*. She is a member of the International Affairs Committee of the Society of American Archivists, the International Council on Archives (Paris), and founding member of the International Council on Jewish Archives (New York—Jerusalem).

Allan MITCHELL is currently Professor of History at the University of California in San Diego. He is the author of *Revolution in Bavaria, 1918–1919* (1965), *Bismarck and the French Nation, 1848–1890* (1971), *The German Influence in France after 1870* (1979); editor of *The Nazi Revolution* (1973), and of *Everyman in Europe: Essays in Social History* (1974). He is currently doing research on the comparative history of France and Germany in the nineteenth century.

John T. PAWLIKOWSKI was born in Chicago in 1940, ordained at St. Mary of the Lake Seminary, received his A.B. at Loyola University, his Ph.D. at the University of Chicago, and is currently Professor of Social Ethics at the Catholic Theological Union at the University of Chicago. He is the author of *Catechetics and Prejudice* (1973); *Sinai and Calvary* (1976); and *What are they saying about Christian-Jewish Relations?* (1980). He has also contributed to numerous scholarly and religious publications. He is a member of the Advisory Committee, Secretariat for Catholic-Jewish

Relations, National Conference of Catholic Bishops; the Academy of Political Science; the American Academy of Religion; and a founding member of the National Interreligious Task Force on Soviet Jewry.

Fritz K. RINGER was born in Ludwigshafen, Germany, in 1934, emigrated to the United States in 1949, and was educated at Amherst College and Harvard University. He taught at Harvard and Indiana universities, and is currently Professor of History at Boston University. He is the author of *The Decline of the German Mandarins* (1969), and *Education and Society in Modern Europe* (1979).

Beate RUHM VON OPPEN was born in Switzerland in 1918, and educated in Germany, Holland, and England. She served with the British Foreign Office, the Royal Institute of International Affairs, and the Captured German Documents Project at Alexandria, Va.; she was a member of the Institute for Advanced Study and the Center of International Studies at Princeton; taught at Smith College and the University of Massachusetts, and is now on the faculty of St. John's college in Annapolis. She is the author of several *Guides to German Records* (1960 ff); *Religion and Resistance to Nazisim* (1971); editor of *Documents on Germany under Occupation 1945–54* (1955); and author of numerous contributions to scholarly publications on international affairs, the German church struggle, and German resistance to the Nazis. She is currently working on an edition of the Letters of Helmuth James von Moltke.

Telford TAYLOR was born in Schenectady, New York, in 1908, and received his A.B. and M.A. from Williams College, and his LL.B. from Harvard University. He served with the Department of the Interior, the Agricultural Adjustment Administration, and the Federal Communications Commission, and has held the offices of Special Assistant to the Attorney General, and Associate Counsel to the U.S. Senate Committee on Interstate Commerce. During World War II he was a military intelligence officer with the U.S. Army, and was commissioned Brigadier General in April 1946. At Nuremberg he served as U.S. Chief of Counsel for War Crimes, 1946–49. After the war he taught at Columbia, Yale, Harvard, and Yeshiva Law Schools, and practiced with Taylor, Scoll, Ferencz, and Simon. He is the author of *Sword and Swastika: Generals and Nazis in the Third Reich* (1952); *Grand Inquest: The Story of Congressional Investigations* (1954); *The March of Conquest: The German Victories in Western Europe, 1940* (1958); *The Breaking Wave: The Second World War in the Summer of 1940* (1967); *Two Studies in Constitutional Interpretation* (1969); *Nuremberg and Vietnam: An American Tragedy* (1970); *Courts of Terror:*

Soviet Criminal Procedure and Jewish Immigration (1977); and *Munich: The Price of Peace* (1979). He has also served as a member of the President's Commission on the Holocaust.

Eugen WEBER was born in Romania in 1925, brought up in England, and served in the British infantry during World War II. He was educated at Cambridge University and at the Institut d'études politiques in Paris, and came to the U.S. in 1956 to teach at the University of California in Los Angeles. He is currently Professor of History and Dean of the College of Letters and Science at UCLA. He is the author of *Action Française* (1962); *Varieties of Fascism* (1964); and most recently *Peasants into Frenchmen* (1976). He is a member of the American Academy of Arts and Sciences.

David WINSTON was born in New York in 1927, ordained at the Jewish Theological Seminary, and received his A.B. at Yeshiva University, and his Ph.D. at Columbia University. He taught at Wesleyan and Columbia universities, and is currently Professor of Hellenistic and Judaic Studies at the Graduate Theological Union in Berkeley, and Director of its Center for Judaic Studies. He is the author of numerous articles on Hellenistic Judaism, and of a commentary on *The Wisdom of Solomon* (1979). He is a fellow of the American Academy for Jewish Research.

INDEX